Burgundy to Champagne

THE JOHNS HOPKINS UNIVERSITY STUDIES
IN HISTORICAL AND POLITICAL SCIENCE

115th Series (1997)

1.

Burgundy to Champagne: The Wine Trade in Early Modern France
by Thomas Brennan

Burgundy to Champagne

The Wine Trade in Early Modern France

Thomas Brennan

THE JOHNS HOPKINS UNIVERSITY PRESS
Baltimore & London

The Johns Hopkins University Press
2715 North Charles Street
Baltimore, Maryland 21218-4319
The Johns Hopkins Press Ltd., London

Library of Congress Cataloging-in-Publication Data will be found
at the end of this book.
A catalog record for this book is available from the British Library.

ISBN 0-8018-5567-5

Contents

Acknowledgments

Having written a book about other people's debts, I find it a pleasure to preface it by acknowledging my own. Throughout my research I have been frequently overwhelmed by the kindness of old friends and complete strangers. I offer them my deepest thanks and this book in partial payment. In many trips to France I have received warm hospitality from Cathie Healey, Alice Brinton, Bob Schwartz, and les familles Rafestin and Traeger, encouragement from Jean-Paul Desaive and Marcel Lachiver, and advice from Thierry Claeys. Each made France more welcoming to me.

Helpful archivists and librarians, especially those at the Bibliothèque Municipale of Epernay and the Archives Départementales of the Yonne and the Marne, provided the keys to my research. The people of the great wine companies—Ruinart Père et Fils, Moët et Chandon, Veuve Clicquot-Ponsardin, Chauvenet, Bouchard Père et Fils, and Champy—offered me assistance and generous access to their documents, as did Jean Nollevalle and François Bonal. Much of this book is the result of their reverence for their past and their willingness to share it with others.

Back in the States, friends and colleagues, particularly those in the Works-in-Progress Seminar of the U.S. Naval Academy's History Department and the Baltimore-Washington Old Regime Study Group, earned my deepest gratitude for reading parts of this book in earlier drafts. Robert Forster, Orest Ranum, Donald Sutherland, Mack Holt, and Fritz Stern did more than their fair share of the reading, for which they have my special thanks.

Grants from the Naval Academy Research Council and the National Endowment for the Humanities gave me encouragement, time, and money to work on this project. The *Journal for European Economic History* published an earlier version of chapter 3. I am grateful for their permission to use the material again.

Finally, my family has been a source of joy and support. I wish to thank Philip and Laura for their patience with the long process of producing a book. No thanks can adequately convey the debt I owe Katherine for her love, advice, and endless readings. This book is hers as much as mine.

Acknowledgments

Introduction

Early modern Europe has been called the age of commercial capitalism, but it is not clear whether the growing sophistication and energy of the long-distance international markets, which have been the focus of most historical study, extended to the vast majority of the domestic economy. How had local and regional markets changed by the early modern era, and did they have a greater impact on the lives of most Europeans?[1] What forces brought people in touch with the market economy, and how did markets shape their culture? These questions are crucial to understanding not only the economy but also the culture and society of Europe. Yet there is little agreement about the answers. There is debate, first of all, about the extent of market exchange. If trade dominated the coasts of Europe and the areas around the large towns, what was its role farther inland and how much of the rural world was involved more than marginally with the market? Questions arise too about the organization of the market economy, as publicly organized and regulated markets gave way to private arrangements and individual enterprise. Debates extend to the impact of the market system, both as an economic and a cultural stimulus. To what degree did the market stimulate production, efficiency, even capitalism? What did it do to traditional social structures and traditional values? This book attempts to answer these questions in France by looking at the early modern wine trade as a particularly precocious segment of an economy that was not yet, in many ways, fully modern.

The debate over the extent of commercialization in early modern France has evolved considerably in recent decades. Not long ago it was an article of faith among historians that most agriculture in France was still part of a "peasant economy" and that peasants resisted capitalist changes in the countryside up to and through the Revolution.[2] Through much of the Old Regime, as Fernand Braudel points out, "an enormous share of the production was absorbed by the self-sufficient family or village and did not enter the market circuit."[3] "The vast majority [of the French in the Old Regime]," according to Pierre Goubert, "still see the perfect state of affairs as a kind of localized autarky relieved by a little 'commerce.' The basis of the economy is 'subsistence' . . . the ideal being to produce everything on one's own land."[4] Even the trade in grain, which was the country's chief commodity, appears to have been surprisingly fragmented and disorganized until well into the eighteenth century, when the commercial circuits were perhaps improved if not much expanded.[5] One study of modern France asserted that "it would be late in the [nineteenth] century before a significant proportion of [French peasants] tied their production to the needs of the market, because it would be late in the century before the market would become significant and accessible to them."[6] The great mass of early modern France and its people, then, is often seen as rural, isolated, and only marginally involved in the market economy.

In their assessments of the economy, many historians of early modern France have emphasized the contrasts between the commercial, outward-looking regions and *la France profonde,* agrarian and static. Herbert Lüthy contrasted an "interior" economy—"essentially agricultural [and] nearly autarkic"—with an "external" economy of commercial capitalism.[7] The Atlantic ports in particular formed a world apart; dynamic, capitalist, cosmopolitan, these ports possessed interests not always in harmony with central France or the central government. Some have even claimed that the ports' "economic ties with the hinterland were inconsequential." The core and periphery of France are seen to have formed a "dual economy" that functioned "in parallel but independently from each other."[8] Braudel offers the image of the outer France "colonizing" the interior, but he does not think that these contacts were sufficient to have united France's divided regional markets.[9]

Historians of the last two decades, however, have amended this view of a noncommercial France with new evidence and arguments for the prevalence of commercial exchange, even though they are still accused of paying inadequate attention to markets.[10] They have identified the subsistence economy as an ideal type, with little historical reality by the late Middle Ages. Guy Bois sees the "peasant holding . . . wide open to the market" and the rapid rise of local trade in the fifteenth century.[11] Even if much of the grain produced was consumed directly by its producers and never entered a market, all but a small minority of peasants had to interact with a market in order to sell their labor, rent their land, or supplement their food production.[12] By the seventeenth and eighteenth centuries, then, much of agrarian society had experienced some level of commercialization.[13] Historians argue for the general "interpenetration" of peripheral and interior France, saying that "it is practically impossible to dissociate interior commerce from the exterior . . . and the 'classic' differentiations are more artificial than anywhere else."[14] The export markets of France, which enjoyed the most spectacular growth in the eighteenth century, contributed most to the expansion of the economy by stimulating production in the interior and indeed relied on this internal market, whose "foundations remain [nevertheless] often badly defined."[15] The question remains: To what extent and by what means did the commercial sectors of France shape the economy?

Recent studies have insisted, in addition, on the importance of market integration for understanding growth in the French economy.[16] Historians looking for an agricultural revolution in France have pointed not to a surge in grain output (they can find, at best, a modest but steady increase) but rather to a growing productivity in the rural sector, based on increased commercialization.[17] Growing specialization in a variety of non-cereal production, especially in grape vines, supplied marketable goods and brought producers into closer contact with the market. Improvements in transportation and credit led to what Le Roy Ladurie has called the "lubrification—[caused] by roads and money—of the internal exchanges of the province, even more than the external commerce."[18] This led to a better distribution of products and to more profits in the hands of rural and urban inhabitants, and so to greater demand for other goods.

The wine trade in France was central to this commercialization, and indeed historians of southwestern France assert that "wine was one of the principal motors of commerce."[19] Although wine production was dwarfed by cereal production in most of France, the vast majority of the wine was exchanged commercially, often over considerable distances. In contrast, Jean Meuvret's magisterial history of the seventeenth-century grain trade underlines the "essential weakness" and "restrained role" given to grain in France's commercial transportation system; grain circulated "interlocally, at best interregionally." He too points to wine as the prominent commercial commodity, both domestically and internationally.[20] Given the much greater commercialization of wine production than cereal, it is possible that the wine market nearly rivaled the impact of the cereal market on the early modern French exchange economy.[21] The wine-producing regions of

France were sufficiently commercial by the early modern period that producers looked to the market as a source of at least supplementary, and in most cases primary, income.

Yet the wine trade discussed in this book alerts us to the complexity of the debate over markets, for the commercial organization of the wine market operated on many different levels, most of them still quite local, small-scale, and unsophisticated. The commercial system, so active around certain port cities and the capital, had penetrated the interior of the country only gradually, and wine markets in the interior developed more slowly. Many viticultural communities remained passively dependent on external initiatives for marketing and financing their wine trade. Through much of the country the wine trade was what anthropologists call a dendritic market system, segregating participants by differential access to demand and dominated by export merchants who controlled the trade.[22] The dynamics of the wine trade changed considerably during the eighteenth century, with the elaboration of communication and transportation networks and the emergence of provincial entrepreneurs. But this book shows that the disparities of economic power created by the commercialization of France provoked social tension and vigorous protest from every level of society.

The Meaning of the Market

The early modern wine trade reminds us that we cannot assume that markets and commercial exchange had an obvious and unitary meaning for those who participated in them. There were many levels of the exchange economy, depending on the range of the commerce as well as the frequency and openness of participation. Much local commerce was carefully regulated by public authorities, whereas long-distance trade tended to create its own dynamics. The regulated or "open" market, as defined by Alan Everitt, "catered primarily for local demand, dealt in relatively small transactions, and reflected the social convictions of the surrounding countryside." Trade at longer distances, between regions and countries, became more sophisticated, more speculative, more "private."[23] Although much local commerce regularly brought producers together with consumers, long-distance trade ended up in the hands of fewer participants.

If we can feel certain that most of early modern society took part in some aspect of the exchange economy, we need still to determine the nature of their exchanges and ask what the experience meant to them. As anthropologists remind us, "Any study of markets must recognize the participants' understanding and conception of their own social and economic activity."[24] Yet here again there is disagreement. For many historians the market empowered participants, bringing economic growth and opportunity, commercialized relationships, and a capitalist mentality.[25] Others see the market as more restrictive and emphasize the mechanisms by which market access favored merchant capital in its relation to producers, or they follow E. P. Thompson in juxtaposing a traditional, "moral" economy to a new capitalism.[26] Clearly there is still need for clarification of the extent and impact of markets in early modern Europe.

Unfortunately, the term *market* enjoys a bewildering range of meanings. For some it refers to all exchanges, others identify it with fully formed capitalism.[27] Perhaps it is best to think of the market as referring to different things in different contexts; it is a place, an action, an idea, and a system, among other things. Each of these refers to a different stage in commercial development, as well as different aspects of the institution. Marketplaces are sometimes identified as the most primitive manifestation of markets, having the greatest importance in societies where market exchange was least pervasive. Through much of premodern history, markets transferred goods but did not make prices and exercised limited influence over economic behavior in the society.[28] Yet the marketplace, as a specific and indeed very formal location, governed by layers of regulation and custom, continued to exist into the early modern world. As commercial exchange became more pervasive it began to organize social life in its own image, drawing more and more activities into the process of exchange. Market actions—the process of exchange—could take place in a marketplace but transcended any given location. Historians have argued that market exchanges gradually freed themselves from marketplaces over the course of the early modern period, slowly escaping from public scrutiny and becoming unregulated, private transactions.[29] Such a transformation occurred earlier in England than in France, but France too experienced the expansion of private marketing.[30] Simultaneous with this transformation the market became an idea, sometimes called the market principle, that worked on an intellectual level to change the language of economic life.[31] Only belatedly did the market become a system, controlling every aspect of economic life.

The transformation of the marketplace into market action, the liberation of commercial exchange from public control of the marketplace, was a particularly contested process. Medieval authorities, seeing the dependency of urban consumers on the market as a source of competitive disadvantage, created urban regulations to protect the urban market from the competitive advantage enjoyed by merchants. Public regulation of markets had sought "pure" competition by maximizing "transparency"—the direct access of sellers to buyers and their general access to information about the market—and minimizing the control any one had over prices.[32] These rules aimed at increasing competition and participation in the market, as well as eliminating fraud and price-gouging.[33] The regulations sustaining an "open market" aimed at the medieval ideal of "just price," which was simply the market price, when the market functioned without fraud or conspiracy.[34] Such regulations also formed part of a town's "provisioning" policies, which identified the good of the community with equity and could privilege local consumers over suppliers.

At the same time there were less defined forces in the early modern world making the market less open and transparent. "New methods of private bargaining were gradually breaking down the protective barriers of the customary marketing system," according to Everitt.[35] The spread of long-distance trade tied to international and metropolitan markets led to "private" trading, which "avoided transparency and control" and reduced competition. Here, Braudel says, "the rules of the market economy regarding, for example, free competition as described in classical economics . . . operated far less frequently" than in the open market. "Here we are dealing with unequal exchanges in which competition—the basic law of the so-called market economy—had little place."[36] As the domestic economy engaged increasingly in long-distance trade it experienced the confrontation of two different market systems, a public and a private one, each obeying very different rules. The asymmetries of knowledge and power in long-distance trade would violate popular assumptions about the way that markets were supposed to work.

Much of the conflict over market practices and principles converges in the person of the intermediary. To measure the development of markets in the French interior, this study focuses on the gradual elaboration of networks of intermediaries and the changes in the way they operated. These individuals—who could be merchants, *négociants* (large-scale wholesale merchants), brokers, or factors, depending on the size, independence, and risk of their enterprise—played the crucial role both in making the market economy function and in symbolizing the disruptive effects of exchange.[37] As the fundamental link between producer and consumer, intermediaries provided credit, transportation, pricing, storage, information, and grading. They had become the conduit through which flowed most of the contacts between local communities and the national market, and they used their position astride these communications to gain considerable control of the market. As a result, intermediaries became the focus of much of the tension created by the transformation of the economy.

A growing number of intermediaries played a particularly crucial role in threatening the transparency of the market. Merchants and middle-men, brokers and intermediaries of every sort, expanded the geography of exchange but by coming between the producer and consumer made the market less transparent. As the putative bearers of capitalism, they were both proponents of fundamental cultural change and the focus of resistance to that change. Since the Middle Ages, the merchant had been distrusted, and "the profession of trade remained characteristically a sor-did business."[38] Even within the liberal movement of the eighteenth cen-tury can be found some of the medieval ambivalence toward commerce and merchants.[39] The physiocrats and their intellectual forebears dismissed commerce as inherently "sterile," particularly when it was "brokerage" or "commerce of a mercenary . . . who finds his subsistence and frequently fat profits merely by being the intermediary of the exchange."[40] Much like medieval theorists, they insisted instead that commerce should only work in perfect competition to bring producer and consumer together, and some even identified merchants as a potential threat to such a mar-ket.[41] Even the archphysiocrat Quesnay accused the merchant of trying to "buy at the lowest possible price and to sell at the highest possible price, so as to make his gain as high as possible at the expense of the nation: his individual interest and that of the nation are opposed."[42]

The spread of intermediaries, long-distance trade, and capitalism chal-lenged traditional ideals of competition and just price. At a time when "commerce" was becoming the preferred metaphor for peaceful and so-ciable interaction among civilized people, the intermediary threatened to derail the community of exchange.[43] The French defended the principle of open markets longer than the English did. Whereas private marketing had become pervasive in England by the late seventeenth century, the French continued to police their markets, and particularly their grain trade, until the second half of the eighteenth century. The deregulation and liberal-ization of French markets occurred in several very deliberate phases in the 1760s and 1770s and with very controversial consequences. Elements from all of French society, from the parlements down to urban consumers, put up a particularly ferocious resistance to the assault on the traditional operation of the grain market.[44]

There is considerable controversy, then, about markets in France during this crucial transitional period. How pervasive were markets in this economy? To what extent had markets gained control of economic life? What was the impact of markets: Were they structuring economic life, did they offer opportunities for improvement, and to whom did they offer opportunities? As old dichotomies—between subsistence and capitalist economies, between moral and political economy—look less and less satisfactory, we must accept a more nuanced picture of the Old Regime economy. There was a range, between and within communities, of engagement in the market, for no one was completely excluded from it and few had completely joined it. There was also pervasive tension, as a consequence, over the impact and implications of the exchange economy.

The spread of long-distance trade and private marketing in the French economy, with all the resulting asymmetries of power, can be seen with particular clarity in the wine trade. The wine trade replaced most government controls with an increasingly sophisticated system of private exchange through the eighteenth century. This precocious liberalization provoked a broad defense of the just price and market transparency, an early salvo in the century-long fight over the government regulation of the economy. This book examines the effects of the expansion and privatization of exchange in an important segment of the early modern French economy. The wine trade demonstrates both the increasing sophistication of this exchange economy and the controversy that attended it.

The Wine Trade

For all of historians' interest in markets, whether as conduits of growth, change, disruption, or modernity, it is odd that so little attention has been paid to the economic history of wine, which has been called the "market product par excellence."[45] There has been some study of the international wine trade, particularly from the port of Bordeaux, but wine exports amounted to little more than 10 percent of total wine production in the eighteenth century.[46] Wine played a preponderant role in France's exports, to be sure, but it was enormously important to the development of the domestic market as well, and the domestic wine trade has been largely ignored.[47]

The development of winemaking, in contrast, and particularly the creation of modern wine, has been the object of much study, by historians, geographers, and oenophiles. Many books have shown how individual decisions, selections, innovations and endless toil on the part of growers, buyers, and consumers over the last two centuries have made the wines of today. In most cases, however, the wine and the vines are the real subject of the careful investigations, and the constant refrain of these studies has been: What was the impact of the winemakers on the wine?[48] As a recent example illustrates, a book with the title *Vins, vignes, et vignerons (Wines, Vines, and Vinegrowers)* is dedicated to the "history of the French vineyards [*vignoble*]" and seems to dismiss the human element, the vine-grower, as "only an intermediary between the vine and the wine."[49] The men and women who made their lives in viticultural societies are merely accessories to the wine, and the dynamics of their communities have been largely ignored.

Historians have too often failed to ask, What was the impact of wine on the winemakers? How did producing wine influence France's economy, social relations, and culture? The wine producers themselves reflected the range of provincial society. Some belonged to local urban elites, which had gained substantial control of the vineyards by the seventeenth century and challenged merchants and middlemen for precedence and power in both the local society and economy. The rest of the winemakers were less inde-pendent and succumbed more readily to the webs of debt and domination wielded by those with commercial power. Despite several fine studies of the vinegrowers in various regions—largely from a demographic point of view—we still know very little about their social and economic relations to the elites and to each other.[50] This lacuna reflects a more general need for research into early modern commerce on the local and regional level.

Wine production was an unusual, and unusually important, feature of French society. No other form of agriculture was so labor intensive, thus offering greater employment and, in many circumstances, greater wealth to vinegrowing communities. The productivity of vineyards meant that viticultural societies were more densely populated; vineyards also tended to be more evenly distributed among the community. As Ernest Labrousse argued, landowning was common in viticultural society, which was more egalitarian and more democratic than the rest of rural society.[51] Vineyards were so much more productive than grain lands that self-sufficiency could come with only two hectares of vines.[52] According to this picture, viti-cultural society stood sharply apart from much of agrarian society, with its huge farms monopolized by a relative handful of *fermiers*.[53] By the measure of land distribution, the viticultural community should have been unusu-ally free of strains.

At the same time, no other form of agriculture was so commercialized, for most of what the vinegrower produced was sold, if not wholesale and at a great distance, then retail and close at hand. Every region grew grain, but few regions sold more than a small percentage of what they grew, and the grain trade was hedged in and distorted by restrictions and regulations.[54] In contrast, wine had always been a commodity, to be bought and sold, and many sections of the country could respond to government questionnaires, with little exaggeration, that "wine is the only commerce in this region." Wine was a valuable resource but also a source of vulnerability, for vinegrowers went far out on the limb of market society, where all are enjoined to exchange or die. They might drown their sorrows in what they produced but could not survive on wine unless they could sell it. Precocious commercialization and the growing role of capitalism introduced their own range of strains and inequalities of social and economic power into viticultural society.

Marketing wine was as crucial to its producers as was growing it, but marketing could not be purely artisanal, not if wine was to be anything more than a marginal part of the local economy. There was some room, to be sure, for the backdoor sale of wine to one's neighbors, or for turning a room into a tavern, especially in villages on well-traveled trade routes. Many parts of France were constrained to such a local market, and winemaking here offered only a supplement to the principal economy. True viticultural communities depended on much larger and more concentrated markets, at the very least on intraregional trade to supply neighboring cities. But the dynamic force in the wine trade of the Old Regime was the growth of interregional and national markets; wine required larger markets, in the distant cities and ports, to flourish. Of course, wine needed transportation, ideally by river, and in some cases by road, but above all it needed a market, someone who would buy it, and finding that buyer was the great challenge.

Marketing was the key to realizing the value of vines, no less crucial than the production of wine, but a good deal more specialized. To the challenge of finding a buyer were added the mysteries of pricing, the complexities of financing the sale—never easy in an economy as illiquid as France's— the burden of fiscality, and the myriad details of shipment. As soon as the humble growers, even the biggest growers in the village, confronted the outside world, they faced crippling asymmetries of knowledge and economic power. Their community was their competition, for the buyer who knew about them knew of the other growers in the village who were growing nearly identical wines and were facing similar economic pressures. In contrast, the buyer had alternatives and, above all, had information: about demand, prices, and supplies. Growers were also hobbled by immediate needs. They often needed money, quickly, for their taxes, debts, and food. Their wine required real costs before it offered them a return, and delays in seeing that return were painful. Yet for all the disadvantages faced by the growers in marketing their wine, they had little choice but to work with them as best they could. To the grower, then, as to the historian, the most pressing questions were the development of the market and how the grower gained access to it.

The domestic wine trade of early modern France, particularly the long-distance trade to Paris, is the focus of this book. This commerce incorporated much of northern France and created one of the largest internal markets in the country. The sources available for Champagne and Burgundy permit the historian to examine the process of market development through the lens of two critical yet different provinces. The first chapter examines viticultural society in these two provinces, considering landholding and wine production as a context to understanding the dynamics of provincial wine markets. The second chapter concentrates on the wine trade in early-eighteenth-century Champagne; it uses trade figures to identify the principal agents and actors in the market. The chapter introduces the commission broker as the chief impresario of the provincial wine trade, the individual who organized supply, handled transactions and transportation, and generated customers as well as controversy. Chapter 3 offers a more global assessment of the broker's identity and location throughout France; it also charts the rapid transformation of that identity around the turn of the century. The next two chapters look to Burgundy for a more detailed analysis of the broker's role in the viticultural economy, as well as the society's response to brokers. A local scandal in the middle of the century that rapidly achieved national proportions helps gauge both the broker's contested identity and the society's ambivalent attitude toward the market. At the same time, the structural changes occurring in the Parisian wine trade, discussed in chapter 6, facilitated the incorporation of new regions, new participants, and new openness into the domestic wine trade, which challenged brokers' control and reintroduced elements of transparency into the market. The Burgundian wine trade went on to experience growth and increasing integration into national and international markets. Burgundy's experience of the wine trade in the late Old Regime is then compared to the situation in Champagne, where brokers transformed themselves and the local wine trade, launching the modern foundations of that province's economy.

The provincial brokers who supplied Paris are the main characters of this study. As the wine trade around Paris increased its geographical range, bringing distant provinces into the capital's market system, Parisian merchants looked to brokers for aid, both in identifying and paying for wine in the countryside. During the late seventeenth century, brokers became specialized traders, intermediaries in the wine-producing community who competed with distant buyers for commercial power and used their position to gain leverage over local producers. Through their control of credit and information, the provincial brokers developed new commercial skills and, above all, new economic power.

Brokers had been official agents, first of local communities, later of the king's state, until the early eighteenth century. The broker's original purpose had expressed the disadvantages local markets experienced in their contacts with long-distance trade; markets were a liminal, dangerous space, particularly when open to the outside world.[55] As official agents, brokers brought security to the wine trade and lowered transaction costs arising from uncertainty about credit, price, and confidence. As local experts, they could vouch for the provenance and quality of wines that might be quite foreign to the purchaser. Brokers also supervised the wine market for the local authorities and reported on prices and quantities at regular intervals. More importantly, brokers reassured wine sellers of the security of their sales by guaranteeing the purchasers' credit. In their official capacity they provided essential assistance to the transparency of the market.

Yet, during a relatively brief period, from the late seventeenth to the early eighteenth century, the role of the broker changed quite abruptly. Official brokers began to act and define themselves differently and to contest the government's treatment and definition of them. Offering their services as proxies for distant merchants, brokers, now acting on commission, took an increasingly entrepreneurial role in the market. And as the invigoration of trade in the eighteenth century brought rapidly rising demands for credit, brokers stepped in to fill this crucial need. After a period of resistance on the part of royal and local authorities, the state finally backed off, leaving brokers as private agents. The result was the emergence of private brokers, unencumbered by public authority, indeed largely unregulated despite a growing tide of resentment against their increasingly hegemonic power over the local wine trade. The new generation of brokers adopted a very different role in the wine trade, abandoning the earlier public office and becoming private entrepreneurs. This transformation entailed a radical shift in their daily practice and relationship with the local community. Profiting from their freedom from local allegiances, they played upon the traditional habits of market exchange to achieve power over the market and its participants. Redefining price-setting mechanisms, capitalizing on their monopoly of information, these brokers refashioned the market and its meaning in the local economy. But they did not do so without facing considerable resistance. Local communities defended themselves, and their image of the market, through direct and legal action.

The transformation of the wine market produced a cultural transformation, in the way wine producers comprehended and responded to it. The growing commercialization of the countryside engendered new economic and social relations, both within the province and between province and Paris. As increasing demand provoked new production and, sometimes, better prices, more of rural society became involved in the wine trade and, so, dependent on those who controlled the trade. This confrontation with commercial capitalism was often awkward and occasionally contentious, as producers chafed against their own impotence. Their contestation expressed itself in attempts to define what the market and its participants were and should be. They fought to defend their self-image as artisans of quality products, as autonomous actors in a transparent market. And, inevitably, the hottest disputes revolved around the nature of the middleman. As economic and cultural intermediaries, the brokers of the wine trade helped transform the economy of early modern France.

Burgundy to Champagne

I

Wine into Wealth

Viticultural society was the creation of a market economy and was formed, fashioned, and maintained by market forces. The development of viticulture in France, even before the Romans, responded to the demands of markets, whether foreign, urban, clerical, or noble. The organization of viticultural society, with its density of population and small holdings, its tendency to egalitarian communities and absence of great disparities of property, depended on the availability of markets in which all could sell their produce. The dynamics of the viticultural economy responded to the growth of commerce, through improved transportation, communication, and financial organization. Behind the markets that turned wine into wealth and the brokers who made these markets work lay the land, labor, and capital that produced the wine.

Commerce brought profits and perils to viticultural society. The wine trade allowed vineyards to support denser, more egalitarian populations than did grain production, though the distinction lends itself to some exaggeration. According to the economic historian Ernest Labrousse, "The wine region is the sector predestined for social peace. Property there is very divided up. The conflict between fermier and capitalist, likely to bring discord on arable or pasture lands, between the cultivator and the proprietor, occurred only rarely in wine regions, where tenant farming [*fermage*] was exceptional."[1] Yet, despite the unusual degree of land ownership in viticultural society, which meant that most owned enough vines to have wine to sell and no one owned very much, there were important social and economic disparities. An increasingly hierarchical wine trade, differentiated by access to local, regional, or interregional markets, produced corresponding distinctions in viticultural society. Local markets suffered most from competition and stagnant prices. Distant markets posed different challenges to local economies; they offered rewards only to those who enjoyed sufficient resources and information to profit from them. In each case, access to markets shaped the structures of landholding and established the form and dynamics of viticultural society.

The Evolution of the Wine Trade

The French wine trade has been central to the French economy for a very long time. The gradual spread of vinegrowing throughout the country during the first millennium of the common era made wine an essential part of the local economy in most medieval communities. Scattered evidence suggests that considerable wine consumption was common among the wealthy, among urban populations, perhaps even among the peasants.[2] In most parts of medieval France, wine was largely part of the subsistence economy, grown and consumed locally. Nevertheless, a vigorous wine trade also linked a few parts of the country to international markets and created a more complex wine market in those areas that exported. The disruptions of the late Middle Ages altered these markets, both local and long-distance. The wine economy that emerged in the Renaissance was more concentrated, less subsistence based, and oriented more toward long- and medium-range trade. Offering greater wealth and greater opportunities than could be gained from supplying purely local demand, the long-distance wine trade would become one of the most sophisticated commercial systems in early modern France, gradually knitting the regions of France into a coherent national market and stimulating the commercial development of French society.

Although the wine trade in France had long supplied a flourishing export trade, domestic markets expanded very slowly beyond essentially local, intraregional commerce. The earliest evidence of wine trade shows a flourishing French contribution to the long-distance Mediterranean wine market well before the arrival of Roman colonies, one organized largely by Phoenician merchants visiting southern French ports. A local market must have grown up around these port cities to supply both distant markets and the tastes of the cosmopolitan port inhabitants. The spur of external demand had pushed vinegrowing into much of southern France by the Christian era. Then, with the gradual spread of wine drinking into the rest of France, more or less accompanying the spread of Christianity, vine-yards emerged in various northern locations to supply local markets.[3]

The difficulties of transportation meant that most medieval consumers tried to have access to wines nearby, in many cases acquiring vineyards to grow their own. Ecclesiastical centers and the courts of nobles and mon-archs demanded wine for the sacraments in the Christian liturgy, prestige, and hospitality. Vines grew near every abbey, cathedral, and church estab-lishment. Monasteries in particular required a constant supply of wine, for both religious and dietary purposes. Important monasteries near Paris, like Saint-Denis and Saint-Germain-des-Prés, had vineyards all around the Parisian area, as far as twenty-five kilometers to the south. The abbeys of Cîteaux and Cluny in Burgundy developed the famous vineyards of Clos de Vougeot and Gevrey. With the emergence of urban communities in the high Middle Ages, vineyards also appeared around cities. But these were not so much commercial ventures as they were attempts at self-sufficiency, a substitute for markets that rarely spanned great distances.[4]

In contrast to the limited development of the domestic wine trade, the maritime wine trade had developed into a flourishing and precocious commerce in the Middle Ages. Markets in harsher climates across north-ern Europe, where vines grew poorly or not at all, turned to France for wines. Among the first exports were the white wines from the area around Paris, the Île-de-France, which passed by way of Rouen to reach the sea. La Rochelle in the twelfth century and Bordeaux in the thirteenth gradu-ally outstripped Paris, with vast quantities of wine shipped to England, the Netherlands, and the Baltic, as would vineyards along the length of the Loire River. The vineyards of the northeast, around Laon and Soissons, sent wine directly overland to Flemish cities. There is no way to mea-sure the volume of all this long-distance trade, but the most flourishing of these entrepôts, Bordeaux, was sending an average of 850,000 hectoliters per year in the early fourteenth century. The only domestic market that showed a similar vigor was Paris, importing some four hundred thousand hectoliters for its own consumption at the same period.[5] For scores of kilo-meters around Bordeaux and Paris a dense landscape of vineyards arose to maintain this wine trade. From a distance of nearly two hundred kilo-meters, the people of thirteenth-century Auxerre "send their wines to Paris by the nearby river . . . [which] provides them with a handsome profit."[6]

The maritime wine trade languished during the late Middle Ages be-cause of demographic and political difficulties but rebounded in the six-teenth century with the arrival of Dutch merchants. Exports from Bor-deaux had fallen to the range of some one hundred thousand hectoliters because of the Hundred Years' War and fell even lower with the fifteenth-century expulsion of the English, who had been the main consumers of "claret." The wines of Poitou, exported from La Rochelle, lost their primary market in the fifteenth century, when their main customers in the Netherlands temporarily joined the lands of Burgundy in dynastic union. The Loire vineyards, sending much of their wine overland or through Nantes to a variety of northern French markets, also lost their vigor. But all these Atlantic regions received a powerful stimulus with the arrival of Dutch merchants, starting in the late sixteenth century. The Dutch offered an enormous market, both for consumption and reexport, as well as strong encouragement to reorganize the maritime vineyards of western France to Dutch taste. Nantes in particular increased its exports a hundredfold, to nearly four hundred thousand hectoliters in the late sixteenth century.[7] Yearly exports through Bordeaux in the sixteenth century returned to 250,000 hectoliters and tripled by the end of the seventeenth century to regain their medieval high point.

For a time the Dutch gained nearly complete control of the wine trade along the west coast and used their position to transform wine production as well. "We must recognize the invention with which these foreigners have established this commerce to their advantage, by installing themselves in the cities where the wine trade is greatest, such as Nantes," noted a writer of that city in the middle of the seventeenth century. "First they offered high prices for our wines, and the Nantais . . . planted their best land in vines, hoping the foreigners would take all their wines at a high price."[8] The Dutch had found that the market for cheap white wine, and for the brandy made from this wine, was more profitable than that for high-quality wine and encouraged the French to replant with a cheaper, high-yielding grape. This same stimulus was felt in the hinterlands of Nantes and La Rochelle, and upstream from Bordeaux, leading to a boom in wine, and particularly brandy, production through the seventeenth century.[9] The Dutch pushed certain parts of western France toward a monoculture tied closely to the demands of the northern market and left the vineowners dependent on Dutch merchants, who gained control of prices, quality, and transportation. "We see how these foreigners become masters," complained the seventeenth-century Nantais, "not only of the commerce within and without the kingdom but are even more the master of our goods than are the owners."[10]

The vineyards of continental France enjoyed nothing like the Dutch stimulus of the late sixteenth century, yet certain areas benefited from changed circumstances. New winemaking areas were able to join the con-

Wine into Wealth

tinental export trade, and interregional trade, particularly tied to Paris, gradually became important enough to encompass much of northern France. Beaune profited from the growing taste for stronger red wines around the fourteenth century, as well as from the political union of Burgundy with the Netherlands that gave it new markets. The current of wine flowing from Beaune to Flanders also helped the province of Champagne, through which it passed. Reims became a major entrepôt for the wines of Beaune in the fifteenth century and added its own wines to this export trade. A notable of Beaune complained in the eighteenth century that since "the distance and difficulties of the wine trade led the Flemish and others to commission the wine merchants of Reims" to buy wine in Beaune, until recently the merchants of "Reims and Troyes were practically the only ones to purchase our wine." Only since the end of the seventeenth century had the Flemish decided that the main roads were good enough, and the cost of working through Reims high enough, to come make their purchases themselves.[11]

Both Burgundy and Champagne benefited from the growth and structural change in the Parisian market. Wine from lower Burgundy, around Auxerre, had always played a role in the Parisian wine trade. Exported from Paris, through Rouen, it figured prominently in the stocks of merchants and tavern keepers in Rouen, Amiens, Flanders, and elsewhere in the north. With the growth of the population of Paris the urban consumption of wine also increased, though the city still drew most of its wine from the vines immediately surrounding it. Then a Parlementary order of 1577 gave a powerful boost to the vineyards of neighboring provinces. The order prohibited Parisian wine merchants from buying wine in a radius of roughly twenty leagues (fifty miles) around the city, in order, according to the Parisian police, "to give the bourgeois and communities [of Paris] the time to make their own provisions."[12] As a consequence, Parisian wine merchants extended the demands of Parisian provisioning to more distant vineyards, which benefited from growing integration into a major market, although at the expense of the vineyards closer to the city. The wine traditionally supplied by lower Burgundy was joined by wines from Champagne, and the wines of the Loire, in particular, flowed now toward Paris. Improvements in transportation and the building of new canals in the mid–seventeenth century also gave substantial assistance to the wine traveling from the Loire to Paris. The ordinance of 1577 encouraged the gradual process of integrating the regional markets of France into a national market.

The domestic market in the north of France replaced the export trade, which, along much of the Loire, was in rapid decline. From a maximum of four hundred thousand hectoliters exported through Nantes in the sixteenth century, the flow had diminished to less than eighty thousand hectoliters in 1698 and would fall even lower through most of the eighteenth century.[13] "The region around Blois, alone, once exported sixty thousand muids [160,000 hectoliters]" by way of Nantes, according to an eighteenth-century report from Tours, but now "it appears that the wines of the Loire that are exported through Brittany do not exceed ten thousand muids."[14] By 1667 the magistrates of Blois were lamenting that "the English and the Dutch only come here looking for our wines when there is a poor vintage in other regions and now, either because of a lack of money or because it is easier to trade with Gascony and Aunis, these foreigners have entirely abandoned the Blésois."[15] The French government exacerbated the damage with an order in 1723 prohibiting exports of wine from much of the Loire to the French colonies, claiming that they did not travel well.[16] The difficulties of royal wars and edicts, combined with a sizable tax owed before reaching Nantes (at Ingrandes), pushed the growers of the Loire steadily away from the Atlantic market and toward commerce with Paris. The vast majority of wine shipments from the region around Blois in the second half of the seventeenth century went to Paris.[17] A very partial survey of wines shipped to Paris at the beginning of the eighteenth century indicates that nearly three-fifths came from the upper Loire, particularly around Blois and Orléans, and the rest fairly evenly divided between Champagne and Burgundy, particularly lower Burgundy.[18]

As the vineyards of northern France were pulled into the orbit of the Parisian market they were gradually but irreversibly changed. Reports from Chinon in the middle of the century noted that "since the time when the wine merchants of Paris have recognized the good quality of the wine of this region [apparently in the early 1740s] everyone has given more attention to his vines, the abandoned vines have been renewed, and new vines have been planted."[19] The most common transformation produced by the increasing access to a new mass market (to a city of nearly half a million inhabitants in the late seventeenth century, when all but a dozen French cities had less than thirty thousand people) was a burgeoning reliance on vinegrowing as a monoculture, as well as some decrease in the quality of the wine.[20] The wine produced in the north of France had long enjoyed a reputation for its quality, but the populace of Paris demanded vast quantities of cheap wine. The good wine had been the result of pinot noir or, in the upper Loire, the related auvernat grapes, grown on the best slopes, which produced a low yield of rich, complex wine. In response to Parisian

Wine into Wealth

demand, the regions within reach of Paris turned increasingly to high-yielding grapes, such as the gamay or gros noir, that could grow even on flat land and make an abundance of cheap, unsophisticated wine.

Strong economic incentives encouraged the spread of vines. Peasants with a little arable land could plant gamay vines to produce a far more profitable crop and enhance the value of the land.[21] On a piece of land that made them hopelessly marginal grain producers they could achieve a measure of self-sufficiency by planting vines. A report from Blois late in the eighteenth century defended the spread of vines: "The arid land in the neighborhood of Orléans, Blois, and Tours is worth less than fifty francs an arpent as arable land, but planted in vines this land sells for five hundred francs, one hundred pistolles, up to three thousand livres per arpent . . . but that is not all, the wages for the cultivation of four to five arpents of vines is sufficient to nourish and maintain a vigneron and his family, thus a parish in vines contains at least twelve times more cultivators than a parish of arable labor."[22] This calculation led to the steady spread of vine-yards through the early modern period.[23] It also made viticultural society remarkable for its homogeneity: It was relatively easy to own or lease a modest vineyard, and few individuals controlled large ones.

The transformation of arable land into vineyards became so widespread in the seventeenth century that the royal government finally stepped in to limit the loss of grain lands. In 1725 and again in 1731, royal arrêts ordered that no one could plant new vineyards without express permission. Some intendants had pushed for the measures to remedy an apparent oversupply of wine, but most of the impetus came from ministers who feared that turning grain fields into vineyards was simply aggravating the shortage of bread.[24] Such strictures were clearly not successful. By the end of the Old Regime vineyards had proliferated to the extent of rivaling cereal land in the major winemaking regions of northern France. But the intendants had not been wrong in their fears of overproduction; wine prices remained relatively flat through most of the century, only achieving a boom in the 1770s that collapsed in the 1780s. In fifteen hundred years of expansion the vineyards of France had concentrated increasingly in certain regions and developed a sophisticated commercial network to supply the country and the world with wines. Yet increasing production kept wine producers constantly on the alert for buyers and would make marketing their single most important challenge.

The geography of wine production in France suggests how much grow-ers depended on access to markets. The only survey that offers any detail about the amount of vines and wine production for the whole country comes from the end of the Old Regime and was created retrospectively by an inquiry in the 1820s.[25] The figures are somewhat anachronistic, being reported by modern départements, and are only a rough indication of the extent of viticultural society—for the end of the Old Regime or earlier—but they suggest at least the general contours. The thirty-seven départements that each produced at least 1 percent of the country's wine formed a rough circle. The rim followed the Loire and Rhône Rivers, the Mediterranean and Atlantic Coasts, though it was heavily weighted toward the south. Transportation, by sea or by river, clearly encouraged wine production.

Production flourished along the coasts and within reach of the biggest cities; the markets in Germany also encouraged production in the northeast. The southwest of the country, the seven départements around Bordeaux in particular, boasted over a quarter of all the wine produced in France. The southern départements along the Mediterranean also made substantial amounts of wine (13 percent), especially the Herault. The western départements, along the lower Loire, were no longer so productive, with less than 7 percent of the wine, whereas the most eastern départements produced 10 percent. Finally a core of départements in the center-north, directly connected to the Parisian market, grew 17 percent of the wine.[26] The geography of production emphasized the importance of export markets. Overseas trade from the south and southwest and continental export markets to the east had clearly inspired considerable commercialization of wine production. The only domestic markets to have a comparable impact were the capital, with a cluster of connected départements, and a smaller cluster around Lyon.

A river of wine, flowing from slopes across France to cities and towns throughout Europe, gave life to a world of producers—a whole viticultural society. There are no precise figures for the population or land area directly involved in producing wine, but it can be estimated at under 5 percent of France's land and some 10 percent of its populace.[27] Viticultural society experienced its own structures and dynamics, distinct from the rest of society. Above all it worked with different manifestations of power, for power in the vines, even more than in agrarian society, was determined not only by access to land but also by access to markets.[28]

Viticultural Society

The precocious commercialization of most vineyards, even if only for a local market, gave viticultural society its own very distinctive features. If the grower could find a market, vines produced more profit per acre than cereals; by one estimate they were some twelve times more productive.[29] Vines also escaped some of the burdensome costs of cereal production, such as leaving a third or more of the land unproductively fallow, reserving as much as a fifth of the grain to seed the following year's crop, and renting or maintaining a plow and plow team. Vine tending, in contrast, required purely human labor and modest capital inputs and produced a crop almost every year. Since vines were particularly labor intensive, they provided full employment to a *vigneron* (vinedresser) with only three or four *arpents* (depending on the region, the arpent was usually equal to half a hectare and 25 percent larger than an acre). From a single arpent of vines, an owner could produce five to ten barrels of wine, although the amount varied widely in different parts of France and in different years. An owner did not need to keep any of this wine for domestic consumption since a thin wine, or *piquette,* could be made by adding water to the pressed grapes and fermenting them again. The barrels of wine might be worth thirty or forty livres apiece, again with wide disparities depending on time and place.

A grower's income in many parts of France could be quite respectable from a small number of vines in a favorable year, and a holding of three or four arpents was usually enough to support a family modestly. As a consequence vineyards were usually divided into smaller plots, and their ownership was distributed more generally throughout a community. Most owners held a very small number of vineyards; someone with more than two hectares is designated a "gros vigneron" by one historian, and it was rare to find an owner with more than five hectares of vineyards.[30] Regions devoted to vinegrowing tended to be more densely populated, with larger villages, than cereal regions, with a population that tended to be more property owning and more egalitarian in the distribution of property.[31]

Yet if commerce increased the value of wine production it also exposed viticultural communities to pressures from the outside world. Where winemaking was particularly profitable it drew outside interest, and notables from nearby towns invaded the countryside to buy up the best vineyards. In some of these regions the vinedressers were left with too few vines to support themselves on their own property, creating a workforce little better off than agricultural workers in general. And commerce introduced inequalities, privileging some groups over others. Those with information about and contacts with the outside world, those with financial resources and better vines gained access to the more lucrative long-distance markets. The rest, the vast majority, competed in the limited local market. Thus it is important to look more closely at who produced wine and how, who marketed the wine, and who profited from it.

The landholding patterns in vineyards were generally quite distinct from patterns in cereal lands. In much of the north of France, particularly in regions producing grain for Paris, the tendency during the last centuries of the Old Regime had been toward the creation of large farms owned by urban elites and leased by enterprising peasants known as "*fermiers.*" Parisians had acquired most of the grain-growing land around the capital by the eighteenth century, which they leased out in huge farms. Farms of eighty hectares or larger were common and created a sharp dichotomy in agrarian society between an elite of fermiers who controlled these farms and a proletarianized peasantry.[32]

Viticultural society, in contrast, often enjoyed a far more egalitarian landholding pattern and often more peasant ownership, creating "a sort of democracy of vineyards" in some areas.[33] Studies of vineyards around Paris and Lyon, two regions with easy access to immense urban markets that encouraged the commercial production of mediocre wine, show a majority of the vines owned by the common villagers, even when they had lost much of the plow land to urban notables.[34] In other regions producing for a local market, like the Roussillon in southern France, the overwhelming bulk of vineyards were also divided fairly evenly among the nonelites.[35] In striking contrast to grain-producing regions, where a few privileged individuals (usually outsiders) typically monopolized the plow land, vines tended to be dispersed in small holdings of four arpents and less among most of the households in winemaking regions; even grain fields were more equally shared in viticultural communities.[36] There is little evidence of fermiers enjoying large leaseholds of vineyards, as they did with cereal land, in part because elite proprietors typically owned small plots as well. "One finds more homogeneity in the wine-growing regions," according to a recent historian, "less submission, more of a democratic spirit, more fraternity."[37]

In general, where wine-producing communities had ready access to a large local market for cheap wine they tended to be fairly egalitarian societies of many small-scale producers. The modest owners of small plots of vines in the immediate vicinity of cities like Paris and Lyon could easily market their wine, since the costs of production, transportation, and taxes could be kept reasonably low. Growers right around Paris could send their wine quickly and cheaply to *guinguettes,* taverns outside the tax barriers of Paris, only a dozen kilometers away.[38] Low costs to enter the market meant that even small-scale producers, with limited financial resources, could sell, and make a living from, their wine.

Viticulture was not, however, a guarantee of an egalitarian society. Vinegrowers in many regions of France found it more difficult to market their wine and hence harder to survive on a few arpents of vines. Distance from markets meant higher transportation costs, which so distorted the price of cheap wines that they were all but excluded from interregional trade. Upper Burgundy, around Beaune, offers the classic example of vineyards so isolated from markets that they were forced to develop superior and expensive wines. But expensive wines demanded greater production costs and paid higher taxes. The grower might well have to advance some transportation costs. The net effect was to create a class of wealthy vineowners in regions, like upper Burgundy, that depended on a long-distance market.

The long-distance wine trade both encouraged and was encouraged by the spread of wealthy vineowners. Many of the vines along the Côte de Nuits, south of Dijon, had been acquired by the notables of that city in the seventeenth century. Buying existing vineyards, often from religious institutions, or planting new vines, they transformed neighboring villages with new houses and cellars and actively sought markets for their wines. In some cases their investments and energy created the long-distance trade, by enhancing the reputation of their wine and mobilizing their networks to sell it.[39] Even here, however, the commoners retained over half of the vines—mostly "inferior" vines on the low lands (*pays bas*)—and nearly every vigneron owned at least a few vines.[40]

The notables of Bordeaux, including parlementary nobles, négociants, and English brokers, were similarly in the process of buying up the vineyards all around the city through the seventeenth and eighteenth centuries.[41] It was particularly the notables of these two parlementary cities who could afford to invest in the buildings and vines and experiment with new winemaking techniques that would enhance the quality of these regions' wines.[42] By contrast, the humble vignerons in these regions became day laborers or, if they owned vines, produced a cheap wine on poor land. They could not compete with the wealthy producers for access to the interregional market and had to make do with limited local trade.

Most of the vineyards in northern France, particularly those in Champagne, the upper Loire, and lower Burgundy that were less than two hundred kilometers from Paris and close to navigable rivers, were neither so hierarchical as the wealthy vineyards of Bordeaux and upper Burgundy nor so egalitarian as the Parisian vineyards. They produced wine for a primarily long-distance, interregional market, but rivers gave them sufficiently easy access to this market that most levels of viticultural society could participate. Urban notables had acquired some of the vines in these regions, but simple vignerons continued to own the majority of the vineyards and to compete in the long-distance market. Nevertheless, the dynamics of viti-cultural society and the wine trade in these regions were closer to the hierarchy of upper Burgundy than to the equality of the Parisian hinter-land and are probably more typical, both of French wine production and of the emerging national market.

The precise patterns of landholding in these northern wine-producing regions are difficult to specify, for contemporaries were most impressed by the incursions of urban wealth into the vineyards and tended to dis-tort their impact. In villages along the Loire, according to a seventeenth-century official, "there are few bourgeois of Orléans without a house in the vineyards, with three or four arpents of vines that are sufficient to maintain a vigneron and his family."[43] In Champagne, Ay's reputation had tempted outsiders to purchase land early on; by the end of the seventeenth cen-tury "the largest part of its best vines belong to bourgeois of Paris, Reims, Châlons, and Epernay." Thus, although the town had a "large number of bon bourgeois, there are also many important outsiders who have country houses [*vendangeoirs,* to be occupied during the vintage] there and come to spend the autumn," observed an official of the tax farm at the end of the Old Regime. "It is then that one sees the luxury of the towns contrasted with the simplicity of the natives of this bourg." The populace complained just before the Revolution in their *cahier de doléances* (grievances) of the "thirty-three houses of nobles and bourgeois of exempted cities [outsiders] who possess the largest places and the best property."[44]

The complaints emanating from Ay contained more than a little ex-aggeration, however, since a list of the "property possessed by nobles, ecclesiastics, and other privileged [outsiders] in Ay" in 1789 reveals only seventeen individuals owning a total of 121 arpents (some 17 percent of the town's vines). Only one of them owned more than ten arpents and nine owned less than five.[45] Indeed, the overwhelming majority of the propri-etors held very modest parcels around Ay: Half of the owners possessed no more than an arpent (equal to 0.43 hectares in this region) of vines, and barely 2 percent owned more than five arpents. Large properties were made quite difficult by the very high prices of vineyards here, which swung to either side of one thousand livres per arpent, depending on the year.[46] Privileged outsiders may have bought up the best vineyards, but they did not own very much of them.

Throughout the wine country of northern France, urban elites were actively acquiring the best vineyards in the seventeenth and eighteenth century. By the late seventeenth century, the "seigneurs and bourgeois of Reims, Châlons, and Epernay" had acquired the "best part" of the vineyards in many of the other important wine-producing villages of Champagne: Cumières, Mareuil-sur-Ay, Moussy, and Pierry. In Pierry, furthermore, "the inhabitants possess very little in the good growths," and in Avenay "two-thirds of the land, and the best part, belong to nobles and churchmen."[47] The marquis de Sillery-Genlis alone possessed 110 arpents in two villages along the mountain of Reims, amounting to a fifth of their total vines.[48] The abbey of Hautvillers, home of Dom Pérignon, owned forty-eight arpents of the best vines in the neighborhood, and its oppressive tithes brought in seven times more wine than the monks produced on their own; the vignerons of Hautvillers claimed to be "more wretched and poorer than anywhere else."[49]

In Avize, on the periphery of the river valley, where a reputation for good wine came somewhat later, the invasion of outside landowners was merely postponed. Early in the eighteenth century, according to a merchant in Epernay, "their vines, nearly all planted in white grapes, produced only a small acid wine with a harsh taste that was reputed one of the least in the region and usually sold for only twelve to fifteen livres per barrel." Avize experienced the same transformation of fortunes enjoyed by others in the region, and, beginning in the early 1730s with the "mania for cork popping, their abominable drink sells for 150 livres the barrel and [value of an] arpent of vines has [quadrupled] to two thousand livres."[50] But the prosperity and "beautiful houses" brought by this new market were shared unevenly. Of three hundred households at the end of the Old Regime, "there are no more than a dozen that live comfortably, the majority [are] overwhelmed with misery." Since the middle of the century, fifty-five bourgeois *forains* (outsiders) had acquired "ninety-eight arpents of the best vines and forty-five houses and other buildings, little by little and successively from the poor inhabitants of Avize. . . . Twenty nobles and privileged [people] possess at least another eighty arpents of vines." The reviled outsiders actually owned less than a fifth of the village's total vines; the key to the protests here as in many places was that wealthy outsiders had bought up the *best* vines, leaving the villagers with ample but mediocre vineyards.[51] They could produce wine but had trouble selling it and getting a good price.

The vineyards of lower Burgundy had experienced the transfer from peasant to bourgeois hands, perhaps to an even greater extent than in Champagne. The vines around Auxerre, which occupied half of the land around the city, were owned by every level of the city's inhabitants: 10 percent by the church and notables in parcels averaging 0.8 hectares and the rest among the city's twenty-two hundred other households in parcels averaging 0.43 hectares. Yet only a hundred or so of the owners identified themselves as vignerons, and their plots averaged little more than a third of a hectare. The vast majority, then, of the city's six hundred vignerons owned no vines and worked for others, mostly for a daily wage.[52]

Auxerre's merchants and notables also owned vines in villages all over the region around it, the Auxerrois. The little villages like Vaux, some five kilometers away, were completely dominated by Auxerre. A late-eighteenth-century tax roll of Vaux listed eighty-eight households, including fifty-five vignerons; it also listed 116 outsiders owning property in the village, of whom seventy-three were inhabitants of Auxerre.[53] And fifteen kilometers away, in the village of Migé, "most of [the vines] belong to ten individuals in Auxerre and the inhabitants own only a quarter of their vines." In a small village like Jussy, with only a hundred households, "the wealth of the inhabitants consists only in a few arpents of vines that they cannot even consider as their own, being nearly all burdened with mortgages whose arrears actually amount to more than the worth of the land, due to the mediocrity of harvests [only 150 to 200 barrels a year], the poor ground on which the vines are planted, not to mention the hail and frosts of recent years."[54]

Larger, more distant communities had not succumbed to outside control of their vineyards, but, there too many vignerons owned little land. In the bourg of Coulanges-la-vineuse, two-thirds of the vines in the late seventeenth century and "the largest part of the [arable] land belongs to the bourgeois of the neighboring towns" of Auxerre and elsewhere. Thus, of 216 heads of households in 1666, fully two-thirds were vignerons, but the intendant found only "twenty-four good [well-off] vignerons, forty other mediocre ones who possess some vines of their own but not enough to keep them employed, [whose houses] we have found well enough furnished according to their condition, and seventy-eight vignerons laborers . . . without furniture, most sleeping on straw." In the bourg of Saint-Bris, the majority of the vines belonged to the inhabitants, of whom three hundred were vignerons. But except for fifty of them, who "worked their own inheritance and another fifty mediocres, the rest [were] poor day laborers."[55] Things had perhaps changed for the better a hundred years later, when the tax farm opined that "if the common people of Coulanges were not dominated by the spirit of chicanery they would be well off for they always sell their wine advantageously; but court cases are ruining them. Still there are some good houses."[56] And a report from the beginning of the next century found three-quarters of the land belonging to "peasants and vignerons" in the region around Coulanges.[57]

Wine into Wealth

The postmortem inventories of some three dozen vignerons in Auxerre, Chablis, and bourgs in between show more precisely how they compared to the vignerons around Paris.[58] All owned some vines, most of them between one and four arpents (the arpent here amounted to half a hectare), and the average a little over two. Where some two-thirds of the vignerons near Paris possessed two to four arpents, less than half of these Burgundians did. Three arpents were barely enough to make a grower self-sufficient, so most of these people had to supplement their income.[59] They did so, in part, by practicing a polyculture of cereal and, sometimes, fruit. These vignerons commonly owned at least as much plow land as vines, plus a little more land that might be woods, field, or—in Saint-Bris—cherry trees. This land made up the bulk of their assets: They might have a house; their livestock, if they had any, was limited to a "mother cow" and maybe a donkey. These people lived simply, with primitive furniture, clothing, and tools. Their mobile wealth, which included such assets as well as wine they might be waiting to sell, averaged little over four hundred livres at their death. This put them at the low end of the range that has been described as "vignerons with a little ease."[60] Most of these vignerons could barely support themselves on the amount of grain and wine they produced.

Given the prevalence of viticultural communities like those in Champagne and Burgundy, it is difficult to agree wholly with those who characterize winegrowing as generally egalitarian. Even if the distribution of vineyards escaped the gross disparities of many cereal lands, they were subject to significant inequalities of land values, size, and, above all, access to markets. For only the best wines could enter the transregional wine trade and seek better prices; only an elite could really compete in the market.

Vignerons

The distinctive landholding patterns in the vineyards meant that viticultural society combined peasant and elite proprietors in a close symbiosis. Most vignerons owned some vines, but not enough to be fully self-employed and so had to work for other vineowners. This might be seasonal work, for a daily wage, or salaried work for a full year of vine tending; usually it meant sharecropping. Salaries in the early eighteenth century ranged from thirty to forty livres for a year's work on an arpent of vines and might include lodging and food.[61] As a vigneron could not normally tend more than four arpents a year, this was not a very good income. Vignerons of Champagne complained in their cahiers de doléances at the end of the Old Regime that they were paid only fifty livres per arpent; "there is no harder profession," they concluded. Others worked for a wage, either by the task or by the day, though this generally involved the least skilled tasks.

Much of the work in the vines was heavy and unskilled: The constant battle against erosion suffered by vines that are normally planted on hillsides meant endless earth moving, the brutally heavy hoppers of grapes had to be carried at harvest time, and the muddy soil needed to be aerated with pickaxes each spring.[62] At harvest time, regular vignerons were joined by an army of women and casual workers who hired themselves out for the day. "To harvest all the slopes, from Chambertin to Chagny, in the space of four or five days," remarked an eyewitness, "an unbelievable number of people come from the mountains and from every side."[63] Vine-growing required considerable labor and relatively little capital; this was its distinctive economy. Vinegrowers were spared the expense of plowing, and so of maintaining plow teams, though there were advantages to having some animals, for most growers manured, despite much debate about the merits of the practice.

Vines were also remarkably delicate plants, threatened by a fickle nature at every moment, and particularly vulnerable in the northern half of the country. Here the spring was the "most dangerous season," according to one treatise, when frosts could burn the new growth as badly as a fire.[64] Such vulnerability made vinegrowers deeply religious, known for their defense of traditional Catholicism in the religious wars and still attached to it in the age of Enlightenment.[65] Against the damage done by worms attacking the vines the town council of Ay concluded in 1733 that "no solution remains except to implore God's mercy with public prayer and the exorcism of the insects."[66] A "dissertation on Burgundy" addressed to an English audience in the early eighteenth century mocked Burgundian vinegrowers for their beliefs:

> When the nights are calm and cold, the most superstitious peasants run to the churches where they ring the bells with all their force, imagining either that God takes account of this religious act, or that the bells' agitation of the air can somehow warm it or change the wind: whatever the reason, they ring the bells in this season so that one cannot sleep; at the same time the priests and monks are occupied in the churches reciting the Passion according to John, for which occupation they make a requisition in every wine press during the time of winemaking, and each vigneron is obliged to give them a certain quantity of wine, by order of the Parlement of Dijon.

Summer storms brought the threat of destructive hail. Thus, "as soon as the vignerons see the least cloud on the horizon, and the air seems to menace the least storm, they return to their bells, and the priests to their prayers, which they only recite in the fear that the people would revolt against them if the hail fell while they were not at prayer."[67]

Vines were vulnerable too in the fall, as harvest approached, to frosts and rain. Anxiety pushed the vinegrower to harvest early, but the harvest time was regulated in many places by a *ban de vendange,* an official opening of the harvest, before which no one was allowed to pick grapes. An exception might be made in bad years, when growers lacked sufficient wine to serve the harvesters. On several occasions, the inhabitants of a village near Auxerre, represented by the "largest and best part," had to appeal to the lieutenant of the bailliage to let them each harvest enough grapes to make a half barrel, before the "general harvest" had begun, to give their workers. But with only a gap of ten days between the early and the main harvest, one can imagine the kind of wine they were planning to serve their workers.[68] The harvest was described as an "occasion of joy and innocent pleasures" by an eighteenth-century jurist. "The cities empty out in this season, the country houses are full of people of every condition, and the walking and hunting parties are more frequent."[69] For the lower classes it was a time of employment and hard work.

But the vinedresser's jobs also required considerable skill. As a southern French proverb said of the vines: "Anyone can dig me, only my master can prune me." Knowing how to prune was the most important qualification, a matter of art, biology, and economic strategy. "Here is the skill and the science of the vigneron: for he must choose which branches to cut and which to save . . . of four or five branches from a single root, they only leave one or two of the best."[70] Vines were also pruned through the growing season; those allowed to grow tall bore more grapes with less quality. Vinegrowers in certain areas were gradually starting to prune low during the eighteenth century. The vinedresser also had to know how to attach the vines to props, using straw. One of his major duties involved knowing how to propagate vines, either by planting new ones or by spreading established vines. A well-run vineyard was supposed to be regularly revived by a method of "layering" (*provignage*). This method of creating new vines involved first preparing long shoots from an established vine, then burying part of the vine stem to make it put down roots near the original vine. It meant that new plants tended to cluster around old ones, forming the distinctive pattern of vines bunched together that was common to all of the Marne valley and elsewhere.[71] Vinedressers have been called "agricultural artisans" because they did a "technical job far superior to that of the cereal grower."[72] With skill came a spirit of independence and resistance.

Because so many vinedressers who hired themselves out to labor on other people's vines were also owners of small vineyards, they were often tempted to steal time for their own vines at the expense of their employers. Employers had been fighting this since the late Middle Ages, when they gained legislation to allow vinedressers to work on their own vines only on Mondays, Tuesdays, and Saturdays, thus forcing them to offer themselves for hire the rest of the week.[73] Royal ordinances had also limited wages to five sous for a day extending from sunup to sundown, in the face of demographic disruptions that greatly favored wage earners.[74] The vignerons around Blois, Auxerre, and Châlons-sur-Marne responded with a variety of tactics, from legal challenges to strikes and threats of property damage, to increase their wages or shorten their workday. The vignerons of Blois were known as the *tintamarres,* for their tactic of banging their *marres* [picks] to signal the moment to down tools and quit for the day. Those around Auxerre kept their resistance alive for several decades of court cases and attempts to defend their interests. In legal briefs, they argued against the length of the workday that they were "free people and a free person cannot be forced to work against his will, for that would be against the nature of liberty." They also uprooted the vines of the lieutenant and other officers of the bailliage court.[75]

Conditions in the vines had improved very little by the eighteenth century, and workers continued to organize strikes. Early in the century several dozen vignerons of Epernay had pillaged the *vendangeoir* (situated near the vineyards) of their employer when he refused to feed them lunch. These men were day laborers, "working ordinarily for several bourgeois of Epernay and particularly for Sieur Moët," who had answered a call for workers from another owner. They claimed he had originally offered ten sous a day, but seeing the numbers who responded had given them only nine sous. They knew he had failed to feed them "because he wanted them to have only two meals during the day and several times he has delayed the lunch hour until nearly 11:00." They had stormed the house to look for the food they felt was legitimately theirs.[76] Vinedressers working for the abbey of Hautvillers in Cumières went on strike in 1760 and fought the police when it came to quell them. Right up to the Revolution, vineowners complained of strikes among the vignerons meant "to push the owners to pay a daily wage higher than the customary usage."[77]

The account book of one vineowner testifies to the venomous rela-

Wine into Wealth

tions between vinedressers and their employers. A late spring in 1755 had rushed the spring propagation, giving owners little time to have their vines layered. Competition for workers to get the job done had pushed up the daily wage of vinedressers, "which had made them so insolent and proud that we see them pour the wine they are given on the vines and wipe themselves with the bread they are given and threaten the bourgeois that they will have to hand over their silver for payment." The account book's author refused to pay to have his vines propagated that year and noted with grim satisfaction that "God who sees the ingratitude of men punished them and us for their audacity . . . with a freeze in May that wiped out all the low vines [belonging mainly to the vinedressers]."[78] In his eyes and, perhaps too, in the eyes of the workers, the workforce was a volatile group that threatened revolution when given the chance. But his is less the outrage of a capitalist than of a traditionalist who sees the "natural" order overturned.

Vineowners who wished to avoid dealing with laborers or wanted to be less involved in supervision of their vines would rent them to a vigneron for a yearly contract. The usual contract was a form of sharecropping, whereby the vinedresser did the work and got a fraction, usually half, of the production. Indeed, sharecropping was by far the most common—in some places the "sole"—form by which vignerons worked on land that did not belong to them.[79] Sharecropping was less entrepreneurial than a money rent but also less risky; it was probably unavoidable in an activity where prices and output could fluctuate so wildly. Historians have castigated the system of sharecropping as "petty bourgeois" and assert that any landlord who rented out land that way was "thinking more of his cellar than of his money-bags."[80] Yet sharecropping also meant that landlords were heavily involved in marketing. Rather than receiving a money rent, they were paid in kind, in wine that they then had to sell. Indeed, the sharecropper often turned the whole crop over to the landlord, in return for advances of food and money. Given the difficulties of finding markets for wine, the sharecropper may well have decided that the landlord had better commercial contacts and a better chance of finding a buyer. The result was a class of landowners who did not work the vines yet were still very much engaged in the exchange economy.

The detailed accounts of a vineowner in Burgundy clarify the nature of the economic relations between landlord and sharecropper. The curé of Volnay, just south of Beaune, let his vineyard out to a series of sharecroppers, vignerons who received half of the harvest for having cultivated the vines.[81] The accounts are filled with small sums the curé had doled out to his vignerons during the course of a year for very specific living expenses—

for meat, for salt, for new shoes, for pain bénit, "for his needs," and for his taxes—to a total of some one to two hundred livres. The curé would also pay off his vignerons' debts to others, in one case as much as seventy-three livres that his vigneron had borrowed from a cooper of Beaune "unbeknownst to me." The hôpital of Beaune advanced similar sums to the many vignerons who worked its considerable vineyards.[82] The curé paid too for the capital expenses, which included vine props, and for the wine given to the basket carriers during the harvest. All of this money was advanced against the sharecropper's half of the vintage, which might not be sold until six months after the all the work had been finished. Perhaps because the sharecropper was usually indebted to the landlord, the vineowner was often in charge of marketing all the wine produced from the vineyard.

The vigneron who worked as the curé's sharecropper exercised little control over the eventual fate of his wine. With only a few exceptions the curé sold all of the wine produced by his vineyards in Volnay—that is, the half belonging to his vigneron as well as his own half.[83] The vigneron's recompense was based entirely on the curé's decisions about when to sell his wine, at what price and to whom. The buyer generally paid the whole sum directly to the curé, who in turn paid the vigneron half of the price he had negotiated. But this was also the moment to settle accounts, for advances and sums loaned to the vigneron, so little money actually went to him. A brief accounting between another priest and his vigneron in Beaune was very similar: advances totaling some two hundred livres in one year, for medicines, taxes, grain, and equipment, and then a reckoning that balanced advances against wines produced by the vigneron but sold by the priest over the previous three years.[84]

The experience of these vignerons was much like that of Sebastien Boulley, who had sharecropped the vines of a previous curé of Volnay at the end of the seventeenth century. Apparently he worked the vines of several people, for he refers at certain points to selling wine from the vineyards of the abbey Saint-Jean-le-Grand of Autun, from the vines of the curé of Volnay, from those of a "demoiselle Tougeat," and "our" wine, which must have come from his own property. He also attempted to add vines from another abbey; his accounts describe traveling to Autun in 1693 with his brothers to ask the abbesse of Saint-Androche for the lease to sharecrop some eight arpents in Volnay, which would have made him a sharecropper on a very large scale. On their return, however, they encountered other vignerons already working these vines, who insisted that they already had the contract. It took several months to settle the case, and Boulley received only a third of the land.

Boulley was evidently not a marginal vigneron, yet his account book reveals his very intermittent role in the market. It noted the harvest date and prices for "good wine" from 1684 on but only occasionally indicated that he sold any wine himself. In 1693, for the first time, he sold seven barrels from the various vines that he owned and sharecropped. The wines were sold to a broker (*courtier*) of Beaune for a price well above the benchmark listed in other sources. Again the following year he sold even more, though at lower prices, to a cooper and broker of Beaune and to two merchants of Lièges. There were no sales for the next years until 1698, when he sold wines from the same assortment of vineyards to a merchant of Ypres, with the assistance of a broker of Beaune. This sharecropper sold his wines himself infrequently and must have let the landowner sell it for him in the other years, probably using the profits to cancel advances.[85] Sharecroppers seem to have been squeezed out of the market, then, at least partly because they were in debt to the landowners. This squeeze appears indeed to have been suffered by many small vignerons.

Access to Markets

Despite the widespread ownership of, and access to, vines in viticultural communities, there were impediments to producing and selling wine that effectively limited general participation in the market. The wine produced by small-scale growers was generally neither so good nor so abundant as the wine of "bourgeois" growers. The inhabitants of Chablis testified in 1724 that "the poorly maintained vines, such as those of the vignerons, could only produce ten to twelve barrels per arpent" that year, whereas the "well-maintained vines of all the bourgeois and others produced sixteen to eighteen."[86] Contemporary treatises also distinguished between the wine made by "bourgeois" and the inferior wine of the small-scale "vigneron."[87] In the case of wine in Champagne, the tax farm noted that "the wine's preparation requires art, and those who use it, such as the merchants and bourgeois, make an exquisite wine whereas vignerons with equally good vines make an inferior wine."[88] Vignerons had neither the time nor the resources to lavish the care on their vines that the notables could; just as importantly their vineyards were generally worth less than the vineyards of notables and produced a mediocre wine.

Vinification imposed further disadvantages on common vignerons. Wine presses were too expensive for most vignerons to own, but "those who do not have a press of their own, are subject to hazards," as the British traveler Arthur Young remarked during his visit to Champagne at the end of the Old Regime, "which must necessarily turn the scale very contrary to the interests of the small proprietor . . . as they must wait the owner's convenience, their wine sometimes is so damaged that what would have been white, becomes red."[89] Wine vats (cuves), in which the grape must was fermented before being barreled, presented other problems. Those who lacked a vat or who produced, in bad years, too little to fill a vat would sell their grapes to other growers. Although a study of vignerons around Paris shows that the proportion of growers who possessed at least one vat grew steadily through the eighteenth century from some three-fifths to nine-tenths, Young asserted that there were "[in Burgundy], as in all the other wine provinces, many small proprietors who have but patches of vines and always sell their grapes."[90] The tax farm warned that these sales took place fraudulently—without paying a sales tax—most often when vignerons had their grapes pressed: "All the affluent people have presses and acquire by this means the wines of the vignerons."[91] The vignerons of Champagne also complained in their cahiers at the end of the Old Regime of having to sell their wines at a "very low price" in the months immediately after the vintage, since "they can find no suitable cellars in the region, those available to the disposition of the population being flooded by the water from the mountain."[92]

The accumulated difficulties suffered by poor vignerons translated into a serious disadvantage in the value of their wines. A grower in Champagne quoted common wine prices in his account book, noting the range offered for three distinct categories: the "best" or "first cuvées," the wines of "bourgeois vignerons," and those of "simple vignerons." The best wines tended to be three, four, and even seven times more expensive than the common wines.[93] Similarly, the best wines of Nuits, in upper Burgundy, were some five times more expensive than the worst wines, from the "low lands" at the bottom of the slopes.[94] These disparities in the value of wine became progressively more pronounced during the course of the century.

It is important to remember that wine prices rarely appeared in official price lists, the *mercuriales,* and can only be reduced to a neat trend with considerable distortion to the real confusion of prices. As the tax farm noted about prices in Champagne, they were "difficult to know accurately in that they varied quite often, depending both on the different qualities and on the affluence of the sellers."[95] The accounts of a "bourgeois" grower in Champagne demonstrate some of the difficulties in tracking the price of a commodity that came in so many different grades of quality. The barrister Malavois de la Ganne kept scrupulous record of the prices paid for his wine, from the finest white wine he sold to buyers in Reims,

Paris, and abroad down to the poorest red he might sell to a local tavern keeper; he also occasionally identified the range of prices common to the region. His wines sold for half a dozen different prices in any one year, and it is not always possible to tell which wine he was selling at any time, so it is difficult to track the price of a given quality over time. As a result, his records give us a range of prices, rather than a neat set of points.[96] Still it is possible to identify several rough trends in the prices of Malavois's wines.

The disparity in the values of Malavois's different wines, particularly the gap between his best white wine and his common red, grew steadily through the century, as it did in other regions as well. The price of his white wine tripled between the 1730s and 1760s, whereas prices for his reds rose by barely a third.[97] No single price index adequately conveys his experience of the wine market; instead, there was a range and divergence of prices. Like those few who produced superior wine for a long-distance market, he enjoyed rapidly rising prices. Like the vast majority who produced common red wines for the local market, he saw little change. The wines of upper Burgundy appear to have experienced much the same divergence in prices between excellent and ordinary wines. The price of the best wines in the Côte de Nuits rose sharply in the 1690s and continued to rise rapidly and with little interruption until the 1770s. The common wine of upper Burgundy, in contrast, gained value rapidly in the 1680s but stagnated for most of the next five decades and gained only slowly after that.[98]

The producers of common wines faced even greater problems in selling the product. Wine was not the staff of life and did not enjoy the same buoyant market that grain did through the eighteenth century. The number of consumers, most of them in cities, was growing during the century, to be sure, but so was the amount of land put under vine cultivation, and so was the productivity of vines, with the introduction of high-yielding gamays. The amount of wine available in interregional trade also grew during the century, as the south became increasingly connected to a national wine trade. For all these reasons, the wine market remained remarkably stagnant through most of the eighteenth century, particularly in the north of France. Nominal prices from the 1690s through the 1750s around Paris and in Orléans and Angers were generally stagnant, and their real-money value declined steadily from the 1690s to the 1730s, only barely regaining their former value in the price rise of the 1760s.[99] The prices of wines in the south were more buoyant, as they gradually joined a national market.[100] The late 1760s experienced a sharp drop in production, linked to unusually bad weather that one historian has called a "series of disastrous years," which caused a rise in prices that lasted a little over a decade.[101] Prices were back to normal by the early 1780s. To the extent that high prices in the 1770s reflected inadequate production, they had done the average vigneron little good.[102] For most of the century, the market rewarded winegrowers, especially the majority that made common wines, with little improvement in prices, at a time when the cost of living was rising noticeably.

An important result of the widespread stagnation of the wine trade was that small producers often failed to market their wine themselves. Their wine was often marginal and their access to the extralocal market limited; few small producers could afford to offer wine merchants credit for their purchases and so had trouble finding buyers. Indeed, they often found themselves holding wine they could not sell quickly enough to meet their own debts and were forced to pay creditors in wine. Thus their wine entered the subcommercial economy, as a universal instrument in barter. As the wine merchants of Orléans explained, the common grower often could not wait for the harvest to cash in his crop, so, "during the year, vignerons borrow from the merchant or the property owner, who help the vigneron with grain and with his family's subsistence, and furnish him with all he needs for growing and harvesting the vines, after which they take the wine as payment, as does the bourgeois to whom the vigneron owes rentes."[103] The tax farm of Champagne accused "bourgeois" of fraudulently acquiring great quantities of wine from the "vignerons, their debtors, for advances they have made during the course of the year."[104] This created a class of rural middlemen who had to convert the wines they had collected from various debtors into cash. An array of people who might not have produced any wine themselves, and were not wine merchants by choice, nevertheless had to enter the market.

Tax farmers took advantage of this state of affairs when they tried to impose a special tax on wine merchants in 1710. They levied the tax on most farmers of seigneurial dues and tax collectors as a matter of course, because

> the farmers of seigneurial dues demand wine from the inhabitants in place of the cash they cannot collect for what the inhabitants owe to the seigneurs. They get this wine at a very low price because they have the power to foreclose (for lack of payments) and have the courts sell the wine off. The inhabitants prefer to give them the wine at this price than to pay the court costs. . . . The tax collectors do the same. . . . These farmers and collectors should be taxed all the more because they get these wines very cheap and then sell them for a high price.[105]

The tax farm made similar accusations against people like the baker of Châteaudun who protested that he "furnished bread to the poor vignerons who, unable to pay him, made him take eighteen barrels of wine" that he then sold. Several grain merchants were also "obliged" to take wine as payment for the loan of grain.[106] A barrister at the Parlement of Paris was likewise taxed for lending money to vignerons and receiving wine as payment, "in the same way," he argued, "that all the wine merchants of Burgundy and Champagne receive their wine by advances they make to vignerons." In his own defense, he insisted that "he received the wine from his debtors because of the vines that they rent from him."[107] The intendant of Soissons warned the tax farmers not to impede such payments in kind for fear that they might "ruin the countryside and the vignerons, who are sometimes not able to sell their wine for a long period and yet have only this commodity with which to pay their debts."[108] Many vignerons were forced into this kind of barter because they lacked the commercial contacts and the financial resources to market their own wine.

The difficulties of the market as well as the vinegrowers' weak competitive position meant that a majority were curiously marginal to the wine trade. They might be small producers, making a dozen barrels or so from their own grapes and hoping to work on someone's vines to supplement their incomes. In the aggregate they might own as much as half of the vineyards, and they contributed the labor and much of the expertise that went into producing French wine, but their role in the market was basically a limited one. They sold their labor but not much of their wine, at least not directly. The wine they made by sharecropping was usually marketed by the vineowner. Their own wine was considered inferior to the wine of the large owners: vin de vigneron as opposed to vin de bourgeois. It sold for less and sold less readily. The vigneron would probably sell it locally, either for local consumption or to a larger vineowner, who had a better chance of selling it farther afield. In many ways it was the elite owner, the bourgeois, who holds the key to understanding the wine trade at its regional level.

The Bourgeois Vineowner

The detailed account books of two well-off winemakers, a lawyer in Ay and a priest in Volnay, plus the more abbreviated evidence of several others allow us to gain considerable insight into the economics of winemaking and the culture of the makers. There is evidence for techniques, for weather, for the output and quality of wine. But above all these account books betray the winemakers' obsession with marketing, with finding a buyer. Despite major differences in format and style, the account books both focus not on the process of winemaking but that of wine selling. Liquidating their liquid, turning their vines into income, clearly presented the chief satisfaction and the greatest challenge to these producers. To judge from their concerns, the art of winemaking was really wine marketing.

A bourgeois vineowner in Champagne, Malavois de la Ganne, helps us understand this very specific, and very important, segment of the winemaking population. As a barrister at the Parlement of Paris, he belonged to the notables of Ay and possessed vines, acquired through his marriage into an old family of the town. A small town along the Marne River, scarcely five kilometers from Epernay, Ay was among the most famous of all the vineyards in Champagne, with a reputation already firmly established in the Middle Ages. Malavois was probably one of the larger vineowners in Ay, though he owned no vines in Ay itself for his first seventeen years there. He began his marriage, in 1730, with his wife's five and a half arpents of vines in the nearby village of Cuis and in Epernay and bought three and a half more in Ay in 1747. Even three arpents was more than nine-tenths of the vineowners of Ay possessed.[109] His five original arpents produced an average of twenty-one barrels (each of roughly two hectoliters) each year, though the actual amounts ranged widely between five and fifty-seven barrels. In his later years, with more vines, he produced as much as a hundred barrels, though a "sterile" year like 1758 made only three barrels. Red wines of various grades usually accounted for three-quarters of his production; the white wine he made was his prize, of which he was very proud, but in certain years he failed to make any. Occasionally he supplemented his own production with purchases from other growers, particularly in years of low output. But like all of his neighbors, he faced the yearly challenge of turning wine into money. His accounts focus quite noticeably on this issue; without ignoring the economics of cultivation or of state fiscality, he devoted most attention to detailing his sales and his clients.[110]

His gross income from wine was never very great: Half of the time it amounted to less than fifteen hundred livres and exceeded three thousand only ten times in thirty-five years. Malavois gave no indication of the costs of producing this wine, nor of the arrangements made for working the vines, though it appears that he oversaw them directly and hired out for various tasks. Arthur Young gave a very high estimates for the cost of producing wine: Between the tithes, vine props, fertilizer, grape picking and pressing, barrels, and taxes, he put the costs at nearly half the total value of the crop, and modern historians have largely agreed.[111] A neighbor of Malavois asserted that an arpent of vines normally required 150 livres to be "well maintained."[112] This would have meant 750 livres spent on Malavois's five arpents, or roughly half of his returns in the early years and a third later on. The lapses in accounting are unfortunate, for a full account of expenses would show just how difficult it was to make a profit from winegrowing. Yet Malavois's accounts suggest some indifference to the calculation of profit. The vines were probably a significant part of his assets—more importantly, they were his wife's assets—and he needed to show that he was a reliable administrator of her patrimony. But his primary responsibility was to sell the wine and so turn these assets into cash.

The accounts said little about the actual process of either growing or fermenting the grapes, though Malavois prided himself on making some of the best wine in the region. Vinification was sufficiently "natural" that it required little comment. His description of harvesting with phrases like "gather in the wine" (*recueillir le vin*) rather than the grapes, suggests the immediate mental connection between harvesting and the final product. If the vinification ever went wrong, and there are occasional years when he describes the quality of the wine in his cellar as only mediocre, the fault was attributed to the weather rather than any mistakes made after the harvest. Only once does he blame the "mediocrity of the price of my wine in bottles on the infidelity of a cooper of Ay who gave me barrels whose wood gave the wine an execrable taste." To judge from the account book, the art of wine producing appears to have been in the marketing. This is what obsessed Malavois, as it shaped the fortunes of everyone in the business.

As a jurist of the early eighteenth century remarked, "Once the harvest is done and the wine is in barrels, it remains only to set some aside as provisions and convert the rest into money by means of commerce."[113] This transmutation was the ultimate and essential stage of winemaking; wine's use value was relatively low to its producers. The wealthy owner might save some for his own consumption, as Malavois appears to have done, but even he was anxious to sell if he could. The common vinedresser expected to save none of his wine for consumption; he drank water, or piquette. Rather, everyone sought the exchange value of wine, entering the market in any way they could to turn their wine into money.

Much depended on how rapidly Malavois could sell his wine, for it cost him with every passing day. The steady evaporation of the wine from its barrels threatened to ruin it, since any air pocket forming in a barrel would turn the wine to vinegar in short order. The proper care of wine in barrels required regular refilling (*ouillage*) by as much as an additional 15 percent of its volume over several months. After several months, the prudent producer would also rack (*soutirer*) the wine. By removing the wine from its lees, racking not only clarified it but also removed potentially harmful bacteria. But the cost was substantial, for the dregs had to be replaced with an equal volume of good wine—usually some 5–10 percent—to keep a barrel full. The wine market was so slow in much of the middle of the eighteenth century that a winegrower of Burgundy frequently noted that "the bourgeois were forced to rack their wine." [114]

After several seasons, and certainly by the second year, the wine was considered "old," and it is far from clear that old wine was an advantage to the producer. Given the generally poor conditions under which it was kept and the fragile nature of the wine produced in the Old Regime, old wine did not enjoy a good reputation and rarely commanded as good a price as new wine. Despite Young's insistence that the key to making a profit in the wine trade lay in being able to store it for several years, an assertion echoed by Labrousse in his study of prices, the only real advantage to keeping wine came from the possibility of the next harvest being poor enough to raise prices. [115] This was not a risk that growers liked to take.

Instead, Malavois made a special note in his accounts of the "advantage" brought by the unusual speed with which he had been able to sell his wine—by October—in 1747. The eagerness or absence of buyers made all the difference to prices and rapidity of sales; a comment like the one in 1748 signaled a banner year: "We see nothing but merchants on every side, especially Parisians, who throw themselves in a mass on the wines of vignerons and buy them with no other examination than tasting them in their barrels and even in the must. The premières cuvées had to wait two weeks without being broached [and tasted], but two weeks later they have nearly all been sold."

The alacrity with which merchants bought wine closely mirrored the state of the market, and they responded quickly to shortfalls in production throughout the country. The fact that the harvest of 1736 was generally "sterile" and produced a third the amount of the year before sent prices to twice their normal range for the best white and brought the buyers running. Malavois quickly sold his three best barrels to a broker of Reims in December. The next time merchants came scrambling for wine, in 1747, was provoked by both the dearth of the previous year and the "sterility" of the wines in the mountain of Reims. Thus prices were excellent despite somewhat greater production around Ay, "with the result that these two years have rendered the inhabitants of Ay extremely opulent and the poorest among them able to take care of their affairs." The fact that the harvest of 1748 was very "abundant did not stop the merchants from showing acute eagerness to buy red wine, so that six weeks later none remained at Cumières and very little at Ay . . . in no small measure because of the medi-

Wine into Wealth

ocrity of the wines of Burgundy, both in quality and quantity, besides the fact that their cellars were largely empty." Good years brought fast sales.[116]

More frequent were the laments: "The merchants have not been buying. . . . [N]o one has seen merchants anywhere, few have sold [their wine]; I have been among the great number of these unfortunates." The market was still suffering, in 1751, from "all the old wines from the preceding years that they [the merchants] are determined should be drunk. . . . The vignerons are finding no buyers, which has caused general misery." Malavois would sell little of his own wine that year, and only through family connections. Such periodic oversupply was less disastrous for a notable than for a vinedresser, but Malavois, too, was anxious to sell his wine and was a determined marketer, sometimes taking four and five years to sell his wine to a score of small buyers.

It is worth considering what Malavois meant when he said he could not sell his wine. Was it ever simply impossible to sell wine? There was clearly a window of opportunity for certain kind of sales: The big buyers, from Paris and other countries, came in a season of selling, usually right after the harvest. Presumably Malavois could have assured his sales at that time by offering a low enough price, but there were strong disincentives to selling too low. Other account books reveal the public condemnation of neighbors whose anxiety led them to sell low, and thus "ruin" the whole market. Instead, sellers were expected to play a tense game of chicken, holding out for a certain price at the risk of selling nothing. Malavois lost that game often enough.

With the departure of the big buyers, the alternatives were limited. A whole local economy remained, yet it represented an enormous step down in economic rewards. The local market was awash in wine and demanded little beyond a cheap red wine for the common buyer.[117] Malavois sometimes had to sell to this market, to tavern keepers and artisans or the occasional wine merchant who might have better contacts. At times even this market failed and sellers had to hang a branch over their doors and sell their wine by the quart to customers in their own houses. Malavois succumbed to this necessity once, early in his career, and preferred other routes from then on. For him, being unable to sell his wine meant hanging on to it, with all the risks and expenses that storage entailed, and looking for buyers on his own. "Slow sales led me to send my wine to my friends," he wrote in 1756. He could also rely on a network of familial contacts: a brother in Paris who found buyers in the great city, and a brother in the priesthood who knew colleagues with a taste for good wine.

Malavois's accounts show how much he depended on long-distance trade. The geographic range of his clientele is striking; he sold wine to everyone, from local farmers to the archbishop of Rouen and the intendant of Bordeaux. His bottled wine in particular went to titled noblemen, royal administrators, men of the robe and the cloth. Wine merchants from Paris, Amiens, and Lille occasionally bought large quantities of wine in barrels. Not surprisingly, Paris appeared more often than any other location, but it was the destination in a minority of cases. He shipped frequently to Reims and other towns in Champagne, such as Châlons, Vitry, and Menehould. Wine went regularly to towns in neighboring provinces — Arras, Nancy, Lyon, Chantilly, and Senlis—and sometimes farther afield, to Bordeaux and Rouen. Although he mentioned in 1748 that "the commerce interrupted by the war has been reestablished and favors us with the shipment of our wine to foreign countries," he listed very few foreign destinations. On the whole his wines ended up in northern French cities, many of them accessible only overland by cart. His clients were a combination of local clergy and nobility with wine merchants from the major cities of the northeast. National and even international markets offered certain winegrowers, at least, a means to overcome the commercial stagnation of the regional markets.

The key to marketing was finding buyers, but the system was informal and personal, and sellers usually waited until the buyer came to them. "Since I was a newcomer," Malavois said of his first year, "not knowing the value [of the wine] as well as knowing no merchants meant that I gave the wine at a very cheap price." Fortunately there were several brokers in Ay who solved this problem for him. Through much of his career he relied heavily on local brokers either to bring merchants to him or to buy for merchants they knew. This was the classic job of the broker: to receive visiting merchants and introduce them to growers. The fact that many of these brokers of Ay were innkeepers indicates that one of the important services brokers offered to visiting merchants included lodging, and indeed one broker is described as the buyer's "host." Malavois's accounts were careful to note if a buyer had bought "in the presence of" a broker for the broker would guarantee the sale if the buyer failed to pay. More often the accounts stated that the broker had bought "for" a buyer, who was not there. The broker in that case not only guaranteed the sale, he also handled the shipment and the payment. For these services Malavois owed them a 5 percent commission. Throughout his accounts, we can see how much Malavois had to rely on these intermediaries to help him find buyers.

Brokers were Malavois's chief buyers; he rarely dealt with merchants one to one and generally did not deal with them even in the presence of a broker. In his early years the brokers came all too infrequently, leaving him to find buyers through friends and family. With time he became known to the brokers, at first the local brokers of Ay and, occasionally those of Cumières and Epernay, later the important brokers from Reims. From 1747 until his death in 1766, practically without interruption and regardless of the market, he was able to sell to brokers from Reims, usually to the same half dozen individuals. In some years they might not come before the spring, and occasionally they might not come at all, but he had clearly established commercial ties to several brokers of Reims that integrated him into a larger market. These brokers, buying large quantities of wine that they directed toward the important markets of northern Europe, contributed greatly to his prosperity.

Malavois enjoyed the social and economic advantages of being a notable producing first-class wine but still found that the market challenged him. His wine was good enough to tempt the palates of elite consumers around the world, ensuring him a good income even from a small vineyard. His contacts with elite consumers were also unusually good, with relatives in Paris and friends across northern France who could help him market his wine. Nevertheless his business was fraught with difficulty, and his wine was often a burden. He rarely sold it quickly enough to avoid the expense and inconvenience of racking, and sometimes even bottling, his wine in the spring. Even with his advantages he found it difficult to work the transmutation of wine into wealth and relied whenever possible on brokers to provide the philosopher's stone.

A Curé of Volnay

The accounts of another bourgeois grower, Delachère, the curé of the village of Volnay in Burgundy just south of Beaune, are also obsessed with the challenges of marketing wine. If ostensibly quite different from Malavois in both his location and station, he was yet quite similar with regard to his wines. Both owned vineyards of roughly similar sizes and among the most prestigious regions in France.[118] Both enjoyed enough income that their wine would have been described as "bourgeois," meaning that it came from good vineyards, that they could invest in their own equipment, could fertilize properly, and perhaps most importantly, could afford to sell their wines at prices they accepted. Unlike the common vigneron, they were not hounded by creditors or tax collectors to sell at distress prices. Nevertheless, historians have stressed the similarity and "solidarity" of curés with the peasants around them, particularly in vinegrowing regions.[119] Like them, the curé cared greatly about his wines and the income he received from them and devoted considerable attention to selling his produce. Most importantly, the curé of Volnay shared Malavois's need to find markets, and in this he was also dependent on the brokers.

Like many elite landowners, the curé used sharecroppers to tend his vines. The curé's sharecroppers changed fairly frequently, rarely staying for more than two years. As we have seen, the curé lent money to his share-croppers and would deduct the debts from the sale of the sharecropper's half of the wine harvest. He did not have much luck with his growers; on several occasions he received reports from two "*prudhommes*" of their fail-ure to layer and bind the vines and assigned a modest fine on the grower. Otherwise, the accounts revealed little interest in vinegrowing and utter indifference to the process of vinification. They listed exactly how many baskets of grapes were harvested from each parcel of vines, and then how many barrels of wine resulted from these grapes, but between the two stages there is an interesting hiatus—the winemaking itself. We know from other evidence that the winemakers of Volnay pressed the grapes very soon after picking, and so left the juice in contact with the skins for a very short time.[120] This made for a light color red, and the wine had picked up little of the tannin that could help age it. Yet, aside from identifying the date of the harvest, Delachère's accounts say nothing about when the grapes were pressed or when they were barreled. The process of fermentation was evi-dently so simple, and so rapid, that it did not merit comment.

The curé was not indifferent to the quality of his wine, however, and paid close attention to certain factors that would influence the size and value of his crop. The weather, in particular, fascinated Delachère, and his accounts were remarkably well informed about the weather in the princi-pal wine regions of France and abroad. Much of the 1730s seems to have been a time of appalling weather around Volnay, and the wine market was very unstable. Storms were frequent, like the ones in 1732 when hail stripped the vines, and torrential rains washed great quantities of earth off the vineyards. No wine was produced in Volnay that year, and subsequent years produced very little because of the fragile condition of the vines. Vines often suffered gravely from frost, sometimes throughout the whole country, as in May 1736; in Volnay the "low vines" were most hurt and the "fine wine" the least. Following a heavy snow in May 1741 that had damaged many vines, wine was "very expensive, not because of its quality but its scarcity."[121] The brokers from Nuits came quickly that October, buying before they knew what price to offer. It becomes very clear that this curé had excellent contacts around the country, for he could report on the weather conditions in Languedoc and Champagne, as well as the neighboring Mâconnais and Auxerrois. He even noted the conditions in Switzerland and Italy that were reported by a broker of Dijon. All of this information told him about the state of the national wine market and so would be valuable in setting a price on his own wine.

Delachère followed the market closely and speculated modestly on certain occasions. In years when the demand was so great that the market was flooded with buyers, then the curé bought and sold too. In 1728 he had sold all of his good wine to his regular broker from Nuits before the price was even set and sold some of his cheap wine soon after. He and a neighboring curé bought a dozen barrels of wine from a nearby village in late November, which he sold three weeks later for nearly 20 percent more than he paid, and he bought more during the late spring. He felt emboldened to trade for himself again in 1730, when he bought five barrels from a vigneron, with a clause that he did not have to take any barrel that he could not sell. Having quickly sold his own wine in 1737, he again bought wine from a local grower. A week later he sold it for 50 percent more than he had bought it. He would speculate in other years when the price was high and the brokers came early.

In most years, however, the demand for wine was less evident, and the curé was lucky to sell even his best wine. At one point he blamed a war waged "for six or seven years with the King of Prussia and England" for keeping foreigners from buying wine, "a huge and irreparable loss for Burgundy." Then he did not buy wine and gave little indication of having sold his common wine; indeed, he was usually rather casual about reporting the fate of his cheap wines. His account book reported the yield of a dozen vineyards in three different categories of vines, as well as his "vin de passion," collected as a kind of tithe. The quantity of grapes in each category was roughly equal, but the quality was quite different. His first category might be worth anything from eighty to six hundred livres per *queue* (in this region, a double barrel of 456 liters), whereas his common wines were rarely worth thirty or forty livres per queue, and usually he made no record of even having sold them. When he did sell the common wines, it was often later in the year and they entered the local market: sold to other growers, to *cabaretiers,* even to other curés. Some of this wine went into a local system of barter, exchanged for furniture with his parents, for wheat with a local grower, for cloth with a merchant of Beaune.

It was his "good wine" that entered an interregional market, the vast majority of it sold to brokers of Nuits or Beaune. Delachère was among a privileged few; he found buyers in almost every year and usually without too much delay. Unlike Malavois de la Ganne, the curé was nearly always able to sell his best wine within three months of its harvest, though in some years he admitted that "I was considered fortunate to have sold my wine." The accounts of François Antoine, a broker of Nuits who bought most frequently from Delachère in his first two decades, suggests how fortunate the curé was. In 1725 Antoine owed twenty-five thousand livres to some two dozen people for wine sold to him, but only a third of them were identified as vignerons, and they were owed less than a fifth of the total. The rest were office holders, *bourgeois,* canons, and wine merchants in Dijon, Nuits, and even Reims.[122] Antoine's evident preference for buying from notables resulted no doubt from the superior quality of their wine, but he was also looking for sellers who could offer him credit.

Delachère's accounts emphasize this need for sellers to be able to extend credit; the curé usually had to wait three months to receive his first payment and rarely received full payment in less than a year. His sales to the Parisian wine merchant Montussaint through the 1740s forced him to live with impossibly slow payments. Montussaint paid the curé much like a broker, in installments throughout the year, but fell much farther behind than a broker would have; there were sums still due from 1751 in 1765. In the summer of 1747, when an accounting showed him still owing thirteen hundred livres, they went to a broker in Beaune who agreed to take over the debt and put the curé "on his books." The broker paid him shortly thereafter with a bill of exchange; Montussaint paid himself for subsequent purchases. Such delays were distressing, but Delachère's ability to wait for the income from his vineyards set him apart from most vignerons and gave him distinct advantages in the market.

In most cases Delachère sold to wine merchants through a broker without knowing who the buyer was, though in 1731 he recorded selling to "Mirey and Bailly, merchants of Madame Millon, broker of Beaune." These two wine merchants were unusually prominent, being both privileged wholesalers, the one a "merchant of the king," the other a "merchant of the queen." This meant they supplied the court and had useful privileges in supplying Paris as well. The privileged wine merchants, of whom there were several dozen, generally handled the most prestigious wines, as in 1722 when one of them brought the "best wines" of upper Burgundy to the king's coronation.[123] They also handled the largest quantities of any wine merchants; Delachère notes in 1742 that Mirey bought fifteen hundred barrels in three days, and Bailly bought six hundred. It is not clear that their broker, Millon, was even present when Delachère sold to them, though she certainly received a commission and handled the finances, paying Delachère for his wines over the course of the year.

As the grower's principal contact with the outside world, the broker might also play the role of grocer and banker. Delachère's most regular broker, Antoine of Nuits, apparently also dealt in other goods, since the curé received small quantities of linen, food, and furniture, in addition to cash for his wines. The cash was particularly welcome since it was often so scarce a commodity. With an occasional injection of cash, the village economy worked on extensive networks of debt. Whether dealing with his own vinedresser or with other growers, Delachère gave and accepted credit. Thus, another service offered by this local broker was in settling accounts with the curé's creditors and debtors for him. He acted to some extent as a local banker, helping to cancel out the web of debts that spanned the community. Except for some barter and a certain amount of canceling debts, Delachère's finances were usually cash. The rare payments to him in bills of exchange seemed to disconcert him, and he quickly passed them on to a local merchant or simply refused them, "not wishing to take it on."[124]

Brokers also played a crucial role in organizing the wine market and, above all, in setting a benchmark price with visiting merchants. Growers were accustomed to pricing their wine in relation to that benchmark, asking so many livres more or less than the benchmark depending on their experience of its relative value. Upon that price depended the fortunes of all wine producers, and its negotiation was a matter of intense interest. Every year the process combined the elements of theater and tournament, publicly dramatizing the relative economic power and status of individual and corporate participants of the wine trade. It challenged these participants, at a moment of maximum ignorance—buyers frantically assessing the quality of the wine, sellers desperately uncertain about the state of the market— to test their strength against each other. The price became a definition of their economic and social identity, a measure of relative power.[125] But the message derived from pricing was usually a humbling one for wine sellers.

The process ideally involved an amicable consensus between buyers and sellers; the privileged merchants, Mirey and Bailly, dining with the curé and "all the bourgeois of Volnay," set the price in 1748. This was evidently "to the satisfaction of many bourgeois," but the curé complained the following year of "the maneuver of Mirey and the brokers who, from the beginning, decried [the wine] everywhere without knowing it" and so forced the price down.[126] Delachère found it difficult to admit the structural weakness of the sellers' position and preferred instead to condemn the frequent examples of brokers' sharp practices. He blamed the low prices in 1727 squarely on a broker of Beaune, "who had as little knowledge of these wines as good faith in his commerce." The broker had talked one of the local notables, the wife of a royal prosecutor in Beaune, into selling her wine for less than half the price of the previous year. He had insisted that the wine was worth even less and had pretended that a convent in Beaune had agreed to sell its wine for the same price. "He had struck her particularly by saying that the wines of Volnay were worthless and would turn to water in less than six weeks." The woman had given in but, feeling somewhat embarrassed by her timidity, had asked the broker to keep their deal a secret. He promptly told all the other brokers and merchants "to gain glory for having set the price of the wines of Volnay."[127] The power of this first price-setting was such that "whatever the bourgeois [of Volnay, Beaune, Pommard, and others] tried to do they had to return to this price and whoever had offered more was obliged to give only that price."

Delachère found himself in a similar position in the 1735. The year had experienced much bad weather, and the grapes, growing on vines still weakened by the disasters of 1732, were not in good shape. He had produced very little wine, of rather dubious quality, but the region had produced so little for several years that he hoped the prices would remain high. He was offered three hundred livres per queue in November but had refused "out of fear of harming the region and from the advice of the barrister Maitrize." Either his sense of duty or public pressure kept him from selling anything that year, and he was obliged to sell it the following summer to a local tavern owner for 150 livres. Evidently Maitrize had persuaded other growers to refuse the merchants' offers and demand "excessive prices." Delachère wrote bitterly of Maitrize having "damaged Volnay by more than twenty thousand livres [in losses] for having demanded seven hundred livres a queue for his wine."[128]

At the same time, the market did not automatically respect a price that had been badly set. The Parisian merchant Geoffroy set the price in 1751 and again the next year, but he set the price too high—at 250 livres per queue—and drove many buyers away. "The Flemish merchants who had been at Beaune for a fortnight were offering 165 livres and left without concluding anything; and if it were not for the price set [by Geoffroy] we might not have received two hundred livres for wines that had little quality." In fact, the wines that year were so green that "the brokers left them on the pomace until April and then paid only 130 livres for the best wines of Beaune."[129] Delachère offered to take less for his wines the next year "to recompense [the buyer] for the loss he had suffered the previous year." Geoffroy set the price at 280 livres in 1752, but the same morning he paid 310 livres for the wines of Maitrize, "which led all the bourgeois whose wine had been marked to ask for three hundred livres, and they got it."

The curé clearly saw pricing as a corporate struggle between local wine producers and outsiders, and he was very hard on compatriots who failed to defend local interests. He accused Maitrize of acting "to the great detriment of the province" again in 1743 and in 1745, both times by setting the price too low. Many, including the curé, had already marked their wine without a price, "fearing that the merchants would not come." The curé had already sold a big batch of his wine to a broker of Nuits for "a *pistole* less than the highest price in Volnay." Delachère would accept a similarly vague formulation for the next years of the decade, but Maitrize "did not wish his wines marked without a price." Panicking from fear that he would be left with his wine, Maitrize "abandoned it for 270 livres" despite the fact that the "council held among the merchants and brokers of Beaune set it at three hundred livres."[130]

Setting the price determined the kinds of profit to be made by all parties and so became a test of wills, of courage and, ultimately, of economic strength, at which the sellers were not very good. Prices were rising in 1752, but the "agitation" of a major seller led him to "abandon his wine" for too low a price and kept prices from reaching their proper level. After all the buying was over, the buyers "could not help remarking that when we have good wine we do not know how to sell it." The curé's disgust in 1762 was equally divided between his neighbors, for the "fear that took hold of the bourgeois' spirits," and the brokers who forced the prices down to 120 livres but then resold the wine for the benchmark price of 205 livres. The brokers "were able to make twenty thousand livres this year, and [there are] some who make forty or fifty thousand." He decried the fact that growers "have to go through the opinions of people so avid and self-interested," and he called brokers "the prime lips of evil" (*prima mali labes*).[131]

Delachère and Malavois had much in common with the moderately well-off vineowners who played the largest role in the wine trade. They did not own a majority of the vines in a region, but they owned the best and made the best wine and had most access to the interregional market. They employed many of the vinedressers and loaned them money and bought their wine to resell it. They scrambled to find buyers, to turn their liquid into money, but they rarely managed to work the market to their will. Instead, they worked through intermediaries, middlemen who might simply facilitate a transaction between wine producer and consumer but more often formed an opaque screen between the seller and the ultimate buyer. Both Malavois and Delachère looked to brokers as the chief agents of the wine market, the "masters" who organized and manipulated the market, the buying agents who gained control of the market. We too will look to these brokers and at their rapid rise to power.

2

The Provincial Wine Trade

Commerce, as we saw in chapter 1, was the heart of viticultural society, pumping life into the provincial economy by turning its wine into wealth. France was experiencing a commercial transformation in the eighteenth century that spread unevenly through the country, one that would contribute as much to the economic growth of France as would any agricultural revolution before the end of the Old Regime.[1] Commercial integration, made possible by improvements in communications and transportation and by the growing sophistication of commercial intermediaries, encouraged the growing specialization of production and commercial involvement of producers. The improvements in transportation, particularly the road and canal building of the seventeenth and eighteenth centuries, connected the different parts of the country more effectively than ever before. These improvements allowed the domestic economy to respond to the growing population and new demand for a range of subsistence and consumer goods. Historians have tended to focus their discussion of the commercial transformation on the rapid increase of external trade and its impact on a growing hinterland.[2] Exports were probably the most dynamic element in the eighteenth-century French economy, both as a source of profits and as a stimulus to commercial activity. But the wine trade demonstrates the rival importance of a domestic market, centered on the capital and radiating out to the far corners of the country, and it is worth considering the commercial dynamics of that trade.

For all the attention paid to France's external trade in the eighteenth century, little work has been done on its domestic trade, much of it tending to downplay the significance of internal commerce. Studies of the interior regions of eighteenth-century France, such as Auvergne and Limousin, have emphasized their autarkic character, producing far more for subsistence than for exchange: "The proportion of autoconsumption within global household consumption appears extremely large in lower Auvergne and it is overwhelming compared to the [commercial] exchanges of nearly all plants cultivated—with wine being the striking exception." With the exception of the markets for livestock and wine, the trade in agricultural produce was limited and local.[3] Such commercial isolation appears to have been the case in the "large majority" of France in the seventeenth century—"all of the countryside, [and] a good part of the bourgs and even of the towns."[4] A study of Provence invokes the limited range of seventeenth-century peasants, who "bought or sold little more than the products raised locally, bringing them the short distance to the local markets, small but numerous."[5]

Markets grew substantially in certain regions during the eighteenth century, depending on their access to demand. It appears generally true that, where transportation linked a region to a source of demand, rural society responded in the manner of a classic vent for surplus by exporting its surplus and even by reorganizing the economy to produce a greater surplus.[6] Aside from the demands of a few large cities, this vent for surplus was normally a port tied to the international economy.

One of the classic examples of export trade acting as a vent for surplus occurred in the southwest of France, centered around the port of Bordeaux. Much of the southwest had been linked up to this market by the eighteenth century, producing wheat and wine for shipment to colonies and countries across the globe. The region connected to Mediterranean ports as well by the eighteenth century. The grain trade of the southwest enjoyed several advantages—ports along the Atlantic and Mediterranean coasts, the Canal des Deux Mers—that both encouraged production for export and facilitated transport over long distances. As a consequence, the region had achieved a level of market activity and integration unrivaled in most of France.[7] Still, a study of Languedoc shows the limits of this market. The province as a whole managed to produce little more grain than it required for its own consumption, and the majority of the grain trade was intraregional, from upper Languedoc that produced an excess, toward lower Languedoc that failed to feed itself, or a bit beyond to Provence.[8] This kind of specialization allowed lower Languedoc to shift much of its agriculture into vinegrowing and producing wine that could be shipped overseas.

The growth and sophistication of the southwest's market system appears to have been a largely isolated phenomenon, cut off from most of the rest of the country. As one study of Aquitaine concludes, "Its weaker relations with the north, center and east of the kingdom confirm the classic notion of an Atlantic France"—that is, the western periphery of France that turned outward and away from continental France.[9] Even within this privileged region there were limits to the impact of the grain trade on internal markets. Upper Languedoc, which produced so much surplus for the region's grain trade, enjoyed little profit from the commercial activity. "The principal profit," explained an official in 1739, "goes to the merchants of lower Languedoc" along the coast.[10] The markets of the interior were still quite unsophisticated and heavily reliant on the commercial direction of the négociants in the major coastal entrepôts. "This external dependence blocked the development of a true commercial network of merchants" in the interior, according to a recent historian, and perpetuated a fundamental dichotomy between the economies of the ports and their hinterlands.[11] The experience of upper Languedoc reminds us that the benefits of a vent for surplus depended on gaining access to markets, which in turn depended on the development of commercial organization.

Georges Frêche's definitive study of upper Languedoc blames the subordination of its grain trade to outside influences on the "handicap" of its "continental position." The interior markets lacked the access enjoyed by large merchants of the major coastal entrepôts to the international grain trade, with its own rhythms, commercial contacts, and capital. As a result, the interior failed to produce independent merchants who worked for their own risks and profits. Rather, grain in the interior was purchased and assembled by small-scale brokers and commissioning agents working at the behest of and subordinate to financiers of the major ports. Frêche dismisses these local brokers as "simple agents executing distant orders." Their role amounted to nothing more than being "transparent intermediaries" between the real economic rivals, the local producer and the distant négociant.[12] "Without a full commercial network," the inland region that produced the grain, particularly around Toulouse, was forced to "surrender its fate into the hands of the merchants of Bordeaux and Marseilles."[13]

The studies of the grain trade in the north of France indicate the importance of a metropolis as a vent for surplus but testify to similar underdevelopment in the commercial network. The impact of Paris on its surrounding countryside, particularly its need for grain to feed over half a million persons, created a commercial system as extensive as the one in the southwest of France. The demands of normal years engulfed the grain fields up and down the Seine River plus the broad plains north and south of the city, to a distance of a hundred miles; in times of crisis the net was spread much farther.

At the same time, it is clear that the commercial system supplying Paris with its food was only slowly gaining sophistication. The seventeenth-century grain trade is characterized by Jean Meuvret as "episodic" and "casual," "fragmented" by the lack of transportation and the lack of credit.[14] The Parisian grain trade in the eighteenth century experienced only modest improvement. A recent study of large grain producers in the region finds them abandoning local markets to carry on trade directly with Paris. The huge Parisian demand for animal forage excited a particularly active commercial response.[15] Despite growing market integration, however, the grain trade in the countryside surrounding Paris was still operated by buyers of a very small scale. "Even medium-sized grain trading . . . was relatively uncommon," according to Steven Kaplan, "and the bulk of the grain trade was 'abandoned' to a multitude of petty dealers." For a series of reasons, including the dispersion of the supply of grain, the difficulties of transportation, the wary suspicion of public officials, and the risks attendant upon a commodity with a volatile price, the grain trade "remained largely local and intraregional."[16]

On the whole, then, the internal market of eighteenth-century France was fragmented, uneven, and—despite the strength in a few regions—quite limited. Those regions that enjoyed most success seemed to have benefited from several factors: in particular, from a powerful vent for surplus in the form of a port or metropolis, a transportation network that integrated the region to the main market, and large merchants, or négociants, who could organize the trade.[17] The first two factors might give a powerful economic stimulus to a region's economy, but the third factor shaped the region's relationship to the larger world and the degree to which it would benefit from this relationship. As upper Languedoc demonstrates, the absence of local merchants of any stature left the region subordinate to outside influences. The existence of all three factors was rare enough to leave most of France struggling to catch up. The one sector that transcended the general mediocrity was the wine trade.

Regional studies, whether of the largely autarkic provinces in the center of France or the more market-oriented peripheries, emphasize the preponderance of the wine trade in the commercial activities of their region.[18]

The Provincial Wine Trade

"Wine was still the major element in the large-scale commerce of Aquitaine and the Charente during the mid–seventeenth century" and would remain so through the next century.[19] Wine represented three-quarters of the cargo leaving Bordeaux around 1700, and a quarter of the nearly eight hundred thousand hectoliters of wine exported from Bordeaux originated "upstream," from vineyards along the Garonne and Lot River as far away as Toulouse. Exports of wine from the southern ports of Sète and Marseille were also beginning to mobilize the wine trade of the interior at the beginning of the century.[20] Studies of the wine trade in the south and southwest, based on port records, have taught us much about the export trade of wine, just as our knowledge of the French economy in the eighteenth century has been dominated by studies of its external trade.[21] Our knowledge of the overall domestic market lags behind, and about the domestic wine trade we know very little.

The export-oriented wine trade of the southwest employed some of the more sophisticated commercial organization in the country. The wine merchants in Bordeaux were actually agents for foreign markets, many of them foreigners themselves, with close connections to merchants in the countries that were the ultimate destinations of the region's wines.[22] They were identified at the time as *commissionnaires,* commission brokers who bought wine at the request of a distant correspondent.[23] Although they would occasionally buy wine on their own and for their own speculation and were identified equally as merchants and négociants, most of their commercial activity was by commission and so dependent on specific demands from distant markets. From their base in Bordeaux these merchants drew wine from a vast hinterland, over whose trade they exercised nearly complete control. The majority of their wine came from the countryside around Bordeaux and was easily accessible. There, merchants had to work through official *courtiers,* brokers who enjoyed the privilege of supervising contacts between buyers and growers. The rest of the wine came from up the Garonne and Dordogne Rivers, as far away as Cahors, Toulouse, and Bergerac. In these regions the wine merchants of Bordeaux operated networks of "correspondents" to mobilize the timely arrival of wines at the port, though these brokers and commission agents appear to have been relatively modest in their scale and autonomy.[24]

Although the wine trade around Paris has not been studied with the same care that the trade in the south has received, there is evidence that its commercial system rivaled the wine trade in the southwest, if not in size then at least in complexity and sophistication. With an important vent for surplus in the growing capital and an elaborate riverine transportation system, the wine trade in the north enjoyed important factors for economic growth. Even in the early eighteenth century, it knit together several distinct regions; by the end of the century it had connected much of the country to the Parisian market. The wine trade was also creating agents of considerable sophistication throughout the hinterland to organize this commercial system. The local agents of the wine trade were crucial to the balance of commercial power both within the provincial economy and between the provinces and the metropolis.

The wine trade in Champagne illustrates the range of market systems already operating in one of the more precocious regions of France. Its exports to cities and courts in Flanders and beyond had flourished since at least the fourteenth century, and this market was still important to the province in the eighteenth century. At the same time Champagne sent much of its wine to an internal market, in Paris. These two markets were organized quite differently by the eighteenth century, and a comparison reveals significant disparities in their levels of commercial development. Export trade had already produced a complex array of merchants, the largest of them firmly in charge of the province's ties to foreign markets. The internal wine trade, linking the province to its metropolis, provided a critical source of demand to Champagne's viticultural community, yet it was only gradually producing the kinds of autonomous commercial agents that were already well established in the export trade.

The Wine Trade in Champagne

The history of the wine trade in Champagne is an example of the triumph of market forces over the limits of climate. The region is far enough north to lie at the extreme range of viable vinegrowing. It is vulnerable to bad weather, and, through the early modern period, it suffered from frequent disappointing harvests.[25] At the same time, Champagne has also enjoyed a significant geographical advantage: The region lies close to major markets, in Flanders to the northeast and in Paris to the west. In this fashion economic factors have balanced physical handicaps, as the spur of urban demand stimulated centuries of winemakers to struggle against the climate.

Thus the history of the wine of Champagne comprises as much the evolution of its markets as it does the development of its unique production. Its markets dominated the economic life of the province and drove the creation of new kinds of wine. Its markets established the wealth and fame of the province, but also held it hostage to the vagaries of taste, fash-

The Provincial Wine Trade

ion, and demand. The endless search for access to markets gave shape not only to the economy of the vineyards but also to local society. We have seen already how the search for buyers dominated the accounts of wine-growers. Only the union of buyer and seller could transform the wines of Champagne into its wealth.

The rich cities of the Low Countries, deprived by their northern location of producing their own wines, imported substantial quantities from France through the Middle Ages. Champagne was rather farther than Laon from the Flemish markets, and so its wines were not initially as important as wines from the Laonnois in provisioning Flanders.[26] In the years around 1400, the counts of Hainaut imported three-quarters of their wine from Laon and only one-sixth from Champagne. At the same time, Saint-Omer, in Flanders, drew its wine from Laon and overseas rather than from Reims. But the buyers from the Low Countries turned increasingly to the wines of Champagne in the fifteenth century. By the middle of the sixteenth century, wines from Champagne, particularly those from Ay, had risen to four-fifths of Hainaut's imports.[27]

The wine's success in northern markets resulted to a large extent from the rising reputation of new wines that were beginning to make parts of Champagne famous. Although there were literary accolades in the Middle Ages for the lightly sparkling white wines made in certain towns along the Marne River, they were made with inferior white grapes that had a tendency to turn yellow and did not last more than a year. As a result of the pinot noir grape, perhaps imported from Burgundy, the vineyards of Champagne started to produce a light red wine that could compete with the wines of Burgundy, already famous throughout Europe.[28] Northern merchants traveling south to look for red wines from Burgundy became increasingly interested in the alternatives from Champagne. Even in the eighteenth century a treatise on winemaking explained that "much red wine has been made in the last years in Champagne; these wines are good for [sending to] Flanders, where they can easily be sold as [wine] from Burgundy." The wine from the mountain of Reims, south of the city, was particularly recommended to those "who are looking for wine to send to distant provinces and foreign countries," since they had "more body and handle being transported much better than wine of the [Marne] River."[29] The mountain wines dominated the export trade even though the river wines were more fashionable.[30]

Because of its proximity to the Low Countries, Reims was the principal gateway for the export of wines both from Champagne and from Burgundy. Since at least the fourteenth century, Reims served as the market for the wines not only from its own neighborhood but from the Marne River, farther away; it was also a major transit point for the wines of Burgundy that were particularly sought by northerners.[31] Figures from this period show that Reims shipped an average of some eight thousand barrels to markets outside the city, in addition to its own consumption that equaled at least a barrel (of roughly two hectoliters) of wine for each of its ten thousand inhabitants. Roughly two-thirds of the wine leaving Reims in the fifteenth century went to the Low Countries.[32] Although local consumption outweighed exports in volume, exports stimulated the most commercial activity. As early as the early fifteenth century, Reims officially claimed that "the commerce of the city is in large part based on the wines which pass through or are brought here . . . [and] are sold by brokers," and the inhabitants of the nearby city of Châlons presented themselves as "occupied for the most part in selling wine to merchants from Picardy, Hainaut, Flanders, Liège."[33]

By the middle of the eighteenth century, Reims and the region around it tied Provence for having the third most valuable wine exports in France, behind Bordeaux and Burgundy, although this amounted to only 3 percent of the country's wine exports (by value) as opposed to the 78 percent exported by Bordeaux. In addition to some four thousand barrels of wine sent out of the country, the region sold nearly ten times that much to French cities north and east of Reims.[34] The city of Reims dominated the region's wine trade, in which its citizens enjoyed a long tradition of active participation, "both the inhabitants who harvest a great quantity of wine from the mountain of Reims as well as from the Marne River, and wine merchants who make it their particular trade."[35] As early as the fifteenth century, the wine trade had been described as a "commerce open to all."[36] The city defended this tradition of widespread involvement at the end of the seventeenth century by buying the privilege of allowing "all merchants, brokers, and the public to participate in the traffic and commission of wines."[37] Thus, in addition to nearly eighty wholesale wine merchants identified at the end of the seventeenth century, many of the town notables were involved.[38]

The eighteenth-century wine trade in Reims was a complex and sophisticated market that involved a range of economic agents. What we can learn of the most important brokers shows them to have been operating on a very large scale, with customers across northern France and the Low Countries. Their commerce was aimed particularly toward long-distance trade. At the same time there were merchants who participated more intermittently and locally, their wine trade subordinated either to larger mer-

The Provincial Wine Trade

chants or to other professions. What emerges from even a brief survey of this market is the extent to which the wine trade supported a vast world of economic activity.

The accounts of one of the more prominent brokers at the end of the seventeenth century, François de la Vieville, indicate both the range and vulnerability of this long-distance trade. Vieville identified himself as a merchant and boasted of a "considerable trade in wines." At the same time, he seems to have operated much as a broker, at the behest of visiting merchants. A servant described having seen "merchants come looking for Vieville to go purchase wines both in the city and the countryside." If Vieville was out, "his wife made the purchases and had them battened and shipped." Vieville had gotten in trouble in 1685 from "great losses caused by the advances he had to make for a number of foreigners who had given him commissions" and had skipped town. He returned later to claim an inheritance and attempted to clear himself and "purge" a death sentence hanging over his head for fraudulent bankruptcy.[39] In his defense he submitted his balance sheet, the "debts due [to him] . . . for wine sold by him to individuals in Flanders and foreign countries that he cannot get paid because of the war." This amounted to fifty-six thousand livres owed him by people in Douay, Brussels, Mons, Condé, and elsewhere, plus a further seventeen thousand livres of "bad debts," mostly in Valenciennes. A sum of this magnitude could easily represent two thousand barrels or more and was only the unpaid part of a larger volume of business. The bulk of this debt came from trade with towns in the Spanish Netherlands, the traditional, and conveniently proximate, markets for wine of northeast France. A small amount was owed by towns within the French borders, and even some in Paris, but Vieville's business clearly faced primarily northwards.

The wars at the end of the century did not disrupt the main commercial orientation of the merchants in Reims, who continued to export their wines to northern neighbors. One of the most important of these merchants, Jean Clicquot, was sending hundreds of barrels to Arras, Maubeuge, Amsterdam, and a dozen other cities north and east of Reims in the 1710s. His closest commercial ties were in France, however, with Valenciennes: Of the forty-five thousand livres still owed by fifty-four merchants at his death, nearly a third was owed by eight individuals of that city. He had also sold large amounts of wine to fellow merchants and brokers of Reims. Judging from the transactions in the months around his death, much of this wine was coming to him from Burgundy. There are payments for shipments of nearly a hundred barrels from Beaune, Chalon, and Mâcon, and very large sums due the major brokers in those cities.[40]

This is in addition to wines bought in villages surrounding Reims, particularly in Sacy.

For all of his long-distance commercial connections, Clicquot was also very much involved in the production of wine and the life of its producers. Among his professional activities he was a master cooper. His account books include a register detailing the "barrels sold, money lent, grain delivered, [materials to] maintain vines" for which he was owed money by local growers. There followed more than 150 individuals, generally owing less than fifty livres. They lived on the mountain and in the plain of Reims, mostly in villages around Verzy and Sacy. These debts show Clicquot's involvement in the lives of common winegrowers, an involvement that may have had beneficial consequences for the growers but that clearly gave him considerable economic power over those who would supply him with wine. Debts like these could also be an important step toward the acquisition of land, as debts piled up and resulted in foreclosure. And these were, in fact, the villages where he owned vines, judging from payments made by the estate to a dozen vignerons to work on his vines in Luddes, Sacy, les Mesneux, and Villers-Franqueux. From the careful control of supplies in his own neighborhood to the flourishing contacts with the businessmen in distant Burgundy, Clicquot exhibited all the signs of a successful broker, yet it is worth remarking on the limits of his enterprises. There is no evidence for wine coming from the Marne River. He drew his Champagne wines solely from the mountain and the plain, and his outlets were the traditional ones of the northeastern frontier rather than the markets at Paris.

Clicquot and Vieville were probably representative of many in the ranks of the most important brokers, at least a dozen of whom were also listed as master coopers.[41] However the city was full of people involved less actively in the wine trade. When the government sold the right to engage in wine brokering at the end of the seventeenth century, it offered three grades to the brokers in Reims, to "famous brokers, to the inferiors of the first, and to those who have little or no practice."[42] When special taxes were levied on wholesale wine merchants and brokers in Reims at the beginning of the century, many claimed that "they only buy and sell occasionally, like all the clergy, gentlemen, bourgeois, and inhabitants" of Reims.[43]

A good example of the more marginal brokers can be found in Jean Mallo, a master cooper of Reims, who was only lightly taxed by the special levies. His accounts describe a variety of services and business relationships that a broker could perform, from the most traditional job of guiding merchants to sellers to much more entrepreneurial activities. Mallo described himself at one point functioning "as a *courtier*," leading someone else to local villages to buy wine. At another time, he had formed a partnership with another broker to buy some seventy barrels of wine from a broker south of the mountain, along the Marne River, and both then sold it for their own accounts.[44] Actually the partner had put up the money for the purchase, and the cooper still owed him money. More recently, he had bought some fifty barrels from villages on both sides of the mountain and all around Reims; most of it was paid for and in his cellar, but a little was still with the sellers, held for him with a small down payment lent him by another cooper who happened to be there. This wine represented a year's purchases—a small amount but evidence of independent enterprise and a fairly large catchment area.

Mallo's biggest business deal had been a commission that left him with only limited independence: He was given ten thousand livres by an investor with which to buy wines from the mountain, worth forty to sixty livres per queue (a double barrel). Some of that money, one livre per barrel, could go to upkeep—half of which was used for renting cellars, and 2 percent of the wine could be used for ouillage. The investor, a judicial official of a bailliage near Saint-Quentin, gave him an account book in which he was supposed to keep a record of his transactions, and of the cost of shipping and taxes, but the broker was not allowed to sell any wine without the investor's order. In return, Mallo was to receive 3 percent of any profit but would suffer no losses. He had bought nearly three hundred barrels and had sold a little of it for a nice profit but still retained some two hundred barrels two years later. This relationship was an interesting hybrid. Mallo was clearly not selling wine as an independent wine merchant would, nor was he buying as a broker who sends the wine to some other buyer. His commission on the profits was unusual for a broker, as was his responsibility for upkeep of the wine. Essentially he was a junior partner to the investor, more of a factor than a traditional broker.[45]

The best example of the fluid nature of the wine trade in Reims, and certainly the most successful of those who dabbled occasionally in this commerce was the cloth merchant Nicolas Ruinart. His account books, which give the modern Ruinart Père et Fils the right to call itself the oldest existing Champagne house, illustrate several peculiar aspects of the wine trade in Reims. Ruinart was not originally a wine merchant, or even a broker, and the account book beginning in September 1729 was dedicated initially to his cloth trade. He sold a barrel of wine in January of the following year and several dozen by the summer of 1731 to wine merchants in Paris and Reims, but his wine business was not a serious one until 1733, with over one hundred barrels purchased in the late fall and sixty-six barrels sent mostly to Lille. Yet his drapery business with Paris was grossing as much in half a year as he spent on wine for the whole year; the wine was serious but still secondary. His purchases were all quite local, from villages that were all within ten kilometers of Reims. All the wine appears to have been red and of reasonably good quality, at an average 115 livres a queue, plus a present or *épingles* of three livres given to the seller's wife, to establish good relations.[46] Ruinart was obviously not a major figure in the wine trade at this point and was probably quite similar to many of the other participants in the city's wine trade.

Ruinart's shipments fluctuated between one and two hundred barrels over the next decade, mostly to cities like Lille, Tournay, and Mons east of Reims. Much of his business involved sending wine to a merchant named Beaufort in Lille, but whether as broker or merchant is not clear. In one case he noted that he was sending Beaufort wine "following his order" and in another paid the tax for wine that Beaufort bought from someone else; both acts indicate he was working as Beaufort's broker. Otherwise there is no indication of who instigated the shipment of wine he sent to Beaufort, and no mention of a commission paid by either one. The accounts mention a commission paid by only one grower. More tellingly, it is clear that Ruinart was making a profit on wines that he shipped out. The 160 barrels of wine he sent out from October 1737 through the following summer were some two-thirds more expensive than the wines he had purchased in the fall. The timing of his purchases also appears to have been speculative, with the bulk of them in a few days in October, but their shipments mostly spread out over several months in late spring.

Ruinart's business changed dramatically during the decade covered by his account book. His cloth business diminished to a trickle by 1737 and had disappeared by 1739. At the same time, the wine business, though not growing much, had become more sophisticated. His purchases drew on a widening catchment area: Originally from a few villages around Reims, he began to obtain wine from the river—from brokers in Hautvillers and Avenay—and even shipped a little wine from Burgundy. He continued to act as a broker, taking his commission from the monks of Saint-Thierry, for example, and occasionally mentioning it for other purchases. But his wine was sent increasingly to two different brokers ("mon commissionnaire") in Lille, "for my account . . . to be sold," that is, no longer to individuals who had requested it but to be sold speculatively. Occasionally one of these brokers sent the wine on to someone "at the agreed upon price," but in general the accounts entered no specific debit against them since Ruinart could not know what they could be sold for him. After a decade in

The Provincial Wine Trade

the wine business, Ruinart was still in the process of making the transition from low-level brokering to full-scale trading. His purchases amounted to little more than ten thousand livres a year. The geography of his sales was still limited, but his supply zone and connections were expanding, as was his own production. He would become a major broker later in the century.

Producing some fifty-eight thousand barrels of wine, worth nearly three million livres, the region around Reims was able to support an extensive and complex wine trade.[47] If as much as half of this wine was sold locally, the rest entered the regional and interregional markets of northern France.[48] The wine merchants of Reims engaged in a range of speculative and commercial activity, and they maintained a lively trade with dozens of cities to their north and east. In particular, two aspects of this trade—its commercial autonomy and the range of its catchment—are worth underlining, since they demonstrate the commercial sophistication of the wine trade relative to the internal wine trade. The principal merchants were clearly operating large-scale enterprises on an international level, and even small merchants participated occasionally in long-distance trade.

The important brokers of Reims had long exercised considerable control over the wines produced both on the mountain of Reims and along the Marne River. Much of the wine exported during the eighteenth century consisted of wine of "the river" that they sold abroad. Reims could still boast in the middle of the century that the town of Epernay "could not deny that the merchants of Reims buy the largest part of their wines . . . not only in their city but in all the wine regions around them."[49] Indeed, the first chapter pointed to the importance of several brokers of Reims, particularly Godinot and Cocquebert, in the accounts of the winegrower of Ay, Malavois de la Ganne. Yet the brokers of Reims had already lost some of their hegemony over the province. With the rise of new markets to the west of Champagne, particularly Paris, during the seventeenth century, the brokers situated along the Marne River were in a better position to meet the new demand. By the eighteenth century it is possible to find a flourishing, if still rather inchoate, system of brokerage along the Marne. These brokers emerged, during the eighteenth century, as potent rivals to the brokers of Reims and exerted a powerful influence on the future of the wines of Champagne.

The Wine Trade of the Marne River

During the seventeenth century the Parisian market reached out to the Champagne vineyards to satisfy part of its huge need for wine. Forced by law in the late sixteenth century to seek wines beyond the immediate vicinity of Paris, outside a radius of some fifty miles, wine merchants found a source of good wine less than a hundred miles up the Marne River. By the eighteenth century the Marne was closely linked to the Parisian market, sending some 15 percent of the city's wine.[50]

The Marne valley around Epernay boasted somewhat fewer vineyards than the region around Reims, but they were already of superior quality in the seventeenth century. A cluster of two dozen villages just north and south of Epernay and stretching westward along the Marne contained the vast majority of the thirteen thousand arpents of vines in the district. In most of these villages vines covered at least one-fifth of the land, and in a few, like Ay, Pierry, Damery, and Dizy that were within some five kilometers from Epernay, more than a third of the land was under vines.[51] If they were not dedicated solely to wine production, most of these villages had as much or more land devoted to grapes as to grain. Barely a dozen villages were described as having "good wine" in 1691; the rest had trouble selling theirs beyond a local market.[52] In addition to this "good wine," which was light red or "clairet," the region began to produce a white or "gray" wine from red grapes. Its gray wines were rapidly recognized as excellent, and their prices climbed precipitously at the end of the century. The intendant's report of 1698 remarked that "the prices of these best wines, which were only two to three hundred livres per queue ten years ago, have increased to five, six, or seven hundred livres and even nine hundred and fifty."[53] By the early eighteenth century, a number of the villages close to Epernay could be said to "hold the first rank among the wines of Champagne, and particularly those of the valley of Pierry and of the slopes of Ay and Hautvillers."[54] Their wines, whether red or white, found a ready market in Paris.

Exactly how much wine took this route, who sent it and to whom, can be known with unusual precision. The *contrôle des actes,* a register listing all notarized documents, contains an entry for every bill of lading for every wine shipment leaving the city of Epernay since 1702.[55] A bill of lading (*lettre de voiture*) was essentially a contract drawn up before a notary between a shipper and an individual who was sending the wine and had "charged" the boats, stating what was shipped, the price of shipping, some or all of the recipients, and specifying that the goods were in "good and loyal" condition. The bill was also supposed to give the price of the wines, but the intendant of Burgundy pointed out that "this price is the secret of [the brokers'] commerce; they have too much interest in hiding it to make it public by putting it in the hands of shippers."[56] The bill of lading not only contracted the shipper, it also served as an official identification of the wines as they passed through various tax jurisdictions. If the sender accompanied the shipper he did not give him a lettre de voiture but was required to fill out a *déclaration* with the same information. Either a bill of lading or a déclaration had to accompany a shipment, so the notary only very rarely kept a copy, and thus these precious documents have seldom survived.[57] But bills of lading and déclarations, along with all other notarial documents, were registered in the contrôle des actes, for a small fee. The contrôle des actes in most parts of the country stated only that a bill of lading was given to a shipper for an unspecified amount of wine, but they are wonderfully detailed in the case of Epernay.[58] Every shipment is there, often several of them in a day, listing the amounts of wine, the shipper, who sent it, and the recipient. Of course, the consistency of the information depended on the clerk who kept the records, and in some years the clerk was deplorable. But with astonishing dedication, the clerks in Epernay put most of the relevant information into the register. With some effort one can trace the daily fluctuations of the wine trade, the changing markets, and the men who exercised control over the sale of wine in Epernay.

The registers of the contrôle des actes in Epernay reveal a flourishing trade with Paris at the beginning of the eighteenth century. Bills of lading for more than twelve thousand barrels, nearly twenty-five thousand hectoliters, were entered in the twelve months following the harvest in 1702, nearly all sent to the huge market in Paris. Epernay sent roughly six to ten thousand barrels a year to Paris in the early decades of the century, some of which probably went beyond the city to be exported overseas from Rouen. This means that considerably more wine was going west, down the Marne, than was exported over the borders from Reims. Only a little of the trade with Paris could have been the white wine sought by the elites; the majority of this trade was undoubtedly in common red wine, meant for the mass consumption of a huge urban market. The Parisian market was clearly enormously important for the wines of the province of Champagne, especially those along the Marne River. As a consequence, those controlling the trade to the Parisian market enjoyed considerable economic power in the province.

The daily entries into the contrôle des actes measure the rhythms of the wine trade and suggest a frenzied urgency in supplying the capital. Wine merchants wasted no time bringing the new wine to market; it barely had time to stop bubbling in its vats before it was loaded on barges in October or November. The port registers of Paris, a few of which survive for 1702, tally the arrival of these same shipments in Paris, less than two weeks after their departure from Epernay.[59] Following a harvest in late September or early October, the shipments to Paris rapidly swelled in volume through November and December; usually half a year's shipments were sent in these three months. From there the shipments gradually diminished to a very low level by April or May and remained at a trickle until the next harvest. The haste suggests something of the current race to deliver the new beaujolais to America, but the urgency was serious enough. None of the wine made in France lasted well, little beyond its first year. The wine merchants' shops, the taverns and guinguettes were becoming desperate for good wine by October to replenish stocks and revive barrels of old wine. The quantities arriving in Paris tripled between October and November, as wine merchants began to clean out the cellars of the best growers in Champagne.

Champagne appears to have been more precipitous in its shipments than other provinces. The very fragmentary records of wines shipped into Paris from around the country for the same period suggest that the bulk of the capital's wines, over half, arrived in the spring, between March and May. The first surge of wine, which did not start arriving in Paris until November, brought only 40 percent between November and January.[60] The wines traveling up from the south of France along the Loire, through Cosne a little later in the century, were even more concentrated in the spring, especially in March, when three-fifths of the river's volume passed through.[61] In contrast, the rush for wines from Champagne was unusually strong, and indeed the wines of the Marne River were especially sought after as a young wine, to be drunk when freshly fermented.[62] There was no waiting for the wine to mature; certainly no one waited for a second fermentation in the bottle come the spring. Although some river growers were making a white wine from red grapes that could become foamy if it was bottled at the right time in the spring, the idea of capturing this late fermentation was quite new in 1700, known only to a few connoisseurs and merchants. Instead, the wine was shipped in barrels, all but a few dozen bottles. Growers might prepare the wine for bottling by racking and fining it, sometimes several times. But the expense and inconvenience of bottling was left to the Parisians, whether they were dealers or the ultimate consumers. It was not until later in the century, as we shall see in a later chapter, that the trade in bottled wine rivaled the wine shipped in barrels.

The volumes shipped in the years following 1702 oscillated wildly but remained at a generally high level through the first three decades of the eighteenth century. A sampling from the contrôle des actes conveys both the wild swings and a rough idea of general levels of trade. From over twelve thousand barrels of the 1702 vintage, sent between October 1702 and the following September, the shipments had fallen to ten thousand from the 1703 vintage, and under three thousand by 1704. An average has little meaning with such variations, but the seven and six thousand barrels sent in the "vintage years" (starting in October and ending in September) of 1705 and 1706 are probably close to normal. In the next twenty-five years, however, the "normal" years were less common than were the exceptions. Champagne was devastated at the end of the decade by several years of appalling weather. Severe cold damaged vines throughout France and particularly those in the northern vineyards; shipments from Epernay following the 1709 vintage amounted to less than a dozen barrels a month. They had returned to barely a thousand barrels for the whole year following the harvest of 1713 but suddenly soared to twelve thousand in 1714. More average yearly levels of trade in the next two decades were interspersed with one of seventeen thousand barrels in 1724, and over twenty thousand in 1719, but only two thousand in 1725.[63] These figures represent a small but still significant part of the wine flowing into Paris from across the north of France.

By the early eighteenth century, Paris was importing over two-thirds of a million hectoliters of wine a year from the northern half of the country.[64] One study of the trade at the beginning of the century has estimated that the majority of this wine came from vineyards along the Loire, but that 15 percent came from the Marne Valley and that over 5 percent originated in Epernay itself.[65] Most of this wine trade was arranged by the vast and powerful Parisian guild of wine merchants and tavern keepers. Its two thousand members enjoyed a virtual monopoly on the retailing of wine in the city, whether consumed in a tavern or taken home.[66] In shops across and around the city, wine merchants provided the populace an essential element in its diet, as well as a space in which most of male, and part of female, society interacted regularly.[67] Although only a few members of the guild identified themselves as wholesale wine merchants, in fact anyone could buy wine wholesale from the provinces, and a great many tavern keepers were likely to have acquired at least some of their wine directly from the countryside.[68] The Parisian wine trade was remarkably democratic, the widespread participation due in large measure to the sophistication of the commercial organization in the provinces.

The contrôle des actes indicates the degree of decentralization, even fragmentation, of this Parisian market. The register lists hundreds of recipients of small shipments of wine. Most entries for a bill of lading identified some or all of the recipients by name, usually noting if they were wine merchants, and often giving their addresses. The vast majority were indeed wine merchants; their shops ranged across Paris and throughout the faubourgs. Even the guinguettes in the suburbs were represented, for the wine coming from Epernay was not meant simply for an elite market. Of course there is some evidence of elite customers. In 1702 over a hundred barrels were addressed to the Jesuit fathers of Paris, and smaller quantities went to the Cardinal de Noailles, Machault d'Arnouville, Chamillart, and dozens of officeholders. Some wine was going directly to Versailles, though less than 10 percent. A few large shipments of thirty or forty barrels even went to the provinces, to several individuals in Abbeville and Caen. The vast majority of the wine, however, was going to wine merchants, whose customers ranged from artisans coming to their shops for a drink to nobles buying by the barrel.

The fragmented nature of the Parisian market can be seen in the volume of small shipments to different individuals. Two-thirds of the three hundred or so shipments in 1702, for example, consisted of less than twenty barrels; nearly a quarter of them were composed of twenty to a hundred barrels; and the rest were huge flotillas carrying more than more than a hundred barrels. The large shipments went to wine merchants, though there was one shipment of 830 barrels to the Invalides in 1729. The small consignments went not only to wine merchants but also to private individuals for their own consumption. The register lists many hundreds of recipients, most of them receiving less than a dozen barrels.

The large shipments, especially those over a hundred barrels, almost never went to a single recipient. Wine merchants preferred to deal in smaller quantities, presumably to avoid the related problems of storage and spoilage. Certain of these wine merchants, especially Mopinot, Moricault, David, and Coquart, show up regularly, however, indicating an active business in the wines of Champagne.[69] These last three belonged to the small group of privileged wine merchants, known either as the "twelve wine merchants following the court" or the "twenty-five cabaretiers following the court," as were indeed many of the most prominent receivers.[70] Another of these, Eynaud, also known as "wine merchant of the king," was sent 250 barrels, for himself and "other wine merchants," which probably meant he was brokering for them in Paris. And one merchant in particular, "Darboulin and company, wine merchant of the king," was clearly a giant. "Darboulin and other wine merchants" received several large shipments, and a shipment of 150 barrels was addressed to him alone. But the main point is that no individual—not even Darboulin—came close to monopolizing this trade at the Parisian end.

Although the Parisian market was largely decentralized, the wine merchants in Paris and at the court still exercised a kind of dominance, acting as a whole, over the trade with Epernay. Practically all the wine sent down the Marne went to a specific recipient in Paris, who had either commissioned or already bought the wine being shipped. There is virtually no evidence for speculative shipments, except for one individual in 1702 who sent six barrels to Versailles "to be sold retail [and] the shipment paid for on [the boatman's] return," when the boatman would bring back the proceeds of the sale. Early the next year two Gossets and another individual from Ay sent ninety barrels "to sell in Paris."[71] There is little trace, otherwise, of shipments that clearly lacked a specific recipient. Nor is there any clear evidence of growers sending wine to the wine market (Halle aux vins) to be put up for sale, though some of the recipients might have been brokers at the Halle. Only in later years was one of the shipments, in 1724, and two, in 1730, explicitly directed there. The contrôle des actes at the beginning of the century reveal the widespread lack of initiative on the part of individuals in Champagne; very few took a chance on sending wine unaddressed down the river in the hope of selling it when it got there. The wine trade along the Marne in this period was very much directed by the demands of Parisian merchants and consumers; buyers in Paris still called the tune, and the brokers and growers in Epernay merely responded.

The destinations of the wine shipped from Epernay changed very slowly, but by the 1720s Epernay was shipping to a distinctly wider range of locations. Rouen and Orival, in particular, show up a dozen times in 1724, from whence the wine were shipped to foreign cities. Other Norman cities, La Rochelle, even Rome are mentioned as destinations. Although the volume of wine shipped to locations other than Paris had not risen to a significant percentage of the total, it suggests a gradual change in the commercial contacts enjoyed by growers and brokers in Epernay. Still, the wine trade was overwhelmingly linked to the market in Paris and to Parisian merchants. One might conclude that the Parisian metropolis controlled the trade as completely as it controlled the grain trade.

Yet, if the wine trade in this province bore certain similarities to the organization of the grain trade, there were important differences. The commercial system described by the contrôle revolved predominantly around the commissioning of wine by Parisians; at its heart reigned the brokers who dominated the commissioning system. The brokers of Champagne were not the "simple agents" or "transparent intermediaries" of upper Languedoc. Above all, they were not the small-time, insignificant agents who swarmed throughout the grain trade. Rather, the wine brokers, both of this province and others, had managed to concentrate control of the market in a very few hands.

Wine Brokers in Control

The commercial system described by the contrôle des actes in Epernay inverts the order found in the grain trades of the north and southwest of the country. Where a few large-scale grain merchants at a commercial center operated through a massive throng of small-scale agents throughout their hinterlands, the wine trade was organized by a few powerful brokers in the provinces who served a large number of Parisian wine merchants of various sizes. Unlike the provincial middlemen serving the grain trade, the wine brokers engaged in business on a large scale. And, although they bore certain generic similarities to intermediaries operating in other commercial systems, the wine brokers were already, in the early eighteenth century, in the process of gaining autonomous control over their trade networks.

The contrôle des actes gives a fairly clear picture of how the wine trade was organized in the provinces through these early years of the century. The wine was sent by several dozen individuals each year, as many as fifty in the early years. They included men of Epernay holding local offices, some of the large growers, and a few individuals from surrounding villages. Even Dom Pérignon, the cellarer of the abbey of Hautvillers some five kilometers from Epernay, was listed as sending a very few barrels. According to their bills of lading they "charged" any one of half a dozen boatmen, based either in Epernay or in the nearby port of Mareuil, to transport the wine down the Marne River at a cost per barrel that oscillated between four and eight livres. The boatmen played a strictly subordinate role in this trade, however, taking little initiative in buying wine or making commercial arrangements. In several cases wine merchants from Paris launched modest shipments back to their own cellars, and the boatmen themselves are occasionally listed as the "stipulants" or expeditors, but these were the exception. Rather, most of the wine was sent by a few brokers.

Most of those who sent wine to Paris did so infrequently and in small quantities; many of them showed up in only a single month with a dozen barrels—their harvest that they had been able to sell in Paris. This small-scale participation tended to occur in certain months, particularly in January and, more generally, in the fall. Otherwise, the bulk of the wine shipped from Epernay—over three-quarters of it—was sent by a handful of individuals, brokers belonging to two of the city's prominent families. These

The Provincial Wine Trade

brokers retained almost exclusive control over the region's wine trade for the first third of the century.

Two men in Epernay were responsible for some two-thirds of the wine trade. Adam Bertin du Rocheret alone "charged" more than a third of the town's wine shipments in the first decades of the eighteenth century. His father and brothers contributed another 15 percent to give the family control of nearly half of the city's trade. Antoine Quatresous charged some 30 percent of the wine, and his uncle, Nicolas Chertemps, sent another 5 percent. This means that in 1702 the two families had arranged the buying, helped to finance, and organized the shipping of over ten thousand barrels of wine. That vintage was unusually large, but even in the more normal years of that decade they were responsible for roughly half that number.

Arranging the finances alone for this much wine meant paying as much as two hundred thousand livres to the wine sellers, for the brokers had to cover most of the purchase price out of their own pockets and then wait for wine merchants to reimburse them. They often had to pay for brief storage in Epernay while waiting to ship the wine and had to provide the initial shipping costs, including taxes. These figures represent an astonishing commitment of time and energy to the wine business, and a particularly daunting financial challenge, just to juggle the flow of payments. The tangible rewards had become significant, however, with a 5 percent commission on every barrel they bought, these two families could earn well over ten thousand livres.

The wine brokers of Epernay exercised considerable control over the wine trade of the whole region, for it is clear that the wines listed in the contrôle des actes of Epernay originated in many of the surrounding towns. The city itself, with eleven hundred arpents of vines, was estimated to produce some three thousand *muids,* or over four thousand of the local barrels, in a normal year.[72] Much of that production, "a good half," according to a letter to the controller general in the middle of the century, would have been an inferior red wine, a *vin de pressoir,* "of which a part is consumed as drink for the infinite number of workers that must be employed on the vines . . . and the rest is sold at a vile price."[73] It might be sold over the counter to neighbors or kept to drink at home but was not usually sent out of town; little of it was good enough to be sent to Paris. Clearly the shipments sent from Epernay included wine produced elsewhere. The wine was coming, in part, from parishes farther away from the river that used the port, and thus the contrôle, of Epernay. Important wine-producing villages to the south, like Pierry, Cuis, Avize, even Vertus, must have been sending their barrels down to the port in Epernay. Wine even appears to have been coming to Epernay from many of the neighboring bourgs with ports on the river, like Cumières, Mareuil, and Ay.

The contrôle des actes of some of the surrounding towns, although rarely offering as much detail as those of Epernay, attest to the domination of the market and brokers of Epernay over the whole region. Despite having as many vines as Epernay, Cumières and Damery sent substantially less wine from their ports.[74] Barely a thousand barrels left from Damery in 1706, and the amount was much lower in the following decade. Although a little of the region's best wine was being exported northeast, it appears that much of its wine was shipped to Paris by brokers of Epernay.[75] Damery's contrôle shows a dozen inhabitants of Damery itself shipping their own wine, but only two sent anything more than very small quantities. Instead, outsiders sent the large majority. Adam Bertin alone sent nearly a third of the wine, and his brother shipped a further 5 percent. Geoffroy, a broker from Cumières, shipped some 15 percent, and several brokers from Reims and Ventheuil accounted for another tenth.[76] Ay had as many vines as Epernay but registered very little wine—four to six hundred barrels—in its own contrôle des actes early in the century.[77] These bourgs were clearly shipping a very small percentage of their wine from their own ports and sending much through Epernay instead.

Epernay was obviously a major entrepôt, a clearing house for much of the wine made in the area. No doubt some of its commercial power derived from the fact that the elites of Epernay owned vineyards throughout the region and collected and stored their wine in the city. Bertin, for example, owned vines in Pierry and Cumières but fermented and stored them in his own cellars in Epernay.[78] In addition, Epernay was a financial and commercial nexus for this trade, drawing the economic activities of smaller towns and villages to its ports and markets. The resources of a large town nearly always gave it an advantage in the wine trade over smaller agglomerations, regardless of quality. Thus Reims, which had no vines immediately around it, had come to dominate the wine producing of an extensive hinterland. But Epernay's power was also a reflection of the commercial power of its brokers, men who were successfully organizing the wine trade of the Marne River.

The Brokers of Epernay

There had been brokers in Epernay for several centuries, performing the same kinds of services as *courtiers* had in the rest of France. They enjoyed considerable authority in the whole region, being called to judge wine, as official *gourmets* in villages all around the city.[79] Yet their commercial role was limited and largely passive until quite late in the Old Regime; documents show them only intermittently involved in wine sales in the late sixteenth century.[80] Instead, the wine trade in this region, as in much of France, had traditionally been organized by wine merchants from outside—from Flanders since the Middle Ages, later from Paris and always from Reims—who visited to make purchases and arrange for shipments to other provinces and other countries. In Ay and Epernay merchants were assisted by brokers, who were still—as late as the seventeenth century—limited to bringing buyer and seller physically together and guaranteeing the selling price. The initiative was left to outsiders to come to Epernay, or occasionally to prominent vineowners to find buyers through family and friends.[81] As late as 1685, a large Parisian wine wholesaler could simply ignore the services of a broker. One of the "privileged merchants of the king," Triboulet engaged one of the biggest shippers in the region to ship "all of the wines that Triboulet and [another wine merchant] have bought and will buy in Epernay or other places around Epernay or in the mountain of Reims and unload them at . . . Paris."[82] This contract made no reference to the help or mediation of a broker, whereas twenty years later few wine merchants failed to work through a broker, who arranged the shipment and charged the boatman with his bill of lading. By the early eighteenth century, the vast majority of the wine trade and practically all arrangements for shipments were arranged by brokers. And, although some merchants still visited vine-producing regions to make their purchases, the wine trade was conducted increasingly at long distance, through correspondence with brokers.

The provincial brokerage system of the early eighteenth century had become sufficiently sophisticated that Parisian buyers no longer needed to travel but could rely instead on brokers to follow their orders and arrange the purchase, packaging, and shipment of their wines. A report of the late 1730s from an official in Epernay asserted that "for nearly twenty years we have seen hardly any merchants from either Paris or abroad take the trouble to come themselves to our cellars to purchase wine on the spot, and instead they rely almost totally on brokers for the choice and purchase of their wines."[83] A broker's business was no longer passive; it was no longer adequate to make himself available to merchants who came looking for him. Instead, a broker sought out clients and advertised his services.

Now brokers competed for clients: One of the Bertins reported back from a trip to Paris in 1690 that he had "debauched [that is, enticed away] some of Chertemps's clients, who will definitely come visit me [back in Epernay] and who are very good merchants." He also reassured his family of his loyalty: "I have not been to see any merchants who go to you or our father in the intention of having them [as clients]."[84] In between regular trips to Paris, brokers kept up a constant correspondence with buyers there, responding to queries about prices and quality and sending circulars with information to prospective clients.[85] The broker's increasingly active role in the trade had made him much less anonymous; where formerly a merchant might deal with whomever he found in a town he visited, he now chose to rely on a particular broker and developed a long-term relationship with him. The Bertin and Chertemps families were particularly astute at this business and, between them, organized the commercial relations with Paris and the outside world nearly, though not entirely, to the exclusion of everyone else in Epernay.

Nicolas Chertemps had been engaged in the wine trade both as a *courtier* and a *commissionnaire* since at least the 1680s. His purchases, on several occasions in the 1680s, of large amounts of wooden "barres" to batten down barrels show him preparing thousands of barrels for shipment, for which there are occasional contracts with shippers in the archives.[86] He and his nephew Antoine Quatresous must have formed a partnership in the wine trade around 1705, and Chertemps sold his wine to Quatresous through the 1710s.[87] By his death he had become an *écuyer, gentilhomme de la grande fauconnerie de France,* an office giving him nobility; he had also become a substantial producer of wine. The inventory made at the death of his widow in January 1721 reveals over twenty-five arpents of vines, most of them five kilometers south of Epernay, in the villages around Moussy. He had wine presses in his house to prepare his own wine, and his cellars still contained some of the wine from the previous harvest: over two hundred barrels ranging in price from ten to sixty livres.[88] But only a fifth of the wine was good quality and two-thirds was very poor; he had probably sold the best wine already.

Chertemps died a reasonably wealthy man; his widow left an inheritance of nearly forty-three thousand livres to be divided by a son and daughter and by Quatresous and his wife, Anne Clicquot, and son Guillaume. The son, Antoine Chertemps, and a grandson, François, continued in the wine trade, with modest but regular amounts in the contrôle des actes through much of the century, though François also became prévôt, juge civil et criminel d'Epernay in 1745.[89] Quatresous, in his turn, left an inheritance of some thirty-six thousand livres in 1732.[90] Wealth like this put the wine broker far beyond the level of provincial agents in the grain trade, indeed, beyond everyone in the grain trade—broker, miller, flour merchant, and all but the largest grain merchants at the port of Paris.[91] Wine brokers enjoyed the substantial fortunes of provincial notables, which in fact they were.

The Bertins came from much the same social level as the Chertemps. Nicolas Bertin was the grandson of a "famous" broker from Reims and had been in the wine trade of Reims before setting himself up business in Epernay in the 1660s.[92] By the early eighteenth century he was no longer particularly active but had three sons, Simon, Robert, and Adam, who together brokered substantial amounts of the area's wine trade. The inventory made at the death of Robert Bertin's wife in 1706 listed some six thousand livres in "movables" (*meubles*), which would have included furniture, clothing, inventories of wine, ready cash, and commercial assets, but not land or other fixed property.[93] This is a modest level for a family of officials, although at this point Robert is described as only a commis du commissaire of the tax farm.[94] Simon Bertin married a woman with a dowry worth over twelve thousand livres, including some eight arpents of vines.[95] This put him well beyond the level of vignerons, whose dowries were often a fortieth of that amount, and close to the dowries of provincial nobles; it was even a match for the business world of Paris and Bordeaux.[96]

The oldest of the three brothers had been the most successful due to his aggressive involvement in the wine trade. By the time of his wife's death in 1721, Adam Bertin du Rocheret was one of the largest brokers of Epernay. A movable fortune of nearly thirty-four thousand livres placed her postmortem inventory well within the average of a nearby rural elite, the fermiers of the Île-de-France, and nearly eighty times more than the average for vignerons.[97] Bertin was extremely cautious about giving any details about the brokerage business in the inventory, but we can learn something of its scale. He identified sixteen thousand livres in bills of exchange from individuals "whose names he did not give but are known to the other [heirs]." He was further owed thirty-six thousand livres "according to his account books, by many merchants and other individuals" whom he would not name. He identified a handful of people whose debts were in such arrears that he was obliged to start judicial proceedings against them. His account books also show him owing forty-five thousand livres, presumably for the purchase of wine, but he does not specify. All of this suggests scale of business that rivaled the largest brokers working in Reims.

In a rather small town of barely thirty-five hundred inhabitants, the principal brokers of Epernay formed a tight and powerful elite. To their business affairs the Bertin family had added judicial offices. Adam was a *président au grenier à sel* and a brother was *greffier en chef de l'élection*. Their sons would have these offices, as well as being *lieutenant criminel* of the *bailliage, président de l'élection*, and *officier chez le roi*. These offices placed them among the *exempts* (officials exempted from the taille) of the city. All owned various seigneuries. The Chertemps owned more seigneuries than offices, until François became *prévôt* in the middle of the century, and Quatresous was an *élu* and *grenetier*, as well as lieutenant mayor. The two main families combined forces in the 1720s, as Adam's daughter married Guillaume Quatresous, now the seigneur de Partelaine, and the two men formed a partnership to broker wine. These families were a hybrid, with a foot in the very lowest reaches of robe nobility and the highest ranks of the national wine trade. They combined social pretension and commercial acumen with political and economic power.

The brokers integrated business with the prestige of office holding, seigneuries, and civic associations like the Company of Arquebusiers. The company offered social ascension to the nouveaux riches of urban society and a rallying point for challenging the established elites.[98] Thus we find Adam Bertin du Rocheret leading a deputation of arquebusiers to the Hôtel de Ville, one day in the summer of 1712, where they bluntly refused to obey the written command of the duc de Soubise, the governor and lieutenant general of Champagne, ordering them to stand guard for the town. When the mayor then tried to summon Bertin to assemble the company, Bertin had replied that he would tell them to assemble when he wished and had no need of the mayor. The mayor self-righteously prepared a complaint to send to Soubise, but the *échevins* and *syndics* of the town refused to sign, threatening him with a lawsuit because he had refused to call the town notables. "This the mayor believed he should not do, because all the notables are arquebusiers," as well as the échevins and syndics. The exact nature of this power struggle is far from clear, but the situation provided the notables of the town with a way to stand up to the mayor. Matters flared up the following month as the company assembled under arms and insulted the mayor at his house. It took several years of arguments before the *conseil d'état* reestablished the mayor's authority over the arquebusiers.[99] In several cities the Company of Arquebusiers became a focus of contention among local authorities, and it is striking that prominent brokers played the role of ringleader in many of these confrontations.[100]

For all of the Bertins' social and official prominence, it is not hard to find them actively and personally involved in the details of the wine trade. In a court case against the chief members of the Bertin family in 1727 two agents of the tax farm reported that they had been furiously and physically

The Provincial Wine Trade

attacked by the senior members of the family while investigating their business practices. The family in turn explained that they had been entertaining visiting officers of the Maison du Roy in the house of Robert Bertin de Bertincourt, by now an officier du grand fauconnier, "following the usage and good style of receiving strangers in Epernay." They served them wine, which the officers liked so much that they bought more. But the tax agents somehow heard about the sale and came to the house with charges that Bertincourt was selling fraudulently and that his guests were "drunk" and causing a "great commotion." The next day the agents confronted Bertincourt's son when he delivered some bottles of wine to a tavern that sold his wine, and they had come to blows. The Bertin cousins insisted that they had weighed in only to separate the men, but the tax men said they were attacked by several in the family and by the soldiers as well. The case became particularly awkward because the assailants were among the principal officials of the local judicial and financial courts, and so it had to be taken before the conseil d'état and dragged on to an inconclusive ending.[101]

The case gives a particularly telling picture of how the Bertins mixed business with their hospitality, as well as how they were involved in the daily affairs of selling wine, both to elite and popular clients. It also reminds us that "receiving strangers" figured among the more valuable services that a broker could offer. Wine merchants coming to look for wine needed help with advice and financing but would also need a place to stay; a broker who could offer accommodations clearly enjoyed advantages over those who could not. As a broker in another location remarked, "The broker is obliged to have a large and spacious house to receive the priests and merchants who travel every year for their purchases."[102] Thus it is hardly surprising to find that one of the brokers in Epernay and several of those in Ay were also innkeepers.[103]

These two families dominated their region because they had the best contacts with buyers in Paris. When a grand lord like the marquis d'Artagnan wished to buy the wines of Dom Pérignon, he bought through Adam Bertin; when a king's minister like Desmaretz wanted the wines of "Hautvillers and some others of the best and most delicate growths," he bought it through Chertemps.[104] Some of Adam's success seems to have arisen from his contacts with the prior and Dom Perignon of the abbey of Hautvillers. Several of his correspondents were anxious to gain the abbey's wine at any price. Many of them were obviously quite well informed about local wine production and choices of wine, discussing the provenance in great detail with Bertin. To the marquis de Puyseulx he explained that he had bought wine from the postmaster of Epernay and offered to get more from a plot adjoining the postmaster's which had been harvested ten days later and was half the price.[105] It is perhaps not surprising that Puyseulx, the governor of Epernay, should be familiar with different winemakers, but this kind of specific information shows up in Bertin's correspondence with wine merchants, the king's librarian, and gentlemen of the court. The brokers' willingness to maintain this steady stream of market information explains much of their value to Parisian buyers of every rank. They assured both a degree of transparency in the market and their ability to control the market by controlling its transparency.

The Brokerage Business

As their prominence in the contrôle des actes suggests, the wine brokers played a crucial role in the provincial wine trade. They were responsible for arranging the shipment of the vast majority of the wine sent from Champagne to Paris. They were also responsible for first choosing, purchasing, and financing the wine. In this process they had to work closely with both the provincial growers and the Parisian buyers, utilizing an intimate knowledge of the local market as well as developing contacts with the capital. The records of several of these brokers show how they operated.

Adam Bertin's son, Philippe, though never an important broker and one of the least active in the family, indicates the importance of communications between the broker and his market. He left a record of much of his correspondence, a voluminous and eclectic miscellany of verses, genealogical erudition, and gossip, mixed in with commercial affairs. His letters reveal his close contacts with a wider world and his careful cultivation of clients, both in the commercial and the political sense. Philippe's correspondence embraced several overlapping worlds: the Parisian world of affairs, an elite provincial world of officials and nobility, and a national network of freemasons, referred to as the *ordre social*. In part this reflects the different hats Philippe wore. He was simultaneously wine broker, judicial official, and scholar.[106] But he made sure that all his contacts served his wine business.

Philippe sent an average of a letter or two a day to people in Paris and Champagne, at least a third of which included information on prices and availability of wines. At the same time Bertin worked at maintaining his business contacts by sending yearly newsletters (*lettres d'avis*) to a long list of wine merchants, both those who regularly received shipments of his wine and some who did not, giving his assessments of the grape harvest and the wines produced, as well as prices and his estimate of the market.

This kind of announcement was more than simply advertising; the broker's role was primarily to stimulate the market, and he did so by providing information that was surprisingly frank. The best he could say about the harvest of 1725 was that "our wines are not as bad as we had feared," and he was willing to admit that "the best use one can make of our new wines will be to use them to revive the old wines that are beginning to fail."[107] In 1727 he advised that "the bourgeois count on selling [wine at] 250 to 300 livres but with [the offer of] some money [cash] they will not stay there." By making the market more transparent through such missives, brokers encouraged business in general, as well as their own role in it.

The accounts of Bernard Guyot, who became a broker in Epernay in the 1720s, offers us a detailed glimpse of the role of a modest, and only modestly successful, broker. His accounts from 1722 to 1730 survive only because he had deposited them with the juridiction consulaire, the regional commercial court that handled, among other things, cases of business failure.[108] Since cases before the juridiction consulaire will be cited from time to time, it is worth noting that such a deposition did not necessarily lead to bankruptcy. As one broker remarked in his deposition to this court, since he was "pursued by his creditors he had been advised to deposit his balance sheet with the . . . juridiction consulaire in order to obtain from [the creditors] a suitable time to be able to satisfy them and let them know the actual state of his affairs."[109] Such depositions might easily be the result of overextension, all too common in the business of brokering. They are, consequently, less atypical than might be thought and are invaluable sources for economic history.[110]

Guyot's deposition allows us to chart his suppliers along the Marne and his clients in Paris; they indicate something of the quotidian practice of a broker's business. He worked on a small scale, shipping seven or eight hundred barrels in good years, but he essentially sat out the 1725 vintage and did little in 1726. Nearly all of his wine went to Paris, to some forty different wine merchants. There is no way of identifying their clientele, but only one of these merchants was among the "twenty-five privileged wine merchants following the court" who was likely to have had elite customers. Another was the "buyer of the Grand Châtelet" and thus furnished an important Parisian institution.[111] It is likely that Guyot represents the trade in "normal" wine from the region that had long supplied Paris and would continue to do so, even as certain wines of Champagne became too expensive for all but the cream of society.

Although typically cryptic, his account books illustrate the range of activities performed by a broker in this milieu. With one important exception, the vast majority of his wine was sent to specific recipients, usually wine merchants in Paris. Occasionally an entry remarks that a shipment is "by the order" or "according to the lettre d'avis" of a wine merchant, but usually this occurred when the wine was going to a third party. Clearly some Parisian wine merchants acted as intermediaries between their Parisian colleagues and their brokers in Champagne. Fairly often some wine was addressed to a bourgeois of Paris "by order of" a wine merchant. On some occasions the entry explains that Guyot was sending wine "that I bought with" the merchant to whom it is shipped. Thus the broker was offering a range of services to merchants from outside: both assistance when the merchant visited to buy for himself and purchases through correspondence.

At the same time, Guyot was much less traditional and, indeed, technically illegal in buying and selling for his own account. Although some of his purchases were recorded as being "with" a particular wine merchant, those that were "for" a merchant might well have been acquired before the merchant's order had come to him. It was usually safe to buy ahead of time, without an explicit commission but with some certainty that orders would follow. Some of his wine had clearly been bought speculatively. There is an entry of a contract made with two growers in Mardeuil in mid-September for "any wine they can harvest this year" for a set (and low) price, and Guyot obligated himself to furnish the barrels. He was obviously speculating, both on how much he would be acquiring and on finding a buyer. These practices appear to have been widespread but were strongly condemned, nevertheless, by the authorities. "There is an abuse [committed] by the brokers [of Epernay] that merits the conseil [d'état's] whole attention," the intendant reported to his superior in 1732. "Despite regulations requiring them to show their commission when they purchase [wine], even to buy only in the company of the merchant, these regulations are ignored, which makes the brokers totally masters of the trade."[112]

Guyot's shipments also show him buying and selling for his own account; at least once a year he sent considerable amounts of wine (one-fifth of his total shipments) to Simmoneau, a "marchand forain at the Halle aux vins to be sold there." The wines sent to be sold at the Halle were his own speculations, for which he paid the entry tax and shipping, and "the profits belong to me," though he left Simmoneau his "ordinary commission." There was also a small amount of wine sent to a wine merchant "although belonging to me [Guyot] which will be sold in Paris under his name and paid back to me." Elsewhere in the accounts was a short list of wines "that I sold in the region coming from my purchases"; this included eight barrels that "I had sold in retail" at a tavern. Most of these wines were cheaper—only twenty livres per barrel—and were sold to individuals at Châlons. And later in his career he established a partnership with a Parisian wine merchant to buy and sell wine. At his death, his cellars held eight thousand livres of wine in barrels and ten thousand bottles of wine belonging to the partnership. The combination of these activities demonstrates the mixture of commission and trading that so provoked authorities but that was clearly a common occurrence.

His accounts of buying wine also identify him as a traditional broker, taking a commission on nearly all of his purchases, unless the wine was bought from a close relative (but a cousin had to pay the full commission). The exact commission is rarely specified, though it is *au sol le livre* (5 percent) in one case, and a few other specific sums work out to that amount. Yet a number of other commissions are less than 5 percent, and he seems to have applied a variable scale. Where it is possible to compare purchases with shipments, the accounts show that the price he quoted to the Parisian buyer matched the purchase price, although—as always—we do not know if he entered false data. The time between buying and shipping tended to be quite short, on the same day in one case, but more often after a week or two.

Guyot bought his wine almost entirely from villages outside of Epernay, generally within a ten kilometer radius and most heavily from Ay and Damery. The amounts tended to be small, less than a dozen barrels on average and from a large number of individual growers. Thus Guyot was going directly to the source, rather than working through local intermediaries. More importantly, the great majority of his shipments were listed in the contrôle des actes of Epernay, even when the wine originated elsewhere. Here is confirmation of an earlier conjecture: The amounts registered in the contrôle des actes were not based on wine from Epernay alone. Instead, it is clear that wine from the whole region was channeled through notaries and—most importantly—through brokers from Epernay.

What really gave brokers their ability to control the wine trade was their invaluable financial assistance to outside merchants, as the accounts of another new broker, Claude Moët, make clear. Although there is much in these accounts about his purchases and sales, they present the business of brokering as primarily financial in its essence. Moët had started brokering in 1716 and had already gained 14 percent of the market by 1725. His identification in the contrôle des actes is revealing; through 1718 and 1719 he was charging modest amounts of wine and described variously as a commissionnaire of Epernay, a "bourgeois d'Epernay," and a "bourgeois de Paris being at present in his maison de vendange at Epernay."[113] We clearly see a man whose identity was split between his two markets, as well as the degree to which brokers had to live within the Parisian world in order to find business. His description in the contrôle had finally settled down to simply "broker of Epernay" by 1720. Through the 1720s he played a modest role as broker, handling less than a seventh of the wine shipped from Epernay. He had increased his market share to 20 percent by 1743–45, though Quatresous still handled substantially more than he did.

Although available only for the decades between 1743 and 1763, when he was already an old man (he turned sixty in 1743), Moët's account book offers a remarkably detailed record of his business. For every entry listing a barrel or bottle bought, or a shipment sent off, there are three describing a payment—from merchants or a financial clearing agent in Paris to Moët, and from Moët to suppliers, coopers, shippers, and tax agents in Champagne.[114] The actual choice of wines seems much less important than paying for it; indeed, Moët usually dealt with a relatively limited number of growers who seem to have been regular suppliers. Nor is there much about his relations with Parisian partners, or the constant flow of information about prices, quality, and availability of wine that fills the correspondence found in Bertin's records. Moët's accounts focus rather on the flow of funds and remind us that the broker was as much rural banker as he was wine expert.

Moët's account book recorded all purchases for which he was responsible, whether made directly by himself, his sons—who now had a very active role in the business—or "our merchants," who bought "under our commission." He took this fiduciary responsibility very seriously and fretted when he was unable to transfer accounts from temporary registers into his journal, which kept an official record of all business transactions. In one particularly busy year he fell so far behind that he gave up the effort, expressing the hope that, "finally I think the register will be sufficient, especially since the old brokers of this canton never made any use of journals, which I will continue nevertheless."[115] Like Guyot, Moët purchased wine both with and for Parisian merchants, helping those who visited and receiving many orders by mail. Even when a Parisian was on the spot to buy for himself, however, he left the financial details to his broker.

Money rarely changed hands at the initial stage of Moët's purchases, and he delayed payments as long as he could. Normally the records of purchases were quite specific, quoting a precise price, sometimes stipulating that the wine must be racked. Occasionally the price was left unspecified: Two barrels would be "at the price that [the grower] will sell [the rest of] his cuvée, as it is commonly practiced," or "The price will be settled, agreeably." Few customers were given a deposit (*arrhes*), though a woman was given a small advance on wines she was going to make. Then he paid a small sum to sellers a little later, probably when the wine was picked up to be shipped. Generally Moët was able to gain some credit from his sellers by delaying their full payment for many months. Indeed, it becomes clear, once again, that sellers who could afford to grant credit were more attractive to brokers, who tried to delay paying them off as long as possible.

The rest of the money was paid over time, depending on the needs of his sellers. Thus he sent his son in March to two villages with six hundred livres to pay off the "sellers who are most pressed" for money; the son was able to return with most of the cash. Moët refers tartly in late 1748, however, to several "disagreeable sellers" in Romery and Cormoyeux who had to be paid in full at the moment of picking up the wine because they "refuse [to give] an honest credit." They had the "harshness," he went on, to insist on full payment, despite being paid "very considerable" amounts before the wine was picked up. Such advance payments Moët saw as a kind of "credit, with all the risks." [116] The art of brokering for Moët lay in juggling a complex chain of credit from the seller to the ultimate buyer.

In normal years, he could delay paying the growers by many months, paying gradually over the course of a year, but the tax farm would not be delayed. All the wines he shipped owed several taxes upon shipment—the *jauge et courtage,* the *courtier* and *jaugeur,* and the *droit de gros;* and Moët faced an "urgent necessity to pay the pay the taxes for the wines . . . since the [tax] bureaus give us only till the end of each month, except some who wait a second month." [117] And in years with abundant harvests— 1748 stood out particularly—his growers needed a great deal of money: A bigger harvest meant more manpower to collect it, the cost of pressing it, more barrels to store it. His growers that year were "nearly all little vignerons lacking money." Not that he was not "already well ahead with [his payments to] them, having paid much beyond what I have received from the [Parisian] merchants," but he was helping "our poor sellers" in order to "maintain the reputation of being a good payer." [118] As a broker in Beaune described the problem in a despairing letter to one of his merchants in Paris, "all of our bourgeois and vignerons have had so little revenues in the past years that they come to me every day to get money; I have given all that I had [but] I have needed considerable sums to pay the tax on exports from the kingdom and the shippers and the coopers, which leads me to beg you not to pay me with long-term [bills of exchange] and to do for your part all that you can." [119]

Moët found himself without sufficient funds in 1748, though "without the large purchases this year, my funds reserved for this commerce would have sufficed." Part of his problem was simple liquidity: The vignerons refused to accept the bills of exchange he offered them and "only acknowledge cash." He was driven by the "dearth of money" to borrow considerable sums from Geoffroy, a secretary of the king in Epernay, and two others in order to pay the "vignerons in need" for their aides or their accounts. He had offered Geoffroy his choice of bills of exchange, but Geoffroy had also refused them and preferred simply to lend him the money. His lack of cash contributed substantially to the complexity of his task, but the real problem was simply that his buyers paid him more slowly than he paid his sellers.

The money from Parisian merchants arrived in a slow but steady stream throughout the year, culminating with a trip made by Moët or his son to Paris "to do accounts with my merchants for the wines sent them since the last accounting, in this same season past, which is the ordinary one for wine brokers of all the wine regions."[120] Moët's trips to Paris in August aimed at collecting outstanding sums directly from his customers in the capital. After his banner year of 1748, he calculated that he was still owed some sixty thousand livres in July 1749 out of a total of some 168,000 livres of wine bought for his merchants. It was also a chance to bring back some cash, often desperately needed. He worried in late August 1755 that his son's delay in returning with money from Paris left him with only twenty livres in cash on hand: "It has been a long time since I was so short of cash."[121]

During the year he was paid with a combination of bills of exchange and rescriptions on the aides and the gabelles, negotiated by his merchants. He noted about his trip to Paris in the summer of 1748 that only a quarter of what he was owed was paid in cash and the rest in bills of exchange "following the usage in this commerce of commission." He faced some challenge in getting rid of these bills, since most wine producers preferred to be paid in cash. Some large suppliers, owed several hundred livres or more, accepted a mixture of cash and bills of exchange. But Remy, the local receiver of the tax farm, helped buy many of the bills from him in October. The receiver general of the aides also took some of these bills in payment for the wine taxes owed by Moët's suppliers, "following the procedure of earlier years." Moët expected to use bills of exchange to pay his largest suppliers, for he noted with some irritation, when one of his more important suppliers refused to accept two bills from him, that "this arrangement is quite common for bourgeois, who take all the bills from brokers, who are commonly

The Provincial Wine Trade

obliged to accept two-thirds and even three-quarters of their payments in bills, which is why the broker is obliged to pay in the same kind, especially to the bourgeois, who are familiar with [bills], unlike vignerons who do not know anything about them and are paid in cash, and if the bourgeois do the same . . . it would be impossible to pay them all in cash." [122]

The money from his merchants came in more slowly than did his payments to his sellers, forcing him to extend credit to a wide range of people in Paris. When a merchant he did not know asked for such credit he admitted to being indecisive about it until he had been "informed if he is good or not, by the ordinary person who will clarify it for us, having asked a friend to find out." These were precautions that he took in every case, he noted, since it was "all too ordinary that many wine merchants, particularly from Paris, try to dupe us from malice and more often from powerlessness, which makes the commerce of commission very dangerous." [123] But those who took the risk reaped enormous rewards in the wine trade. In the middle of the century Moët was the second largest broker in Epernay, and his heirs were the largest by the end of the century.

By combining financial reserves, reputations as "good payers" among the local wine producers, and assiduously cultivated contacts with buyers in Paris, a handful of individuals had gained practically complete control of the wine trade in Epernay and its environs by the early eighteenth century. The Bertin family in particular represents an important model of wine brokering in these early stages. The family used its social status and its money to good effect: At a time when Parisian merchants were looking for credit help, these men had money that was not tied up in other productive activities. More importantly they could parlay their status into credit from wine suppliers. At a time when the wine from Champagne was still establishing a name for itself in the fashionable society of Paris and Versailles, these men could use their literary and professional connections at court to find customers. And yet they are not quite businessmen. Their correspondence depicts each succeeding generation increasingly caught up in the overlapping worlds of the regional judiciary, Parisian belle lettres, and local society. By the middle of the eighteenth century, wine appears more as a footnote to their preoccupations. This family did not go on to become a famous Champagne house. Although members of the family could be found active in the wine trade through much of the eighteenth century, they did not pursue the business with the same single-mindedness that produced a half dozen houses of renown by the end of the century, houses that have gone on to commanding positions in the modern wine trade.

One of the striking features of the early-eighteenth-century wine trade in Champagne was the clear dichotomy between its export market and its Parisian market. The province seems to have been divided by the mountain of Reims: To the north the growers and brokers looked north and east, across the French border and within it. To the south, growers and brokers aimed their wines westward, toward the burgeoning urban market of the capital. Despite individual exceptions, the evidence suggests that the two halves of the province were not well integrated, at least in the early century. Brokers in Reims might acquire some of their wine in the southern province, and had long done so, but they did not send it to Paris. Similarly, the brokers of the Marne drew on local growers and developed their trade purely downstream to Paris and a little bit beyond. This lack of integration may have had its origins in the relatively recent commercial relations with Paris; the northern market was established and flourishing long before trade with Paris and continued to concentrate its efforts on its traditional clients. It took some time and a commercial crisis, as we shall see, to unite the markets of this province later in the century.

Whatever the reasons, Champagne's two wine trades, the two commercial systems based in Reims and Epernay, were fundamentally different. Not only did they face in different directions, serving two very distinct markets, but more importantly, their relationship to their markets was quite dissimilar. And the intermediaries who served these markets offer the greatest contrast. Where Epernay was wedded to a single market, Paris, Reims traded with a vast geography of customers. Unlike Reims, with its cast of nearly a hundred merchants and brokers engaged in the wine trade, Epernay's subordination to a single market had resulted in this trade being funneled through the very narrow gate of a half-dozen brokers. Unlike the merchants of Reims, who freely combined speculative trading with commissions, the brokers of Epernay appear to have relied largely on commissions from Parisian merchants. Indeed, they identified themselves differently—as commissionnaires in Epernay and as both merchants and commissionnaires in Reims. There will be more to say about this distinction in nomenclature, but it does appear to have captured an essential contrast between the independence of the intermediaries in the two markets. Finally, the differences in markets and in commercial relationships to these markets meant that the wine trade in Reims enjoyed a level of competition vastly beyond that in Epernay. Although there was a clear hierarchy among the merchants of Reims, the whole horde participated to some extent, and many who began only marginally expanded their commerce significantly. Competition can be found in Epernay, of course, but among a mere handful of players, most of whom were related or intermarried, and the brokers of Epernay found little difficulty in gaining control of the local wine trade.

Another feature of the wine trade in Champagne has more universal significance for the country as a whole. The wine trade was clearly dominated by brokers, provincials who chose the wine, paid for it, and shipped it to distant merchants. Theirs was a delicate role, a mixture of subordination and independence which was becoming volatile. The brokers of Reims had become merchants as much as brokers by the eighteenth century and clearly traded for their own accounts. The brokers of Epernay were less precocious, having only recently established themselves and not yet replacing the merchants of Paris as the primary buyers in the region. They became négociants by the end of the century and dominated the wine trade for the next two centuries, but their rise to power—in Champagne and elsewhere—must be examined in greater detail.

3
From Public Office
to Private Entrepreneur

To premodern society, the market was fundamentally ambiguous; at once communal and agonistic, it brought life as well as dangers. It met people's needs and exploited them, it served the community and threatened it. The market was among the most public things in medieval society, a common locus of the commonwealth. A "policed," or well-ordered, society had long been defined as one whose markets served the needs of the community. Public authority, however privately held in feudal society, bore the responsibility for erecting, maintaining, and protecting a marketplace.[1] The market brought the community into contact with the outside world, and with it brought the risks of treachery, pollution, and dependency. To protect the community from these dangers, markets were carefully regulated in the Middle Ages, physically and legally enclosed and set apart, supervised and policed. Only with the rise of the modern, capitalist world did the market become private and self-regulating. The transformation was not without incident, particularly in so prominent a market as the wine trade.

Treatises on seigneurial and royal power early in the seventeenth century portrayed economic regulation as the chief policing obligation of public authorities. For Charles Loyseau, "*la police* consists principally in three parts . . . [relating] to provisions, to trades, and to streets and roads."[2] Similarly, Cardin le Bret defined *police* as "the laws and ordinances that have always been published in well-ordered states, to regulate the public economy of produce . . . to remove the abuse and monopolies that can be committed in commerce."[3] According to these theories of *police*, public authority regulated the traditional economic activities that supported the life of a city, along with the transportation network that physically united these activities. Although *police* became a singularly important concept in the late seventeenth century's definition of civility and its awareness of an emerging public order, its original meaning focused on the urgency of publicly regulating the economy.[4]

Viticultural communities depended on commerce more than most; only by contacting the outside world through markets could they transform their surplus into wealth and relieve their deficiencies of grain. The market might be marginal, even liminal—as some historians have described it—yet it needed to be integrated into communities, especially those that produced wine.[5] But the market had to be contained and neutralized, and the community shielded from its dangers. The wine trade was particularly intrusive, for it operated typically through the initiative of merchants from the metropolis introducing themselves into the local wine markets in search of wine. The response in viticultural communities was the *courtier*, an official broker or intermediary who shielded the community from the risks introduced by the outside world, by absorbing them into his person. Or, in the terms of contemporary economic analysis, the *courtier* was the community's response to transaction costs.

Transaction costs refer to the costs of performing any economic exchange.[6] They arise from insufficient knowledge about both the commodities being exchanged and the participants to the exchange. In the case of the wine trade there were costs every time a buyer's ignorance about where wine was found and, more importantly, about local grades and measurements, led him to make a mistake. Both the buyer and seller risked losses in their exchanges if either party cheated, a risk that increased when the parties were not known to each other. Visiting wine merchants had to rely on the seller to deliver the agreed-upon wine, sometimes well after the merchant's departure. The seller had to trust the merchant to pay up, usually over many months. All of these risks and unknowns added difficulty and expense to the wine trade and limited its growth.

If Douglass North is right that "success stories of economic history describe institutional innovations that have lowered the costs of transacting and allowed more of the gains from trade to be captured, thereby permitting the expansion of markets," then the wine *courtiers* must be seen as a success.[7]

Since the Middle Ages, the outsider's contacts with local wine producers had been mediated by the *courtier*, who purified these contacts by substituting himself for the outsider. Offering information, security of bargaining, and enforcement of contracts, the *courtier* diminished transaction costs. The *courtier* was an agent of "police," bringing order to the public market and protecting the well-ordered community. But *courtiers* abandoned this public role for a private one, quite abruptly, in the seventeenth century, and with their defection the viticultural community lost much of its ability to control the market.

The *courtiers'* transition from public official to private entrepreneur made them the key figures in the wine trade during the eighteenth century. Traditionally, their role had been a completely passive one of waiting for merchants from Paris and abroad to seek out their services as guides and tasters. Their primary responsibility lay in protecting the interests of the local viticultural community. *Courtiers* changed their role fundamentally in the late seventeenth century by becoming commission brokers. This meant replacing the merchant physically and, more importantly, taking over the financial arrangements of the wine trade. They came increasingly to represent the interests of the larger commercial world in competition with those of the local community.

The *courtiers'* emergence as active and independent agents was a major step in the development of the wine trade and the achievement of a more sophisticated division of commercial functions. They gradually gained control of much of the sale of local production and took over the contacts between local producers and their chief markets, making them the critical nodes in the wine trade. This process involved the gradual transformation of a "public function" into a private enterprise and illustrates not only the dynamics of the wine trade, but also some of the changes occurring in the wider economy.[8] Several investigations of the wine trade undertaken by the government in the early eighteenth century allow us to analyze this evolution with much greater precision. After briefly examining the brokers' development up to the early eighteenth century, we will use the royal tax records first to consider how brokers had arrived at a basic divergence in the way they defined themselves and then to construct the geography and function of their market networks.

A Public Function

The medieval wine brokers in France, known as *courtiers* or *gourmets,* served in an official role as market regulators.[9] Since their origin, they had assisted visiting wine merchants in locating local wines and helped them arrange credit, usually from the seller. They smoothed the potentially awkward relations between a local economy and the outside world by giving outsiders access to local information and, in turn, guaranteeing the buyer's solvency for the seller. Their primary role consisted of uniting buyers and sellers: buyers, on the one hand, who came from out of town and knew little about local wines, sellers, or customs; sellers, on the other, who were often local inhabitants with a small cellar. "They should lead visiting merchants to the *caves* and cellars to taste and buy wines," as a later police treatise explained. If a dispute later arose between buyer and seller over the quality of the wine, the broker was a principal witness; if the dispute involved sums of money his testimony was binding. The broker was also liable for the cost of the wine that he had brokered and could be imprisoned if the buyer failed to pay.[10]

Wine brokers performed what was essentially a policing function, in their role as guarantors of contracts and wine quality and generally as supervisors of markets. The wine brokers of Beaune and Reims, for example, were originally town agents, chosen yearly and carefully tested by the échevins. By helping visiting merchants find wine in the town and by tasting it to guarantee its quality, they promoted the town's exports and protected its reputation. A description of the brokers of Beaune to a British audience early in the eighteenth century emphasized their skill and reliability. Brokers were

> public intermediaries, . . . connoisseurs who, from antiquity and from father to son, have a certain knowledge of every wine, and of every region, parcel and canton from which they come, and all the good cellars. . . . Having received their commission they visit the bourgeois and take samples of different wines that they find in the good cellars . . . which they take home and examine them closely and in the different changes of taste and color they see the future colors and qualities of the wine. They make another experiment with this wine, pouring it through filter paper and drawing solid conjectures as to the future taste, color, and the color's duration.[11]

They certified acceptable wines with the town's mark on the barrel and, every two weeks, were expected to report the buyers, sellers, quantities sold, and prices to the town magistrates.[12]

The *courtiers* of Bordeaux were created in the early sixteenth century for the purpose of bringing order to an increasingly chaotic wine trade. Foreign merchants, particularly English commission agents, had apparently caused considerable disruption by their bankruptcies and fraudulent practices and were denounced as "spies and scouts who seek out the weaknesses in our commerce . . . and triumph with impunity from their larceny and monopolies."[13] *Courtiers* regulated every transaction to prevent the abuses and frauds committed by these outsiders. They also had to guarantee the payment of various fees and taxes, as well as the solvency of the purchaser. The city of Bordeaux controlled these officials carefully, limiting their number and testing their proficiency, which included knowing one of the languages common to the merchants who frequented the port, typically English or Dutch. As late as the eighteenth century, regulations in Bordeaux enjoined wine brokers there to help the city "stamp out fraud and abuses in commerce."[14]

As a consequence of their office, the wine brokers' economic activities were strictly circumscribed and subordinated to their public responsibilities. They were expected to reside in the communities they served and to "be present at the market [*étape*] during the days and hours when wine is sold." In order to avoid competition among them, *courtiers* were expected to share their fees.[15] As late as the seventeenth century, the wine brokers of Reims and Beaune were allowed to receive a fee only from the local seller and not from the visiting merchant, to avoid having their loyalties seduced away from the interests of the town and its inhabitants. They were obliged to wait for the merchants to come to them and could not make purchases for an absent merchant without receiving special permission and could not make payments for him to the seller. Such statutes made it theoretically impossible for brokers to perform as commission agents, that is to say, filling orders for merchants who only corresponded with them, and they forced merchants to come to the town themselves.[16]

The essentially passive nature of the brokers' role also expressed the realities of medieval commerce. The wine trade was organized by outside buyers, often from Paris or cities and courts north and east of France, who came looking for wines. From the fourteenth through the sixteenth century in Dijon, according to one study, merchants visiting from elsewhere "dominated" the wine trade, largely to the exclusion of local merchants.[17] The foreign merchants' "preeminence" strengthened the commercial role of the broker, as their assistant, but it was a very subordinate role as brokers had to wait for the merchants to visit. Studies of Auxerre's wine trade in the fifteenth and sixteenth centuries and Beaune's in the seventeenth century similarly emphasize the dominance of outside merchants and the limited and largely passive character of the wine broker's office.[18] Foreign merchants or their agents exercised the same control over the wine market of Bordeaux, leaving *courtiers* merely to assist them.[19]

Despite restrictions on their activities, wine brokers in many parts of France began to transform their economic role at the end of the seventeenth century by gradually becoming *commissionnaires*. Commission brokers "bought merchandise for the account of someone else," according to a contemporary definition.[20] This meant that they bought wine in the name of distant merchants or "correspondents" and financed the purchase, whether or not the merchant was present. Brokers gained a significant financial role, advancing the money for the purchase, or persuading the seller to grant them credit, and waiting as much as a year for the merchant to repay them. Then, in addition to replacing the merchant financially, brokers might replace him physically, handling purchases for merchants who gave their orders by mail. The absence of the merchant left the brokers responsible for a range of tasks: They found and tasted the wine to be purchased, much like a *courtier,* but they also had to arrange payment and shipment. As brokers substituted their finances and their choices for those of the merchant they became the principal sources of demand in viticultural communities. And with growing independence and responsibility for organizing the wine trade came greater power in the local market.

An eighteenth-century lawyer offered one version of the transformation of wine brokers from the passive police agents of the Middle Ages to entrepreneurial intermediary, as he had observed it in the Beaujolais. Parisian wine merchants, who only began to visit this region late in the seventeenth century, originally sought help from "simple artisans" in Beaujeu and Mâcon to "guide them to the best cellars" and to "arrange transport to the Loire." But the greatest help that visiting merchants demanded of brokers turned out to be financial assistance. "They soon sought services of much greater importance: the affairs of a négociant are always infinitely hindered when he can only conduct business with cash; credit is the soul of all commerce." Brokers either provided the credit themselves or guaranteed the wine merchants' solvency to growers who offered credit. As brokers became more sophisticated, he charged, they persuaded wine merchants not to visit but to conduct business by correspondence, giving them the chance to gain a monopoly over the wine trade.[21] This appears to be a speeded-up but basically similar version of the process that had occurred a bit earlier in other provinces.

The wine brokers' transition to private enterprise did not occur everywhere at the same time, or with the same ease. In Reims, the town ordinances of 1654 had defined the office in traditional terms and prohibited *courtiers* from working for particular merchants, but by 1692 a royal arrêt referred to the officials in Reims as "*courtiers* and commissionnaires" and described them "buying for others" and working for "correspondents."[22] Already in 1632 the town of Blois was protesting the "monopolies" practiced by those who have the office of *courtier*, who "buy wine at a vile price, put it in their cellars and then sell it to wine merchants . . . in such a manner that they combine the office of broker and merchant." They were also accused of "preventing wine merchants from coming [to Blois] themselves as they had been accustomed to come and make their purchases."[23] The town of Beaune reacted to the transformation of its brokers with more vigor. The town council of Beaune complained for the first time in 1674 of individuals "calling themselves *courtiers* or commissionnaires" who were certifying and shipping wines with no official sanctions and later forced a broker to choose whether he would continue as courtier or commission agent.[24] The brokers fought back, however, and presented a very different image of their public function.

What was a simple issue of public order for the authorities of Beaune appeared to be altogether more sinister to some of the wine brokers' powerful allies in their struggle against municipal regulation. During the 1670s, the "twelve and twenty-five privileged wine merchants following the court," assisted by the "principal wine merchants of Paris," challenged what they insisted was an injurious attempt by the town of Beaune to reinforce its control over the town's brokers. In briefs to the conseil d'état, they claimed that

the mayor, échevins and principal inhabitants of Beaune, having recognized that for several years their wines were no longer so sought after because they have taken more care to make a lot of wine than to make it good, have wished to make themselves the master of the sale of wine in order to sell their own wine when they wish and in preference to the wine of other inhabitants [and] to that end they have renewed several years ago the ancient statutes [governing brokers] which had once been rejected and have even made new ones by which they pretend to introduce a monopoly over Beaune.

The offending statutes included most of the regulations traditionally imposed on the town's brokers: forbidding the function to anyone not chosen by the town and obliging brokers to reveal what commissions they had received from outside merchants as well as the purchases they had made. The wine merchants also complained that the town had "enjoined these same brokers to bring the merchants with them to buy the wine, even though it is often in the merchant's interest not to be present so as not to give rise to an increase in the price of the wine."[25]

Parisian wine merchants dismissed the brokers' public function, perhaps fairly, as a ploy to further the interests of the town notables. But it must be recognized that maximizing competition by maximizing the number of participants in the market had traditionally been a central goal of the well-policed market.[26] Both Beaune and Blois objected to the way Parisians used commission brokers to organize the market for them, so as to minimize competition by replacing a hoard of buyers with only a few agents. This clearly violated the townspeople's interests, regardless of their status.

The wine merchants objected further that the town showed itself too lenient with regard to one troubling innovation—it accepted the 5 percent fee (the *sol pour livre*) that brokers had taken to charging the sellers for their service. Since the broker's fee increased with the price of the wine, they pointed out, "he will be led to buy the most expensive wines that he can and so lack fidelity" toward the wine merchants.

The town's "hatred" for several wine brokers of Beaune who had served the Parisians as brokers "for a long time and faithfully," according to these Parisians, led the "principal inhabitants of Beaune to form a public conspiracy against them, to defame them in circulars that they wrote to all the wine merchants of Paris and in foreign countries, and to bring criminal charges against them in the parlement of Dijon where they have much credit because of their many relatives and allies." The Parisian wine merchants protested these measures in the name of "facilitating the abundance of wine in Paris" and insisted that "the supplicants should be free, as they have always been, to use whatever persons they judge appropriate for the purchase of their wine."[27] They intervened in the various trials and persuaded the conseil d'état to overturn the criminal verdicts, though they failed to reverse most of the town's regulations. Nevertheless, Beaune rapidly lost control of its brokers in the eighteenth century.

By the eighteenth century the big foreign wine merchants usually relied completely on commissions by correspondence, according to a Dutch treatise in the middle of the century, although "some, and not the least instructed in commerce, come themselves to travel through the wine regions of France at harvest time. . . . Still it is rare that the presence of the wine merchant excludes that of the négociant-commissionnaire; it even happens often that the wine merchant limits himself to the choice [of wines] and leaves the commissionnaire to take care of the price."[28] As commission agents for distant buyers, often embodying the aggregated demand of dozens of merchants, brokers became the most significant purchasers in many viticultural communities. Even when acting for merchants who came to visit, their legal obligation to guarantee the buyer's purchase had gradually transformed them into the principal source of credit on the local market, paying sellers up front and being paid at the buyers' convenience.[29] The wine broker performed an extremely valuable service in a market that was still dominated by the mercantile power of a few major economic centers but was experiencing a growing need for credit and cooperation from an increasingly complicated supply zone.

Whether they were called *courtiers,* commissionnaires, or both, brokers constituted an increasingly central part of the wine trade by the late seventeenth century. Dissuaded from trading for their own account by law and by a substantial tax imposed on all sales, they bought only in the name of other merchants and played little role at all in local retail marketing. Their sole raison d'être was working with and for "foreigners"—merchants from outside the community—whether the outsider presented himself or corresponded. Thus brokers delineate the long-distance trade, and their presence points to the importance of external demand from merchants at distant entrepôts who had taken the initiative in buying the wine and came themselves, in some cases, to oversee the acquisition. Such long-distance trade, whether linked to markets in major French cities or to overseas markets through maritime ports, was certainly the most important economic stimulus in the wine trade. As brokers became increasingly dominant in the long-distance trade they came to represent the most dynamic element in the wine trade.

This process of transformation from *courtier* to commissionnaire, never completely sanctioned or clearly accomplished, turns out to have been more complicated than a few examples would suggest. Different markets required different kinds of agents and resulted in distinct combinations of the brokerage and commissioning functions. These distinctions, revealed by a government investigation at the beginning of the eighteenth century, offer a clue to the dynamics of the long-distance wine trade and to the role of brokers.

Royal Control

The wine broker's official status, combined with his pivotal role in an increasingly lucrative commercial activity, proved irresistible to the state's desire for revenues. The royal government had gained the right to choose several of the brokers in Auxerre by the early sixteenth century, but later in that century it tried to turn all of the wine brokers in the kingdom into royal venal offices. The creation of official brokers was both an expression of the state's growing desire to ensure order and "police" in society and its urgent need for money. As the king asserted, "We have . . . created . . . the office of *courtiers et commissionnaires* to have them provided by Us with men of probity and good life and morals."[30] Yet while calling the position of broker an "office of police" and insisting that it regulated the office in order to "take care of the abuses and malpractices that are committed in the function" of wine brokering, the state also turned brokers into tax collectors.[31] It sold the office to brokers and gave them the right to a tax on each commercial transaction. The brokerage fee became another way for the state to tax the substantial revenues generated by the wine trade or, as an eighteenth-century report noted about brokers, "some police functions [that were] voluntary both for those who performed them and those who sought them served as a pretext for [state] finance."[32]

Yet the government found that it was surprisingly difficult to maintain its control over commercial activity in the wine trade. According to most customary law, operating in the northern half of France, the buyer could dispense with a broker's service if he wished, and the state was inclined to allow the same discretion with regards to the royal brokers. But repeatedly through the seventeenth century the government found occasion to complain that wine merchants were choosing to work with a variety of unofficial brokers. An edict in 1627 complained that "all sorts of people and particularly coopers and other artisans" were involving themselves in brokerage. These "guides" would "lead merchants and tavern keepers who were visiting vineyards . . . to storerooms and cellars," but arranged sales "without the ministry of the established *courtier* and in this way defraud them of their fees." The king also regretted the fact that wine sellers were "forced to pay up to fifteen or twenty sous to the [unofficial] guides for the sale of each barrel, otherwise the guides use their artifice to keep merchants and cabaretiers from buying wine from those [sellers] who do not pay them the brokerage fee at their discretion."[33] Unofficial brokers had no right to the official brokerage fee but found it easy to extract a payment from wine producers anxious to make a sale.

Despite the government's regular attempts to impose official brokers on the wine trade throughout the seventeenth century, unofficial brokers obstinately ignored the official monopoly on brokering and continued their informal business arrangements in the face of royal bans. An edict of 1656 charged that "many people undertake to continue the functions of broker without title or our permission . . . [and] they demand considerable fees of our subjects." Evidently these unofficial brokers continued to dominate the local wine markets. The government threatened to fine those who had practiced brokerage unofficially but complained again in 1691 that it had "come to our attention that many people still continue . . . the functions under the title of commissionnaire, *courtier, gourmet* [and] demand considerable sums from buyers and sellers, and most of them being men without reputation or means, many problems arise [that are] harmful both to our subjects and to the foreigners who employ them."[34] Such massive resistance was possible, in part, because of the increasingly personal and pivotal role played by individual brokers in the wine trade.

The government cracked down hard on the unlicensed brokers in the summer of 1691. All those who had been involved in brokering were obliged to acquire a royal office or they were fined and excluded from the business. An edict demanded that all official brokers were required to set up a common bureau at which they would all work together, keeping a common register of clients and sharing their profits by putting half of their fees into a "common purse."[35] This stipulation was partly a clever device to encourage interlopers to introduce themselves into the trade; a newcomer who lacked any contacts or business experience might share effortlessly in the wealth generated by his fellows. At the same time, the idea of a common bureau reveals that the government still understood the broker's function as a very traditional, essentially passive, role of simply waiting for visiting merchants to present themselves in the town and be guided by a broker to the appropriate seller. The broker then had the right to a tax, which was imposed on all transactions involving a wine sale.

This system worked nicely to tap the enormous volume of trade engendered by wine consumption, but the edict misunderstood the nature of the brokerage system as it had already evolved by the late seventeenth century. Brokers were no longer minor functionaries who could interchangeably and anonymously serve whichever merchant presented himself at a bureau. The wine trade was rapidly becoming a very specific and personal service that an individual broker offered to a select clientele that he had carefully cultivated. This is clearly illustrated by the example of Bertin du Rocheret, among others in the previous chapter, who maintained constant epistolary contact with scores of clients. Not surprisingly, the requirement of a common bureau was resisted by many of the brokers, despite subsequent exhortations from the conseil d'état.[36]

The sale of offices caused considerable anxiety to the existing brokers, as can be seen in the correspondence of the Bertin family of Epernay. A profession that they had freely practiced for some years was suddenly closed

From Public Office to Private Entrepreneur

to anyone not provided with one of the few, expensive offices. Their decision to buy an office was complicated by several factors. The price was subject to negotiation, of course, but more serious was the question of whether it needed to be paid at all. One of the family wrote from Orléans that everyone there was resisting the office, and that "only two have committed this folly [of buying the office] and [they are] not of the region." The opinion there was that the office "is only for the money they wish to trick from us and they are laughing at us."

Nevertheless the Bertins had to be interested, for the offices were limited to eight for Epernay and might tempt someone to achieve a monopoly by buying up all of them. One of the family was in Paris through much of the summer that the sale was announced and kept warning his father back in Epernay to be "absolutely discrete and avoid all cabals . . . act as if they had not created the offices. There is much misery in this region." Advice came from other friends, who warned the family to "keep the thing secret and reveal yourself to no one but trusted people." Finally, the government threatened to levy a fine on those who had practiced this profession previously, and only buying the office would avoid this fine. By October the Bertins had acquired one office, "so as not to fall into some disagreeable consequences," under which several in the family could work. But that was not enough, and through the following year the intendant pressured others in the family to buy an office by garrisoning troops in their homes and pursuing them with fines.[37]

The creation of royal wine brokers also threatened the ability of important municipal centers in the wine trade to exercise their power over regional commerce. To maintain local control over these crucial offices, many towns preferred to buy them wholesale from the king. As early as 1576, with the first royal creation of this office, the town of Blois agreed to pay for the suppression of the office since it was "of such great importance to the public liberty of this town, where there has never been anything like it [official brokers] before."[38] Auxerre paid 120,000 livres in 1627 to keep control over its brokers.[39] Reims was forced to buy off royally appointed brokers on several occasions, paying 150,000 livres in 1691 to assure "the conservation of the wine trade . . . which the royally appointed *courtiers* could diminish, and to conserve the jurisdiction that the [town council] has always exercised."[40] In 1692 the estates of Burgundy paid 200,000 livres, Nantes paid 140,000 livres, and Bordeaux offered 126,000 livres to free their regions from royal intervention.[41] Evidently these offices had become sufficiently crucial to the wine trade that the state could use them to extort considerable sums from wine-producing regions.

It is easy to be skeptical of the government's claim that these officials provided needed "policing" of the wine trade, for the state multiplied their numbers by the end of the seventeenth century with transparent greed. In its desperate scramble for revenues the crown abolished and re-created positions, multiplied new ones, and held old ones ransom to their owners. The crown's attempt to control this activity finally came to a head in 1704 with a massive effort to identify and punish the interlopers who had taken over the brokerage of wine. Although motivated by a desperate need for revenues to conduct war, this investigation of unlicensed brokers is an early and striking example of the government's growing desire and ability to identify and measure economic activity in its own kingdom. The results provide an unusual survey of the state of the wine trade.

Claiming in an edict of November 1704 that unofficial brokers had once again been ruining the wine trade, the king abolished the official position in order to start over. The edict chided official brokers for having "only taken up the office to acquire the taxes attributed to it," which they levied "whether they were present at the sale or not" and having left the actual task of brokering to a "great number of former commissionnaires, *gourmets,* and others without title [who] perform the functions."[42] In many of the major wine regions the province had already paid to have the official position suppressed, in order to let anyone perform as a broker, but the edict insisted that the resulting "confusion was greater than before." The edict then created the offices of *courtier-commissionnaire* again and offered to sell them to the highest bidder.

The government justified the office on the grounds of the public trust confided in brokers. As the *traitant,* who actually administered the new tax for the government, argued, it would be "an advantage to the public and to commerce if the people who handle public wealth [*le bien public*], as the wine brokers do, were to have a title, which should take the place of a kind of security and pledge to those who entrust them with their wealth." Official control of brokers was particularly necessary in some cases, such as the brokers of Nantes "because being foreigners for the most part, it is politic to secure them in France with offices." Turning brokers into quasi-public officials would guarantee their behavior and so bring confidence to the market. But he also thought it relevant to point out that brokers were in a profession "in which we have seen so many people make considerable fortunes."[43]

The edict caused enormous consternation among the communities that had struggled so hard to maintain control over their wine trades. The chief wine-producing regions, in particular, flooded the controller general with

From Public Office to Private Entrepreneur

petitions challenging various aspects of the edict. The estates of Burgundy objected bitterly that they had already paid to suppress the office of brokers created in 1691, fearing at the time that these new offices "would remove the liberty and confidence that merchants can take in their brokers." Now they complained of the disastrous impact the new offices of 1704 would have on the wine trade, "in which consists all the wealth of this province." Those who bought this office would be "only clerks who are not known, [because of] not being from the region." As a consequence, these outsiders "had not established a reputation for their [financial] resources so no one would accept them as guarantors for merchants from other countries or provinces." The wine trade would be ruined since "the majority of wines are sold on credit." [44]

Officials in Champagne agreed that the wine trade "would end suddenly if these offices were once possessed by men without experience," since it survived "only through the brokers' credit and by the confidence with which foreigners correspond with them." [45] The intendant at Bordeaux had already cautioned his superior in 1691 that the creation of official, mandatory brokers would only drive business away, since foreign merchants insisted upon choosing their own brokers. Now he warned that the "establishment of brokers would be the ruin of commerce," for it would give them "immense profits and crush commerce under a monopoly." [46] In each city's protest, the broker was identified as someone who had to have experience and be known and trusted by his clients. If the king could install unqualified people in the function, the wine trade would be ruined.

The traitant expressed suitable concern for the harmful possibilities of the new offices and graciously agreed to let the wine-producing regions buy him out, as of course he had planned to do all along. He blandly announced that "if the estates of Burgundy believed it should involve itself, it had only to acquire the offices, with the right to entrust them" to whomever they wished. That is exactly what Burgundy did, for eighty thousand livres. Other provinces reached the same conclusion and paid lesser sums to have the offices suppressed. [47]

The government was going after bigger sums, however, with another feature of the edict. The edict announced that those who had practiced brokerage without an official title were guilty of cheating the public and were liable to prosecution. It even threatened to make them turn over all of the commissions they had earned. But the traitant offered to let them pay a fine that would absolve them from prosecution. Provincial intendants were given the responsibility for drawing up a list bearing the names of all those who were guilty of brokering "without title" and assigning a sum to be paid. Such a list of trespassing brokers was valuable to the tax farmer for a second reason. These interlopers were expected to be the primary purchasers of the new offices, and the fine they faced was an incentive to buy. Buying the office was one way of absolving themselves of the fine, for "this clause [the fine] was put in the edict," according to one of the memoirs addressing the case, "with the design of making those who performed the functions without title acquire the offices of *courtiers commissionnaires*."[48] The whole point of the tax scheme, then, was to force the towns and individuals who controlled the wine trade to pay in order to maintain their control.

The fines levied on unofficial brokers prompted a howl of protest from the principal wine-producing regions, which claimed that the threat of judicial action would disrupt the whole profession. The head of the farm of indirect taxes (*aides*) in Champagne objected that the tax on brokers without titles would "suddenly stop the commerce of wines in this province, which would be a considerable prejudice to the farm of the aides." Even worse, the government applied the fine aggressively to anyone involved in brokerage, with little regard for legitimate claims to the office. To the brokers of Tonnerre who demonstrated that they had acquired the office in 1692, the traitant retorted that they were still culpable because they had charged more than the official tariff. The city of Reims complained that, when it had offered 150,000 livres to suppress the last batch of official brokers in 1691, the arrangement was supposed to have made "all merchants, *courtiers,* and the public free to perform the trade and brokerage of wines." The traitant backed down in this case to the extent of agreeing to discharge all those on the roll of fines who had been officially recognized as brokers by the town of Reims.[49]

Contested Identities

At the same time, a few of the most international market centers challenged the government's fine on unofficial brokers as a fundamental misconception of the commercial system. Many of the wine merchants of Nantes had appeared on the lists of unofficial brokers who owed fines. Joined by the estates of Brittany and the "wholesale wine merchants of the province," they complained that the traitant did not understand the nature of brokerage and had implicated them unreasonably in something that was not their affair. Although admitting that they acted as commissionnaires, they insisted that they were not *courtiers* and hence the edict did not apply to them.[50] Their defense rested on a subtle distinction that reveals the sophistication of their commercial system. More importantly, their protests reveal a profound gap between the business culture of France's periphery and its interior.

In their appeal to the king's council, these "négociants of Nantes" asserted that, despite the traitant's attempt to "confound the ambiguous term of commissionnaire with that of *courtier*," there was an "essential difference" between them. "In effect, the négociant performing the function of commissionnaire" acted on the behalf of men who were absent, buying or selling for them when they could not come in person. This kind of commission was the "négociants' greatest and surest commerce, [and] to want to forbid its liberty would absolutely destroy commerce because it only subsists by [commissions]." In contrast, the *courtier* "does not work for absent people, [rather] he serves those in his own town." He bought wine for merchants who hired him, going out to the "countryside to taste [wines] and mark [barrels]." For this work he simply received a salary rather than a commission, that is, a flat fee rather than a sum proportionate to the value of the merchandise. The *courtier* was "a trade that the négociants do not perform and is much beneath the commerce that they do."[51]

The judge and consuls of the merchants' court of Nantes, appealing to the controller general because of the "attention they owe to commerce and in the interest of numerous wholesale négociants, of retail wine merchants and of coopers," made the same arguments and distinctions between "the négociants commissionnaires and the *courtiers*." They agreed that "these mutual commissions [between merchants] are so necessary and so important that commerce cannot subsist without their help."[52] Elsewhere, the intendant at Bordeaux had already warned the controller general, over a decade earlier, that "all the merchants [at Bordeaux] are commissionnaires, who work sometimes for the accounts of foreigners and sometimes for their own." But that was a very different activity from the *courtier*'s, and the négociants of Bordeaux informed the traitant that they had "always regarded this profession [of *courtier*] as incompatible with theirs."[53] The government was conflating two commercial activities that were considered to be quite distinct by merchants in the large Atlantic ports, but the subtlety seems to have been lost on the head of the king's finances.

In several letters to the king's council, négociants in Nantes joined the judge and consuls in emphasizing an even more important distinction between the négociant and the *courtier*. Whereas the négociant's profession was "the most distinguished in commerce," that of *courtier* was "the most vile, since he can be considered in some ways as servile." The consuls added that the *courtiers* in Nantes were "all men without fortunes, nearly incapable of [paying the tax]." An appeal from several of the most heavily taxed brokers concluded, "Being wholesale merchants-négociants it would be demeaning [*un déclin*] to act as a *courtier,* who are only men of low extraction whom we use and treat in matters of commerce as our valets."[54] The intendant at Marseille made the same point in a memo-randum to the controller general: "The function of *courtiers gourmets* is completely mechanical [meaning also unskilled] and has never been filled except by wretches and men in debt from whom one would have trouble getting anything."[55] These expressions of contempt for *courtiers* may have been rather exaggerated, for *courtiers* obviously needed experience at tast-ing wines as well as contacts among vignerons. Yet they were sincerely scorned, apparently because they could not act independently.

These protests from France's major port cities reveal important differ-ences in the development of brokerage between the interior of France and its peripheries. The brokers of the interior had only recently evolved from their medieval origins as purely local middlemen, as *courtiers,* who had little scope for independent action, and they were gradually adding the role of commission agent to their duties as *courtiers.* The government's treatment of the two functions interchangeably clearly aimed at this hybrid, for it de-scribed the joint office largely in terms suitable to *courtiers.* The edict said nothing about working for merchants on commission or by correspon-dence. Instead, brokers would have an "office in each town . . . to receive the individuals, merchants, négociants, and others who will have need of their ministry."[56] The official description depicts them as passive and local and sounds nearly identical to the Nantais' description of a *courtier,* as someone who worked for a merchant present in the same town. The edict clearly corresponded to the kinds of brokers emerging in Auxerre, Beaune, and Epernay. It is worth remarking, too, that none of the wine-producing regions of the French interior protested the edict's conflation of *courtier* and commissionnaire in the way that merchants and officials at Nantes, Bordeaux, and Marseille did.

In the port cities, however, the brokers' functions had evolved alto-gether differently. The *courtiers* of Bordeaux were a fairly recent office, cre-ated in response to the established power of commission merchants. The commission agents in the major ports overlapped with merchants rather than with *courtiers,* and *courtiers* remained a subordinate, even subservi-ent, position. The difference appears to be due to the existence of foreign wholesale merchants in the major ports, who took it upon themselves to provide the important service of commission agents and kept the local

From Public Office to Private Entrepreneur

brokers in their place. These merchants were also much more in tune with the international practice of commissioning.

The merchants in the port cities conceived of brokers in much the same way as did the commercial treatises of the day. A generation before the Nantais' appeal, Jacques Savary verified their fundamental distinctions between *courtiers* and commissionnaires. Savary treated commissionnaires as "négociants . . . who buy merchandise for the account of négociants living elsewhere" and are "all forbidden to sell, buy, or exchange for foreigners without the mediation and the company of an approved *courtier*."[57] His description had the international commerce of the major ports very clearly in mind: "There is nothing that maintains commerce so much as commissionnaires or correspondents; for through them merchants and négociants can trade throughout the world without leaving their shops or counters."[58] A hundred years later, Condillac's treatise on *Commerce and Government* also equated commissionnaires with merchants and asserted that they were entitled to the same kind of profits accorded to a merchant. Like the merchant, the commissionnaire operated "between the producer and the consumer," and any exchange involving merchants Condillac termed *commerce de commission*, because the merchants "establish themselves as commissionnaires."[59] It is instructive to see how much closer these treatises came to describing behavior in the peripheral economy than in the interior.

The commission brokers in the port cities may have enjoyed the support of international practice and commercial theory, but they came into direct conflict with the interests of the royal tax system. Since 1360 every sale of wine in barrels was attended by a "wholesale tax" (*droit de gros*).[60] As brokers were exempted from paying the sales tax when they bought in someone else's name, the farm was greatly concerned that a purchase by commission not be secretly a separate sale and so taxable. Hence *courtiers* and commissionnaires were expressly forbidden to act as merchants, that is, to buy and sell for their own account, and wine merchants were explicitly forbidden to act as "commissionnaires [who] have wine arrive under other names than their own, under pretext of a service to a friend or otherwise." Thus wine brokers were deliberately excluded from normal practice of combining commissioning with other mercantile activity.[61] Yet they evidently did so in the most international centers like Bordeaux, Nantes, and, as we saw in the previous chapter, Reims.

Evidently the tax farm and the government had not been able to block the commercial imperatives of international trade, where merchants needed to help each other as brokers. The wine merchants of the port cities, who insisted that they acted both as merchant and broker, were precocious, however, for nowhere else did merchants admit to this. This suggests the greater sophistication of merchants involved in overseas trade, especially those connected to Holland.[62] Indeed, most of the brokers on the list of négociants who protested in Nantes in 1704 had foreign names, many of them Dutch. Although some of these had been naturalized, their presence in Nantes reflected the Dutch preeminence in the wine trade of the French west coast.[63] One list of brokers in Bordeaux identified twenty of them as citizens of England, Holland, and several German ports.[64] As a consequence, the major French ports were very different markets, and differently organized, than the rest of France. The brokers in the domestic market supplying Paris did not make use of the Nantais' distinctions and may not have even understood them.

Geography of Brokers

Despite the protests and the confusion over terms, intendants throughout the country moved with remarkable speed, in early 1705, to draw up lists of brokers in most of the major—and many minor—market centers, along with the amount each would be fined. These rolls of fines are an invaluable source of information about the brokers in many parts of the country.[65] Giving name, location, and the amount of the fine, the rolls allow us to map the density of brokers and indicate the scale of commercial activity in different regions. They give a rough overview, unique before the nineteenth century, of the wine trade and the geography of brokerage markets. Like radioactive isotopes injected into the bloodstream, the concentrations of brokers identify the viticultural markets that had been quickened by access to long-distance trade. There we can see the principal arteries of the interregional wine trade, where the viticultural economy had achieved its greatest vigor.

Details about the location and activity of wine brokers revealed by this tax elucidate the regional patterns of market networks and the growth and articulation of this commercial system. In addition to the rough topography of markets, they offer evidence for a typology of brokers that largely matches the different development of *courtiers* in the ports and the interior. The contrasts of organization and scale in different regions, particularly between purely domestic trade networks and those connected to international trade, suggest that brokers had achieved markedly different levels of economic power and control over their markets. The markets around the country's outer edge exhibit the greater sophistication and economic power that came with links to international commerce, compared to the interior zone that was still in some ways inchoate and undeveloped. Thus regional patterns in the wine trade illustrate the division, argued by Braudel and others, of France's economy into a core and periphery.[66]

The tax on brokers allows us to survey an important aspect of the wine trade over a national area, although it is less comprehensive than one could hope. Intendants in several areas, particularly in the south, failed to provide a list of brokers and seem, in a few cases, to have actively engaged in subverting the whole process. The tax lists give no precise indication of the wine trade in Languedoc, Provence, or La Rochelle. The tax also shared a typical problem of the Old Regime in being apportioned from the top down. The traitants had assigned overall fines to each generality, based no doubt upon information gleaned from the existing taxes on the wine trade. They then left it to the intendants to divide the fines locally as well as they, and their local assistants, could.

On the whole, however, the intendants seem to have been quite thorough; their lists correspond well with the active brokers that can be identified in several regions. The list for Epernay certainly identified the right people: Adam Bertin du Rocheret owed four thousand livres, as did his father and two brothers. Antoine Quatresous owed six thousand livres, as did his cousin Nicolas Chertemps; his uncle's widow owed two thousand. The two families owed two-thirds of the fines on brokers in Epernay, but the list had dragged in four others who seem, from the contrôle des actes discussed in the previous chapter, to have been more marginal to the wine trade. Of the eleven brokers named in Ay, several, like the two Testulats and Pierre Louis, appear with some frequency in the contrôle des actes, but there is less evidence for the rest having been serious brokers.[67] The brokers of lower Burgundy, discussed in the following chapter, were also well represented on the tax rolls.

The lists seem to have been overly inclusive, for some individuals protested their assessment, usually denying that they were ever involved in brokering. A hotel keeper near Paris wrote to contest his fine of two thousand livres, blaming it all on the "pure imagination or supposition of his enemies." He had "accompanied those who had asked him, carters among others, to buy wines and transport them on their return from Paris to the provinces of Brittany and Normandy . . . [but] purely in the office of friendship without even the benefit of a sous." He included certificates from local officials and the mayor of Mantes attesting to his statements, but they admitted that he accepted "some small tip [*gratification*] to reimburse him for carrying letters and the trouble he takes to load the wine." The traitant pounced on the evidence about tips: "Nothing more is needed to be convinced that [the hotel keeper] falls under the [provisions of the] edict."[68] He had merely acted informally, but the edict addressed both formal and informal brokering and essentially conflated them. By and large, the protests suggest that the roll was fairly accurate, if heavy-handed. If this procedure provoked complaints from its victims, it also offers us a more comprehensive picture of who was involved in the wine trade.

The intendant was expected to determine not only who had engaged in brokering but also how much they were liable for. Despite the complaint that "the taxes carried on the rolls are proportionate neither to the commerce nor the resources of those who are included," it is clear that they were meant to be both.[69] Even if we must dismiss some brokers from the list as the victims of envy or excessive zeal, the rolls contained over a thousand names and can certainly be trusted as indicative on a large scale. The sums that brokers owed were occasionally contested and could not have been precise measures of liability, yet the fines give us a sense of relative commercial activity, both between and within regions.

Although the size of the fines was meant to bear some relation to the level of wine trade in a region, and probably to an individual's involvement in the trade, there are limits to what it tells us. Evidence from Nantes suggests that fines were matched to ability to pay as much as to any precise activity in the wine trade. For some, unspecified, reason the traitants produced two rolls for Nantes: One gave the fines for each of eighty-two individuals, and the other gave their "resources" (*facultés*). This second list, entitled the "Condition of individuals who function as brokers," provided an estimate of the wealth (*biens*) of the brokers, mostly rounded to the nearest thousand livres.[70] It was probably drawn up to justify the list of fines, in the face of intense criticism by the Nantais. The two lists together show that fines correlated quite closely with the estimates for wealth. The bottom half of the brokers, taxed only five hundred livres, had all been assessed at less than ten thousand livres of wealth. Most of those fined one and two thousand livres enjoyed between eight and twenty-five thousand livres of wealth, and those in the highest bracket, owing three thousand livres, had anywhere from twenty to eighty thousand livres.[71] The estimates of wealth were probably an ex post facto rationalization of the original tax role, but the point is that fines appear to have been linked with wealth, rather than with any attempt to estimate individual commercial activity.

As a result we must be careful not to attach too much importance to the individual fines. They are at best a rough approximation of the brokers' business activities and their ability to pay. Rather than being a simple

From Public Office to Private Entrepreneur

value-added tax, the fine was more in the nature of blackmail: a sum to be paid in exchange for freeing the city's brokers to continue their business. It was calculated on the basis of exceptionally detailed information available to the government about the wine trade throughout the country. The wine trade was so closely supervised for good reason. A city's total fine, then, reflected the traitants' estimate of what the brokerage trade was worth to its participants. The relative weight of a city's tax is probably a good indication of the relative activity of the brokerage trade there. The total fine was then divided among the participants by the local subdelegate, probably in much the same way that Nantes reveals.

The brokers who were identified, then, delineate the major markets in the long-distance wine trade of France. A table and map showing the total fines owed by brokers in each city assessed at least three thousand livres indicate the general configuration of this trade (table 3.1, figure 3.1). They omit information about individual brokers that will be considered later, but they identify regions or clusters of market networks. The city of Bordeaux and its hinterland was the region paying the largest fine, bearing almost a quarter of the kingdom's total tax, with Reims and Champagne close behind. If the whole Loire is taken as a single region, its cities paid more, but one can distinguish two fairly distinct regions in the upper and lower Loire, divided roughly at Tours. The Loire from Tours down was taxed roughly one-fifth of the total, and that above Tours owed about one-tenth. Then Burgundy, with 15 percent, could also be divided between lower Burgundy around Auxerre, paying two-thirds of the burden, and an area from Dijon south paying the rest. The Île-de-France had to pay another tenth of the total tax.

The map indicates the relative involvement of different wine-producing regions in long-distance trade. Many regions of France produced wine but were isolated from long-distance trade; they denied having brokers and escaped the tax. The intendant in the Limousin had already warned the controller general that the region only had a dozen parishes with vines and that the wine was consumed locally.[72] About the generality of Bourges the traitants noted that "there are very few *courtiers* in this province . . . and those on the roll are not very opulent." The province had been assessed twenty-five thousand livres, but "we do not expect to get more than eight thousand livres." They had also been warned by the intendant of Provence that "those who perform these functions are miserable men incapable of paying any tax."[73] In the whole of the generality of Poitiers there were only "some brokers of brandy in certain locations," and in the generality of Lyon, "we do not presume that there are many brokers." Distance and

Bordeaux: 344 [180]
  Bordeaux: 313 [135]
  Sainte-Foy: 5 [7]
  Bergerac: 3 [5]
  Libourne: 3 [5]
  Preignac: 3 [5]
  Saint-Macaire: 3 [5]
Lower Burgundy: 140 [50]
  Auxerre: 39 [12]
  Chablis: 30 [6]
  Tonnerre: 19 [10]
  Saint-Bris: 12 [5]
  Vermenton: 9 [2]
  Joigny: 6 [2]
  Epineuil: 5 [2]
  Coulanges: 5 [1]
  Champs: 4 [3]
  Irancy: 4 [1]
  Chitry: 3 [3]
Upper Burgundy: 82 [22]
  Beaune: 45 [9]
  Chalon: 15 [5]
  Mâcon: 9 [3]
  Auxonne: 7 [3]
  Dijon: 4 [1]
Champagne: 337 [205]
  Reims: 174 [94]
  Epernay: 44 [11]
  Ay: 24 [11]
  Damery: 12 [7]
  Cumières: 11 [7]
  Château Thierry: 9 [6]
  Avenay: 7 [4]
  Reuil: 6 [3]
  Essômes: 5 [5]
  Saulchery: 4 [3]
  Dormans: 4 [2]
  Venteuil: 4 [2]
  Trélou: 3 [3]
  Châtillon: 3 [1]

Île-de-France: 153 [360]
  Laon: 17 [19]
  Meaux: 13 [29]
  Villeneuve Saint-George/Ablon: 12 [8]
  Soissons: 9 [11]
  Mantes: 9 [5]
  Argenteuil: 5 [8]
  Limay: 4 [2]
  Quincy: 3 [4]
Lower Loire: 304 [167]
  Nantes: 95 [82]
  Saumur: 44 [16]
  Angers: 30 [18]
  Chinon: 25 [6]
  Châtellerault: 23 [8]
  Chemillé: 18 [6]
  Tours: 11 [4]
  Fresnay: 8 [3]
  Rablay: 6 [3]
  Niort: 6 [2]
  Ligré: 5 [1]
  Vouvray: 4 [2]
  Chouzé: 4 [1]
  Jallais: 4 [1]
  Doué: 3 [1]
Upper Loire: 183 [113]
  Orléans: 54 [55]
  Blois: 53 [19]
  Mer: 14 [7]
  Sancerre: 12 [4]
  Beaugency: 6 [8]
  Muides: 6 [3]
  Saint-Denis: 6 [3]
  Saint-Dyé: 6 [3]
  Châteauroux: 6 [2]
  Montliveaux: 4 [2]
  Pouilly: 4 [2]
  Suèvres: 4 [2]

Total: 1,543 [1,097]

From Public Office to Private Entrepreneur

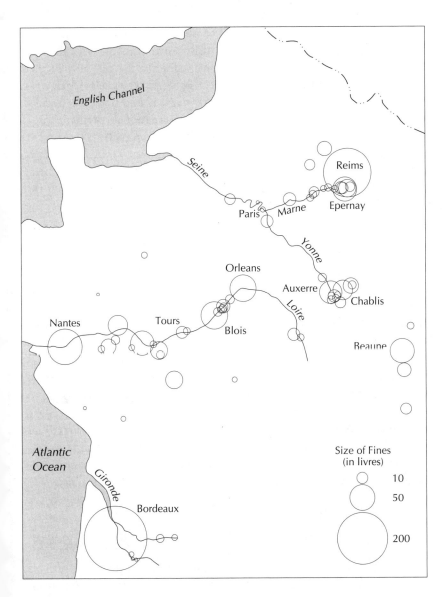

Figure 3.1
Level of Fines on Brokers in Specific Towns

lack of transportation hindered access to upper Burgundy, and the wines of the Mâconnais and Beaujolais were still mostly consumed locally and did not circulate beyond a narrow regional market at this point, as indeed was true of much of the wine produced in France.[74] The existence of brokers, in contrast, tells us where local wine markets had been successfully connected to larger currents of national and international commerce.

As the map indicates, much of the brokerage activity lay on what Braudel has called the border zones of the kingdom, by which he means both its maritime and its continental frontiers.[75] Here were the commercial centers catering to the export trade.[76] The two large cities along the west coast, Bordeaux and Nantes, were the most striking markets on the periphery. They had long been the chief centers of the export trade toward the Atlantic, each dominated by foreigners who connected them to the markets of northern Europe. They were joined by Reims in the northeast corner and, on a much smaller scale, by Beaune along France's eastern border, both centers of export to a vast number of continental markets. These four cities alone gave employment to nearly one-third of all the brokers in France and were assessed at 40 percent of the kingdom's total levy. If intendants in the south had cooperated with the traitants, a fourth and possibly fifth entrepôt of substantial size might have been identified in Montpellier and Marseilles.[77] The preponderance of this export trade is only properly measured if we add the brokers along the lower Loire to those on the periphery, for most of the long-distance trade in that region was aimed at Nantes and thence overseas. Brokers thus linked directly or indirectly to the export trade bore nearly 60 percent of the total fines.

There is little surprising in the fact that long-distance trade was so connected to international markets: International commerce was already old and well developed by the eighteenth century. What is surprising is the evident strength of the long-distance wine trade for the domestic market. Paris drew on markets in the upper Loire, lower Burgundy, and much of Champagne; the capital was already the focus of a large and sophisticated market system that grew steadily through the century. The brokers in these markets owed almost a third of the total tax burden—40 percent if we include the more marginal brokers in the Île-de-France. This tax provides one of the first measures of the capital's importance as a stimulus to the development of a national market. The dynamic element in France's wine trade, what lifted it above local and intraregional commerce, had long been the result of exports, but now it was increasingly rivaled by a growing domestic market.

From Public Office to Private Entrepreneur

The Function of Market Networks

The map of brokers clearly indicates several separate market systems and suggests, more importantly, that brokerage was organized quite distinctly in different regions. The geography of brokers—the proximity of subordinate or competing market centers, the degree to which brokers were concentrated or dispersed among a region's towns—depended upon the dynamics of the regional wine trade. All these factors illustrate differences in the development of the foreign and domestic wine trades and shed light on the mechanics of wine brokering.

The size of the supply area on which brokers could draw is an important indication of their financial and commercial strength. The classic method for determining catchment areas relies on account books for individual brokers to chart the location and range of their suppliers; the next chapter will make that kind of analysis.[78] The map of brokers' fines offers an alternative method of estimating catchment areas: The number and density of brokers in neighboring market centers suggests competition with and limits to a city's catchment area. Where brokers were most concentrated—in Nantes and Bordeaux, for example—the city faced least competition and the greatest catchment area. In contrast, the dispersion of brokers through a region, as can be found in many parts of the interior, indicates contested catchment areas and more circumscribed supply zones.

Commercial organization in the domestic markets distinguished them from the export trade in several important ways. Brokerage activities in export centers were not only unusually intense, to judge both by the number of brokers and by their tax burden, but the brokers were also unusually concentrated. In the export entrepôts, particularly Bordeaux and Nantes, the tax rolls discovered great numbers of brokers who exercised their economic sway over extensive hinterlands. The tax also identified a pronounced hierarchy of fines among these brokers, indicating a sophisticated division of labor. Here brokers had most fully developed their commission business. In contrast, the brokers' dispersion and lack of hierarchy throughout the interior markets of lower Burgundy, the Marne, and, to a lesser extent, the Loire point to their recent origins as *courtiers*. Since the transformation of *courtiers* into commission brokers entailed a change in the organization of their markets, the map can help us pinpoint the stages of this evolution.

The different organizations of the brokerage systems found in the interior and the periphery illustrate the differences in their origins. In those cities where commission brokers had long distinguished themselves from *courtiers,* as they had in the export centers, they had also developed large catchment areas. Their business was to organize the bulking up of wine from a whole region for the convenience of their correspondents. In contrast, the very local nature of the traditional *courtiers,* officially serving a single town and a little of its neighborhood, meant that they were initially scattered among the wine-producing locations without much interaction.[79] The brokers of Beaune, as late as 1683, were carefully restricted to serving the winemakers of the town and precluded from conducting merchants to neighboring villages.[80] The dispersion of brokers throughout the interior of France appears to be a legacy of their origin as parochial public servants. As such they had little reason to compete with brokers nearby and little incentive to expand their catchment areas. But as brokers took to buying on commission for absent merchants, they expanded their purchasing to a larger area. No longer working simply to sell the wine of their town, they worked for merchants to assemble wines from a whole region. The distribution of brokers in lower Burgundy and the Marne suggests this gradual evolution toward a market organized by commission brokers. The brokers along the Loire appear to have already moved somewhat farther in this direction.

Bordeaux offers a striking example of the concentration of the brokerage trade of a whole region in one location. The port city lay at the edge of a huge wine region, including the basins of the Dordogne and Garonne Rivers. Three-quarters of the region's one hundred and eighty brokers were based in the city, and the city's brokers owed nine-tenths of the fine levied on the region, which suggests their complete domination of the wine trade in the area. To some extent the dominance of the city's brokers reflects an earlier reality, based on the carefully constructed privileges that had long discriminated against "upriver wines" (*vin du haut*) in favor of the "city's wines" (*vin de ville*) from around Bordeaux. But the city had lost its monopoly in 1675 and was gradually reaching out to bring these upriver wines into its market.[81] In the early eighteenth century vin du haut already accounted for nearly a quarter of wine exported from the region. There were also serious brokers in the outlying towns, among them Brière of Saint-Macaire, who is described in a recent monograph as a wine producer "who seems to have organized a veritable assemblage of wine" for a négociant of Bordeaux.[82] By the middle of the century there is evidence of a thriving and independent wine trade in upriver towns, like Bergerac.[83] Nor was Bordeaux the only port from which wine of the region was exported. Libourne and Blaye were gradually increasing their exports, embarking a

From Public Office to Private Entrepreneur

third of the region's wine shipments by 1716.[84] Yet the brokers in Bordeaux in 1705 still maintained considerable control over brokerage in the area.[85]

The brokerage market in several other export entrepôts exhibited basic similarities to Bordeaux. Like Bordeaux, though on a much smaller scale, Nantes had also gained domination of its immediate hinterland, a radius of some seventy-five kilometers, and was the focal point for all the export trade from half a dozen substantial market centers along the lower Loire. Nantes's hegemony was reinforced by a toll imposed on wines descending the Loire, sixty kilometers from Nantes, at Ingrandes. Many winegrowers upstream found the toll so high as to "absolutely prohibit commerce," though producers of expensive wines could afford the added cost.[86] Reims too was an ancient export center, sending the wines of Champagne and Burgundy to the major markets of northern Europe since the Middle Ages and continuing to receive a host of foreign wine merchants through the seventeenth century.[87] Owing more than half of the fine imposed on the generality of Châlons, the city of Reims dominated its hinterland but had not engulfed it like Bordeaux. A strong market system along the Marne River and centered around Epernay had developed an independent commerce with Paris. Reims was an international market, with a flourishing trade to the important markets of the north, at the same time that Epernay and Ay were still largely interregional markets, within the Parisian network.

The individual fines levied in Nantes, Reims, and, to a lesser extent Bordeaux and Orléans, distinguished a clearly differentiated hierarchy of brokers, with many only marginally involved in brokering.[88] Nearly all of the twenty-eight brokers identified in the first roll to be drawn up for Reims had to pay between four and six thousand livres each. A subsequent roll discovered a host of small brokers in the town—sixty-five of them—half of whom owed less than five hundred livres.[89] For example, Vieville and Clicquot, mentioned in the previous chapter, owed three and four thousand livres; Mallo only owed one hundred and fifty. Even more hierarchical than Bordeaux, the upper quartile in Reims paid three-quarters of the tax, and those in the bottom third were clearly marginal. Similarly, the top quartile of Nantes's eighty-two brokers owed between two and three thousand livres, whereas the majority paid only five hundred livres. This hierarchy, found in few markets in the interior of France, resulted from the more competitive nature of commission brokering in the international markets.

Like the other major markets, Paris had no intermediate markets in its immediate hinterland but was unusual in being surrounded by a dense penumbra of marginal brokers upon whom it relied for huge amounts of wine. In scores of towns and villages within the "twenty-league distance" from Paris (the zone from which Parisian wine merchants were excluded) and around Soissons, three hundred and sixty brokers were fined an average of barely four hundred livres. Their locations closely match the villages producing most of the wine just west of Paris and downstream along the Seine.[90] Only two dozen of these individuals, in the towns of Mantes, Meaux, and Villeneuve-Saint-George, owed as much as a thousand livres. There were no brokers of any real stature, and the vast majority were on such a small scale as to be trivial. With almost a third of all the country's brokers the generalities of Paris and Soisson bore a tenth of the fines.[91]

Indeed, brokers in the immediate vicinity of Paris hardly deserved the title. Wine producers around Paris enjoyed relatively easy access to a large and growing band of "suburban" taverns, the guinguettes just outside the tax barriers of the city.[92] Their proximity meant low transportation costs, and wine going to the guinguettes was cheap and avoided the entrance taxes paid by wine going into the city. Thus the wine trade right around Paris required substantially less financial resources than that elsewhere in France. Almost anyone in the immediate vicinity of Paris could afford to act as a broker, and so many individuals of very modest means engaged in brokering on what was apparently a very small scale. The interregional markets in the rest of France and the international markets along its peripheries presented vastly greater financial challenges that severely limited the number who could participate as brokers and raised the costs of competing. Unlike the brokers around Paris, the brokers in the rest of France formed a financial and commercial elite.

The Parisian wine trade extended to a second provisioning crown, at a distance of some hundred and fifty kilometers, in which the brokers were altogether more serious than those closest to Paris, yet were organized quite differently from the brokers in the periphery. Over two hundred brokers in lower Burgundy, the upper Loire, and along the Marne River owed an average of more than two thousand livres.[93] Their fines made them equal to the major brokers in the country's export centers, but they lacked the concentration and hierarchies found in Bordeaux or Nantes. In contrast to the regional hegemony exercised by the export entrepôts, brokerage in the second provisioning crown around Paris was dispersed among many small- to medium-sized market centers, each connected to the metropolitan market. Unlike the hierarchies found among brokers in the big ports, most of the brokers in this zone were subjected to major fines. Their limited catchment areas, densely dispersed throughout their region, characterize a supply zone still organized by *courtiers*. Such a pattern bore little resemblance to the vast catchment areas controlled by commission brokers in the export entrepôts.

The towns in lower Burgundy, in the region around Auxerre, differed most strikingly from the concentrated market systems of Bordeaux or Nantes; this area is the best example of a brokerage market dispersed throughout a contested catchment area. Fifty brokers, owing an average of nearly three thousand livres, could be found in a dozen towns in a twenty-kilometer radius. Auxerre clearly enjoyed primacy, with twelve brokers, half of whom owed fines of five or six thousand livres.[94] But the city owed only a quarter of the total fine for the region and competed with brokers in bourgs and villages like Coulanges-la-vineuse, Saint-Bris, and Irancy, where brokers owed at least a thousand livres, and most over two. Only twenty and thirty-five kilometers away, Chablis and Tonnerre were large ... id Tonnerre were large ... owing ... quarter ... half ... of Auxerre's fines, re- ... owed the largest fines ... in France. The situation of these neighboring bourgs, on navigable rivers and fine wine regions, made them important wine markets as early as ... century ... continued into the eighteenth century ... were only slowly expanding ... to confront with brokers who ... their brokerage over the whole area.

Records from this period attest to the ... mentation of the markets in the extended supply zone around Paris that resulted from the enduringly parochial character of brokering. In 1713 a Parisian wine merchant visited both regional brokers and very local ones in more than a dozen towns and villages in Burgundy and the upper Loire in his search for wines. The bulk of his purchases came from the large regional markets, such as Auxerre, Chablis, Blois, and Orléans, where he dealt with brokers who had in turn acquired wines from the smaller centers in their areas. The broker in Auxerre, for example, had acquired other wine in the neighborhood, particularly from Saint-Bris and Coulanges. He had also acted as a shipping agent for wines going from Beaune through Auxerre to Paris, though these were wines that the Parisian had acquired himself in trips to Beaune.[96] At the same time, however, the Parisian wine merchant visited and made purchases directly from brokers in several smaller centers, like Irancy and Beaugency. His purchases tended to be greatest in the biggest markets, but he either could not, or chose not to, dispense with visits to the smaller markets. Rather than having one contact to handle all his purchases, the Parisian merchant worked with several brokers in each region. His itinerary indicates that brokers in the intermediate markets had not yet taken over the markets of the smaller towns, that no entrepreneur in the regions he visited had emerged with sufficient initiative or power to dominate the brokerage of a large area.

Similarly, the part of Champagne supplying Paris, where a dozen small towns along the Marne River owed substantial fines, appears to have been a region of intense competition among brokers. The eleven brokers of Epernay certainly stood out, with individual fines of close to four thousand livres and owing, collectively, more than a third of the region's penalties. Yet in ten other villages along the Marne, within fifteen kilometers of Epernay, another forty brokers owed an average of nineteen hundred livres, not one fined less than a thousand livres. These figures exaggerate the brokers' dispersion, however; the contrôle des actes examined in the previous chapter show that the brokers of Epernay had gained greater control over the region than the tax suggests. The tax list reflected an earlier stage in the region's commercial development, based as it was on "infringements" over the previous two decades. Now brokers in Epernay were engrossing much of the commission business with Paris at the expense of other *courtiers* along the Marne, much as the brokers in certain well-established markets along the Loire had already done.

The patterns of brokerage along the lower Loire were similar to other interior regions, yet not so dispersed. In sharp contrast to the insignificant markets upriver from Bordeaux, the lower Loire had a number of important intermediate markets, including Saumur, Angers, and Chinon, that linked the region to the primary entrepôt in Nantes. Most of the brokers in the main commercial centers of the Loire owed three or four thousand livres, and those in the surrounding villages owed at least two thousand. Yet the brokerage system along the Loire was also more nucleated than that in Champagne or lower Burgundy. Covering a much larger area, the main brokers were concentrated into a few cities that controlled larger catchment areas, with noticeably less competition from each other and from small centers. Because these markets exerted uncontested control over such large areas, the brokerage system along the Loire River comes closest to the model identified by anthropologists as a "dendritic system." A trade network is dendritic when it connects rural producers to a metropolitan capital or port through a series of intermediate bulking-up centers that draw on smaller market centers in their hinterland.[97] Anthropologists point out that the hierarchical aspects of a dendritic system give merchants in the intermediate centers the advantages of monopolistic control over price information and credit.[98] Such advantages concentrated brokering in the intermediate markets along the Loire.

Despite the government's conflation of *courtier* and commissionnaire,

From Public Office to Private Entrepreneur

it is evident that the two offices provided very different services and so assumed a very different geography. Where commission brokers had the longest experience of a distinct identity and practice, especially along the coast, brokerage had acquired the longest reach and largest catchment area. Brokerage elsewhere still showed the traces, to a greater or lesser extent, of its origins in a parochial police function. Brokers in much of the interior remained dispersed, continuing to operate in the small markets, in the shadow of intermediate markets. As *courtiers* became commissionnaires they extended their reach and commercial power and gradually established a hierarchy among these markets, as the map suggests that the brokers along the Loire had already done, and as the contrôle des actes suggests that the brokers along the Marne were doing. Brokers in the interior of France were evolving rapidly, gaining sophistication, wealth, and control over the wine trade as they abandoned their public function and became private entrepreneurs.

Triumph of the Private

Public authorities, both municipal and royal, tried to maintain brokers as public servants but failed. Whether from a desire to protect a town's economic interests or to tax the wine trade, governments had regulated the numbers, licensing, and commercial practices of wine brokers. But they had lost control of the brokers' commercial practices in the late seventeenth century, and now, in the early eighteenth, they lost control of their licensing.

Letters back to the traitants show that their attempt to organize and control wine brokers met overwhelming resistance from every level of society: from the intendants down to the vigneron selling wine. Those in a position of power criticized the tax assessments or simply refused to comply. They scrambled for ways to avoid royal control of brokers and to maintain existing brokers without disruption. Those without power resorted to fraud and violence to thwart any attempt to impose new middlemen on the wine trade. A report reviewing the situation shortly after the creation of the tax rolls shows us that the traitants knew they were in trouble.[99] Although they had "estimate[d] at least 150,000 livres from this generality [of Orléans] it being one of those where there is the largest commerce in wine and spirits and where the brokers have the largest fortunes," they had to admit that the city of Orléans had been recalcitrant and (initially) refused to turn in a roll of fines. The intendants of both Soissons and Tours were also causing problems, refusing to verify their rolls for various reasons, but "the excuses of the intendant [of Tours] do not appear truthful." Here the traitants were beginning to revise their goals: The roll for Tours had reached 182,500 livres in fines, but they acknowledged that they could hope for little more than half of that. The estates of Burgundy had sent a request "containing poor arguments," and there too the estimates were being lowered. The traitants had come up with a total of 344,500 livres in fines for Bordeaux, but the intendant had suggested they ask for only 126,000 livres "as in 1691." Yet Bordeaux was the "best department for our affair and the place where the *courtiers* have made the largest fortunes" so the traitants hoped still for two hundred thousand livres.

Perhaps the most common problem facing this whole system was the resistance it faced from the private market. The controller general received numerous complaints from newly created official brokers about the private brokers who flouted the law, continuing to conduct business, and about the wine merchants who abetted them. The two men who had acquired the offices of broker in Villeneuve-Saint-George and Ablon (south of Paris) were writing to protest the violations that had been going on since they took office in June 1705. They named six men "and others" who were still interfering in their function of broker and "have not ceased taking commissions from wine merchants from Paris and abroad." All six of the interlopers had already been fined between one and two thousand livres for acting as brokers without title before 1705. The plaintiffs cited numerous reports of violations since then and claimed to be "without functions and frustrated from [gaining] their fees, which made it impossible to pay the traitant."[100] Eight official brokers of Meaux had to complain to the conseil d'état that the "former *courtiers* who did not wish to acquire [the office] boast of selling and buying and shipping wines despite the supplicants."[101] In the same way, former brokers had driven the new owner of six offices around Chablis and Irancy to appeal to the king for help. "They have threatened to destroy and burn the houses" of his clerks and procureurs "if they got involved in wine brokering." Of course, this is exactly what the plaintiff had paid 17,050 livres to be able to do, but he faced stiff resistance from the whole community. "All the inhabitants, wine merchants and vignerons have treated his clerks with contempt, saying that such an establishment [the official broker] was capable of ruining the wine trade and that they would only deal with the former brokers." Against such hostility "he has earned nothing useful since . . . he had made this acquisition."[102]

A striking triumph of private arrangements over official brokering occurred in Tonnerre, not far from Chablis, somewhat after the issue had been resolved throughout the rest of the country. Two women and one of

From Public Office to Private Entrepreneur

their sons had been among the ten brokers from Tonnerre each fined two thousand livres in 1705. The two women were the widows of men who had paid the countess of Tonnerre (the marquise de Louvois) since 1687 for the right to act as brokers and to collect five sous on every barrel sold in the county for this right.[103] By 1709 the women were paying the countess two thousand livres a year for the collection rights, indicating a commerce based on well over eight thousand barrels. The countess had earlier forced the conseil d'état to recognize the right of certain seigneurs to choose their own official brokers and to exempt the pair in 1691 and their widows in 1705 of any fines. A right won from the crown was not necessarily worth much in situ, however, and she encountered implacable resistance from the inhabitants of her own county when she tried to impose her choice of broker on them. A new pair had bought the right to broker from the countess in 1715, but to their chagrin they found that the old brokers would not stop their activities. The countess took the interlopers to court, but the case quickly took on much larger dimensions and principles.

The inhabitants of Tonnerre intervened to plead the cause of the accused women and, more importantly, to defend their own rights. They complained that the countess's claims to control the choice of broker were ill-founded, that documents from 1631 showed that, as early as 1261, the inhabitants had gained the right to choose the brokers whom the counts would then name. The counts could only name brokers who were "agreeable to the inhabitants," and this practice could not hinder in any way the "liberty of commerce." These official brokers "have never had the right to stop any other person from involving themselves in the same function. . . . They were only introduced because of the need to have people always in place who are capable of arranging the sale of wine, which is the principal or rather the unique revenue of the region." The fight over the two widows was important because they were crucial to the wine trade, and the local growers "were used to delivering their wines to the said brokers [the two widows] on credit and without collateral, for a price and to persons [that is, buyers] that they can trust, and they recognize the commendable experience of the widows in the wine trade." But a more fundamental issue of rights lay at the base of this case: "The wine trade in Tonnerre has always been as free as it is everywhere else in France where all those who have the confidence of the buyers and sellers have functioned as brokers without trouble or hinderance."[104]

Viticultural communities needed brokers who had their "trust" and "confidence," as well as "experience" and sound credit. The function of broker was too critical to be left to the incompetence of venal interlopers. A judicial memorandum reviewing the situation later in the century suggests that, for the rest of the country, the attempt to recreate the post of official broker had simply been abandoned: "This edict [of November 1704] appears not to have been entirely executed, except in Paris. . . . It was not executed in the rest of the kingdom."[105] Brokers had relinquished the role of the public servant to become indispensable entrepreneurs in the increasingly private market. The offices were officially suppressed by an arrêt du conseil in September 1706, for the last time, and brokers were now on their own.[106] The government tried to police them on occasion in the future, but it abandoned any attempt to turn them into officials.

4

The Brokers of Burgundy

There is a profound irony in the response of communities and wine producers to the government's attempts to control wine brokers. The creation of royal offices had ultimately foundered on the concerted resistance of viticultural society, from municipal leaders to humble vignerons. Invoking the ideal of commercial liberty and the good of the wine trade, viticultural communities insisted on the importance of the broker's role and defended their right to choose their own brokers. And the government had been forced to allow the brokers' liberation and privatization. But this liberty soon appeared excessive in the eyes of these very same people who had called for it so loudly. The wine brokers quickly asserted their independent role in the market, a role that gave them enormous economic power.

Studies of the early modern economy, particularly the rural textile industries, emphasize the varieties of ways in which economic power was acquired and wielded; some of these insights are useful for understanding the wine trade. There has been much debate over the role of merchants in petty commodity production and proto-industrialization. The classic argument, presented by Jürgen Schlumbohm, underscored the advantages of the "successful trader [who] could achieve considerable profit at the expense of the small producer who had no direct access to the distant market."[1] Where merchants enjoyed superior access to markets they could pressure producers to sell at lower prices. It was only a series of small steps between this "exploitation through trade" and the introduction of merchant capital into the production process that resulted in the true putting-out system. In contrast, William Reddy and Tessie Liu have argued that there were "so many dealers and local markets that cottagers had little to fear from monopsony" in the regions they study.[2] The only way that merchants could compete with producers was to insert themselves into the production process and to gain control of the producer by gaining control over raw materials. But there were other factors that might lead producers to surrender some of their independence and income to a merchant; many allowed merchants to handle their marketing out of a desire to lessen risk. Both Liana Vardi and Schlumbohm argue that weavers "saw the advantages of relying on local merchants" and so "lessened their marketing risk by giving them commissions."[3] To summarize, the principal features of the struggle for power in rural textile industries revolved around the goal of controlling both the process of marketing and producing, though there are disagreements about which was more important and came first.

Much of the work on proto-industrialization alerts us to ways of understanding the sources and articulation of power in the wine trade. Despite obvious differences between proto-industrialization and viticulture, the two shared similar needs for markets and raw materials. It will be argued in this chapter that access to markets provided the principal advantage enjoyed by wine brokers, but that some of them were slowly beginning to insert themselves into the production process. Distant wine markets presented a series of challenges to wine producers that privileged the role of brokers in the wine trade. Although they had lost the royal monopoly of assisting, and being paid for, every commercial transaction, the services they now provided made them even more indispensable to the wine trade. Their access to credit and consumers essentially allowed them to dominate access to markets. By the early eighteenth century they had turned their control of markets into real economic power, which they used as a springboard for a limited but increasingly important role in the production process, through their loans of money and barrels to producers.

During the late seventeenth century, wine brokers began to assume the function of commission agents, which required considerably more financial, mercantile, and entrepreneurial skill than the office of *courtier* had formerly. No longer merely arranging a meeting between local seller and a buyer from out of town, the broker was usually acting for the buyer in a variety of ways. The broker might well have to represent a buyer who had not come and had sent an order by mail. This gave the broker even greater latitude in the choice of wines and thus greater control over the local market. Even if the buyer were present, the broker would attend to the financing of the purchase, both by providing credit and by soliciting credit from the seller. Typically the broker could delay payment to the wine seller for several months but was forced to wait almost a year before the buyer repaid him the bulk of the sum. Account books examined in this chapter reveal many variations on this arrangement, but all show the broker carrying substantial debts from a host of buyers and owing lesser amounts to a range of sellers. Thus the broker had become a financier on a significant scale, requiring considerable financial resources to float much of the wine's value as well as to maintain the confidence of his sellers.

The broker's responsibility for wine shipments further taxed his financial resources and his managerial skills but rendered his services even more valuable. The process of getting the wine from the seller into the hands of the buyer entailed, at the very least, arranging transportation, often from the seller to the nearest port and then certainly from the port to the buyer's city. The simplest transaction also included preparing the wine for transportation, by securing the barrel and possibly clarifying the wine. Transportation also meant a myriad of taxes, to be paid initially by the broker. But the broker was lucky who could promptly send a purchase to its ultimate buyer; there were delays that might result from impediments to transportation, such as low or high water, storms or ice, but which always proved expensive. The long list of financial and mercantile responsibilities gave brokers unparalleled control over the viticultural economy.

Brokers derived power both from the services they offered buyers and from their relations with the sellers. Their assistance to buyers, both commercial and financial, gave them unique access to sources of demand, making them privileged conduits to the crucial markets in Paris and beyond. Demand was the first thing they offered winegrowers and so saved them the costs and uncertainties of speculation. But brokers also offered financial assistance to growers, many of them too poor to bear the significant delays between paying for the wine's production and enjoying the ultimate return on its sale. Brokers were generally obliged to pay growers the value of the wine they brokered before they themselves received full payment from Parisians, particularly when the grower was poor. It will emerge that brokers offered credit to growers on a much wider and more systematic basis, whether in the form of cash or in barrels needed for harvesting. We will investigate the webs of debt and assistance that made brokers indispensable to buyers and sellers alike.

The analysis in this chapter draws primarily upon the inventories made after the deaths of brokers and their wives. The contrôles des actes of the region offer none of the details of the wine trade to be found in Champagne.[4] Rather, the webs of debts owed to and by the broker left traces at his death because the heirs usually requested an inventory of the assets and accounts of the household. These records, which exist in profusion in the Burgundian archives, reveal the elaborate networks of debt that bound the urban and rural worlds together. Happily for the historian, most debts were repaid so slowly that debtors lingered in account books for enough months to be renewed by a new harvest and subsequent debts. Long lists of wine merchants in Paris and elsewhere who still owed money for wine sent by brokers sketch the geography, if not the precise volume, of markets served by brokers.[5]

The broker's inventory was equally obliged to attest to the money he owed producers from whom he had bought wine. We must pay particularly close attention to the catchment areas mapped out by these creditors, for they offer evidence of the broker's sources of wine that no contrôle des actes ever can. The extent and nature of the catchment area turns out to distinguish a clear hierarchy among the brokers of lower Burgundy, from those in villages who worked close to the small-scale vigneron, bulking up the modest quantities produced by many individuals, to the urban brokers drawing larger quantities from brokers and buyers around them. This hierarchy is further reinforced by the evidence of the many ways in which brokers built up dependencies in the rural population, through loans of money, food, and barrels, or through the more elaborate contracts for *rente* or partnerships in animal raising (*baux à cheptel*). The village brokers were more involved than their urban counterparts in financing wine production through these loans, perhaps as compensation for less direct access to markets. Thus power in the wine trade, as in proto-industrialization, derived from different combinations of superior access to markets and intervention in the production process. The postmortem inventories of some dozen brokers in lower Burgundy during the first quarter of the eighteenth century will allow us to refine the modeling of the wine trade begun in previous chapters as well as to develop our understanding of the dynamics of viticultural society.

The Wine Trade in Lower Burgundy

Lower Burgundy was among the oldest sources of wine in France and had supplied excellent wine to Paris since the Middle Ages. It is probably one of the best and earliest examples of the "colonization" of the French interior by market forces; the merchants of Paris had caused the hills for miles around the lovely town of Auxerre to be turned into vineyards at least by the thirteenth century. Yet the wine trade in lower Burgundy shows the limits of this colonization, for the trade continued to be dominated by outsiders until the seventeenth century. Only gradually did the indigenous population move beyond simple production to attempt to trade in their own wines, in the face of the monopolies and advantages enjoyed by Parisian merchants. Even in the eighteenth century, the financial obstacles to this trade continued to restrict provincial enterprise. Yet the provincial brokers, taking advantage of their unique access to Parisian buyers and provincial growers, replaced Parisians as the conduits to the long-distance trade and profoundly altered the dynamics of this commercial system.

For centuries lower Burgundy produced a large quantity of wine that was both highly prized for its quality and readily accessible to the Parisian market. Boats full of wine could leave the docks of Auxerre and, traveling a hundred and fifty kilometers down the Yonne and Seine Rivers, reach Paris in less than two weeks. With this ideal combination of quantity, quality, and access, the wine from this region had flourished to the point in the thirteenth century at which the Franciscan Salimbene could observe that "the hills, slopes, and plains of this vast diocese are covered with vines, as I saw with my own eyes. The people of this region do not sow, harvest, or store [grain]. It is enough for them to send their wines to Paris by the nearby river . . . [which] provides them with a handsome profit."[6] In Paris and throughout the north, the wines from the region of Auxerre were so much better known than those of Beaune that medieval references to the "wine of Burgundy" meant lower Burgundy rather than the Côte d'Or.[7] The villages of Coulanges-la-vineuse and Irancy shared with Beaune, Epernay, and Ay the distinction of being singled out in the sixteenth century as "delicate and excellent wines."[8] The white wines of Irancy, in particular, were rivaled only by those of Ay, according to authors in the sixteenth and seventeenth centuries.[9] The excellence of lower Burgundy's wines justified the cost of transporting them to Paris, or beyond, and made wine the most important feature of the region's economy.

The city of Auxerre was surrounded by vines, some thirty-six hundred arpents (equal to half a hectare in this region) or half of the land around the city, at the end of the Old Regime. Its reputation, and prices, remained high in the eighteenth century, although more and more growers were turning to the lesser-quality gamay vine. The prices for the wines of the best vineyards around Auxerre—la Chainette, for example—rivaled, at 350 livres per muid (of 268 liters), the wines of Epernay. But most of the forty thousand hectoliters of wine produced, on average, around the city in the second half of the eighteenth century were sold for a half or a quarter of that.[10] The wine trade so dominated the city and its inhabitants that the intendant could remark in 1698 that "their application to the cultivation of their vines occupies them so greatly that they think of nothing but making them profitable."[11]

A vast expanse of vineyards unfolded across the hilly countryside to the south and east of Auxerre. A survey near the end of the Old Regime calculated that the region generally produced 115,000 hectoliters of wine, but described nearly a third of that as either "bad quality, cannot be sold wholesale," or as "too far from routes to be sold wholesale" and so could only be drunk by locals in their taverns.[12] Much of the rest, however, was "excellent quality, quickly sold [to] wholesale [merchants]." In particular, a band of vineyards extending from Chitry, through the small towns of Saint-Bris, Irancy, and Coulanges-la-vineuse, produced some fifty thousand hectoliters, much of which was "excellent quality" wine that was "always [sold] wholesale and very rapidly" to merchants of Paris. The "merchants and bourgeois of Paris" bought a further twenty thousand hectoliters from Chablis and the villages around it. Other figures, from the toll on the river between Auxerre and Paris confirm the annual passage of some eighty thousand hectoliters in the 1650s and 1690s, though this would have included some wine from upper Burgundy as well.[13] Statistics from early in the nineteenth century show that lower Burgundy exported slightly more than half of the two hundred thousand hectoliters it produced.[14] Little wonder that a seventeenth-century intendant had reported the economy of the region as having "no commerce except the wine trade."[15]

The complete reliance on a monoculture like wine could make the region's fortune but also left it vulnerable to weather and markets. Irancy's "common people, though very hard working, are unfortunate, particularly when the vines do not produce or the wine does not sell, for it is their only resource."[16] With barely one thousand inhabitants in 1666 and perhaps fifteen hundred a century later, Coulanges consisted of little besides vines: no meadows, very little woods or grain fields, so that "they do not harvest enough wheat to feed the inhabitants for two months." And when a "universal frost of their vines" struck in 1677, "if the king had not given the inhabitants a respite from paying their debts there would have been no inhabitants left. But to their misery is . . . added the sterility of the year [1691] that has produced no wine . . . which is the sole occupation of the inhabitants."[17]

Lower Burgundy depended entirely for its prosperity on its ability to sell its wines and, thus, on those who facilitated this commerce. Paris was its chief market, though the cheapest wine remained to compete in the local market, already awash in cheap wine. But the proximity of Paris, its legal privileges, and the economic strength of the Parisian wine merchants also meant that the metropolis completely dominated commercial relations with the province. Few growers took it upon themselves to seek markets for their wine directly in Paris, and few provincials ventured into the long-distance wine trade. Instead, growers sold their wine to visiting Parisian merchants, who thus controlled access to the Parisian market.

Parisian hegemony in turn privileged the role of the merchants' intermediaries, the Burgundian brokers who worked with them. First as *courtiers,* arranging the visits of Parisian merchants to provincial wine cellars, and increasingly from the late seventeenth century as commission brokers, taking over the buying and financing from Parisians who now sent them orders, provincial brokers came to dominate the wine trade with Paris. Without a contrôle des actes like those in Epernay, it is difficult to make as clear a case for the dominance of brokers in the Burgundian wine trade. Nevertheless the evidence suggests that most of the region's long-distance wine trade passed through their hands. And as they replaced Parisian merchants, both financially and physically, they gained control over access to the Parisian market.

The Parisian domination of the provincial wine trade was the product of carefully constructed privileges. Parisian merchants enjoyed a virtual monopoly of the river traffic along the Seine since the creation of their guild, or "compagnie française," in the Middle Ages. Any provincial merchant who wished to send his wine beyond Paris to Rouen, and thence overseas, needed to buy the permission of the guild. The records that survive for the fifteenth and sixteenth century indicate how infrequently the Auxerrois themselves—or any provincial—organized the shipment or trade of their own wine. According to a sixteenth-century official, "The inhabitants of Burgundy are not accustomed to bring or send wine beyond the bridges" of Paris.[18] Nor did they play a big role in provisioning Paris itself; a historian of the late medieval wine trade in lower Burgundy insists that "very few Auxerrois devoted themselves to the wine trade."[19] Instead, Burgundians sold the vast quantities of wine they produced to Parisian merchants visiting the province.

Provincial reluctance to take their wines to Paris also resulted from their lack of the important privilege, monopolized by Parisian merchants since an edict of 1192, of unloading their unsold wines at Paris. Any wine they brought speculatively to sell in the city had to remain on the boat that had transported it until it was bought. Parisian officials recognized that this restriction "exposed provincial traders [*marchands forains*] to great inconveniences and often to considerable losses, from heat, floods, and ice."[20]

Indeed, the inconvenience and expense was undoubtedly meant to discourage provincials from bringing their wine to Paris and to leave the wine trade in the hands of Parisians.

Burgundians were apparently more willing to accept the risks of speculative trading by the seventeenth century. Some hundred and fifty "provincial traders and vignerons" of lower Burgundy petitioned the Parlement of Paris in 1648 that they were "accustomed to bring the wines that they have produced from their vines and bought from poor vignerons down the Yonne to Paris."[21] Traders from lower Burgundy played an active role in persuading the king to overturn the Parisians' privilege and allow private entrepreneurs in 1656 to build a covered market, or Halle aux vins, at which provincial traders could unload, store, and sell their wines. Dozens of traders from Auxerre and the villages and towns around it sent legal suits and petitions in 1661 asserting that they shipped wines to Paris and had an "urgent and pressing necessity" for such a market.[22] Without the Halle, they complained, "when the provincial traders bring their wine to Paris the [Parisian] wine merchants buy them and . . . make themselves the masters, having the advantage over bourgeois and provincials alike . . . [because] the provincials are forced to sell their wine cheap to avoid the danger to their persons, and the risk of losing all their wines from staying [too] long on the water and from . . . the great heat which ruptures the boats."[23] The petition from Auxerre insisted that "the Halle is necessary as much for the relief of the bourgeois of Paris as of the provincial traders of Burgundy, Champagne, and elsewhere because with the Halle the wine merchants will be sheltered from great heat, great cold, and ice, which will let us bring a [greater] quantity of merchandise for the bourgeois of Paris, and we will no longer be subject to the great expenses of [longer] boat rentals, guarding the wine and other taxes that increase the cost of the wine by more than eight or nine livres for each muid."[24] Clearly there were a number of provincial traders who aspired to play a role in the Parisian wine trade, though there is little other evidence about them, or about the scale of their commerce. Yet for most of these traders the wine trade was less a profession than a temporary expedient, given the fact that few of the names from the petition of 1661 figured among the three dozen "provincial traders bringing wine to Paris" from lower Burgundy who were involved in a case before the Parlement ten years later.[25]

The Halle may have facilitated the wine trade with Paris, but it failed to inspire a surge of commercial participation by provincial merchants. The records that have survived for the early eighteenth century reveal that the Halle was not yet a very busy place. Through the first decade of the century provincial traders sent a yearly average of forty-seven thousand hecto-liters to the Halle compared to thirteen times that much wine (614,000 hectoliters) brought to the city by the wine merchants of Paris.[26] At least through the early eighteenth century, the overwhelming dominance enjoyed by Parisian merchants over the wine trade with lower Burgundy changed very little. The vast majority of wine arrived under the auspices of merchants in Paris sending commissions or going out to the provinces, and working through brokers.

Not only did the provincial traders form a very minor part of the overall provisioning of Paris, it is clear that they played only an intermittent role in the wine trade. When growers produced a surplus, the "forains" helped get rid of it; as the tax farm noted, "the forains are for the most part simple peasants who come to sell some carts of wine."[27] Following the disastrous frosts of 1709, when Parisian wine merchants protested that "for three years there has been almost no wine, so that merchants have had to look for it in the farthest provinces," the forains practically disappeared from the market. During those three terrible years, the amount of wine brought into the city dropped by half, to 318,000 hectoliters, but the wine brought by provincial traders to the Halle almost evaporated, dwindling to only eighty-five hundred hectoliters. As the tax farm reported from this period, although the usual number of provincial wine traders from all of the wine regions supplying the city was "about twenty-five by their own account, [now] only two could be found."[28]

Even in times of surplus, the cost of sending wine to Paris dissuaded most growers from even trying. The process of sending wine to the Halle in Paris was very expensive and highly speculative, and once it reached the Halle there was no assurance of finding a buyer or a decent price. Getting the wine to the Halle required a series of expenses: It usually had to be racked and the barrel reinforced (*reliage*), and it had to be carted to the nearest river. Then the cost of the boat itself was usually four to six livres per barrel. The provincial trader was obliged to put up the money to pay for the transportation, the taxes, and the space at the Halle, unless he could find someone to lend it to him.

The cost of transportation and especially the cost of the "entry tax" (*droit d'entrée*) levied on wine going into Paris rose continually through the last two centuries of the Old Regime, making it increasingly difficult for growers to send their wine speculatively to the capital. From three livres per muid of wine in 1636, the droit d'entrée had risen to eighteen livres by 1680 and sharply again to twenty-three livres in 1719, when the average muid of wine was worth less than fifty livres. "The obligation to pay the entry tax in cash," according to one observer, and to pay before the provincial traders could enter Paris and look for a buyer, "forced many of them to borrow, at exorbitant rates the sums that they needed, or to sell their wine at a vile price at the instant of their arrival."[29] The rapid increase in wine taxes during the seventeenth and early eighteenth centuries only served to discourage the speculative involvement of small traders and vinegrowers.

Provincial growers turned to a variety of sources for credit to pay the costs of sending their wine to Paris. They might pool their resources into an "association," like the one formed among vignerons of Irancy to go and sell a hundred barrels at Paris.[30] Another vigneron of Irancy commissioned the boatman Maujot to "go in his place to sell his wine in Paris," which "because of his indisposition he could not take" himself. Maujot was to sell them at the Halle, "at whatever price he judged appropriate to merchants and bourgeois of Paris" and return with an account.[31] A spate of court cases in the 1720s and early 1730s found boatmen suing several dozen provincial traders and growers from some of the villages around Auxerre and Chablis for small sums of "money advanced for rebarreling and carting" as well as the cost of shipping. Most of these people were sending wine to Paris at their own expense and initiative. They generally owed less than a hundred livres, though "marchands forains" could also owe several thousand livres.[32] Some of these growers had made an arrangement with a boatman whereby he had "lent and advanced" them small sums (between six and thirty livres) "for the promise that they would cart and have carted their wines to the ports of Auxerre to load them on [the boatman's] boats in order to ship them to the Halle aux vins at Paris."[33] Such a system guaranteed him business and perhaps gave him a monopolistic price on his services; it also reveals how marginal some of those supplying the Parisian market really were, if they needed loans just to get their wine to market. But boatmen in Auxerre, as elsewhere in France, seem to have been relatively small businessmen who could offer only limited help to growers trying to get to market.[34]

A well-known example of one grower who took his wines to Paris reveals the actual limits of this trade. Edme Rétif was a rich peasant of the village of Sacy, seventeen kilometers south of Chablis, who decided to put some of his large farm of fifty hectares into vines during the 1710s, at which point viticulture was apparently quite a local innovation. His decision to take his wine to sell in Paris in 1725 was even more daring. Only his relative wealth permitted such an experiment, just as it provided the wagons and finances for his speculative trip to Paris.[35] His successful venture failed, evidently, to persuade others to emulate him or to transform the village into a viticultural center, for its wine production was still extremely modest by the end of the Old Regime.[36] The risks and costs of the business put it beyond the means of anyone less wealthy than a rural notable like Rétif.

The administration of the Halle was sufficiently concerned about taxes having discouraged trade to establish a "caisse de crédit" at the Halle aux vins in 1719 to help the provincial grower or trader "who cannot send wine to Paris because he is unable to advance the money for the droits d'entrée and the shipping."[37] The caisse offered loans to "all marchands forains and others in the wine trade [in order to] have the liberty to borrow on the value of their wines, the credit they need, . . . for the payment of taxes and the cost of shipping . . . [for] His Majesty has been informed that different individuals were undertaking to loan money at the ports and the Halle and were profiting from the often pressing needs that forains found themselves in by demanding usurious interest rates."[38] As one of the administrators explained to the controller general in defense of this system, the credit would also help "the owner of vines [who] is no longer forced to sell his wine with difficulty in the provinces and can send it to Paris with the same liberty as the provincial trader."[39] The caisse de crédit at least addressed the speculative challenges faced by provincial traders and growers, even if it did not soon solve them.[40]

Despite the efforts of the Halle and the occasional speculation of a Rétif, the long-distance wine trade in lower Burgundy remained tied to the purchases made by Parisian merchants, working through local brokers. As one of these brokers reflected in 1739 on the differences between the late seventeenth century and the mid–eighteenth: "Forty or fifty years ago . . . there were only several hundred Parisian wine merchants then, who came to buy [wine] with always enough money to pay at least half the cost and paid the surplus within two months at the latest. The vignerons [of Auxerre] brought their wines to Paris in boats, for the [droit d']entrée was only some twenty livres per barrel, and there was no need for large sums in advance; today the advances, both for boats and entrée, runs as much as fifty-five livres."[41] Increasing costs had made the speculative shipment of wine to Paris more expensive than most provincial growers and merchants could afford and hence, the broker pointed out, increasingly rare. Instead, Parisian wine merchants bought most of the wine for Paris and, indeed, "pretend to be the only ones with the right to furnish Paris with wines. Hence they are obliged to make advances through the brokers and to employ the brokers' credit" in order to buy wine in the provinces.[42] As Parisian wine merchants relied increasingly on brokers to arrange the purchasing, financing, and shipping of their wine, the brokers gained several advantages over

The Brokers of Burgundy

others in provincial society who might wish to trade in wine. Buying in the Parisian merchant's stead, the broker had nothing to fear from fluctuations in prices or from delays in finding a buyer. His sale was certain, and his risk was limited to the possibility of the merchant's default.

By the early eighteenth century, provincial brokers had not only become indispensable to the wine trade, they were increasingly independent of Parisian control. As another broker of Auxerre explained about changes in the wine trade: "In the past the Auxerrois produced less wine, and much less wine was generally consumed . . . so the brokerage of wine could not constitute a trade on its own, capable of occupying an individual and being a profession. . . . Besides there were official *courtiers* to sell wines." But with the abolition of this office and the growth of the wine trade, at the beginning of the eighteenth century, wine merchants and bourgeois looking for wines faced a problem. "Bourgeois looking for modest provisions could not afford the expense of travel. . . . Merchants have to visit too many wine regions and find it too expensive to have factors in all of them." Thus brokers relieved merchants of the need to travel and gradually replaced them as the local buyer. "Finally, the vigneron . . . delivers no [wine] without cash, and often the wine merchant has none with him. Such are the hurdles and inconveniences that have led to the establishment of commission brokers in Auxerre and all the wine regions."[43] The combination of local knowledge, financial resources, and orders from Parisian buyers gave the broker a role of growing importance in the region.

The Brokers of Auxerre

The continuing dominance of Parisian merchants over the provisioning of the Parisian market ensured the power of the provincial brokers who worked with them. "The only industry to prosper" in the early eighteenth century, according to a local historian of Auxerre, "was that of the region's wine brokers, who . . . held the whole business of wine production in their hands."[44] As the royal investigation discussed in the previous chapter suggested, lower Burgundy was full of wine brokers, some fifty of them in the vicinity of the town of Auxerre. Their fines indicate a thriving wine trade and a significant amount of brokerage business. The tax also found the brokers dispersed among a dozen towns and villages of the region, suggesting their recent status as local officials. We shall see that some of these brokers were gradually emerging as intermediaries doing business on a provincial scale, and that even the most local of them had acquired a crucial role in the economic life of the region.

Already in the Middle Ages the overwhelming domination that merchants of Paris had exercised over the wine trade in lower Burgundy meant that the agents who worked for Parisians, and other outsiders, played a much greater role in the local economy than vignerons or merchants acting on their own. *Courtiers* were found in Auxerre as early as 1346, when the comte de Chalon agreed to choose them in conjunction with the town's officials.[45] Those of the nine *courtiers* of Auxerre in 1623 who can be identified were already involved independently in some aspect of the wine trade.[46] In particular, Jehan Robinet, the youngest one of them at age twenty-eight, was involved in "very many contracts connected to the wine trade and possess[ed] a quantity of vine plots in the finage of Auxerre and its environs, as well as a 'port in the city of Auxerre, called the port au diable, to put his wines.'" He sat three times on the prestigious consular court in the 1640s and 1650s and, in 1668, became the governor of the hôtel de ville of Auxerre.[47] He and three others of the nine—Guillaume Navarre, Germain Drinot, and François Ragot—founded dynasties of brokers. Their descendants included the wealthiest five of the twelve brokers of Auxerre fined in 1705, who owed two-thirds of the city's total fine between them, as well as a broker owing one of the largest fines in Chablis.[48]

The brokers identified by the fines in early-eighteenth-century Auxerre belonged, on the whole, to families of substantial stature and mercantile power. But they show how incompletely the brokers of lower Burgundy had made the transition from *courtage* to commission brokering. Of the two groups defined by different levels of fines, only the top group, fined at five or six thousand livres, had fully adopted the practice of commission brokering. These brokers were nearly all descended from the *courtiers* of the early seventeenth century and, like the brokers in Epernay, combined commerce with municipal and royal offices. Each had been chosen three or four times to fill one of the three seats on the powerful consular court, a yearly appointment that conveyed both unusual prestige and prominence in the community.[49] These brokers included a Drinot and son and two Robinets, identified more often by their municipal offices than as brokers, but still involved in trade. Another, Etienne Navarre, became "captain of the bourgeoisie" (the militia), an honorific position indicating his prestige rather than any martial talents, but he was still identified as a merchant broker at his death. Of the top brokers, only Edme Liger and a son were a "new" family in the trade, though he had been active in the wine trade since at least 1691.[50]

The other group of brokers, who owed less than two thousand livres in fines, were as much *courtiers* as commission brokers and only marginally involved in either activity. Linked by marriage and business, they had engaged in little commission brokering; Potin's postmortem inventory included only a few debts to people who had sold him wine and only one outstanding sum of five hundred livres owed him by a Parisian merchant for whom he had bought wine. Villain had worked with Potin "for courtage alone," that is, as a *courtier* rather than as a commissionnaire, collecting the royal tax. Potin had also formed a partnership in 1698 with the other modest broker, Caillant, "to make a commerce of wine," for which the heirs still owed Caillant nearly seven thousand livres.[51] Potin's accounts show these brokers dabbling in commerce, courtage, and commission without being particularly active in any one. Two boatmen, fined less than a thousand livres, were clearly even more marginal to the wine trade.

The most important brokers engaged in a scale and volume of trade that dwarfed the *courtiers*. In the company, and increasingly in the absence, of Parisian merchants they acquired wine from the whole of lower Burgundy and beyond. They handled a volume of wine, judging from fragmented records, that rivaled the commerce of the biggest brokers in Epernay. One of the Robinets figures prominently in the account book of a Parisian wine merchant, doing business on the same scale as brokers in Blois and Orléans. Robinet had arranged the purchase of over a hundred barrels of wine from Auxerre, Saint-Bris, Coulanges, and Tonnerre for this one merchant in 1713. His catchment area was impressive, though he reminds us of his agent status by carefully passing on many of his costs, like carting, rebarreling, refilling the barrels, and some taxes.[52] The networks of debts and services summarized in brokers' inventories after death depict a similar range and scale of catchment.

The inventory of Etienne Navarre's wife and his own, two years later, show clearly that he was buying on commission for absent merchants and that his purchases extended to much of the region. Even in his last years, in 1717 and 1718, he was actively engaged in the wine trade, and the inventory's accounts of "wines bought for his merchants" was still current, although he had passed some of the burden on to a nephew who was assisting him. Most of the twenty-seven thousand livres of debts still owed to him in 1717 was for wine sent to a dozen wine merchants, some officials, and two religious houses in Paris. This sum represented nearly a thousand barrels, though he had obviously sent more wine that had already been paid off. The entries were careful to note that the debts were for purchases "following [the debtor's] order," showing the broker to have been buying in response to an absent merchant's request and for his account.

The Brokers of Burgundy

Similarly the fifty barrels of wine from Chablis, Tonnerre, and Saint-Bris, waiting at a port of Navarre's to be shipped, already "belonged to the Sieurs Aumel, Aurillon, Henicque, and other" wine merchants. A debt he owed his nephew Germain Navarre "for having led merchants [to various buyers], made the purchases, and the expense of taking care of the wines in the ports" also shows him operating in a traditional relationship to merchants who actually came and looked for the wine themselves.[53] As the broker, however, he made the purchases and owed the sellers their money and handled the shipments. This, even more than his knowledge of who was selling wine, was most valuable to his merchants.

Navarre's acquisition of wine indicates that he had abandoned the traditional *courtier's* service to the growers of his own town and now acquired wine from an extensive catchment area. An "[account] book for purchases of wine belonging to the bourgeois from the vintage of 1718" shows that Navarre bought some of this wine from other brokers at Tonnerre, Chablis, Saint-Bris, and Coulanges. He also drew heavily on local notables, including doctors, canons, officials at the grenier au sel and the town hall, each one noted as still owing Navarre a commission for his services in arranging the sale of their wine. Their sales to Navarre probably included wine that they had acquired from others, in the myriad small transactions by which growers paid off debts with barrels of wine.

Navarre's accounts portray him as a businessman who dealt with large producers or with other middlemen rather than cultivating ties with local vignerons. His business seems to have worked through a network of townsmen and notables who acted as small-scale buyers and had already bulked up a volume of wine from individual growers. This gave him the ability to reach across the whole region for his purchases. Indeed, his business operated at an interregional scale, for several of the Parisian merchants owed him money for "purchase and transportation of wine from Beaune," and the accounts listed a few barrels of wine from Beaune that were waiting at the port of Auxerre to be shipped to Paris.[54] Navarre was a crucial link in the wine trade of a whole province.

Another broker of Auxerre named Sallé, who entered the trade shortly after the investigation of 1705, shows that, like Navarre, the brokers of the city had developed a large catchment, with suppliers and networks that transcended the purely local arena of Auxerre and Paris.[55] His business, at its height, shipped vast quantities of wine to Paris and beyond. He had traveled to Paris and Arras on several occasions to see to accounts, staying three months in Paris in 1715 to collect 118,000 livres in debts. This figure alone represents several thousand barrels of wine and suggests a huge level of trade. But by 1718 he had run into financial trouble and was asking his creditors for a grace period.

His creditors, and the wines he bought from them, delineate a catchment area that extended to most of the vineyards of Burgundy. Of fifty people to whom he owed thirty-six thousand livres, mostly "for the rest of the wine" that he had bought from them, a slight majority lived in Auxerre. These local suppliers were city notables—the lieutenant criminel, a conseiller au presidial, priests, barristers, the Benedictines—who probably owned considerable vineyards and could acquire wines from lesser growers. Except for four thousand livres that he owed for barrels and wood to make them with, most of the other debts were for wine from villages through lower Burgundy: from bourgeois of Coulanges, Saint-Bris, and Cravant, the priest at Augy, the seigneur of Coulanges, and a broker of Chablis. He owed three thousand livres for wine from a broker in Beaune and thirteen hundred livres to several brokers in Chalon. Again the suppliers were notables and probably large producers or, if they lived more than fifteen kilometers from Auxerre, brokers. Like Navarre, Sallé operated at the pinnacle of the bulking-up process. His accounts give no evidence of economic ties to the common people or small producers in the way that we shall see other brokers doing.

Like Navarre and another big broker of Auxerre, Robinet, Sallé was also handling wine shipped from Beaune and Chalon for Parisian wine merchants.[56] On at least one occasion Sallé had accepted wines "addressed to him by Milliard, broker at Chalon[-sur-Saône], for the account of Guenon, wine merchant of Paris," that had been carted to Auxerre to be sent on by boat.[57] But his debt of six hundred livres to Milliard indicates that he had bought the wine from him or was at least handling the financing as well as the shipment for the Parisian. In various ways, upper Burgundy relied heavily on Auxerre for its contacts with Paris.

Sallé's career, and his financial troubles in 1718, also illustrate the pitfalls that awaited a broker. He had shipped eighty barrels of wine to a Parisian merchant who turned out to be insolvent, and the boatman who had taken them to Paris, Maujot, had sold them at a loss. Two Parisian wine merchants had died owing him money for wine. Several other Parisian wine merchants had somehow backed out of a deal, leaving him to sell over a hundred barrels at a loss and to spend considerable amounts litigating the bills of exchange that they would not honor. Indeed, the costs related to litigating and paying interest on various bills of exchange came to at least a third of the thirty thousand livres that he was writing off as losses and expenses. Yet none of it can be obviously attributed to his own business ventures. There is no indication that he bought wine to sell for himself, and he sold wine only when left with it by a correspondent. The losses he incurred when forced to sell wine for himself indicate the disadvantages faced by any winegrower who tried to take his wines to Paris on his own. Acting on commission from a buyer, the broker was usually assured of the buyer taking his wines at an agreed upon cost. The risks run by brokers were essentially those of a banker, who lends money to a wide range of clients, rather than the risks and uncertainties attendant upon a speculative commercial venture. The volatility of the wine market made this an obvious choice, though Sallé's misfortune shows that brokering was far from foolproof.

Brokers in the Villages

Despite the importance of the brokerage business in Auxerre, the brokers there did not dominate the region's wine trade as thoroughly as those in Epernay appear to have managed. Rather, the wine trade was dispersed among brokers in many smaller markets. It is clear that the brokers in Auxerre worked through several layers of subordinate buyers, both in the city and in neighboring villages, to assemble the wines they sold. Many of these small-scale buyers were probably dependent on the big brokers for their contacts with Paris, but not all. The brokers in some of the more important villages surrounding Auxerre—principally Saint-Bris, Coulanges, and Irancy—sent their wines both through the brokers of Auxerre and, more frequently, directly to Paris on their own. Brokers in half a dozen villages and small towns within fifteen kilometers of Auxerre also appeared on the list of brokers fined in 1705. They too had independent contacts with Paris. Another sixteen brokers conducted business somewhat farther away from Auxerre, in Chablis and Tonnerre, small towns sustaining an important wine trade in their own right. More than half of the region's fifty brokers, and nearly two-thirds of the region's total fines, were found in the three largest towns. But around each was a penumbra of individuals, distinguished by large-scale fines, in a dozen villages. Ironically the vineyards of these villages have long outlasted those of Auxerre. They are particularly interesting both because they competed with the larger towns on their own terms and because they organized their local brokerage in a distinct manner.

Coulanges-la-vineuse, a "little bourg" ten kilometers south of Auxerre, had only one broker—Millon—in 1705, but he was fined the large sum of five thousand livres. Considering the scale of the Coulanges's wine production, the fine was probably fair. Its own vines made over six thousand hectoliters of wine, which were described as "excellent quality, always sold wholesale [that is, exported to Paris] and very rapidly." With the wine made in the hamlets around Coulanges, the broker there could draw on nearly half as much wine as was produced in Auxerre.[58] The broker of Coulanges, like those in other bourgs of the region, might easily handle the same volume of wine as brokers in Auxerre, yet he drew on a much smaller catchment area and passed some of his wine along to local intermediaries—in the bigger towns—as well as to Paris. His accounts also reveal him to be an entrepreneur who was more intimately involved in the agricultural life of his communities than the city brokers were. In some ways he exercised even more power over his neighbors than the bigger brokers had.

Claude Millon was originally from Sens, the son of a merchant there. He had moved to Auxerre sometime before 1688, when he married the daughter of a wood merchant of Coulanges. The bourg's broker at that point was also the lieutenant of the bailliage; another broker had been forced to flee ahead of his creditors, leaving a wife and several sick children.[59] Millon quickly took up wine brokering in Coulanges but also became an important fermier for some of the principal estates in the region. He took over as receiver of a local estate from the previous broker of Coulanges and later added the seigneurie of Coulanges and a lease on the port and château of Vincelles. He also served a term as governor of the village's hôpital.[60] Both as broker and as principal lease-holder he was clearly a coq du village, a man with enormous power in his local society. His inventory after death, in 1718, in which he is called a "merchant commissionnaire," allows us to see this power as well as the differences that distinguished the brokers of Auxerre from those of the villages in its orbit.[61]

In the first place, the volume of Millon's economic activities was every bit as impressive as the brokers in Auxerre, even though the geography was on a smaller scale. His books show that he was dealing in considerable amounts of wine. Judging only from the accounts that were still open, of the people to whom he still owed money, he had bought a minimum of fifty-two thousand livres of wine (worth roughly two thousand barrels) in the previous year or two.[62] Most entries noted that he had already paid the growers something, after deducting for the taxes he had paid and for his commission. He still owed nearly twenty-four thousand livres to thirty individuals, some of whom—where they can be identified—were vignerons from Coulanges and from several villages within five kilometers. Yet the six given a "Sieur" to their names were clearly not humble vinedressers (one was a notary), and the largest creditor was his sister-in-law, the widow of a broker, for ten thousand livres.

Then there were dozens of vignerons who owed him small sums of money and would probably pay their debts in wine. Fourteen of them from Coulanges came forward to acknowledge a total of 753 livres for "settlement of accounts" or for "barrels delivered before his last harvest." One vigneron said the debt was for "money lent, meat and food for children." Millon's papers also included more than a dozen "debts" (*obligations*) from vignerons of Jussy, only two kilometers away. The sums are small and ambiguous. It is not clear, for example, whether these debts obligated the vigneron to sell only to the creditor. Three of the vignerons mentioned that they had sold their wine to a broker of Auxerre who had agreed to pay some of their debt to Millon. Nor can we be certain whether these debts were exploitive. Another broker of Coulanges, twenty years later, insisted that "if he loaned money to some, it was not with the idea of an advantageous sale of his barrels or to take over their wine but from charity."[63] The debts attest, in any case, to the strength of Millon's economic ties to local vignerons.

Millon also strengthened his ties to, and his control over, the local growers by a lively business selling barrels. One account book entitled "barrels delivered beginning 27 June 1718" shows that, in little more than three months following that date—in time to prepare for the harvest—he delivered 1,294 barrels to fifty people. This amounted to more than a third of the barrels used by the town of Coulanges in a normal year. Roughly half of the barrels went to six people, particularly the 200 to his sister-in-law, 233 to Madame de Coulanges (the local seigneur?), and 80 to a bourgeois of Coulanges who later sold him wine. The rest were listed only by name but can be identified in many cases as vignerons from Coulanges and Jussy.[64] The same book indicated the sale of thousands of vine props (*paisseaux*) to many of the same individuals. Millon was very seriously inserting himself into the production process by dealing in two indispensable products needed for the creation of wine.

The lack of alternative sources of barrels made it much easier for Millon to gain such a large share of the market. There may have been a dozen coopers in Coulanges who regularly contracted to provide barrels for growers, but many of them insisted on the modesty of their condition. They were "only simple merchants with neither the ability or capacity to make new barrels," they claimed in 1692, in a plea to have their taxes reduced, and "the quality that some wish to attribute to them of 'coopers' consists only in spending a month repairing the vessels that the inhabitants use during the harvest, when they only work for a daily wage as laborers, the rest of the time cultivating the land for bourgeois of neighboring towns."[65] The only real alternative was for vineowners to supply themselves from merchant coopers some distance away (Saulieu and Pouilly) who occasionally visited Coulanges to solicit business.[66]

The elaborate network of debts maintained by brokers like Millon may represent the benevolent succor of a patron for his economic clients, but they were portrayed in a harsher light by some contemporaries as a form of bondage, especially when the brokers had lent barrels. A court case between a grower and a later broker of Coulanges reveals the economic asymmetry caused by such debts. Whereas the broker's testimony described a simple exchange between the two—he had purchased seven barrels of wine at a price agreed to by the grower—the grower had presented certain "contradictory facts." Because he was indebted to the broker, the grower explained, for several years' back payment for a rente of seven and a half livres (the interest on a loan of 150 livres) the broker had seized his wine as surety for payment. The grower had offered to sell it to him for forty-five livres a barrel, but the broker responded "if you [*tu*] do not give it to me for twenty-four livres I will have it sold by the courts." In despair at the court costs this would entail, the grower had answered, "Take it for thirty sous rather than have it sold." He was forced to accept the broker's offer, though the transaction wound up in court for other reasons.[67]

The high-handed tactics of another broker, later in the century, provoked several growers in Irancy to appeal to local justices for clarification and protection. What was the custom, the widow Geau wanted to know, regarding the loan of barrels? The broker Boyard had threatened her with a "monstrous suit" for having sold wine, in barrels that he had loaned her, to other buyers, "under the pretext that custom [*usage*] obliged her to save [the wine] for him." Boyard had similarly told a wood merchant that he could not sell the dozen barrels loaned by Boyard, or the wine in it, to any broker but himself. The justices responded that, although "the fact that the brokers of Auxerre sell and loan numbers of barrels was known to them and a matter of public notoriety, the sale or investment [*placement*] obliges no one to sell the wine put in the barrels to the said brokers unless there was a promise or express agreement."[68] Yet clearly a debt placed the debtor under implicit obligations to the creditor.

Millon's object in acquiring all of this wine was clearly to pass it along to wine merchants in Paris. There are numerous references to letters written by and to merchants there, as well as memoirs about "purchases of wine by [Millon] for X, merchant at Paris." One book summarized "what is due to

The Brokers of Burgundy

me by the merchants up to now, 6 October 1716," with a list of "many wine merchants of Paris," some of whom appeared in the other book, and their debts. There followed forty-eight merchants owing forty-three thousand livres, nearly half of it owed by only five of them. Extracts from one "book of merchants" beginning in 1713 and going through 1717 identified fifty-four individuals, most of them Parisian wine merchants, to whom Millon had sent at least forty thousand livres of wine.[69] A little of this went to brokers in Chablis, Tonnerre, Epineuil, and Auxerre, and a vague reference to "accounts in Sallé's hand of what he owes and has paid Millon" suggests that Millon had regularly supplied the broker of Auxerre, Sallé, with wines. Millon was simultaneously brokering for bigger brokers around him and brokering directly for buyers in Paris. The address of one merchant was given as "la halle," presumably the Halle aux vins, where Millon sent only seven hundred livres of wine. Rather than making speculative purchases, however, his books sometimes state explicitly that he "bought the wine for" a particular merchant or that the merchant had actually bought it himself. Evidently Millon was quite firmly and independently linked to the Parisian market, and, although drawing on a smaller catchment area than brokers in Auxerre, he largely dominated it. He may well have been handling as much as a half of all that Coulanges produced each year.

Millon was probably quite typical of the village brokers around Auxerre. He clearly worked at the lower levels of the wine trade, bulking up from individual growers. This wine he passed on both to brokers in Auxerre and to buyers in Paris. The government had found a dozen other brokers like him in villages and small towns around Auxerre. Half of them lived in small villages—Chitry and Champs—with only 150 households and were barely taken seriously. Both villages were clearly subordinate to their neighbors, and the brokers there owed fines of only a thousand or fifteen hundred livres. But the five brokers in Saint-Bris owed two to four thousand livres, and one in Irancy owed forty-five hundred livres. What little we know about them resembles Millon's activities and points to strong ties to Paris.

Both Saint-Bris and Irancy were already well known in Paris for their excellent wines. A more tangible trace of their commercial activity can be found in the contrôle des actes of Saint-Bris, which is unusual in the Auxerrois for including the details, if only briefly, of the wine shipments from the town. The entries are intermittent except for the twelve months following August 1697, during which time a minimum of 950 barrels were shipped to Paris by an assortment of boatmen of Auxerre.[70] Among the rare senders who were identified, Soufflot, Jodon, Sourdeau, and Regnauldin figured prominently if not unambiguously. Each one illustrates important aspects of Saint-Bris' economy, above all its close connections to the larger worlds of the province and Paris.

Soufflot and Jodon were fined two and four thousand livres as brokers of Saint-Bris in 1705. Edme Jodon had been a broker in the smaller bourg of Coulanges a dozen years before and had promoted himself to a larger market.[71] The Soufflots had been lieutenants in the bailliage of Irancy since at least the early seventeenth century, and several had also been identified in notarial documents as merchants of Saint-Bris.[72] A broker identified as "someone named Soufflot," was also fined forty-five hundred livres for brokering in Irancy.[73] He was probably a different member of the family than the one brokering in Saint-Bris, but the point is the family united the wine trades of several small towns, all within five kilometers of each other.

The Sourdeau and Regnauldin families illustrate the close ties between Paris and this province. Neither one was fined as a broker and may not, indeed, have been sending wine from Saint-Bris (the contrôle des actes is not entirely clear about whether they were sending or receiving the wine in Paris). But they clearly conducted a considerable amount of business between the town and the capital. Jacques Sourdeau was described in notarial documents at various times as both a merchant of Saint-Bris and a wine merchant of Paris. He maintained a house and enough vines in Saint-Bris to produce over forty barrels of white wine.[74] He had probably married a sister of Henri Regnauldin, the procureur fiscal of Saint-Bris, who had in turn married a Sourdeau. Regnauldin's sons were both wine merchants of Paris, a profession in which it was advantageous to have a base in both the wine's market and its origin, so they maintained houses and lands in Saint-Bris. His grandsons returned to Saint-Bris, however, one of them becoming a broker there.[75] The way these families straddled the two worlds of the capital and province accounts for some of Saint-Bris' ability to deal directly with Paris, rather than going through intermediaries in Auxerre.

As an illustration of Auxerre's economic penetration into local affairs, one of the five brokers of Saint-Bris was the son and brother of several prominent boatmen of Auxerre. Pierre Boyard was the first in the family to dedicate himself to wine brokering, and he began in this new trade by initially setting himself up outside of Auxerre, in the smaller market of Saint-Bris. He had married the sister of a local wine broker and was already identified as a bourgeois of Saint-Bris by 1702. He and his brother-in-law, working together as partners, played an important role in the bourg's wine trade, particularly evident in the disastrous year of 1709, when they were able to foreclose on many of the local vignerons in distress. The weather in 1708 had already been very harmful to vines: Frosts and rain had kept the harvest to a minimum. But 1709 had begun with a month of killing cold that destroyed much of the vines in northern France, and many growers found it the last straw. Boyard and his partner were able to buy up over five arpents from a dozen different growers as they became desperate through the summer and autumn months.[76] Other brokers in the bourg, like Jean Duché, were also buying land. Boyard did not stay in Saint-Bris, however, and returned to Auxerre by 1715 to continue his brokering on a larger scale.

The small bourgs directly around Auxerre demonstrate the complex relationships that existed between the capital, a provincial entrepôt, and the small markets surrounding it. Individuals regularly shifted their operations from one market to another, generally moving from a smaller to a larger market over time. Their families and landholdings tied them to several communities, leaving them with roots in the smaller markets even after they had left and moved on. But there were limits to the range over which this integration worked. Lower Burgundy contained several large entrepôts, particularly Chablis and Tonnerre, that remained essentially independent of Auxerre.

The Brokers of Chablis

The size of Chablis' total fines in 1705 was surprisingly high, particularly given its proximity to a major market center like Auxerre. Despite the small size of the town, and its modest output, it owed a total that was nearly as great as that owed by the brokers of Auxerre, and its six individual brokers had the highest fines in France, between four thousand and sixty-five hundred livres. They formed a commanding and closely interconnected elite in Chablis whose control of the local wine trade remained largely unshaken through the century. Because of the serious hurdles to trading between Chablis and Paris the local growers had even less opportunity to market their own vines and relied even more on brokers than elsewhere in lower Burgundy.

Years ago, Roger Dion's magisterial history of vines made a special point about Chablis' unusual situation. Explaining the survival of Chablis' wines into the twentieth century, almost alone among all the ancient wines of lower Burgundy, he pointed to the disadvantage Chablis suffered from being so far from the Yonne River: "Beyond a certain distance from water routes, when the cost of carting [wine] to the nearest river port passes a certain price, the exportation ceases to be advantageous for wines of little value and can only be contemplated for wines of quality. Hence the vineyards of Chablis, inaccessible to commercial shipping, remained faithful to the pinot blanc grape, a vine of quality that many of the vigerons closer to the river routes had abandoned in order to respond to the demands of Parisian commerce."[77] Chablis was unable to join in the progressive degradation of the wines produced for a mass market in Paris because transportation costs added too large a percentage to the costs of its wines. This same geographical disadvantage gave brokers even greater control over the wine trade of Chablis.

Unlike the many wine-producing villages in Auxerre's immediate orbit, Chablis was almost completely independent of its influence and maintained vigorous ties with merchants in Paris and elsewhere. One of the brokers of Chablis fined in 1705 was, indeed, the son of a prominent wine merchant in Paris, "one of the twelve privileged wine merchants following the court," who had only recently moved from Paris to Chablis. Charles Alexandre, protesting his own fine on the grounds that he had only "established himself" in Chablis since the summer of 1704, had just married—in Paris—the widow of a broker of Chablis, Giraut, who was also being fined. Alexandre was willing to admit that his new wife had acted as a broker since her husband's death in 1702, but only from "necessity . . . because of her husband's engagements with some Parisian merchants to retrieve the funds that were due to his succession."[78] It seems reasonable to suspect that Alexandre was one of Giraut's clients and that his contacts with Chablis were neither so recent nor so innocent of brokering as he claimed.

The four other brokers in Chablis were equally connected by marriages and formed a small elite with remarkable control over the local wine trade. Edme Petit had married the widow of Jean Soufflot, a "merchant *courtier* of wines" of Chablis. Jean Soufflot had been the brother of Jacques, the sole broker fined in Irancy in 1705. Jean appears to have held a minor official post in Irancy before moving to Chablis. One of his daughters, raised by Petit, married the son of another broker of Chablis, Jean Chapotin, who received one of the two highest fines in France in 1705.[79] The other broker fined that much, Louis Ragot, had also married the widow of a broker of Chablis. Much like the major brokers of Epernay, these men— and their wives and widows—monopolized their community's commerce with the outside world. The glimpses of this commercial system that remain in their inventories show their wine trade spanning several countries yet deeply embedded in the local community.

Chablis' wine trade in the late seventeenth century, as seen in Soufflot's inventory at his death in 1689, was still limited to supplying Paris.[80] He was owed seventeen thousand livres by twenty-nine "merchants of Paris for the purchases of wine that he made from individuals of Chablis of the harvest of 1688." The debts and language indicate that he was already working as a commission broker for these merchants. He in turn still owed eight thousand livres to a dozen people, a third of them widows, for the wines he had bought. Many of them were local notables, who had sold him large quantities—especially the widow of an officier du roi who had sold him 165 barrels. There is little evidence that he bought from small-scale producers and no sign of the loans of money and barrels with which Millon of Coulanges tied vignerons to his interests. Rather, Soufflot's commercial contacts with the local peasants appeared in dozens of *baux à cheptel,* an arrangement whereby a peasant lent an animal could keep its offspring in exchange for caring for the mother. The bail à cheptel could be very useful to a vigneron, of course, but gave the broker less direct control over the winegrowers and their products.

Soufflot's widow soon remarried, to Edme Petit, already a broker of Chablis. She brought more than thirty thousand livres to the new marriage, including seven arpents of vines around Chablis and at Irancy. By her death in 1704, the couple had doubled their vineyards.[81] She appears also to have brought with her Soufflot's relationship to the local peasants, for she had a large quantity of baux à cheptel at her death. Her second husband was more orthodox than her first, however, in his patronage of local vignerons. Instead of baux à cheptel, the inventory at his death, in 1717, recorded forty-five hundred livres in "barrels, money, and other goods" leant to seventy-five growers in Chablis and the surrounding villages, which they would probably pay back in wine. This suggests a closer commercial relationship to the lower levels of growers and vinedressers than Soufflot's, but his accounts leave little evidence of his purchasing patterns. His inventory included only eighteen thousand livres in credits and bills of exchange for wine sold to thirty individuals—indicating that he had largely abandoned the wine trade by his death. Yet the fact that four of his debtors were merchants from Rouen and Fontainebleau shows broader commercial contacts than those of the typical broker of Auxerre. Petit's estate was worth one hundred thousand livres, making him the equal of the powerful fermiers of the Île-de-France and probably one of the richest men in town.[82]

By the early eighteenth century, the brokers of Chablis were trading with markets across northern Europe. A better sense of this reach comes from the accounts of Petit's colleague Edme Rathier, who had been fined like Petit in 1705 and died the year before him.[83] Rathier's enterprise had been operating at a larger scale than Petit's at the time of his death, though his wealth was put at only a quarter of Petit's. He was owed nearly forty thousand livres for wine sent in the previous two years, much of it to a dozen merchants in Liège, Reims, Béthune, Rocroi, Troyes, and Rouen. His sources of wine were also more extensive than those of his colleagues. He still owed twenty thousand livres to some seventy people for well over a thousand barrels of wine, drawn heavily from Chablis and the villages immediately around it, but also from somewhat farther away in Tonnerre, Poilly, and Sainte-Vertu. His purchase of wine from so many individuals suggests close contacts with the small winegrowers in the area. At the same time, his debts from previous years show that he had acquired substantial quantities of wine from Soufflot and Millon, the brokers in Irancy and Coulanges. Thus Chablis, like Auxerre and in competition with it, acted as a bulking-up entrepôt between the lower-level villages in the region and the ultimate buyers.

Edme Rathier's widow, Elizabeth Froment, substantially expanded her husband's enterprise after his death.[84] With the help of another broker, Claude Lambert, she had been acquiring substantial amounts of wine that, although drawn from only a local catchment area, were going to more than just the Parisian market. Through the fall and spring of 1718–19, Lambert had purchased 3,657 barrels, for each of which Froment owed him a commission of five sous. This amounted to forty-nine hundred hectoliters, when Chablis itself produced only sixty-seven hundred hectoliters. According to her accounts in June, Froment owed a further thirty-five thousand livres to sixty-nine "individuals of Chablis and surrounding places who have sold [her] wine." Earlier inventories show her owing larger debts totaling almost fifty-three thousand livres. Half of this wine was sold by a top quintile of large-scale sellers, individuals who had already bulked up considerable quantities. They included a canon, a shoemaker, and Claude Millon, the broker from Coulanges. The rest were small-scale sellers, averaging barely three hundred livres, or roughly a dozen barrels.[85] The vast majority of this wine went to wine merchants of Paris and Versailles, but a little also went to merchants at Béthune and Liège, and a broker in Reims. Despite her reliance on the help of another broker for much of her acquisitions, Froment was clearly able to maintain her husband's business at a booming pace.[86]

The brokers of Chablis drew their economic strength less from their far-flung markets, for, indeed, they traded mainly with Paris like other brokers in lower Burgundy, than from their overwhelming control of the economic life of their own region. The accounts of Louis Ragot, who had to pay the highest fine of all the brokers in France, suggests how they had gained their control. He had married the niece of another broker, Jean Navarre, whose widow had settled some land upon the couple.[87] By the time of his

The Brokers of Burgundy

wife's probate inventory, in 1724, they owned twenty arpents in Chablis and right around it, including vines in the grand cru "Grenouilles."[88] Not only were they large proprietors, Ragot dealt in large quantities of wine for "foreign" merchants. Within a few weeks of the harvest he had already shipped off twelve hundred barrels, most going to Paris by way of Auxerre, but a few carted downstream to a port at Bonnard.

Ragot's purchases represent a large portion of the local market; the 1,796 barrels of wine he bought in 1723 amounted to a quarter of the total production in Chablis and villages right around it—Fleys, Milly, Chichée—where he was buying.[89] They also show him working closely with small-scale producers. He had bought wine from over a hundred people, the great majority of whom were identified as vignerons; a few were listed as an officier, a procureur, a merchant, or a butcher. Most sold him relatively little, a dozen barrels, except for a top quintile that sold more like forty barrels. The prices ranged between thirty-five and thirty-nine livres per muid for wine from Chablis and between thirty and thirty-four livres for wine from Fleys and Milly. But the vast majority of the wine had been given no price. He had bought it for sixty-six individuals, most of them Parisian wine merchants who bought an average of only eight muids. Four of the wine merchants, however, had commissioned half of the purchases, at an average of 117 muids apiece.[90] The inventory referred to forty-three thousand livres owed by fifty wine merchants, plus another six thousand livres owed by merchants from Namur and the Savoie.

His records are unusually clear about his services to wine merchants, as well as the financial burden they entailed. The purchases are entered chronologically in a book and identify in each case which merchant the wine was bought for. Brokers were repeatedly enjoined to buy their wine for specific merchants and keep careful records to that effect. Ragot is one of the few who did. Many entries mentioned that the price of the wine had not been fixed but detailed the costs of rebarreling (fifty sous per muid) and carting the wine either to Auxerre (four livres per muid) or to Bonnard, downstream from Auxerre (5.5 livres per muid). These costs and the local taxes he paid up front and charged to the wine merchant. They added some 20 to 30 percent to the cost of the wine, just to get it to the Yonne River.[91] He also financed the cost of the wine, as his debts to local vignerons makes clear.

Ragot's role in this community went well beyond buying their wines for Parisian merchants. Nearly all of the people who had sold him wine appeared in his accounts of "loans made by Ragot . . . both in money and in barrels." Between late April and October 1724 he had lent over twenty-three thousand livres in barrels and money (the accounts do not distinguish) to two hundred people, vignerons from the same few villages where he got his wine. There were only a few coming to him for help in the spring; a dozen came to him in May and June, gradually increasing to three dozen in August, and the average loan dropping from two hundred to one hundred livres over that period. We may easily suspect that these were the indigent vignerons, who could not get through the summer on what they had. Yet with few exceptions, those who had borrowed in the spring and summer repaid the loan in the first half of September, well before they could have delivered their wine to a buyer, indeed, earlier than the harvest that year.[92] The implication is very clear that these growers repaid him by selling him their wine on the vine; early September was probably the earliest he could estimate their value. In fact, the "loans" recorded in his accounts may well have been little more than advances for such purchases, disguised because buyers were forbidden to purchase wine before it was made. If Ragot was indeed buying wine speculatively before the harvest, it was also a serious breach of the laws that forbade brokers to buy wine before receiving a specific commission from a merchant, but this practice was becoming increasingly common.[93]

Then in September the number of loans Ragot made to vignerons suddenly shot up, caused no doubt by the needs of the harvest; 127 people borrowed fourteen thousand livres worth of barrels for their wine, food and money for their workers, and money to pay their taxes. They included a range of people, from vignerons to the curé of Fleys, and a bourgeois or a merchant of Chablis borrowing five hundred livres. A few had paid quickly, but most still owed Ragot by mid-October.

Ragot and, to a lesser extent, the other brokers of Chablis enjoyed the enviable position of being the sole intermediaries for a large and productive vinegrowing region. Their control was made more certain by the difficulties of transportation. Chablis was not easily accessible to Paris by water; the local stream had never been navigable, and efforts to make it so had always been blocked downstream. To be shipped from either the port at Auxerre or Bonnard, the wines of Chablis required expensive haulage over roads that had been described at the end of the seventeenth century as "so broken that, unless they are soon fixed, will become immediately impracticable, especially in winter, and closed to commerce."[94] This haulage increased the already prohibitive costs of sending wine to Paris speculatively and gave a further advantage to brokers with greater resources than the small vignerons. Vignerons did not stop trying, but the court cases

The Brokers of Burgundy

discussed earlier show that they had trouble putting up the initial costs and turned to shippers for help.

The brokers of Chablis, in contrast, had the financial resources to overcome the impediments of their location, as well as the near certainty of buyers in Paris. They could afford to pay the myriad costs of shipping and ran little risk of having their wines left unsold in Paris. Their economic power gave them an advantage in commercial affairs, but it also gave them substantial control over local producers through webs of dependency and debt. Brokers not only helped finance the wine trade for Parisians and merchants from abroad, they were also important sources of rural credit. Vignerons' inventories in the mid-1720s show nearly all to have relied heavily on brokers to buy their wines and lend them money and still owed substantial sums that were "remaining [after] the deduction of the wine that [the broker] held" from them.[95] Small wonder that these brokers dominated this market.

The brokers of Burgundy represented a series of bridges: between producers and merchants, between province and capital, between the local and national economies, and between the modest circumstances of the rural landowners and the vast wealth of international commerce. It is impossible to say exactly what fraction of the provincial wine trade they controlled. A rough estimate would give the brokers of Chablis a huge proportion, at least three-quarters of the long-distance trade from their neighborhood. The brokers in and around Auxerre may have carried less; with greater accessibility to the Yonne River, more producers could manage the trip to Paris on their own. But brokers dominated the commercial dealings of the Parisian wine merchants, which still provided the surest long-distance market.[96] Their financial assistance facilitated the capital's trade with the provinces, making it possible for even modest Parisian wine merchants to engage in commerce. This effectively increased demand in the province, although it did not increase the number of buyers, since a few brokers were increasingly replacing a multitude of merchants in the market.

Providing the links between distinct geographical, financial, and economic worlds, brokers brought the stimulation of the capitalist economy to their own viticultural communities. They mobilized a vast system of provincial credit, arranging a complex combination of loans offered to vignerons to help them support the costs of making wine until they could sell it, as well as loans that allowed merchants to pay off their purchases over the course of a year. But these intermediaries did not fit easily into their communities and faced increasing hostility. With fortunes of less than one hundred thousand livres, brokers could not compare themselves to the négociants of the Atlantic ports. Still, their wealth put them above all of their village, and most of their urban, neighbors, and their ties to Parisian markets gave them leverage over producers that provoked growing resentment. Above all, the ambiguities of their economic status, as they made the transition from public official to commission broker and, gradually, to independent négociant, challenged the viticultural community's assumptions about how the economy should work.

The Brokers of Burgundy

5
Power in the Vines

The rise of commission wine brokers had occurred in a comparatively short time in the late seventeenth and early eighteenth centuries, with far-reaching results. They quickly became central to the interregional wine trade through their credit and their contacts and established themselves as the chief conduits between provincial growers and Parisian merchants. The financial and commercial assistance they offered to both buyers and sellers made them indispensable to the wine trade. Their utility gave them considerable power over provincial markets, which made them controversial figures. Controversy throughout the eighteenth century, but particularly at the end of the 1730s, offers us a rich source of information about the scope of brokers' economic power and their evolving role in viticultural society. It also sheds light on contemporary definitions of commercial liberty and equity and on debates over the market economy, and it allows us to rethink early models of economic legitimacy.

The Moral Economy Model

The penetration of capitalist markets into early modern France provoked a long-term crisis, a crisis of conflicting market models and discourses.[1] Government officials, philosophes, and the populace struggled bitterly to define markets in different ways and, through definition, to sanction very different forms of practice. Historians studying the evolution of market discourses in France have largely limited their investigation, however, to the single contested issue of the grain trade, thus missing broader debates over the nature and role of the market occurring in the society.[2] Disputes over the grain trade, although undoubtedly central to public policy for much of the eighteenth century, were not the only problems raised by the growing commercialization of French society and should not exhaust our historical treatment of the period. For, unlike grain, the wine trade was substantially liberalized early in the century, particularly with the privatizing of the brokers' office. The effects of this liberalization disturbed a broad cross section of viticultural society and provoked widespread protests. If these protests did not threaten the regime as "flour wars" did, they reveal, nonetheless, the enduring potency of premodern market models.

For all that has been written about popular economic attitudes, our understanding of popular conceptions of the market is still quite one-dimensional. The "moral economy," with its *taxation populaire,* its hostility to grain horders and engrossers, its belief in "the right to be fed," and its demand for royal regulation of the grain trade, has gained a central place in historians' descriptions of popular culture, due to much fine work in the last thirty years. But this model, and its revolutionary cognate of the sans-culottes, express only the outlook of consumers, and largely urban consumers at that.[3] Despite some excellent recent work on artisans, there is much less understanding of the market models held by women and men, whether urban or rural, as producers.[4] As for the views of merchants or the middle class, we know very little.[5]

The government's shifting position on the proper functioning of the market is perhaps better understood. It was caught up in the debate over the grain trade and was obliged to explain its support for, and then gradual abandonment of, market regulation. Despite historians' tendencies to dismiss official discourse as camouflage for fiscal self-interest, the government articulated a coherent view of its role in the market.[6] Here again, however, the focus on the grain trade can lead to distortion. The political volatility of the grain question clearly provoked a political response from the government, anxious to soothe urban crowds. As a consequence modern historians tend to reduce market regulation to the police of provisioning and to lose sight of other, and perhaps more fundamental, principles of equity that informed the ideal of policing. Where historians of the Middle Ages perceive Christian and Aristotelian ideals of commutative justice producing commercial regulation out of a pervasive anxiety about monopoly and markets, the early modern state is presented as motivated largely by statist ambition and fear of urban bread riots.[7] Did ethical imperatives embracing the equity of all participants in the market disappear, or at least become submerged by concern for purely political considerations of "social control?"[8]

The discussion of legitimizing principles that operated in early modern France is usually confined to issues of the grain trade and concern for consumers, despite E. P. Thompson's admonition that the "moral economy" was only a "selective reconstruction" of a more general ideal of "market supervision."[9] This emphasis on the consumer orientation of regulations has led to a misunderstanding of broader social and political attitudes about the market economy. We need to remember that what Louise Tilly has called the "conscious popular model of how the economy should work" was not restricted to the "problem of subsistence," for hostility to those who wielded economic power transcended producer and consumer, town and country, state and subject.[10] As anthropologists remind us, every market is "a contested field of power" that provokes "moral responses on the part of market agents to the potential imbalances of power engendered through exchange relations."[11] To understand the broader conceptions of, and responses to, the market economy, we must investigate other power asymmetries in the early modern market. The wine trade offers a particularly clear example of a moral response to profound changes in the balance of rural economic power, as wine producers and the government invoked an ancient market discourse of transparency and equity.

The medieval ideal of commerce had been an "equivalence between what is received and what is given," where value was determined by a transparent, and so perfectly competitive, market.[12] Such equivalence was vulnerable to monopoly, however, and merchants, in particular, were seen to pose a threat to the proper function of competitive markets.[13] Governments from the Middle Ages to the Old Regime, defending the ideal of "open markets" through regulation, made an effort to protect markets from merchant monopolies.[14] For example, market towns frequently kept merchants from buying on market day until after townsmen had first pick of wares, and Paris kept grain merchants from provisioning within ten leagues of the city and wine merchants within twenty leagues, to avoid competition with inhabitants who wished to buy.[15] Steven Kaplan has defined this ideally transparent market as the "marketplace," which embodied notions of "social responsibility" and "just price." The concept of the "marketplace" enshrined the ideal of market regulation to limit monopolistic practices—defined loosely as ways of gaining control of a commodity in order to control its price. Such regulation translated a general belief that the unregulated market permitted merchants to "use their enormous leverage to 'promote public misfortune' in order to profit from it."[16]

Beyond protecting the transparency of markets, the authorities felt a particular responsibility to ensure a community's subsistence, which usually meant keeping bread prices from rising too high. They were convinced that merchants and middlemen in the grain trade employed "monopolistic" practices to drive prices up, so regulations aimed at limiting their ability to manipulate the market.[17] If the regulation of the grain trade benefited consumers, it was due both to the fact that grain was perceived as a "common good upon which society had certain claims" and to the recognition that consumers were vulnerable to the economic power of merchants and suppliers.[18] There were fundamental political considerations behind the police of provisioning, based on the desire to avoid social disruption and the bread riot, for the bread riot was one of the few occasions when the common people forced themselves on the public stage of politics, and the elites were anxious to avoid repeated performances. There were also clear ethical imperatives as well, expressed by the populace as a "right to be fed," and by the police more generally as paternalist obligations to defend the urban community.[19] And in their concern for urban consumers, the authorities were clearly willing to sacrifice the interests of grain producers and sellers.

In reaction to the state's regulatory policies everything from provisioning policies to mercantilism came under increasing attack in the late seventeenth century. Political reformers and merchants called for free trade, arguing that "liberty is the soul and element of commerce."[20] Their ardor for liberty was somewhat tempered in the first half of the century by a contradictory desire for protection, the "protection of a regulator State, guarantor of individual rights and founder of social order through laws that conform to the natural order of things." Their recognition of the "contradiction between private interest and general interest" has led Simone Meyssonnier to identify the early phases of the free trade movement as "egalitarian liberalism."[21] Thus early economists like Forbonnais expected the "legislator [to] reestablish the [economy's] equilibrium to prevent misfortune," at the same time that they criticized mercantilist policies.[22] And Montesquieu, a proponent of free trade, would not extend laissez-faire to merchants: "The freedom of commerce is not a power granted to the merchants to do what they please. . . . The constraint of the merchant is not the constraint of commerce."[23]

By the middle of the eighteenth century, the physiocratic movement demanded not only free trade but also assailed the traditional ideals of "police," especially the police of provisioning. The physiocrats rejected any role for the government in the market. There was no need for regulation, they insisted, since free trade and monopoly were, by definition, "contradictory." Commerce, for them, was inherently a direct and transparent exchange, with no tendency toward monopoly; according to Quesnay, "trade is only an exchange of value for equal value."[24] For all the echoes of scholasticism in that formulation, it involved very different assumptions about the need for public authorities to protect the open market. Physiocrats accused government action of actually being the source of the problem, for "it is the legislative precautions against monopoly which cause the terrible monopoly which could starve us all."[25]

The physiocrats attacked the police's conceptualization of the market for focusing too narrowly on the consumers' interests, and the indictment has recently been leveled against modern interpretations of the policy of provisioning and the moral economy. One recent critic has charged that the government caved in too easily to moral and political claims made by urban consumers for market regulation, which "served narrow regional professional groups at the expense of the general interest."[26] But bread prices do not exhaust the implications of the "marketplace," nor was government regulation motivated solely by consumer interests and pressures. Proponents and critics of the moral economy model alike are missing important aspects of the government's policies.

Consumer advocacy was not the only goal of government regulation, and much of the work on moral economy has lost sight of other legitimizing notions that inspired both popular protest and the government's regulations. There is evidence, however, that producers mobilized to protest against intermediaries whose economic power threatened to give them a monopoly and that the government shared their concerns.[27] A commercial scandal in the eighteenth-century French wine trade illustrates the confluence of both state and popular action to defend the interests of producers, within the larger economic ideals of equity and the open market. Provincial wine brokers, who had traditionally played a very subordinate role in the national wine trade, had emerged as intermediaries of considerable economic power in the late seventeenth century. They were now attempting to flex their entrepreneurial muscles to take control of regional commerce, at the expense of local winemakers. The very brokers who had once been responsible for protecting the openness of the public wine market were now accused of subverting it. Viticultural communities indicted them for supplanting traditional buyers, making clandestine purchases for their own accounts, and obscuring the mechanisms of sale and pricing, thereby gathering enormous economic power into their hands.

The evidence in earlier chapters from Champagne and lower Burgundy shows that brokers had become the major purchasers, shippers, and creditors of wine sent from the provinces to Paris. They used their position astride this axis to gain greater control of the wine trade and the power to manipulate prices and commissions. They defended their use of this power as a reasonable effort to limit the risks inherent in the business. But they violated a widely held understanding of how the market was supposed to operate and provoked winemakers to protest the middlemen whose economic power jeopardized their place in the market as producers. Both perspectives offer valuable insights into assumptions and judgments about the way in which markets and commercial agents ought to work.

The controversy over brokers finally drew the participation of the government, acting first in a local scandal and finally in an investigation across the kingdom. The government's intervention reveals a fundamental desire to limit any group from gaining disproportionate economic power over others and to protect the interests of producers as well as consumers against monopoly. No "right to drink" or fear of urban unrest appears to have motivated government involvement. Instead, government officials acted upon a normative vision of the broker's commercial role and his relation to the producer. Their opposition to change was not the obscurantism that has so often been decried but spoke, rather, to concerns expressed by many people involved in the wine trade. In so doing, it used the language of just price, of community interest and the open market, as well as expressing hostility to middlemen, forestallers, and commercial power. This was a vocabulary of the "marketplace," with roots deep in the civic, religious, and political consciousness of the Middle Ages and persistent echoes as late as the Age of Reason. The language of the marketplace continued to shape attitudes, not just toward issues of bread prices and the grain trade, but to the function of the whole economy as a distributive mechanism. It is a language that infused the debate over the wine brokers of the eighteenth century.

Brokers on Trial

The government took decisive action on the issue of wine brokers in October 1737 when the royal prosecutor (procureur du roi) of Auxerre publicly charged an unnamed wine broker with having "totally disrupted the wine trade" by his "excessive greed and very blameworthy schemes."

In a *monitoire* (official notice) to be read from the pulpit of every parish church in the bailliage and even posted in Paris, the prosecutor announced that he had information about a "certain person" who had been working in Auxerre for some fifteen years as a wine broker, buying wine from growers in the region "for the accounts of merchants and several Parisian religious communities." The monitoire called for witnesses to come forward with information about the affair but already indicted the broker with a list of fraudulent business practices. The broker was demanding a 5 percent commission on the wines he bought for others, he neglected to leave receipts with the sellers, and he was selling the wines to his customers at prices higher than he had paid. Furthermore he was using the "money of the Public that he has in his hands" to buy barrels and forcing wine-makers to buy them from him at a profit of one-third. He had also bought a "large quantity" of vines "in secret" and sold his own wine as coming from better growths. Finally he had revealed the "traits of his character and his avidity" by sending a letter to merchants in Paris claiming falsely that the region's grape harvest had been ruined by hail and urging them to buy up the previous year's wines, of which he had a great quantity.[28]

The first two indictments were rather obscure violations of the local customary laws.[29] Official *courtiers* of the previous century were traditionally limited to collecting a fee of ten sous per barrel from sellers. The monitoire admitted that, since the abolition of the official *courtiers*, brokers followed the "tolerated usage" of collecting ten or even fifteen and twenty sous per muid. The accused, however, was demanding a 5 percent commission (sol pour livre) that produced "as much as five or six livres per muid, which was a very dangerous example for his colleagues." The local custom also enjoined the broker to leave a signed receipt with the seller. The unidentified person's failure to follow this rule made it easier for him to charge an excessive commission and to report an inflated price to his buyers, yet "no one dares complain about this, for fear of never selling his wine." The monitoire made no reference to the local codes for the rest of the violations since they were transparently fraudulent practices. The defendant's actions, it asserted, particularly the letter to Parisian merchants, "threaten to ruin the whole region."

Everyone in town could easily identify the "person" talked about in the monitoire, though legally a monitoire accused no one and could only ask for information in a very general way. As the man himself, Edme Pierre Alexandre Villetard, angrily pointed out, everyone knew that he was the only broker to have moved to Auxerre fifteen years before, and there was already gossip about the crimes he was supposed to have committed.[30] His indictment was soon formal enough, along with an indictment, on lesser charges, of eight other brokers from Auxerre and bourgs in its vicinity. Of the nine, several were considered very wealthy men, and four had served on the prestigious consular court (the juridiction consulaire) during the previous decade.[31] Yet their wealth gave grounds for suspicion. As one brief against them noted, "Of the twelve brokers who are in Auxerre, there are four who were born without wealth and began this commerce without fortune, leading one to believe by the beautiful and vast houses they have built, by the manner in which they are furnished and decorated, and by their expenses, that they have made very considerable profits."[32]

Indeed, many of the accused were new men, coming either from out of town or from different—and inferior—trades. Edme Villetard was a Parisian, the son of a wine merchant of Paris who bought substantial amounts of wine from lower Burgundy and clearly had close ties there, for Edme had been baptized in Auxerre and was listed in the city's tax rolls as a resident broker by 1725.[33] Four of the other defendants began their careers in the nearby small bourgs, and three were there still. Germain Soufflot was not only broker but also lieutenant of the bailliage of Irancy, as his father had been. He claimed to be "accustomed by [his father and ancestors] for nearly two centuries" to the wine trade. He had also married the daughter of Claude Millon, the important broker of Coulanges.[34] Pierre Boyard had been fined as a broker in Saint-Bris in 1705 but had later moved to Auxerre—or rather returned, for his family had been boatmen of Auxerre for generations. He had become a very successful broker, sitting frequently on the consular court and buying as much as a million livres worth of wine in recent years, if "public rumor" can be believed.[35] Germain Monnot, a nephew of Boyard's, was the son of a merchant boatman, as were several of the other indicted brokers.[36] The older brokering families seemed to have kept a certain distance from the new; of the seven families in Auxerre who had been identified as serious brokers in 1705, not one could be found among the culprits in 1737. Some of these families, particularly those like Navarre, Robinet, and Liger, with the biggest fines in 1705, were still involved in brokerage in the 1730s but had avoided the scandal. Indeed, scions of two of the original families, Roch Liger le jeune and Robinet de Villeme, were probably responsible for blowing the whistle on the new men.[37]

The original impetus to this affair is a bit obscure, but there is evidence that local rivalries played a role. Even before the monitoire officially opened the brokering affair, Villetard had formally sued Liger and accused him and Robinet of having started the rumor that he had written to Paris about hail destroying the year's grape harvest. Witnesses testifying for Villetard agreed that Liger had stated as much in the public square. One witness (admittedly a broker who would soon be implicated with Villetard in the brokerage scandal) claimed that Liger had been publicly complaining that Villetard had "stolen more than fifty of his merchants." Liger, he added, had threatened that "when he learned that one of his colleagues was writing to these merchants he would bring a complaint to the royal prosecutor on the basis of what he was learning about his colleagues."[38] But whatever role rivalry between brokers played in this affair, it quickly became clear that resentment against the accused was widespread throughout much of viticultural society.

Other witnesses described this story about the letter as a "public rumor," and there is evidence that it had mobilized much of the public in protest. For the "rumor" about the letter had already provoked popular violence within the larger community, whose interests were also hurt by slanders about their harvest and who objected just as strongly as Liger to such tactics. Villetard complained that as a result of these "calumnies . . . the angered [common] people discharged its fury on [his] vines," completely destroying them. Vines were a vulnerable and particularly tempting target for acts of retribution. There is a kind of poetic justice in ruining the harvest of somebody who had falsely reported the destruction of others' harvests.

Villetard had tried to bring the perpetrators to justice, "but this crime being the work of the [common] people, who regarded it as an act of legitimate violence, all those who knew about it felt justified in keeping their silence."[39] The remark is striking, for we must ask ourselves: What could legitimize the wholesale destruction of another's vines? Villetard was alluding to something more fundamental than an act of irrational revenge, to some system that the common people clearly felt had been violated and needed defending. First in direct and violent action, later through legal proceedings, the winemakers, whether common or not, defended the economic principles of the open market.

Indictment of a System

In the suit that followed, through the depositions of scores of witnesses against the accused, the striking fact is the breadth of hostility to all of the brokers and to their practices. In Auxerre and in the bourgs around it, among vignerons and bourgeois, the wine producers of lower Burgundy turned out to condemn Villetard and the rest. Of the eighty-six witnesses whose depositions remain, just over a third called themselves either *vigneron* or *laboureur* (well-off farmer). Most of these came from a string of bourgs and villages extending fifteen kilometers to the south of Auxerre. Another third were bourgeois or "merchants" from Auxerre or the towns nearby. A quarter held public office—everything from a local tax official to a councillor at the highest court in the region—and a few were even noble.[40] Nearly all of them had sold their wine to brokers and complained about something the brokers had done.

Their evidence is rich but obviously partisan; it is useful, nevertheless, for what it reveals about attitudes and assumptions concerning the wine trade and the market in general. The condemnations expressed widespread beliefs about how a market ought to work and how intermediaries ought to behave. These brokers were accused of having broken specific laws, but much of the testimony vented outrage at their having violated certain norms that tacitly regulated behavior in the market. Witnesses repeatedly blamed the brokers for having transgressed the principles of just pricing and fair competition. The brokers' attempts to vindicate themselves must be viewed in the same light, as expressions of shared norms or, occasionally, appeals to different standards of economic activity. These economic norms allow us to determine the relevance of the "marketplace" ideal in the changing economic realities of the eighteenth century.

The evidence also sheds light on the way the provincial wine trade worked and reinforces the argument made earlier that wine brokers had become figures who wielded great power in viticultural communities. Testimony identified certain levers of economic power that were widely regarded as giving brokers an advantage in the market. Brokers were attacked for their power, above all, power that they were held to have acquired illegally and used improperly. Whether or not their rise to power had been illegal, however, it was clearly deemed to be illegitimate. The fact that they enjoyed superior access to buyers, to information about prices, and to well-organized systems of credit privileged their role in the market. But what may seem to us as reasonable advantages struck contemporaries— the vignerons and wine producers of every social level—as unfair.

The depositions supported the royal prosecutor's accusations of fraud but went well beyond them. They indicted a whole system, contending that a series of innovations were allowing the wine brokers to shift the balance of commercial power in their favor; they had made themselves "masters" of the winemakers and gained an "empire" over the wine trade.[41] Easily the most common complaint arose from the brokers' failure to leave receipts with the sellers. Without a receipt, sellers had no proof of the verbal agreements they had made with brokers and so suffered "every day a thousand inconveniences." The commentaries written on the local customs of Auxerre by a barrister at the end of the seventeenth century reveal that the problem was actually an old one; even then "the observance of this article [requiring receipts] is much neglected."[42] Presumably a verbal agreement and trust was once enough to allow the system to function, but no longer.[43]

Now witnesses were very bitter about the lack of receipts, and many recited instances where they had agreed on a price with the broker but had been paid less when the wine was delivered or the debt finally settled. A widow of a bourgeois of Auxerre explained that one broker had promised her husband over one hundred livres per muid, but, after his death when she wished to collect, she was given only ninety livres, which she was "obliged to accept in the hope the broker had given her that he would pay attention to selling her wine in the future." But he had never offered to help her again. Other witnesses found that brokers did not pay them fairly or claimed to have paid them money that they never received. A laboureur and his wife had gone to the broker's house for sixty livres he owed them and had stood outside his window making a "great noise . . . nevertheless they lost [the money], not having a receipt." Even years after the fact, depositions reveal the bitterness such treatment caused. And when it happened that a grower and his broker did not agree on what the price should be or what had been paid, the grower noted sadly that "he was advised to approach [the broker] gently . . . without bringing a suit against the broker, since he did not have a receipt."[44]

Winegrowers were particularly vulnerable because the whole system of setting a price was actually quite informal and even a bit chaotic. Not only did brokers rarely leave receipts, they often bought from the grower without specifying a price. A vigneron in a village near Auxerre simply asked that the broker "pay him what he would pay the others in the area from whom he bought . . . as was fairly customary."[45] A procureur fiscal, an attorney in the seigneurial justice system, had not been willing to sell his wine without a price, like "all the others" in his village and had asked instead to be paid the same as a particular neighbor. But when he went to Villetard's house to collect, he was offered half the sum he expected and found others from his village who were also protesting. Knowing the legal system better than the average peasant, the procureur took Villetard to court and won a small increase in the price.[46]

Despite abuses, the system of waiting to set prices made a good deal of sense. The wine market involved too many distinct stages for a price-setting mechanism to work quickly; brokers had little idea what prices were being asked elsewhere in France or what was being offered in Paris. The winegrower obviously had even less information about prices. A Burgundian lawyer argued, several decades later, that the typical grower "paid attention only to the difference between his price and that of others" in the area; price was as much a matter of pride as of profit.[47] A parish priest agreed with Villetard not to specify a price, as long as he "bought it at the same price that he charged the [Parisian] merchants, which would be a higher price than for the wines of [a village three kilometers away] since he knew there were no wines [there] that surpassed his in quality."[48] But the system of selling without a fixed price lent itself to abuses.

Practically in the middle of the court case, in the fall of 1739, Villetard was sued by one of the Robinet family for duplicity in pricing.[49] Villetard had brought several Parisian wine merchants to Robinet's residence in Auxerre to purchase the two cuvées he had made in Chablis. Robinet had not visited Chablis since the harvest, however, and did not know what price wine there was selling for. Harvests had recently been quite disrupted by poor weather, so the market was in considerable turmoil and prices were fluid.[50] In such a situation, growers were often forced to sell without having agreed to any fixed price.

A man of Robinet's stature could resist the humiliation of having to accept whatever price the broker offered him, but he needed some benchmark to compare his wines to. The wines sold by the abbey of Pontigny, which owned a large part the vineyards around Chablis, seemed the obvious referent, although Robinet was sure that his wines were "much better." Without knowing the exact price the monks of Pontigny were getting that year, a figure Villetard refused to divulge, Robinet tried to sell his wines for ten livres per barrel above their price, "believing that Messieurs de Pontigny would have sold [their wine] at a price proportionate to preceding years." After "some contestations" he was forced to "abandon" his wine for only two livres above the abbey's price and agree to pay for carting the wine to Auxerre. Only then did Villetard reveal that the monks had sold their wine for a mere thirty-eight livres per barrel, at which Robinet was "so surprised that he could not stop himself from showing his chagrin to Villetard." Robinet subsequently learned that the buyers had gone on to Chablis and had bought much wine using his price as a benchmark. Of course the incident illustrates more than Villetard's deviousness, which could have been no real surprise to Robinet, whatever he claimed. Robinet had tried to set his price well above the benchmark and had failed;

he was a victim both of his limited access to price information and of his poor bargaining position.

Testimony reveals many of the wine producers to have been both naive and heavily dependent in their relations with the broker. Men and women from all social levels indicated that they routinely sold to brokers on trust, accepting their word on prices but having little recourse when a broker tricked them. Only a few thought of asking for receipts or for a more sophisticated accounting. Several witnesses also complained that brokers bought wine and then left it with the grower for extended periods of time, forcing the grower to bear the costs of upkeep. Since barrels needed frequent filling to keep out the air as the wine evaporated, this maintenance could be a considerable expense, as well as a contravention of the customary laws.[51] But it was hard to complain if brokers helped growers sell their wine.

Growers also accepted a dependent relationship by buying barrels from brokers on credit. Many of the witnesses bought barrels on credit before the wine harvest and paid the brokers back when they sold their wine. They complained in their testimony that brokers frequently charged above the market price for these barrels yet they continued to buy from them. Some of those buying barrels were of obviously modest means, laboureurs and vignerons who mentioned that they also borrowed money from brokers before the harvest and clearly could not afford to pay for barrels before the harvest. Yet some were even men of standing, who might be expected to avoid the debt; nevertheless, "they are too happy to buy [barrels] from the [brokers] because of the hope the brokers give them of facilitating the sale of their wine and of according them some preference."[52] In a buyers' market, the brokers benefited from their knowledge of and direct access to the all-important Parisian buyers. Sellers were willing to buy the broker's services in a variety of ways.

The brokers' trade in barrels also gave them an excuse to be considered as merchants, according to the royal prosecutor, and thus made them eligible to sit on the consular court. They were regularly chosen to serve on this court, "so that these brokers, who are frequently indicted before this court find there all the credit and every way to have their frauds authorized by their confrères [sitting on the court] and always obtain a judgment exempting them from their debts."[53] Thus was informal, economic power reinforced by institutional.

In contrast to the raw anger excited by the brokers' manipulation of prices of wine and barrels, most witnesses expressed resignation about the

5 percent commission they were forced to pay for the brokers' services. In nearly every case, people noted simply that the broker had taken his commission "with his own hands," and a few said they had paid it voluntarily. But, as one witness put it, "Although having given the commission voluntarily he had paid it with no less constraint than if they had demanded it by force, in the fear that he would not be able to sell his wines, which make up the principal fortune of this region."[54] The problem, according to the prosecutor, was not simply that the individual broker never returned to buy more wine from someone who refused to pay; "he even warns all his confrères of the person's refusal and so by a common accord among the brokers it is settled that the person will never again sell his wine in the future."[55] This accusation, that brokers worked together to enforce their control, recurred throughout the testimony.

The original indictment had also charged brokers with buying and selling for their own account and selling wine for more than they had bought it. This aroused comparatively little anger among witnesses, but they offered evidence of such transgressions. Growers reported that various brokers had brought merchants to their cellars to taste the wine the brokers had already bought but had not yet collected. The brokers had enjoined the growers not to reveal the price for which they had sold their wine, should the merchants ask. The growers subsequently learned that the brokers were charging the merchants more than they had paid the growers. More damaging evidence came from Claude Bazot, who had served as Villetard's agent (*facteur*) in the important wine-producing village of Coulanges-la-vineuse. He recalled that in 1730, after he had helped Villetard visit growers and buy some nineteen hundred barrels of wine, Villetard had expressly forbidden him to tell anyone how much he had paid for the wine. Villetard had then sent a series of merchants to Bazot, with instructions to have them taste particular wines, and they vainly tried to pump Bazot for information about the price. He had to admit that he never learned what price Villetard charged the merchants, but clearly implied that the merchants were paying more.[56]

The issue of overcharging merchants went to the heart of the brokers' powerful economic role. Brokers (*courtiers*) in every trade were forbidden to "traffic for their own account." This prohibition, reiterated as recently as Colbert's Commercial Code of 1673, was based on the fear that "*courtiers* can abuse the confidence that [merchants] are forced to have in them, by taking advantage of the good deals they make for others."[57] Knowing the prices at which the merchants were willing to buy and the growers were willing to sell, the broker could profit from any disparity by buying

at one price and reselling at another. Wine brokers were especially prohibited because of the sales tax on wine. Brokers buying wine in the name of
a merchant paid the sales tax on wine only once, whereas if they were buying and reselling the wine it was subject to the tax twice. As recently as
1721 an arrêt de conseil had been forced to reiterate the specific injunction
against wine brokers and admonished brokers not to buy wine until they
had a specific order from a merchant, which they should dutifully enter in
their registers.[58] But in practice they were obviously buying large quantities of wine in the expectation that some merchant would subsequently
express an interest in it. Many witnesses explained that brokers had bought
wine and left it with the grower until they could find a buyer. Much of the
brokers' buying activities were clearly prior to, and independent of, any
commissions they would receive. This was entrepreneurial behavior, in an
activity that was closed to entrepreneurs.

Scores of witnesses provided evidence that brokers had indeed broken
the law in a variety of ways. Yet the fundamental theme running throughout the testimony was a protest against a perfectly legal fact: that growers
had become so dependent on brokers. If growers felt abused by the brokers' behavior they had little recourse because they had come to rely so
completely on the brokers' credit and access to markets. They acquiesced
to the price gouging, the cost of commissions and maintenance, and the
duplicity over prices because they needed brokers in order to survive in
the market. But they could not reconcile themselves to the central role
now played by intermediaries.

Thus the brokers were accused of having gained enormous power in a
classic combination of collusion, debt, and their control over access to and
information about markets. Their power broke no laws, but it violated
the belief that middlemen should be a transparent screen through which
buyer and seller communicated directly. More than that, growers resented
brokers for their ruthless exploitation of traditional practices, such as not
leaving receipts and not setting prices, that seems to have taken the rest of
society by surprise. Witnesses clearly expected that they should be able to
trust brokers and were slow to adjust their own behavior. To their surprise,
the broker had stopped being the reliable town agent and had become an
aggressive entrepreneur pursuing his own self-interest.

A System Defended

The brokers defended themselves vigorously, both in the court and
then in printed briefs, or *factums,* that presented their side of the story to a

public, indeed, national audience.[59] They denied many of the accusations without challenging the underlying assumptions about proper practice, yet they defended some of their behavior in ways that reveal a new conception of the wine trade.

In his own defense, Villetard admitted to taking a 5 percent commission but insisted both that the practice was older than his introduction into the trade and that the article of the customs of Auxerre prescribing a much lower rate had been ignored for over a century. Indeed, the court of the prévôt des marchands of Paris sitting in Auxerre considered the sol pour livre to be reasonable enough that it backed up Pierre Boyard's demand to be paid that much in a suit that he brought in 1730.[60] As to the injunction to leave receipts, Villetard argued that it applied to *courtiers* rather than commissionnaires who did not need to leave receipts "because commissionnaires are merchants, who have [account] books" in which they recorded their transactions. Villetard explained the irrelevance of the local customary laws by pointing out that "since they were written down, over two hundred years ago, the state of the province had changed considerably and these changes have necessarily abolished old usages and introduced new ones." There followed a brief description of the evolution of the wine trade, as understood by one broker.[61]

"In the past," Villetard explained, the Auxerrois and neighboring provinces produced less wine and much less wine was generally consumed. The brokerage of wine was on too small a scale to give full occupation to an individual, "and besides there were official brokers [*courtiers*] to sell wines. Subsequently, these offices having been abolished, and the wine trade having since grown considerably," wine merchants sought assistance both in finding wine and in paying for it. Credit was particularly important since "the vigneron . . . delivers no [wine] without cash, and often the wine merchant has none with him." Such problems had led to the emergence of commission brokers in all the wine regions. Brokers were justified in demanding a 5 percent commission because of all the expenses they incurred in their business. They were "obliged to have a large, spacious house to receive, at their expense, the religious and merchants who . . . travel for their purchases," as well as large storage facilities and stables full of horses. They hired agents, *gourmets,* to help them look for wines and factors to take care of shipments. Brokers had to pay the vigneron quickly after the sale but might not be reimbursed by the merchant for over a year, unless, as sometimes happened, the merchant went bankrupt and the broker was never paid.[62] Thus the 5 percent commission had become standard

Power in the Vines

not only in Auxerre but in the "Orléanais, in Champagne, at Tonnerre, Chablis, and the rest of Burgundy."

Villetard refuted the charges of fraud in some detail. The letters to wine merchants, he repeated from an earlier trial, were never produced, and one witness had recanted. Villetard admitted that he had bought wine for his own provision, which he occasionally sold to friends out of "pure consideration." But he emphatically denied buying wine in order to resell it. He claimed, on the one hand, that "commissionnaires are merchants" but denied behaving like a merchant. Most of the accusations to that effect he dismissed by impeaching the witnesses. His agent Bazot, he asserted, had been fired for dishonesty (Bazot contested this vigorously), and "it is obviously to avenge himself for this shameful expulsion that the witness has imagined his deposition."

Villetard was especially sensitive about the "atrocious calumny" that he was price-gouging on barrels and using the loan of barrels to exploit growers. He recognized the accusation as one of the most volatile in the popular mind and insisted that "he was only charged with it in the hope that the populace, who were carefully stirred up against him with false rumors, would passionately seize this occasion to satisfy its resentment." Another of the defendants, Soufflot, also reacted vigorously to this charge, behind which he saw an equally nefarious purpose. "Who will not imagine that in the city of Auxerre one can find some interest in drying up the sources [of barrels] advanced to the vignerons of the countryside?" he asked. Soufflot was a broker in Irancy and was appealing, no doubt, to the villagers' resentment of the local city. And he pointed to other commercial forces at work: "Reduced to such scarcity [of barrels, the vignerons] would see the citizens of Auxerre become absolute masters and take over the whole wine-producing region, as well as drawing the wine trade tighter under their hands, whereas the brokers extend commerce; the citizens would be able to take possession of their harvests at a vile price."[63] Without the brokers' credit, many of the poorer vignerons could not afford to make their own wine or were forced to turn to others in Auxerre for credit. Soufflot could point to his father-in-law, Claude Millon, for evidence of scores of vignerons relying on brokers for loans of money and barrels to get them through a harvest. He identified his own loans as "charity" and presented brokers as the allies of the small grower and the champions of free trade.

Other defendants rejected their indictments in more limited terms, attacking the witnesses' credibility, denying any coercion in taking the commission, challenging the relevance of the customary laws, and trying to clarify the recent changes in the wine trade. They blamed the whole affair on "the jealousy of idle people who see with envy that brokers make some small profit" but offered little challenge to the assumptions underlying their accusers' indictments.[64]

Soufflot, however, expanded on his defense and took an even bolder step of attacking the authorities for impeding free trade: "Commerce cannot be constrained, and to deprive or restrain its liberty is to kill its germ, above all for things that are necessary for life, like wine." He also defended himself by invoking an important commercial treatise, Savary's *Le parfait négociant,* which offered a very different model of brokering activities than the government's. "In these sorts of occasions," he argued, "it is the evidence from merchants that ensures what is useful or not."[65] Like Villetard, Soufflot insisted that he was a commissionnaire rather than a *courtier* and pointed to the passages in Savary that described the broker's commission as a percentage of the price, rather than a flat fee. He also noted where Savary had accepted the fact that brokers would inevitably be left with merchandise that they must sell on their own.

Indeed, Savary sketched out a greater degree of freedom for brokers than anything the government had envisioned. During the times when business was slow, he explained, and merchants were not buying, rich brokers would buy cheaply and stock goods until their correspondents begin to buy again. At that point these brokers were not obliged to pass the goods along at the price they paid, "since they had advanced the money and ran the risks." Rather, they should charge something between the current price and the bargain prices they had paid, for "it is just that their correspondents participate in some way in the profit made by the brokers."[66] Savary was offering a good picture of the commercial organization found in many places of international trade. Merchants at the large ports of France and the north of Europe frequently engaged in both commissioning activities and trade for their own account.[67] This commercial model, invoked by wine brokers in the Atlantic ports during the investigation of 1705, evidently represented the telos of provincial brokering as well. But provincial wine brokers were still embedded in a different model, the *courtier* as public official, both in general perceptions and in their own practices.

The French wine broker could not legally be a merchant, and his relationship to the merchants for whom he worked was unusual.[68] Like the normal commission agent, he was independent of the merchant, but as guarantor of the payment to the seller, he shared the financial risks of the buyer, which the commission agent normally did not.[69] And unlike the merchant or any of his agents, the wine broker took his commission not from the buyer but from the seller, for whom he still theoretically worked. Wine brokers exercised an ambiguous function, combining the identity of both private and public agents. They continued to collect the old fee from the seller but without official sanction; the rhetoric of accusations emphasized their public responsibilities, but they defended themselves in terms of a private, free market. The wine broker was a curious hybrid of commercial functions—an unstable hybrid in the process of evolving.

Even the local judge in charge of the case in Auxerre found the issues to be perplexing. On the strength of the witnesses' testimony, the royal prosecutor had asked him to make out a warrant for Villetard's arrest. In a long letter seeking advice from Joly de Fleury, the prosecutor general (procureur général) of the Parlement de Paris, the judge explained that the case could have "very dangerous results if it were not handled with care." He summarized, with some sympathy, the brokers' justifications for asking the 5 percent commission and pointed out that "we have always placed our confidence in these brokers to the point that we deliver the wines they buy without receipts or promises; we rely on their good faith and must admit that there are rarely any problems." But the economic consequences of the fact that "the principal wealth of the city and its environs is in vines, and wine is the sole commerce" were clearly uppermost in the judge's mind. The brokers were currently "at the height of buying wines" and an imprisonment would "interrupt" their trade. Such an interruption would hurt everyone in the region, for the brokers had become "the masters of the fortune of each and every one, which they can put to bad use. . . . It is important therefore to conserve this commerce and to take care of those who are in it." Whatever the merits of the case he was unwilling to issue the warrant and finished by asking for instructions on his course of action.[70] In the end he found the brokers guilty but handed down lenient sentences, with small fines.

There is a profound irony in the judge's reasoning. The brokers' commercial power, the very issue that caused so much resentment in the community, compelled the judge to treat them with circumspection. This was ultimately the treatment accorded to brokers across France, who —it will be seen—were gaining similar power over their own communities.

A National Scandal

The revelations about the wine trade uncovered by the scandal in Auxerre around 1738 were sufficiently troubling that they provoked a royal investigation into the practices of wine brokers in the rest of the kingdom. The results of this investigation are revealing: Auxerre was in no way unique; indeed, even worse abuses were claimed in several of the major markets in northern France. Reports from around the country allow us to survey the perception of the brokers' position and power in other provinces and demonstrate the near universality of certain themes in the official discourse of market transparency and regulation.

The affair of the wine brokers of Auxerre did not end with the mild sentence passed in 1740. When word of the case got back to Paris it provoked considerable reaction. It was brought up in the king's council early in 1738 and came to the attention of the controller general, Orry, who prepared a declaration condemning new "abuses, frauds, and extortions that have been introduced into this commerce for some years," without referring specifically to Villetard's case. In fact, the declaration did little more than repeat earlier injunctions: that wine brokers register themselves with a local judge, keep their books in order, obey the local laws, not buy and sell for their own account, and charge no more than twenty sous per barrel for their services.[71] Orry had the proposed declaration sent to officials in Paris to get their reaction and was persuaded by Joly de Fleury to consult officials on the state of the wine trade throughout the enormous jurisdiction of the Parlement of Paris.[72] It is purely speculation, but the government's sharp response to this affair certainly coincided with, and may have been spurred on by, an extremely serious grain shortage in the years 1738–41. Orry and the Parlement were soon popularly accused of manipulating and profiting from the dearth.[73]

Almost certainly Joly de Fleury had also been hearing about similar misbehavior by wine brokers in Beaune. The town had prosecuted several brokers in 1732, and the governor of the province had gone to Beaune to "order the brokers to fulfill their duties with more fidelity or be driven from the town." A memorandum for the inhabitants of Beaune in 1735 explained that because "the town of Beaune and many others of the same province have no other resource and commerce than the cultivation of their vines and the sale of their wine, they have been forced to establish brokers, both to attract foreign merchants and to procure the sale of this kind of produce. But to the extent that they have felt the need to use [the brokers'] services, they have also recognized how important it was to prescribe limits to their cupidity." Since the late seventeenth century, however, these brokers "have dared to undertake anything in the belief that the immense wealth they have acquired by all sorts of indirect means and the alliances they have contracted would give them impunity and cover from all investigations."[74]

The mayor and échevins of Beaune had finally prosecuted several brokers in 1732 for "fraudulent" behavior. In their case against one of them, they noted "the prodigious fortunes of most of these brokers" and pointed out that the "superb houses, magnificent furniture, and excessive expenditures" could not have come from their brokerage fee alone. The brokers were formally accused of selling wine at a profit—"how many times have we seen these people sell wine to foreigners for four times more than they bought it"—and of buying without setting a price or even offering a receipt. "We have kept silent about this," they added bitterly, "because the vineowners did not dare complain. . . . Who among all the proprietors would be so foolish as to stop [the brokers] from marking their wine and arbitrarily regulating its value and price? who among them has even dared ever open his mouth to ask for a receipt? a word, a gesture, a movement of disquiet would have proscribed them for ever, no broker would ever again enter their cellars."[75] The authorities assailed the practice of setting the price at some vague benchmark, a "highest price" to be determined. The brokers had ways of then fraudulently setting the benchmark at a very low price.[76] If the sellers objected, they risked the "indignation of the broker, who never again puts his foot in the seller's storeroom, [and] the rest of his confrères imitate him in order to keep the bourgeois in slavery."

The town accepted both the justice of paying commissions to brokers in return for their guaranteeing the buyers' debts and the need for wealthy brokers, since those "without wealth" could not honor their purchases. But it argued in another memorandum that "it would be desirable to triple the actual number of brokers because it is more difficult for a great number of people . . . to make a monopoly to the detriment of the public, which has happened only too frequently for the last thirty years."[77] The brokers had "promised solemnly that, in return for setting aside the prosecutions and allowing the liberty of commerce for three years, they would give the public the marks of their affection and fidelity." But in 1735 the bourgeois of Beaune were officially protesting that the brokers "have not changed their conduct: the present year has seen the height of their cupidity."[78]

Because of events in Beaune and Auxerre and elsewhere, wine brokers in the major markets were increasingly perceived as out of control, and Joly de Fleury became so concerned that he launched a widespread investigation into fraudulent practices in the wine brokerage trade. He prepared a report setting out the government's case against the brokers' abuses, with a brief summary of their rebuttals, and sent it out to a score of important cities in the northern half of France asking for comments.[79] The memorandum was similar to the indictments in Auxerre but it revealed the government's preoccupations by arranging and defining the brokers' offenses somewhat differently.

Where the indictment from Auxerre began by condemning the 5 percent brokerage fee, Joly de Fleury condemned buying and selling for the broker's own account, first and unambiguously. This practice was objectionable for several reasons: It threatened to cheat the tax farm of its sales taxes, yet it is striking that neither Joly de Fleury nor any of his correspondents referred to that issue. Instead, they objected to the power such behavior gave brokers to control the market. Joly de Fleury reiterated the objections raised by the Commercial Code to brokers in any trade trafficking for their own account: They violated the "secret and confidence" of both the buyer and seller because the broker "knows the price [at which] the seller wishes to sell and at which the buyer wants to buy." Thus he knew the "extent of the profit" to be made and would "buy for himself when there is an advantage . . . and for his correspondent when there is none." The broker "enjoys every advantage; he will abuse the secret of others to gain all the profits." In this concept of an "advantage" enjoyed by the broker over everyone else in the market, Joly de Fleury seems to have identified the most troubling aspect of the wine brokers' behavior.

A second abuse, closely related to the first, lay in buying wines in advance of orders from correspondents and of failing to keep clear records of these purchasing orders. The memorandum also condemned the failure to leave receipts with sellers and the 5 percent commission, much as the indictment in Auxerre had. Finally, it decried the "commerce of vine props and barrels that gives brokers such an ascendancy over the wine trade that they are nearly the only ones to profit."[80]

From the provinces, the responses to Joly de Fleury's investigation came back filled with ringing condemnations of all that he had described. Across much of France, the wine brokers had done as much, it appears, and worse. Letters came back from royal prosecutors in most of the major towns in the wine country of northern France to the effect that brokers had indeed gained control of the wine trade. Although written by the local royal prosecutor or his assistant, they often noted that their reports were the result of consultations with prominent winemakers and notables. There is evidence that the local procureur was passing copies of the draft to some of these notables.[81] Even the intendant of Burgundy received the memorandum and responded in a lengthy and detailed letter.

The intendant of Burgundy was absolutely convinced that brokers bought for their own account and had heard of brokers making up to fifty thousand livres that way. He condemned this and all other "wicked schemes . . . [that] they invent every day to engross their fortunes at the expense of the Rich and unfortunate, seller and buyer." Like others, he objected to the advantages this system gave the brokers: "In a word, if . . . they buy and sell for their account, having the secret of the seller and the buyer, they will always work without risk and their profits will always be as certain as they are illicit." They enjoyed, in other words, a monopoly over information. He also denounced the power that brokers derived from their schemes, especially of advancing barrels, "by means of which brokers make themselves masters of all the trade." Perhaps it was the innovation that was most offensive; he denied any distinction between the new unlicensed broker (commissionnaire) and the old official one (courtier) ("for the words are a synonym") beyond the important difference that "the brokers of the past did not rise above their estate as do those of today."[82] This blast, and the other responses, show that Joly de Fleury was not alone in being concerned by the brokers, although the provinces were more disturbed by some aspects of the case than by others.

Provincial Protests

In a score of responses to Joly de Fleury's questionnaire from cities in the major wine regions came trenchant condemnations of wine brokers' economic power and how they acquired and wielded it. Not all accused brokers of buying on their own account, however. The correspondent in Beaugency accused them of it, and Anger confirmed it with anecdotal evidence, but the reports from Mâcon and Saumur claimed it was not a problem there.[83] The response from Blois was particularly bitter: "For a long time now the brokers of the Blésois have been buying wine and brandy in their own name without orders from their merchant." The royal prosecutor of Blois added that brokers had been manipulating credit by delaying their payments to winemakers and so increased their buying power. Thus "in addition to their own funds they use the public's money to make their purchases, from which they then fill the orders from their merchants as they are addressed to them." Since the brokers were the "masters of this kind of commerce, and [because of] the necessity people found themselves in of getting rid of their wine . . . one does everything [the brokers] desire."[84]

At the same time, there were cities that could report no problems with brokers, and their geography is interesting because it confirms the evidence of the 1705 survey. A great arc of towns, running from Mantes, west of Paris, to the south through Dreux and Chartres, and west down to Château-du-Loir and Baugé, north of Saumur, claimed little involvement in interregional wine trade and so knew nothing about brokers and their fraudulent practices. In most of these places "the wine is of such poor quality that it is not traded," or "the wine is consumed locally and strangers do not come for it," or "I have been assured that the problem only bothers Burgundy."[85] The brokers of Château-Thierry had developed no independence from Parisian wine merchants: "They make very few purchases without the wine merchants being there and do not make prices with the bourgeois or vigneron; they only take care of sending the wine." These towns, along with the region around Troyes and Bar-sur-Seine, between Champagne and Burgundy, had to admit that they were too cut off from long-distance trade to experience the depredations of wine brokers.[86]

In the major wine markets polled by Joly de Fleury, however, the brokers had gained enormous power. As in Auxerre, one of the chief grievances in many reports focused on the abuses of pricing and receipts. "We have never known the use of receipts like those spoken of in the memorandum," complained the correspondent in Blois. But, he added wistfully, "it appears that it would be very advantageous to establish it everywhere." Brokers in Mâcon and Blois had been in the habit "for a long time" of buying wine from growers without agreeing to any specific price. They were accused of buying the best wine unpriced and setting the benchmark price with wine bought from "those in need [of selling] and country men," who sold at distress prices. The town of Blois had finally held a general assembly in 1733 and persuaded the lieutenant general of Blois to pass an ordinance forbidding this practice.[87] "Wine merchants and brokers are the masters over giving this merchandise an arbitrary value, which destroys the nature of the sale," the town argued, "it wounds the first principles of equity." The issue was reported to the Council of Commerce, which was told that "the seller finds himself obliged to follow blindly the law that it pleases the buyer to impose on him. . . . The richest, the best informed are forced to follow the torrent, convinced by experience that their wines will not be sold if they insist on setting a price."[88] But the brokers obtained a suspension of the ordinance from the intendant, arguing that the practice was common in the major northern wine regions, and the matter was still not settled by the time of Joly de Fleury's inquiry.[89]

Power in the Vines

The brokers' power over price-setting appears to have been equally serious near Beaune. Joly de Fleury's survey does not, regrettably, extend to this region, since it lay outside the jurisdiction of the Parlement of Paris, but the account books of the curé of Volnay referred frequently to the abuses and power of the brokers: "these fellows who, against order, are rather merchants than brokers." Their hold on the market was so complete that they could enforce a benchmark against widespread dissatisfaction. In 1764, "The majority of the bourgeois of Volnay . . . complained greatly over the price set at Beaune," which was then imposed on Volnay. But the brokers could tell "those who make the slightest difficulty, 'if you do not wish to sell your wine at this price you can keep it,' a compliment to no one's taste. . . . The brokers decided to take only the wines already marked and to force the bourgeois to lower the price of their wines." When the Carmelite convent refused the official price, the following year, they were left with a cellar full of wine.[90]

The involvement of brokers in the barrel trade provoked even more outcry in other provinces than it had in Auxerre. In most of the important wine markets the brokers had clearly gained considerable control over barrel making and selling and used it to manipulate the prices of these crucial vessels and to put growers in their debt. The problem was so serious around Beaugency, however, that the coopers of that town sent their own report to Joly de Fleury complaining about the brokers there and around Blois. "Under the promises they make to the inhabitants and vignerons of getting their wines sold," they wrote, "[the brokers] furnish them with barrels . . . to the prejudice of the plaintiffs, at an exorbitant price."[91] Elsewhere in the Loire, the vinegrowers of Vendôme had already been forced, in 1723, to complain to the government about brokers buying up barrels.[92] Around Angers the brokers did not bother to engage in barrel making, but they did lend barrels to the winegrowers, "which gives them credit and thus they have the wines of the poor people at a bargain."[93]

The brokers of Blois had actually been involved in barrel making for over half a century, or at least had been fighting about it for that long. The police had seized barrels from a woman identified as a broker (*courtière*) in 1685 and hauled the broker Guignace into court for the same thing in 1696. This time the brokers of Blois, all eleven "in league against the coopers' guild," intervened in the case, to protect their interests, without success.[94] Half a dozen brokers, who are all identified as major businessmen a decade later, were forbidden to engage in the barrel trade or to join the coopers' guild.[95] The memorandum from Blois in 1739 agreed that the brokers had ruined business for the master coopers, who were "very numerous and very poor" because of the brokers. But the real problem at Blois, as elsewhere, was the economic power this barrel trade gave to brokers. If brokers were kept from the barrel trade "they would no longer have the means to make themselves masters of the wines of the country people to whom they sell the barrels and who are their debtors for considerable sums."

In contrast with the anger over the brokers' economic leverage, the size of the commission they charged bothered few of the local procureurs. The royal prosecutor of Vendôme argued that "the fee [sol pour livre] is too high and must be reduced," although he also noted that "considering that [brokers] are responsible for [the money owed by] their correspondents the fee should be more than ten sous." In Mâcon the vignerons had apparently tried to resist the rising fees, but the brokers "paid themselves out of the [vignerons'] money that they have in their hand and left [the vignerons] to cry."[96]

In general, however, the largest trading centers took a markedly tolerant stance on the question of commissions. Unlike the profits from manipulating markets, the broker's fee was earned, a just recompense for a job that was increasingly recognized for its commercial importance. Not only were the royal prosecutors accustomed to the 5 percent commission, but they found reason to praise it. "The profession of broker is excellent," said the man in Epernay, "[with] considerable, even sudden, fortunes, but . . . it is even advantageous that they be rich." Since the broker was the guarantor of the payment to the vigneron, the "sol pour livre established by usage does not appear to be something needing reform." The royal prosecutor of Blois also supported the increases in commissions paid to the broker. As he noted, the wine trade was "once" handled by merchants, and the brokers were "country people" (gens de la campagne) who only made 7½ sous per tonneaux. But then they had not been "capable of guaranteeing the price of wines in case the merchants went bankrupt," and now "they are responsible for the whole price of what they buy for others, the vineowners only know the broker and do not even know the name of the merchant to whom their wine is addressed." As a consequence, he argued, "it would perhaps not be too much to leave the brokers their sol pour livre."

The report from Orléans spoke up most firmly in favor of the brokers' commission. They charged 2 percent when they did not stand guarantee to the vigneron for the wine merchant and double that when they did, although the report added "the sol pour livre had been introduced so long before and was so common that all went along with it voluntarily." A large fee was justified by the danger of bankruptcies and the advances brokers made for their correspondents. Furthermore, brokers who found advanta-

166   *Power in the Vines*

geous fees would bring considerable business to the province and help the wine owners. In general, the cities that did the most business with brokers defended their fees most resolutely. They invoked the charges borne by brokers and market responses. The sympathy shown to the brokers' charges by notables in the towns at the major nodes of the regional market contrasts strongly with attitudes in towns on the peripheries of this market.[97]

In fact, the report from Orléans, alone among all the responses, offered a defense of practically every aspect of the brokers' behavior. This city, unquestionably the most important center in Paris's principal provisioning crown, examined the brokers' behavior in terms of a different market model, one that resembled the commercial system to be found in major ports of the Atlantic Coast far more than the commerce of the domestic market. Like the petitions from port cities at the beginning of the century, the report from Orléans insisted on "a great difference" between commissionnaires and *courtiers*. Commissionnaires were exempt, Orléans claimed, from many of the rules cited in Joly de Fleury's report. Without denying that the combination of broker and merchant in the same individual was technically an abuse, it was clearly comfortable in seeing the two functions combined. Rather, Orléans asserted that "what is most important to examine and decide is whether in tolerating abuses . . . the public does not gain a greater advantage than if one absolutely reduced négociants to the sole quality of either merchant or of broker." The modern broker found himself receiving orders from merchants that were "never exact and precise enough." He was "accustomed to have or expect many commissions, for which he could only take the precaution of buying in advance and so facilitate the sale of wine and procure a better price." Inevitably he found himself with wine left over that he sold for himself. Above all, "it is certain that commerce must have complete liberty and once one has no profit or reduces it with constraints that are too limited one destroys it."[98]

Orléans also urged a more balanced consideration of "the most serious abuse," that of overcharging for barrels. Only those brokers who "sought to ruin the bourgeois and vignerons" should be blamed. As for the rest, if "vignerons and bourgeois whose resources are meager find themselves obliged to sell their wine to the broker who had advanced them barrels, nevertheless this gives them an advantage in the credit that they have received." The broker offered credit at comparatively generous terms: "If they had bought their barrels instead from a cooper they would find themselves pursued immediately after the harvest either by the cooper or their creditors and so find themselves without resources and forced to sell their

wine at a very low price, or see it consumed in costs." Orléans emphasized other "advantages" to the sellers: "They have the pleasure of seeing
their wine sold promptly, and the broker secures their debt and succors
the vignerons and bourgeois. . . . [T]he goods of the earth are only harvested in order to be sold and everyone runs after buyers and is delighted
to be relieved of the care of maintaining wine; nothing is so costly as an
abundant harvest, and no one should be surprised that we tolerate any
terms that brokers have demanded." For these reasons "all are in unani-
mous agreement that one ought to leave the same liberty to brokers that
they have had in the past."

Rather more lukewarm support appeared in the report from Villefranche, which complained about the local control gained by brokers, who
"with their interest in view work as hard as they can to [persuade] merchants never to appear, by making them believe that their presence would
cost them dearly." The report argued, nevertheless, that "I think that we
can close our eyes to the brokers' practices [of buying for their own ac-
count]." The broker inevitably found himself with his own wine to sell,
whether from his own vines or because a merchant had not taken a shipment, and the broker had to sell it. Furthermore, "if the broker had to
await a commission from his correspondent he would often see himself
frustrated by other brokers from getting the wines he preferred and on
which he counted." In general, this report maintained that "since liberty is
the mother of commerce . . . it seems that we ought not to take too many
precautions to avoid all that can trouble it."[99]

Although a few cities joined the brokers' call for free trade, most
equated deregulation with commercial abuses. Above all they feared the
power that brokers had gained over local markets, their "empire" over the
wine trade. "There is more deference for the broker than for any merchant," according to the account from Angers, "because the broker buys
wine from his friends every year whereas merchants, who only visit rarely,
were not so well known." This gave brokers "an authority in commerce
that one could call despotic and harmful to the négociant and the bourgeois." In the absence of other merchants the broker had come to monopolize contacts with the regional market. "For the last twenty years,"
the correspondent in Epernay wrote, "we have seen practically no merchants, whether Parisians or foreigners, take the trouble to come here
themselves to buy wine." Instead, these merchants "rely almost totally on
brokers for the choice and purchase of their wines," and so "brokers have
become practically the masters of making the choice" of wines. "This lib-

erty to give their favors to those they judge worthy makes the friendship of these people extremely necessary."[100]

As a consequence of the brokers' domination the royal prosecutor of Epernay had found it difficult to persuade any of those involved in the wine trade to cooperate in his inquiry, for "very few of them did not fear that they would be thought to have taken part in the measures" against brokers. The royal prosecutor in Angers had encountered the same concerns, for he noted that those he asked for information "apparently fear that the brokers would leave them behind and not come to their cellars, so that no one would instruct me . . . although one agrees that these abuses occur or can occur, if not in the region of Anjou at least in the provinces of Touraine, Orléanais, Bourgogne, etc." Indeed, the Touraine was troubled by brokers who had established a "tyranny" over wine owners. "A small number of brokers," according to the correspondent in Tours, "keep merchants from coming themselves [to buy wine and] preclude in this way the multiplicity of buyers." It would be preferable, he argued, if "commerce was conducted immediately, and not by commission." Short of that he asked for strict laws, so that "in limiting the liberty of this trade, one can at the same time put limits to the abuse and fraud with which it is filled."[101]

Wine brokers and their defenders argued persuasively that they were victims of an anachronistic situation, caught between local customary codes that had preserved sixteenth-century practices and an eighteenth-century market system that reflected the complexities of international capitalism. Liberty, for them, meant the abolition of antiquated regulations. Yet, they were criticized for more than merely trespassing a few old rules. Nor were public authorities in Paris and the provinces merely fighting to defend the dead letter of the law. They joined witnesses from every social rank to condemn the brokers' economic power and their control of the market just as much as their illegal practices. Their rejection of economic power and "empire" expressed a larger vision of the market, an ideal of the transparent market in which all competed without advantages. Intermediaries in this ideal market were to be the most transparent of all, facilitating exchange and competition in the public interest. Little wonder that the authorities looked to regulations to accomplish this goal.

The Aftermath

It cannot be said, however, that the state was particularly successful in its effort to limit the innovations practiced by wine brokers. The government continued its efforts to halt abuses, but apparently abuses continued. Evidence from a variety of locations confirms the basic point that brokers gained increasing power throughout the wine trade. Officials and private citizens in Languedoc in the middle of the century objected to the brokers' growing power, particularly to keep prices they paid to growers as low as possible. Where the inhabitants of one town used to assemble to find a "common and reasonable price; . . . today [1752] we depend supremely on the price offered by the brokers."[102] The Cour des Aides followed the case in Auxerre with an arrêt enjoining wine brokers to keep account books, but Joly de Fleury's son had to aim another arrêt de Parlement against brokers falsifying their registers in 1747.[103] The Cour des Aides and the Conseil d'état filled the 1740s with injunctions against wine merchants and brokers combining each others' roles.[104] Attempts at regulation made little impact, and brokers acted increasingly like merchants and gained greater control of the regional and long-distance trade.

Brokers refused to give up their use of barrels to exert control over growers and continued to participate in the barrel trade. The brokers of Mâcon appealed to the intendant in 1753 for the right to break the coopers' monopoly over barrel making, though without much success.[105] The long-running dispute between coopers and brokers in Blois over brokers selling barrels reveals how important the issues were. In 1751 the master coopers brought suit against their rivals, at least two of whom were grandsons of brokers condemned in the 1680s for similar abuses.[106] This time the coopers were complaining about brokers who had joined the coopers' guild and combined both activities. These "audacious adversaries" had "devoured" the livelihood of sixty coopers with shops in Blois and more than five hundred journeymen in the surrounding countryside. The coopers wished to forbid all brokers from making or selling barrels and to force brokers in their guild to choose one or the other profession. In this way, coopers could "regain the honest mediocrity that is the share of the licit and laboring arts." The essence of their argument was simple: A broker never had been allowed to traffic in what he brokered; brokerage in wine was also, necessarily, brokerage in the barrels the wine came in, hence wine brokers were not allowed to traffic in barrels.

The police of Blois agreed, but the brokers, including several who were not coopers, appealed to the Parlement. The coopers' statutes allowed anyone to buy and sell barrels, the brokers pointed out; there was "no incompatibility between the state of brokers and coopers," and coopers could become brokers if they wanted to. Furthermore, the public interest was well served by the brokers, for the coopers, "who are poor for the most part, will not suffice to provide the province with barrels in the abundant years." They also produced certificates from Tours and Orléans and from the lieutenant general of the bailliage to the effect that "brokers are used to trading in barrels and this liberty is of great utility and advantage to the public." Most interestingly, however, the brokers challenged the premise of the coopers' argument. No law, they insisted, forbade them from trading in wine; they were prohibited only from "being the merchant for the same shipment for which they had been broker [*courtier*] and had received a salary."[107] Clearly brokers had never accepted the legal limits to their profession.

The coopers seized on this last of the brokers' arguments with bitter sarcasm: "Let us grant that [the broker] will warn his correspondent that he owns the merchandise [that he is sending to the merchant] . . . the hypothesis presents a truly sincere mortal; but this mortal will certainly prefer to send his own wine rather than go elsewhere to buy better wine for less." In other words, the broker who trafficked would always place his interests before those of his correspondent. This abuse had become a "common disorder in the large wine regions where there are many *court-iers*; . . . the commissionnaires of all large towns work together to profit over the buyers and sellers." They concluded that "the only people in the kingdom who do not accept the prohibition against trading and brokering in the same commodity are the brokers; and perhaps only the brokers of Blois have yet had the sincerity to admit it and the security to pretend it is legal." Unfortunately for the coopers, the town council of Blois voted to uphold the brokers.[108]

The coopers had complained about several individual brokers, including Cousin who was "judge of the grenier à sel, *courtier,* and cooper, without ever in his life having constructed a barrel or a [judicial] sentence," and Coullange who was "master [cooper], it is true, but without ever having tried the least piece of work in the profession; the arts and crafts do not need honorary masters."[109] In fact, the records of a partnership formed by Joseph Coullange, "négociant" of Blois, ancien échevin and conseiller de l'hôtel de ville, and his son in 1747 show the construction and trade in barrels to have been quite important to his business.[110] The partnership was "for the commerce of wine, brandy, barrels, and other articles" and began with an inventory that included over six hundred empty barrels and the wood to make as many more. The assets also consisted of money that a dozen Parisian wine merchants owed the father, who had been buying wine on commission for Parisians since the 1720s.[111]

The Coullanges mixed commission and speculation, agreeing that either partner could sell wine to the partnership, individually and for his own profit, but that the "profits from commissions that would arise" from this wine would be "common to both of them." They would also pay for all voyages and any factors the partners might employ and "for expenses of merchants who will come." [112] Like brokers elsewhere, they offered hospitality to visiting merchants and charged commissions on the wine they bought. Their records retain traces of their speculative buying; there were still a few barrels that had been purchased but "remained to be placed" at the end of the partnership. The vast majority, however, of the some eleven hundred barrels of wine, bought for nearly forty thousand livres in the last two months of 1749, was already "placed" with Parisian wine merchants by late December, even when the wine had not yet been picked up from the vigneron. If the buying was originally speculative, it was quickly covered by merchants' orders.

The tax farm's report on the wine brokers of Blois, twenty-five years later, had a familiar reproach to make: "The vignerons who have become the brokers' debtors over the course of the year, by provisioning themselves with barrels in which the brokers all engage in wholesale trade, find themselves forced to give them their wines at a very low price as soon as the harvest is finished." The brokers' control of barrels allowed them to "profit from the discomfort of the vignerons." Brokers were still being accused of trading in wine for their own account: "Everyone knows that they deliver their wines at a higher price than they bought them; they always gain considerably on these sorts of deals." [113] And the coopers' guild was still suing wine brokers in the 1780s for "having made a great quantity of barrels and selling them for three times their worth." [114]

The most common complaint against brokers continued to be their manipulation of wine prices. In a bitter footnote to his accounts of 1754, Malavois de la Ganne of Ay had especially harsh criticism for the "merchants of Reims," referring to the brokers who had maintained an important position in the markets along the Marne. They had bought up quantities of wine from 1752, he noted, but the wine had gone bad. "In the desire to correct its bad quality, they cut it with good wine from 1753, principally red, whose quality was excellent." Probably this kind of mixing was common; Malavois tried it on several occasions, but he pointedly condemned their decision as a "discordant marriage, which only gave them . . . very mediocre wine." Faced with such a drug on the market, the brokers "decided to write to all of their correspondents that the wine of 1754 was worthless, with the intention of getting rid of the preceding [year's] wine, and this was enough to mislead all the merchants against the excellence of this year's wine, which they had not yet bought." He sold nothing that year until the spring and received little help from Reims. In what looks suspiciously like collusion among brokers on an interregional scale, the brokers of Beaune were accused of using the same ploy that year.[115]

An indictment of the wine brokers written by a lawyer in the Beaujolais in 1769 suggests that viticultural communities had not conceded the basic principles upon which they had stood thirty years before. Brac charged that the brokers of Mâcon "form a single exclusive partnership, destroying all competition; they have become the sole masters of prices." He based his critique on traditional principles of equity and transparency in the market: "All police regulations have the object of favoring direct contacts between the one who has harvested and the consumer." In the past, when the merchants of Paris visited the province "in a large gathering at the same time [which] formed an advantageous competition, wine sold nearly at its [proper] price." But the brokers persuaded the merchants not to visit: "To succeed more surely, they break all communication between producer and consumer . . . these are the wasps of society." By obscuring the transparency of the market, they had found "the secret of getting the wines at the price they wished." Like the wholesale merchant, they "buy only to monopolize produce, to make themselves masters and then resell it . . . at the highest price possible," Brac asserted. When suspicious Parisians inquired of the wine producers about the original price, the producers were "forced by the empire that the brokers had gained in the Province . . . to make no response, for fear that, by the understanding that began to prevail among brokers, they would be left with their crops."[116]

The principal harm done to growers, according to Brac, lay in the brokers' efforts to lower the price that they gave for wine:

> In effect, to be able to pass the shipments [of wine] to the merchant at a price that he is willing to pay, and will not complain about, the broker uses every means to reduce the price of the wine . . . to make lots of shipments, it is necessary to attract the merchant with excessively low prices; for it is certain that the lower the price, the more the buyer buys and the more shipments the broker makes; to have the wine below its value, there are no ruses that brokers have not practiced and the proprietors have only been too easy to take in.[117]

It is only fair to note that Brac was scapegoating brokers for passing cost-cutting pressures along to the wine producers. Brokers could do little to keep prices up if the merchants were unwilling to buy, but Brac clearly expected them to try. However, brokers were also driving prices down, according to Brac, because they were buying and selling for their own account: "They have bought [wine] without commission . . . and when the commissions arrive, they have placed the wine that they bought for their own account, and at very different prices than what they bought it at." Brac was appalled by the brazenness of this behavior. "The brokers believe that they are permitted to buy and resell for their own account with such good faith that they do not hide it and call these operations speculations; but if they had some notion of the first rules of commerce they would know that these pretended speculations . . . are real crimes."

Brac objected most fundamentally to the brokers' betrayal of the province's interests. In the good old days, which he identified in the first half of the century, the "broker did not regard himself entirely as the merchant's man; the interest of the Province, especially that of the cultivator was dear to him."[118] Here he echoed the sentiments of the curé of Volnay, who bitterly condemned the selfishness and lack of local patriotism of these "brokers, who look only to enrich themselves by impoverishing the bourgeois." Delachère blamed the bad prices of 1772 on the "bourgeois of Volnay who sell their wines to brokers [who are] more friends and confederates of the merchants than the bourgeois."[119] The curé had developed a good relationship with one broker, Antoine of Nuits, and could write with real regret of the broker of Beaune, Gombaut, on his death, "We will not find his like again, to support the interests of the bourgeois and to make the merchants and sellers listen to reason." But at the same time he condemned the majority of brokers for their lack of devotion to the interests of the local community. "What a misfortune for this land," he lamented, "to have business with these sorts of people who, like public plagues, ravage a region in a moment and who, to the prejudice of honesty, often dupe bourgeois and merchants. It is not surprising to see them become rich all of a sudden. Commerce makes them rich when good faith is excluded."[120]

As brokers turned into commission agents, and then into négociants, they resorted increasingly to these maneuvers, talking prices up or down in order to acquire wine or get rid of unsold stock. The level of prices became increasingly important to the brokers' business as they turned gradually to speculative buying. But they did not make the transfer cleanly, as the government wished, choosing to be either merchants or brokers. Rather, they combined both operations more and more openly. A broker from the Beaujolais in the 1760s combined wines bought on commission with wholesale operations right at the Parisian wine market. The majority of his wine had been ordered by big Parisian wine merchants, but he brought some to sell on the spot, much as any wine merchant would.[121] Similarly, a report written about the brokers of Reims in 1759 asked, "Can we see . . . persons of every estate, merchants, councillors of the city and others mixing brokerage [courtage] conjointly with commerce in wine . . . [and] demanding the sol pour livre . . . without worrying whether the [wine] sellers suffer?" Only in 1766 did the brokers of Reims constitute themselves the "corps des marchands de vins" and stop using the title commissionnaire.[122]

It must be understood that the nature of the market discouraged brokers from abandoning their former profession for a new one. The risks of speculation in a perishable commodity like wine, made vastly more dangerous by the expenses of transportation and taxes, gave considerable advantage to the commission system, where a buyer was assured. Hence brokers attempted to mix the two systems in various ways, either fraudulently by raising prices on wines they had bought on commission or merely illegally by conducting speculative and commissioned buying simultaneously.

Compared to the century-long debate over the police of the grain trade, the brokerage scandals of the eighteenth century were hardly earthshaking. Bread riots brought down ministries, and royal experiments with provisioning policies substantially weakened the paternalist image enjoyed by Old Regime monarchy. In contrast, the wine scandals appear to have agitated winegrowers and public prosecutors only intermittently. They expressed their animosity toward brokers but probably learned to deal with them on new terms and carried on. The government tried to reinforce the old police of the wine trade through the 1740s, but without much rigor, and gradually let the issue die out. We may speculate, nevertheless, that the wine scandal made waves beyond the relatively small pond of the winegrowers' interests. For here, in the behavior of a limited number of wine brokers, the agencies responsible for policing the economy found confirmation of their deepest suspicions. Middlemen had clearly attempted to achieve monopolistic power over the wine trade and had nearly succeeded. They had broken the rules to set prices at the levels they wished, to dominate the producers, and to corner the market. If the consequences for the country of a pact of wine brokers were less important than the pacte de famine, the wine brokers reinforced the suspicion that a trade left unpoliced was vulnerable to greed and abuses. Many of the same institutions that protested against the wine brokers in the 1730s would later, with Joly de Fleury's son at their head, denounce the engrossers and monopolists in the 1760s. The physiocrats dismissed their fears as imagined, and historians have found little evidence either, but it is not too much to wonder whether the wine scandal had not left a bad impression that lingered for decades.[123]

Despite pressure from winegrowers and sellers, and from merchants and lawyers, the police of the wine trade never became the juggernaut of regulation that controlled the grain trade. The state fulminated periodically against brokers but accomplished little more than the slowing of their gradual transformation of the wine business and their role in it. The state's ultimate failure to halt brokers is evidence, perhaps, of the limits to any policing that was not spurred by the political imperatives of collective urban violence. A more certain impediment was surely identified by the judge of the case in Auxerre: Serious sanctions against brokers threatened to disrupt the wine trade and thus the crucial revenues that the state derived from the wine trade. But just as important is the evidence that the state made the effort to regulate, and tried for reasons that have little to do with fiscality or urban consumers. The state intervened to defend the principles of equity and transparency in the market. The police of the wine trade reminds us of a larger agenda that encompassed the regulation of both the wine and the grain trade, a conception of the public good that spanned the Middle Ages and the Revolution.

6

Toward a Transparent Market

There was much discontent with the changes occurring in the provincial wine trade, voiced at many levels of provincial society and administration. But if we shift our sights from the provinces to Paris, it is not hard to find evidence of the brokers' positive contributions to the wine trade. Wine brokers had contributed to a growing sophistication of the provincial wine trade, organizing provincial markets more efficiently, offering financial resources to Parisian merchants and provincial growers, and allowing smoother communications between the capital and its catchment. As early as the Middle Ages wine merchants had found minor officials willing to offer their knowledge about the location, quality, and grades of local wine. *Courtiers* had answered the Parisians' need for information and security, lowering transaction costs and making distant provinces more transparent to visitors. Then in the late seventeenth century Parisians had called upon *courtiers* for far more serious help, asking for massive financial assistance to arrange credit, either on their own, or—through their own security— from the sellers. They had asked *courtiers* to represent them as commission brokers and relieve them of the need to travel to each source of wine. The result was a transformation, not only of the provincial wine trade, but of the Parisian market system.

Wine brokers opened viticultural economies to a more efficient relationship to the outside world, facilitating the penetration of long-distance trade and helping to create a national market. The Parisian market grew, as a consequence, probably by volume, and certainly in the size of the provisioning crown.[1] By the end of the Old Regime the Parisian crown embraced much of the kingdom and drew heavily on regions that had been remote and, in some cases, barely existed a century earlier. Brokers made it possible for wine merchants of even fairly modest means to acquire wine from the provinces that produced it. They were given credit for as much as a year and access to more choices than any one individual could have managed on his own.

Furthermore, other Parisian institutions emerged in the second half of the century that contributed to the growing transparency of the market in ways that both reinforced the brokers' central role and undermined some of the sources of their power. New publications disseminating information about the wine trade emphasized the brokers' position as chief conduit between consumer and producer. But the spread of information about the wine trade reduced the brokers' control over such information and inhibited their ability to achieve speculative profits from their knowledge. The elaboration of brokerage at the Parisian Halle aux vins further contributed to the openness of the market and encouraged independent initiatives to speculative trading on the part of provincial growers and traders. Provincial brokers, acting as négociants, participated as well but now competed in a jostling world of many speculators. There was less room for them to exploit the "secret of the buyer and seller" in the evolving wine trade.

Revolutions in the Wine Trade

The medieval wine trade in Paris had been an "open" market, subjected to many of the same rules that regulated the grain trade, but it shed most of them during the eighteenth century. The city had long supervised all wine sold in Paris, as a trade "involving public order," and channeled it to several "public places," in order to "facilitate the provisioning, not only of the bourgeois of Paris but also of tavern keepers and others selling wines at tables, who were forbidden to seek provisions in the provinces."[2] Wholesale merchants supplying the city were obliged to sell their wines at these public places, which included the Port Saint-Paul and the Place de Grève by the fifteenth century, and to which several other ports were added by the seventeenth century. Regulations ordered all merchants who brought wine to Paris to make at least one-third of it available for wholesale in the Staple, at the Place de Grève, or on their boats at the ports in order to provide bourgeois and tavern keepers alike with a steady supply of wine

Toward a Transparent Market

and prevent large wholesale merchants from controlling the wine trade. The Staple was regulated like any public market: No deals could be made before the official opening of the market, prices could not be raised once the market opened, the quality of the wine could not be lessened by mixing.[3] The prévôt des marchands of Paris was still trying to force the wine merchants to bring a third of their wine to the Staple as late as 1722.[4]

The Parisian wine trade became so much more efficient at getting wine to the city during the eighteenth century that wine merchants of Paris called for the end to regulations. By the middle of the century, the wine merchants' guild announced that "the various revolutions that have occurred in the [wine] trade have led to the abandonment of the old rules [of the market], now become useless and even impractical." In a petition addressed to the government shortly after 1756 they described some of these changes: "It is common knowledge that hardly any *bon bourgeois* is accustomed to provision himself at the Staple or the Halle. The wines brought there are usually tired and of little quality. It is infinitely easier today for him to get his provisions directly from the provinces."[5] Thus, there was no point in demanding that wine merchants leave a third of their shipments at the Staple, they argued, since everyone who wanted wine in Paris could now arrange for their own provisions, presumably through provincial brokers. Few wine merchants bothered to send anything to the Staple and most now sold everything wholesale from their own shops since they were dealing in better wines than the kind that went to the Halle: "Luxury and delicacy have introduced the more frequent use of certain wines that cannot support the fatigue [of being left out] at the Halle and Staple." The wine merchants insisted that "they do not fear admitting publicly that the old rules are no longer executed." Instead, private enterprise was meeting the city's needs and keeping its markets supplied. The wine merchants pointed to the "increasing flood" of provincial traders bringing wine to the Halle: "It is common knowledge that the Staple and the Halle are always sufficiently provisioned, both by provincial traders and by a certain number of Parisian merchants who continue this trade." In any case, they explained, Parisian wine merchants now brought an average of 250,000 muids a year to the city, and "it is evident that these two places could not hold a tenth part" of all that wine.[6]

The guild's remarks on the wine trade were clearly self-serving. Wine merchants were resisting an effort to force them to send their wines to the Staple as they once had been obliged. They insisted that they had long since gained the "public right" to trade privately. But they justified these changes by pointing to the greater ease of provisioning the capital, emphasizing the greatly improved links between Paris and the provinces: "The construction of new routes and canals communicating with rivers has made it easier to bring wine from provinces farther away."[7] The capital was in such close contact with the provinces, both because of improvements in transportation and communication, and the sophistication of brokering, that the old system whereby wine merchants were forced to bring wines to the Staple at Paris disappeared.

Figures for the amount of wine brought to the Halle at the beginning of the century, discussed in chapter 4, portray a still marginal market and only a few merchants supplying it.[8] The creation of a *caisse de crédit*—a fund to help marchands forains finance their shipments to the Halle—in the 1720s probably encouraged more traders to bring wine. As an official argued in 1739, "A merchant who does not send [wine] to Paris because he is unable to advance the entrance tax and pay shipping will freely send his wines when he is assured of finding the funds."[9] By the second half of the century the guild of wine merchants expressed contempt for the wine brought by outsiders to the Halle, but portrayed it nevertheless as a flourishing market. There is no direct evidence for this commerce until near the end of the Old Regime, at which point it is clear that the Halle had contributed greatly to integrating the provincial winegrowers and traders into the commercial system of Paris. The correspondence and account books of a broker at the Halle in the 1770s and 1780s suddenly plunge us into the midst of a feverishly speculative wine trade with the capital. A range of growers and provincial traders and négociants were actively engaged in supplying an important market with their own and other people's wines.

Since at least the early 1770s, a M. Moreau, variously described in correspondence as a commissionnaire, marchand commissionnaire, and *courtier-commissionnaire,* operated as one of a number of brokers at the Halle aux vins.[10] His most important duty lay in receiving and selling wine sent to the Halle from the provinces, but he served much as the provincial broker to disseminate information about the Parisian market back to merchants in the provinces. Like provincial brokers he contributed greatly to the transparency of the market. By making the Halle so much easier to deal with, he helped to create an effective rival to the commercial system dominated by Parisian wine merchants and their provincial brokers.

Moreau assisted anyone who wished to sell wines speculatively at the Halle. His clients included a small number of men who were major négociants and brokers of Orléans and sent him large shipments throughout the year.[11] The account books of marchands forains of Burgundy show them also sending some of their wine to brokers at the Halle.[12] But Moreau

Toward a Transparent Market

helped many who were not provincial wine merchants to enter the Parisian market as well. Other clients included the royal notaries of Jargeau and Beaugency, who had extensive vines, and other vignerons with their own wines to sell. One large producer of Blois, with vines in Sologne, boasted that he "could send you at least 800 barrels without [acquiring it] from anyone other than my children, brothers, and nephews."[13] Most of the clients lived in Orléans, a few in Blois, Saumur, and Saint-Dyé, though he handled a little wine from Juliénas, in the Beaujolais, and from Chichée, near Chablis. Clients looked to Moreau to sell their wine "as promptly and advantageously as possible" and to arrange payment, by bills of exchange. Through his assistance, the Halle became more readily accessible to those who wished to risk a shipment of wine in the Parisian market.

With an agent at the Halle, a whole new range of entrepreneurs could speculate with shipments of wine. A wood merchant wrote Moreau in 1773 to ask him to become "my broker at the Halle" and to begin sending him the prices of red and white wine, old and new. This regular news was a crucial service, but so was Moreau's ability to sell the wine. By the next spring he was getting a disgruntled letter from the wood merchant for his failure to sell the man's fourteen barrels quickly enough: "I have never heard of such a thing happening. . . . I have even more trouble understanding it since this week I sold twenty-three barrels to a broker in Blois." Moreau got rid of the wine quickly after that, and the merchant's letter two months later offered to send another two dozen barrels depending on the "sensation that the bad weather is creating" at the Halle. His letters at other times asked, "How much can one sell a barrel [of wine of Sologne] for these wines cost us sixty livres; . . . if I can make a profit I will send you a dozen carts of wine."[14]

Moreau's clients also included very small-scale producers, like the vignerons and coopers of les Ricey who each sent anything from one to ten muids of wine, "to be sold at the Halle by Moreau, at whatever price and to whatever person he judges appropriate." Their letters stipulated that he should "pay and advance the costs of carting and other taxes that the wine will be charged with, the said advances being deducted from the price of the wine [when it is] sold."[15] Moreau was offering important financial assistance: He advanced the money to pay the boatmen for most of the wine he handled, amounting to some seventy thousand livres in 1780, plus the entrance tax of some 350,000 livres, plus *"remplissage"* and maintenance work by coopers. To offset these enormous loans, Moreau had the use of the money from the wine he sold, until his clients withdrew it from him, usually through a bill of exchange written against him. He also charged a brokerage fee of two livres per barrel, amounting to some 2 percent of its sale price. In addition to finding them buyers, Moreau supplied small producers with the money needed to get their wine to Paris, a sum that otherwise would have prohibited many of them gaining access to this market.

Like other brokers, Moreau was a financier as much as a merchant. His correspondence is full of negotiations about the complicated financial arrangements between capital and provinces. A royal official of Orléans handled much of the financial arrangements between Moreau in Paris and his correspondents in Orléans. Moreau let his accounts with Grammont fall behind at times; he owed more than eight thousand livres in September, before the new wine came in. At all times he was strapped for cash: "You cannot believe how hard it has been to find cash in the last two to three weeks. . . . All the merchants receive wine and so need their funds rather than wine, which means that sales are going badly."[16]

Unfortunately we have Moreau's records only for the early 1780s, when the wine market was suffering a slump in prices and demand. Still, his accounts for 1780 show him selling over seven thousand barrels (15,750 hectoliters), worth over six hundred thousand livres, that had been sent to him by dozens of individuals, most of them in the region from Blois to Orléans. He was clearly receiving only part of what came to the Halle and must have been one among a number of brokers at the Halle operating in similar ways. This wine was, in turn, sold to hundreds of carefully recorded individuals, rarely in quantities larger than half a dozen barrels at a time. Unlike the city's principal ports, where wine merchants received shipments they had ordered in the provinces, most wine arrived at the Halle speculatively, looking for buyers. And in contrast to the ports, where we shall see that large merchants were increasingly dominant, there is little evidence for large buyers figuring prominently at the Halle. Aside from the wholesale merchant Chagot, who bought over two hundred barrels, and a few others like him, the visitors to the Halle bought little overall. Rather it seems to have been the repair of small-scale retailers and consumers who purchased in small amounts.[17]

The Halle was still a place where growers could bring their own wine to sell on their own. "Many vignerons have been coming these days," Moreau wrote at the end of summer in 1782. "They have sold promptly, though at eighty-seven to eighty-eight livres [per barrel, rather than the low nineties]," for they could not afford to hold out for higher prices. Unfortunately, these vignerons "give up their wines at a low price, which hurts the [marchand] forain." He usually expressed scorn for the quality of their wine—"those that the vignerons bring are not good"—though

Toward a Transparent Market

he conceded that "those of Ingres have sold [their wine] briskly enough." Again in late September, "many vignerons have come these days, but most have wine that has been badly cared for and not cellared, which always harms the market since they sell it cheaply and some even abandon it at eighty-five livres."[18] By early October these vignerons were selling for even less, as "the time presses them to leave and [return to] harvest." By mid-October they had all left. Moreau competed only indirectly with the mass of unnamed "vignerons" who brought their wine to the Halle on their own. He competed more directly with other brokers at the Halle, writing to one client "I am angry that you sent your wines to [Mme. le Sage], I could have sold them as easily as she and would have received more value for them." To another he complained that le Sage sold her wine on credit, getting no cash "not even paper [bills of exchange]." He spoke up bluntly for his own interests, and, indeed, one of his correspondents ventured to say that "I would have sent five or six carts of wine to another broker if I had not feared to distress you."[19]

Moreau and the other brokers at the Halle represent a crucial evolution away from the Halle as it functioned a century earlier. Provincial-based marchands forains had originally been the principal users of the Halle, in the late seventeenth century. They appear to have brought more than their own wines to Paris, though they were usually described as small-scale merchants. They probably had to stay at the Halle for extended periods, to sell their wine, but they did not base themselves in Paris and returned sooner rather than later to the provinces. These were undoubtedly some of the small merchants whose complaints about financing the transportation and taxes on wine going to Paris had led to the creation of a caisse de crédit to help them out in the 1720s. These minor traders continued to bring wine to the Halle, but the emergence of brokers like Moreau effected a fundamental change in the provinces' access to the Parisian markets. It was now possible to have detailed and almost immediate information about the state of the market, to have someone to maintain the wines in the Halle, and to find merchants to buy the wine, all without leaving the provinces.

With an eye on wines coming to Paris from everywhere, and correspondents around the country, Moreau was a privileged clearinghouse of information about the market. "Sales are going badly," he wrote in late September 1780 to one correspondent. "We will surely sell more next month when it is learned that the new wine is not good, as we have seen by the wine we have received so far and by what we have learned from other regions, that the grapes are green and rotten, and around Paris they want to sell their wine very expensively, and the Parisian merchants who counted [on buying the wines around Paris cheaply] to sell it at eight sous [per pinte in taverns] are mistaken."[20]

In return, Moreau received long chatty letters on a weekly basis from a variety of clients, describing the weather, the condition of the vines, the quality of the wine, their speculations on the market. They passed along gossip about their neighbors and news they had picked up from merchants traveling through. "I had an occasion to enter a cellar and taste the wine," wrote one. "I did not find one barrel that was healthy. Thus I resemble [doubting] Saint Thomas. One thing is certain, the white wines of the côtes de la Loire are green."[21] At the same time, Moreau was beset by constant letters asking for information. "I ask you to write me immediately the prices of old and new wine and particularly the price of vignerons of Chaigny since I have sent some carts of wine from them and I told them I would pay them what the wine sold for in Paris and want to know if they [the carters] will tell me the truth when they come back."[22]

Moreau's correspondence depicts a business man similar in many ways to the brokers in the provinces. Like any broker he worked at the behest of clients, though at times his clients sound like they are working for him. Shipping invoices from provincial merchants that began "Following your orders, I am sending you" a shipment of wine suggest that Moreau was initiating the shipment.[23] Indeed, his letters to producers sometimes demanded that they send him wine to sell. "I am astonished that you have sent no wine for two weeks," he wrote a client. "We must sell in order to make money, for which we have need especially at the end of the month."[24] There is almost no evidence that he bought or sold for his own account. On a single occasion he referred to wine in the provinces that he had bought with a provincial merchant; otherwise he dealt only with what provincials sent to him or what Parisian merchants asked to have sent.[25] At the same time, the tenor of his letters show him to have been anything but a pliant middleman. There are many instances of his advice and even criticism directed at clients who needed encouragement or correction.

Moreau's letters were far from those of a passive agent; he had to take the pulse of the market and directed his correspondents accordingly. "In general white wine will have greater demand than red given their strong color," he notes at one point, "and besides many more merchants, even of Paris, have made black [*noir*, actually dark red] wine." After asking for a shipment of red, he added, "As you know it is necessary to have merchandise with which one can make money; that ought to be the principal goal that should guide us." His letters were full of basic (and fairly obvious) advice about the market: "I still have seven barrels of your wine to sell, not because of neglect but because it is impossible to force merchants to buy what they don't want . . . judge how much we will be left with if the new wine is good [this in late August], the old will be absolutely neglected." Moreau also chastised his correspondents for failures of judgment and lack of enterprise: "It is truly maladroit on your part not to have sent some red wine before the price of transportation went up. . . . I am angry not to have two or three carts of red wine from Orléans."[26]

More often Moreau wrote encouragingly to his correspondents, urging them to send him wine. Even when he admitted that sales were slow, he suggested a wine that might spark interest—a really good wine from Sologne, for example, or one from Blois with a strong red color. "I will give you some advice," said one letter, "a cart of black wine would be good. . . . [Y]ou would also do well to send some new white wine, but it has to arrive early or you will find [it] in abundance." Clearly Moreau needed the business to make his commission and to generate cash, but he had to worry about selling the wine once he received it, so he could not be foolishly optimistic. He mentioned to one client that the guards of the Halle came through periodically and rounded up all the "bad wine" by tasting and then seizing it, to make vinegar of it. His references to specific requests from individual wine merchants in Paris mean that only some of the wine brought to the Halle was speculative; it is not clear how much. Moreau's clients, with hundreds of barrels and thousands of livres at stake, tended to express their anxieties about their speculation quite frankly in their correspondence. They demanded rapid turnover and railed against Moreau if he failed to sell their wine: "I am astonished that you are not selling my wine when I am told that sales are very good at the Halle."

Certainly his clients engaged in highly speculative behavior, facing increasing risks through the summer and early fall as they bought old wine whose value fluctuated with the level of people's fears for the new harvest. "You say you are going to hang on to the [wines of] Bourgeuil until a later season, but be careful," he warned a négociant of Orléans. "There is a lot of old wine and with the new wine being cheap there cannot be such a big difference in the price of old wine to make much profit." "I am persuaded," he added, "that when the wine arrives from high and low, [prices] will really fall."[27] As a client from Orléans wrote him in the spring, "You warn me that the fine weather has dissuaded merchants from buying in the hope of a diminution, which you say is already being felt, still the good [wines of] Anjou are holding up. It is a bit chilly, which led me to buy some in the hope that you can sell them, and having found a good deal on a carter I arranged to send you twenty-one barrels of good anjou. . . . I ask you to look out for my interests [for] these wines are good and I think you can sell them for 133 to 135 livres, so I ask you to act as if for yourself and leave you the master." The letter added, "When you expect to be able to sell good red [wines of] Chinon at 138 to 140 livres please let me know."[28]

The late summer became increasingly tense, as the new vintage approached. Unfortunately the weather in the fall of 1780 was good, "which raises everyone's hopes for the quality of the wine, so the merchants are only buying [old wine] when they have great need." Moreau commented gleefully on the bad weather leading up to the vintage of 1782: "Here is some weather that gives us a little hope; the old wine will be able to be sold and I am persuaded that [their prices] will rise. . . . This weather should please anyone with a lot of [old] wine; I think it will be impossible to harvest before October." By early October there was news of frosts, which had "caused some sales of [old] wine here. . . . I suspect that when the news of the frosts gets about, if it occurred in other regions, it will cause a sensation."[29]

Dealing as he was with so much "old" wine, Moreau dispensed much advice about the care and maintenance of the wine itself, for most wine did not remain good for as much as a whole year. More generally Moreau provided expert advice about the tastes of the Parisian market and was clearly involved in doctoring the wines to improve their appeal. "The way to pass off your hot [strong] wines at the Halle," he informed one client, "will be to send a barrel of new black wine with lots of brandy [in it] and mix that with the wines." The letters could be brutally frank about the quality of the wine Moreau received: "The auvernats you sent me are not pleasing. You cannot say they are natural; one tastes the brandy on the mouth." "You have absolutely denatured your [wine of] Bourgeuil both of color and taste," he complained, "and the brandy or hot wine you mixed with it is unpleasant." To another he warned, "Your [wines of] Vouvray no longer seem like anything next to those of M. Ladureau." Of course he had to be aware of what his own buyers thought of the wine and did not wish to be burdened with wines he could not sell. "M. Pinel, to whom you sent six barrels of red wine, brought me some to taste," he informed a client, "and I found it falsely colored, dry, green, and little vinous. He complained bitterly to me."

Much of this correspondence addressed the problems of maintaining the wine, for the speculator who sent wine to the Halle had to accept the need to wait for buyers, and wine was a tricky commodity to store. Hence he had ready advice about the way to "improve" the quality of the wine

Toward a Transparent Market

he received and offered to mix new wine with old to revive barrels still in his inventory. "Send as much of the fresh wine as you can," he wrote in September, "so we can refresh the others [old wine] with the new." His customers were frequently speculating on old wines, whose value could suddenly rise if the new vintage failed, but which took extra maintenance. "It will be necessary to buy some [new wine] with a cleaner taste," he advised a client, "and cut your old anjou [wines] with it in order to get rid of them." And there was always the problem of color: "The auvernats, with a little vin noir to keep up their color, always sell." [30]

The art of mixing wines was delicate for many reasons. The police criticized wine merchants for their use of chemical additives that threatened the health of their customers, but even mixing different wines was considered underhanded.[31] Yet Moreau passed along requests—from a wine merchant—for "seven barrels of good vin noir nourished with about 20 pintes of brandy."[32] "Your wine was and still is good," he assured one client, "but I would have preferred it to be more vinous; a little more brandy would have done it much good." Moreau clearly had no problem with such mixtures, though he urged restraint. "I had asked for some barrels of vouvray and . . . since this article is in [good] reputation I beg of you to try to send some by the first shipment but of the first quality in order to accustom the merchants to finding them good, after that you can put in a little white wine of the region."[33] Moreau's services as broker included his skill at making the wine taste right for the market. "I know that you are very capable," he wrote soothingly to one correspondent, "but you should believe that we have some knowledge and must adjust to the taste of the merchant, which is, as you know, capricious."

By facilitating the all-important task of finding buyers, the brokers at the Halle made it increasingly possible for provincials to enter the market as long-distance traders, a function once largely monopolized by the Parisians. In a variety of other ways, Moreau made the Parisian market accessible to provincials, who probably did not know much about Parisian tastes and needed information about the current state of the wine trade. He offered them financing, advice, price quotes, and salesmanship. His services went to a fairly traditional geography of wine producers, principally the regions of the upper Loire that had long maintained close ties to the Parisian market. But he assisted provincial growers in dealing directly with this market and dispensing with provincial brokers or merchants. The growing wine trade to the Halle represents an important evolution in the nature of Old Regime commerce: From a market dominated by Parisian wine merchants and the provincial brokers who worked for them, the wine trade was gradually becoming a speculative market operated increasingly by provincial growers and négociants.

A Growing Public Sphere

Other innovations were opening the rest of the wine trade to greater participation. The growth of a public press in the second half of the century encouraged greater transparency in the wine trade and made it even easier to dispense with the traditional commercial networks. One of the earliest periodicals, the *Annonces, affiches et avis divers,* first published in 1752 in Paris, devoted itself to a curious amalgam of public announcements, book reviews, social gossip, and classified advertising.[34] Advertisements for houses, farms, seigneuries, and other immovable goods appeared prominently on the front page of each of the weekly editions; they distinguished this new periodical from its older rivals, the *Mercure galant* and the *Journal des Trévoux.* The important place given to economic exchange, amid the traditional references to cultural and social events, nicely expresses the emergence of an independent commercial culture in the eighteenth century, a world of exchange conducted among private individuals. Jürgen Habermas has defined this world as the "public sphere of civil society"— not, perhaps, the happiest phrase, since the withdrawal of the economy from the public sphere of the state into the private world of individual exchange is what makes this such an important process.[35] Still, Habermas has recognized the importance of the emergence of this autonomous sphere to the development of western capitalist societies. The full flourishing of such a sphere required the transparent exchange of a bourse or coffeehouse (in England) that could be found, in embryo, in the *Affiches.* The *Affiches* of Paris became a model for dozens of provincial journals with the same title that appeared later in the century. It is of some interest, then, that this new text should devote some of its pages in its first years to a discussion of the wine trade.

Judging from the kind of information the editors offered about the wine trade, they apparently saw themselves serving both an educational and commercial function. They ran advertisements for individuals with wine to sell, like the barrister of Auxerre with "excellent old wine" or the owner of "considerable vineyards" in Chambertin who advised readers to address themselves directly to him for some "veritable wine of this growth."[36] In addition to advertising, however, the journal offered information of a much more general nature. The issue of 16 October 1752 announced that the harvest of Burgundy's "fine wines" was concluded: "It has been abundant; the connoisseurs think the wine will be excellent. There were not enough cuves to hold all the grapes in the Chalonnais. . . . This great abundance gives hope that the wine will not be expensive. Nearly all the wine of Burgundy has already been spoken for by the brokers of Beaune and its surroundings. We will be sure to inform the Public of the exact prices of different wines as soon as they are set."[37] This was not advertising; it offered no precise information about these brokers. The readers were clearly expected to be able to make their own contacts with brokers or perhaps to buy from merchants in Paris. Rather, the journal was offering precious information about the price of wines, a gesture of transparency though perhaps, too, a threat to the brokers' ability to manipulate prices between the buyers and the sellers.

Several weeks later the journal returned to the subject: "We promised to announce the prices of different wines of Burgundy to the Public . . . which will, we think, be usefully served in being given at the same time some details of different *climats* where the wines grow, most of which are only known under general denominations." There followed a tour of the region and a rating of its different wines, according to how long they could be kept. The "vins de primeur," the lightest wines, to be drunk soonest were those of Beaune, Pommard, and Volnay; sturdier wines came from Dijon, Corton d'Aloxe, Savigny, Monthelie, Auxey, Chassagne, Monjot; those to be kept longest were from Nuits, Premeaux, Vosne, Chambolle, Morey, and all the wines of the Chalonnais; and lastly the white wines of Montrachet, Meursault, Corton blanc, Aloxe, Clos de Citeaux, and Côte de Pouilly.[38] The report continued with a detailed discussion of prices as they had been initially set and noted the ensuing price increases. The prices were generally very high, running around sixty livres for a barrel of Chalonnais, to 150 livres for those around Beaune, and five to six hundred livres for a barrel of Montrachet and Romanée. This was not wine for the populace.

The "Public" addressed by this journal was evidently quite wealthy and interested in acquiring the best wine of Burgundy, but it needed some advice about the intricacies of the region. It had the contacts or wherewithal to make arrangements for this wine without help from the journal, for no details about the "brokers of Beaune" were offered. In late November a report from Auxerre described the wines of lower Burgundy as "excellent this year; the best, from the grande côte, are selling for two hundred livres per barrel. . . . [T]he wines of Chablis, a vignoble with a reputation, four leagues from Auxerre, are selling as much as 150 livres a barrel." Prices for Coulanges and Tonnerre were also listed, along with "useful" information:

"Once this canton [Tonnerre] only made white wine or wine the color of partridge-eye; today it makes excellent red wine." A week later, the journal gave a short report on the wines of Arbois, but never turned to the luxury wines of Champagne, much less the common wines of the Loire.

The *Affiches* provided general information about the conditions and quality of the wine but little help in acquiring it, beyond a casual reference to the brokers of Beaune and the occasional advertising by individuals. It did not continue to run such interesting stories but offered a place for individuals to advertise their wine on occasion. And as local papers began to emulate the formula created by the *Affiches,* printed in most provincial capitals by the end of the Old Regime, they too offered local vinegrowers a chance to inform the larger world about their produce.[39] Wine was advertised in the *Affiches d'Orléans* more often than anything but horses and carriages, and by a wide range of sellers who included vignerons and other small-scale traders.[40]

Other publications showed a more comprehensive interest in the wine trade, however, and offered more information about acquiring wine. The *Journal du commerce et de l'agriculture,* the *Journal économique,* and the *Gazette du commerce,* starting up at different times during the 1750s and 1760s, ran articles on many aspects of the viticultural economy, reviewing and excerpting books on winemaking, the wine trade, and wine taxes. They published letters suggesting a "bureau for the perfecting of winemaking" or reporting on the condition of the wine harvest around Beaune or publicizing the benchmark price set by the brokers of Beaune. The *Journal du commerce* devoted two long articles to the wine trade in its first year, 1759. Asserting that "the wine trade is one of the most interesting branches of European commerce" and that "among the wines of France those of Burgundy and Champagne hold first place," the journal offered a very detailed discussion of the wines produced by upper and lower Burgundy, with short references to the wines of Champagne and the south. The articles looked much like the discussion in the *Affiches* in their concern to distinguish the wines produced in the different viticultural villages by their quality, taste, durability, and price. The *Journal* devoted far more space to practical advice about purchasing and transporting the wine, however.[41]

In surprisingly partisan terms, the *Journal du commerce* condemned wine merchants and encouraged its readers to acquire their wine through négociants. Declaring its sympathy with "the Public's complaints against retailers" who alter and ruin the wine they handle, the journal strongly endorsed négociants, about whom "there is no example of their furnishing other than natural wines." Consumers were urged to "take care to avoid the hand of the wine merchants, who manipulate the wine, who are not only unfaithful about the qualities asked for, but even multiply the wines of Burgundy by adding foreign wines." In contrast, "the good négociants of Burgundy cannot be suspected of infidelity." The *Journal* then provided the names of one or two négociants in Reims, Auxerre, Beaune, Mâcon, and Chalon-sur-Saône by whom "buyers can be directly instructed." It sang the praises of the firm of David, père et fils, and Barbizote, for example, "which has long ago acquired a reputation for great probity and exact fidelity and enjoys a foundation of extensive credit." It identified Boyard of Auxerre and noted that De la Motte of Reims "justly enjoys a good reputation and great credit. Public interest does not permit us to defer to their modest request not to be named in this Journal. It is clearly not the only one in Reims that merits the Public's esteem and confidence. We will name the others when they wish to be known."[42] This blatant offer to advertise should not obscure the subtler message. Readers throughout France and, indeed, Europe were being given a way to transcend the local scope of their commercial world, to bypass the layers of intermediaries and go "directly" to the source of their wine. The négociant in this account emerged as the champion of transparency in the market.

The *Affiches* and *Journal du commerce* made important introductions to the complexities of the wine trade available to a wide audience. Many of the new wines being developed in upper Burgundy were explained for the first time, and anyone wishing to acquire this wine was given a rough idea how to go about it. Clearly the journals expected their readers to be able to contact these brokers with little trouble. Within a few years information about brokers became even more readily available in commercial almanacs. These useful little reference books offered concise information about the wine trade and precise advice for acquiring wine from lists of négociant-brokers. They also give us a quick glimpse of how the brokerage system had changed over the course of the century.

By the 1770s, someone interested in wine was less likely to find information in the *Affiches* than in commercial almanacs, like the *Almanach général du commerce, des marchands négociants, armateurs de la France,* that provided even more help in opening up the national market to the sophisticated buyer. The information continued to span the most obvious and most arcane, appealing to an audience that might wish to arrange the most detailed shipments of wine to Paris, but just as easily might not know where the wine could be found. The wines of a town like Beaujeu were praised as being "as much esteemed as those of Mâcon," but nothing useful was said about acquiring them. The wines of Beaune, in contrast, were identified in great detail. The almanac gave the villages producing the finest wines in the neighborhood and followed with prices from the previous year for the finest wines, a note about local measurements, the price of shipping from Beaune to Paris, and the names of two brokers. The "famous" wines of Epernay received less attention, although nine of the "principal négociants" in town were identified. Instead, the almanac developed its discussion of the wines of Champagne under the listing for Reims. The best villages of the mountain of Reims produced a wine that was "a quality superior to Pomart, Nuits, and Vougeau and more healthy." The entry also noted that Ay was "the first vignoble of Europe, where Henry IV and Sixtequint both had harvest houses," and produced "exquisite reds" in addition to vin mousseux. It then identified four of the town's vignerons but no brokers. There was considerable detail for the wine trade in Reims, however. A list gave four dozen "proprietors selling their wine" (of whom a dozen were identified as widows) to whom buyers paid cash, plus thirty "commissionnaires proprietors," who accepted bills of exchange and a final fifteen "commissionnaires courtiers" who sold for credit and were "consequently more expensive because of the risks."[43]

The almanac offered a rather more comprehensive survey of the French wine trade than had the *Affiches*. The finest wines still received considerable attention, but now the bulk wines produced for the urban mass markets also had a place. Thus the wines of Blois were explained in some detail: The finest included the auvernat, "very heady, agreeable, and to be reserved for desserts," and those from Sologne "in certain years [which are] so sweet they seem to be made from honey." But the almanac also gave current yield figures for the region (six barrels per arpent in 1778), which had more to do with the common wines marketed in this town. More than a dozen négociants and brokers were identified who could facilitate this market. The wines of Tours and Orléans also received a brief mention, along with a few brokers, but the entries for other towns along the Loire barely noted their wines and gave no clue about brokers.

Several hundred towns of France merited at least a brief mention in the almanac, with the number growing steadily in the last decade of the Old Regime, yet scarcely two dozen of these towns appear to have had brokers. Particularly in the early years, the almanac was rather haphazard about offering information for the wine trade. The 1774 *Almanach* identified brokers only in Auxerre, Blois, Chablis, Chalon, Mâcon, Orléans, Reims, Tonnerre, and Tours: an absolutely minimal list and revealingly tilted toward Burgundy. The issue of 1778 ignored the brokers and wine trade of Auxerre but identified three brokers in Chablis and detailed the opening of a new

Toward a Transparent Market

route from Chablis to a point beyond Joigny that avoided the tax at the bridge there. The following year rectified the oversight with a long discussion of the wine trade in Auxerre, which was "nearly the only [trade] of the region, and worth drawing the attention of those who trade wine to the northern provinces or even individuals who provision themselves." It identified the prices of four different grades of wine from Auxerre and recommended they be aged before drinking and bottled after a year or two. It ranked the wines produced by two dozen villages in the region and gave the names of a dozen brokers in Auxerre and several in Saint-Bris.

Here was a mass of useful but specialized information made available to a wide reading public. The details about shipments and trade routes, about brokers and the ways to pay them, about the wines of each region and where they were generally shipped, had been known all along by a small circle of wholesale merchants and brokers. Now it was accessible to anyone who wished to engage in the wine trade, whether to provision themselves directly or to engage in the wine trade as an entrepreneur. If we can assume that the almanac was responding to some demand, some need on the part of its readers, then it seems clear that "the public" was involving itself increasingly in the wine trade, at the very least as consumers. Recommendations like "One can write to the brokers of Auxerre to procure the wine of Coulanges" or simply "write to Beaune" were showing neophytes how to make the system of provincial brokers work for them. Evidently these consumers looked no longer to their local wine merchants to arrange for their supplies; instead, they planned to contact the provinces directly and needed both information and addresses to facilitate this new system. The almanac responded increasingly to this need.

During the last decade of the Old Regime, the almanac added considerably to its scope. Several additional cities with a wine trade were discussed: Chinon, Saumur, and Roanne were finally recognized for producing large amounts of "passable ordinary" wine going to Paris. Orléans, which had always enjoyed an entry, finally earned proper recognition for its "very esteemed" wines and for twenty-six of its négociants and brokers. The almanac also gave Parisians access to brokers in a dozen towns of the southwest, such as Cognac, Blaye, Cahors, Angoulême, that were not in the city's normal commercial orbit. The almanac had sections devoted simply to clarifying the different grades of wine produced by Burgundy and Champagne. "This rich production having become an object of speculation for an infinity of négociants from France and Europe, we have felt obliged to offer the public a table where it can see at a glance the good wines" of these provinces. The authors coyly refused to "pronounce on the great question of whether the wines of Champagne are of a quality superior to those of Burgundy" but opined that those of Champagne were preferred by young people and women and those of Burgundy by "the French of a ripe age." The English, "who have more need than any others for a light drink," also preferred those of Champagne, whereas the Dutch and northern Europeans looked instead to Burgundy.[44] Here again was a collection of basic information that offered consumers valuable insight into the functioning of the wine trade. The almanac's evolution over the last decades of the Old Regime suggests that it was changing to meet demand for greater details about the wines of France and, more importantly, for information about the wine trade and how to operate it.

To the extent that this commercial almanac offers an accurate survey of the merchants and brokers in France just before the Revolution, it shows that the brokerage system in Burgundy and Champagne had evolved substantially since the survey at the beginning of the century. Many of the smallest centers in lower Burgundy like Irancy, Cravant, and Champs no longer had brokers; instead, the almanac advised readers to write to brokers in the intermediate centers of Auxerre and Chablis to handle their purchases throughout the whole area. Even these larger centers, like Auxerre and Tonnerre, had fewer brokers than in 1705.[45] The almanac also informs us that the commercial system in upper Burgundy had changed, though in different ways. The number of brokers had doubled since 1705, with a sharp increase in the number at Beaune and Mâcon and the addition of Nuits and Roanne as brokerage centers. The almanac provided not only the names of seven brokers in Nuits, but also of fifty-five individuals with "large properties" in Nuits, who sold their wine to brokers and foreign merchants. Simple numbers of brokers, with no fines like those at the beginning of the century to indicate the size of the enterprise, are ambiguous, of course. They argue, nevertheless, that the economic activity of the wine trade in upper Burgundy had expanded, both in old centers like Mâcon and into new ones, like Nuits.

Elsewhere, the almanac revealed a concentration of business in fewer hands. In Champagne, only Epernay, Reims, and Vertus continued to have brokers listed.[46] Along the Loire, the region around Orléans and Blois still listed significant numbers of brokers, with a few more along the lower Loire in Chinon, Amboise, Chatellerault, and Angers, but there were fewer brokers, in fewer locations. Long-distance trade now worked through an orderly hierarchy, and Parisian readers had no need to contact the lowest level of supply centers directly. This evolution represents both a tendency to consolidation and an increasing efficiency in the supply network, but it

Toward a Transparent Market

also entailed greater control in the hands of intermediate brokers, many of whom were in the process of founding commercial houses that still flourish.

The editor "permitted" himself "some reflections" in the last edition on the almanac's emphasis on wine brokers when discussing the wine trade, admitting that "some people find it strange that we have not identified proprietors before" and that "we have received many complaints from proprietors." The broker was essential, he argued, to international commerce. "Let us suppose that a négociant of Amsterdam or London needs five hundred barrels of champagne or burgundy; if he addresses himself to his broker, the shipment will be prompt, otherwise it becomes impossible." A buyer faced the problem of visiting many proprietors to make small purchases of each; the proprietors themselves had no way of knowing whether the purchasers were financially solvent and ran a much greater risk of "terrible losses" than did a négociant who had the "powerful interest in, and facilities to, check the finances" of a partner. He recognized, however, that brokers were accused ("perhaps wrongly") of shipping ruined or adulterated wine, which "would be a crime of lèse-nation or lèse-patrie." They also used "veiled schemes" to get the better of foreign merchants and to dominate proprietors. But he pointed to the example of Bordeaux, where "exports are made entirely through commercial intermediaries [brokers]," as having "great weight." In the end he had included the names of a few proprietors, "since the wine is theirs before it is the state's."[47]

Despite the belated references to proprietors, the almanac attested to the centrality of brokers to the wine trade and enhanced their business by making them known to a wider public. But the brokerage trade had subtly changed as a consequence. It could no longer be the recondite world it had been at the beginning of the century. As consumers were given more information about prices and transportation and the grades of wine it proved increasingly difficult for brokers to use their specialized knowledge to their own advantage. The possibilities for fraud, or even for speculation, became more limited. And brokers were now competing in an increasingly national market. Almanacs offered consumers access to most of the vineyards of France and facilitated their contacts with even the remotest of them. In this expanding and progressively transparent wine trade, the broker would have to struggle for any advantages.

Clear evidence for the increasing transparency and sophistication of the wine trade can be found in the expanded range of the Parisian catchment over the course of the eighteenth century. With better access to brokers around the country and improvements in communications and transportation, Parisian wine merchants turned to wines from much farther away to supply the city's markets. A comparison of wines arriving in Paris at the beginning and the end of the century demonstrates this evolution. Registers from the chief wine ports of Paris, particularly Saint-Paul and La Tournelle, give a rough idea of the wine trade in 1702–5 and again in 1788–89.[48] The wines arriving at these ports were identified only by the origin of the boatmen who transported them—not a precise indication of the wine's provenance, but a good suggestion of its general region of origin. Neither set of registers gives more than a sample of the total wines arriving in Paris, but they offer a useful picture of the wine trade's general outlines and the expansion of the capital's provisioning crown.

The Parisian catchment area at the beginning of the century relied heavily on vineyards within a fairly short distance, particularly along the upper Loire (see table 6.1). Fully a quarter of the wines came with boatmen based in Orléans, plus another 5 percent from villages nearby. Boatmen from the region around Blois brought another 27 percent of the wine. The lower regions of the Loire—the Touraine and Anjou—accounted for only 1 percent, though it is quite possible that their wines had been transhipped to the boats of merchants in Blois or Orléans. Wines from Champagne came a distant second, at 15 percent, arriving with boatmen of Epernay and Château-Thierry. Lower Burgundy sent another 12 percent, mostly with boatmen of Auxerre. As we have seen in an earlier chapter, these boats may well have carried some wines from upper Burgundy, for the brokers of Auxerre arranged shipping for their colleagues in Beaune and Mâcon. The preferred route for the wines from farther away in the southeast, however, appears to have been through two towns on the Loire, Roanne, and Digoin, which sent 9 percent to Paris. The wines of the Beaujolais, Mâconnais, and the Rhône arrived at the southeastern reaches of the Loire through these two ports. All told, only 12 percent of the wine came from various parts of the southeast.[49]

The general outlines of this trade suggest certain influences shaping the Parisian catchment area at the beginning of the eighteenth century. Clearly transportation was a crucial constraint: the great rivers of France brought

Table 6.1
Arrivals of Wine at Parisian Ports (in percentages)

	1702–4	1788–89
Lower Burgundy	12	6
(Auxerre)	(10)	(6)
Champagne	15	0
(Epernay)	(6)	(0)
Île-de-France	2	0
Upper Loire	57	24
(Orléans)	(26)	(0)
(Blois)	(19)	(10)
Touraine	1	9
Anjou	0	6
Southeastern Loire	9	42
(Cosne)	(0)	(26)
(Saint-Thibault)	(0)	(8)
(Roanne)	(6)	(4)
(Allier)	(2)	(10)
(Unidentified)	(0)	(2)
N =	37,505 muids	77,176 muids

wines to the ports of Paris. Just as certainly, the primitive transportation network between the Saône and the southeastern Loire severely restrained the amount of wine available to Paris from upper Burgundy and the south. The port registers indicate that the Parisian catchment area was not yet very extensive at the beginning of the century. The vast majority of wines appear to have come from a provisioning "crown": a band extending from 120 to 200 kilometers around Paris. This crown supplied the bulk of the wines brought in to the city by wine merchants, to supplement the local wines of the Île-de-France. The essential change over the century would be the growth of this crown.

The wine arriving at the port of Saint-Paul in the twenty months beginning in January 1788 came, on the average, from much farther away.[50] Rather than a sample of the port's traffic, as were those registered from the beginning of the century, the seventy-seven thousand muids (some two hundred thousand hectoliters) of wine registered in 1788 probably included all the wine arriving at that port. The contrast with the port records of eighty-five years before may be somewhat exaggerated because the relative dearth of wine at the end of the 1780s forced merchants to seek farther afield for supplies, but it points to profound changes in the range and organization of the wine trade.[51]

The port records demonstrate the important geographical expansion of the wine trade of Paris at the end of the Old Regime; the bulk of the wine at the port came now from much farther away. The Loire had lost some of its preponderance, but Paris had incorporated much more of the great river into its provisioning crown. The upper Loire—from Blois to Orléans—had been reduced to less than half its former contribution, though the almost complete disappearance of wine from Orléans is anomalous. The prominence of wine from the upper Loire in the accounts of Moreau at the Halle aux vins may explain some of this shift, for much of the wine from Orléans was apparently now going there. The lower Loire, from the Touraine to Anjou, had increased its shipments substantially. Reports from the end of the seventeenth century presented the chief trade of the lower Loire as being still with the Dutch, by way of Nantes, though this commerce was apparently already much in decline. By the middle of the eighteenth century, the region had reoriented itself toward the Parisian market. Reports from Chinon spoke of Parisian wine merchants discovering their region in the 1740s. By the 1760s, a report identified the region between Tours and Saumur sending 22,500 barrels of red wine to Paris and only 14,000 barrels, mostly white wine, to Nantes.[52]

The wines of Champagne had also declined, indeed, had almost disappeared from the port records. Little more than a hundred barrels from Châlons and several hundred bottles from Dormans were registered, a complete collapse of the wine trade along the Marne that had existed at the beginning of the century. The wine from Auxerre had also decreased somewhat, to 6 percent of the port's traffic. Based on these three regions, the principal provisioning crown of the early century, lying at a radius of less than two hundred kilometers from the capital, had experienced a precipitous decline in its control of the Parisian wine trade. From providing nearly five-sixths of the port's wine, the regions of Champagne, lower Burgundy, and the upper Loire had been reduced to less than a third.

The wine now came from much farther away, particularly from the southeast, which had more than doubled its contribution, to roughly half of all the wine at the port. Some 6 percent came from the important transhipment points along the southeastern reaches of the Loire—at Roanne, Pouilly, and Digoin—more or less as it had at the beginning of the century. These ports still functioned as the places along the Loire where wine from

the Mâconnais and Beaujolais were put in boats, having been carted overland from the Saône River.[53] The area now known as Saint-Pourçain had
shown real growth, however; some 10 percent of the wine was brought by
boatmen from towns along the Allier, particularly Moulins and Puy Guillaume.

The single greatest change from the earlier record occurred in two villages along the southeastern Loire near Sancerre. Fully a third of the wines
at the end of the Old Regime had been brought by boatmen from Cosne
or Saint-Thibault—and Cosne alone accounted for a quarter of the wines
at the Parisian port. Clearly the stunning emergence of this area owed less
to the good fortune of the few vinegrowers around Sancerre than to the
local boatmen, who were picking up the wines from the southeastern parts
of the Loire, where it had been transhipped from regions farther south
and east.[54] Their activity, along with that of the boatmen around Roanne,
indicates the expansion of the provisioning crown to include a more distant zone, extending three to four hundred kilometers from Paris.

The wines of the south had slowly gained importance in the Parisian
trade during the century. The records of the river toll (péage) at Cosne
listed the passage of nearly forty-six thousand barrels of wine in 1733.[55]
The amounts traveling the southeastern Loire rose to fifty-four thousand
barrels in the late 1750s.[56] This already constituted some 15 percent of the
wine brought into Paris. Among the wines that passed through Cosne,
those of the Mâconnais and Beaujolais became an increasingly important
part of the capital's provisions. Indeed, estimates in 1769 of the amount of
wine sent from Beaujolais alone went as high as eighty thousand barrels.[57]
If accurate, this amounted to almost a fourth of the wine that Paris drew
from beyond its immediate provisioning crown. The wines from farther to
the south, from Dauphiné, remained largely outside of the Parisian market. With the exception of the wines of Vienne and l'Hermitage, most
were considered too fragile to travel or be stored for long.[58]

In addition to representing a pronounced expansion in the provisioning crown, the changes in the wine trade along the Loire underscore the
proliferation of boatmen from smaller towns and villages in the commerce
with Paris. Where a few boatmen in Blois and Orléans had once handled
the huge majority of the trade connecting the river to Paris, there were
now boatmen from at least sixteen locations along the river, all competing to supply the capital. Their competition arose from the improvements
in transportation and commerce across the century. The amelioration of
canals between the Loire and Paris had made it comparatively easy to transport wines.[59] The burgeoning number of boatmen along the southeastern

Loire also depended upon improvements of transportation facilities, this time of the land routes between the Saône and the Loire.[60] This link had fundamentally changed the wine trade along the Loire. Improved communications also brought Paris in closer contact with businessmen in the provinces and facilitated commercial arrangements.

The port records indicate that this geographical expansion was also due, in part, to the efforts of large Parisian wholesalers, who had gained a far more prominent place in the Parisian wine trade. The port records from the beginning of the century reveal a host of small-scale receivers to whom the wine was addressed and for whom it had been ordered. None of the Parisian wine merchants at the beginning of the century received large shipments at any time, and few appeared frequently; rather, the wine trade within Paris seemed to have been largely dispersed among many small dealers. By 1788 the majority of the receivers still collected small quantities of one to two dozen muids from the shippers, much as they had done under Louis XIV. But now, at the end of the Old Regime, nearly half of the wine went to only two dozen people, usually in shipments of one to three hundred barrels. The large wholesale wine merchants, particularly Davidan, Seguin, and Vée, each received over a thousand barrels of wine in some sixteen months, and two of the privileged "wine merchants of the king," Jacquier and Boudaille, received three and four thousand.[61] Only these individuals had the resources to bring large quantities of expensive wine to Paris, to pay for their shipments from ever greater distances, and to cover the various entrance taxes (now more than sixty-five livres per muid). They too relied on provincial brokers, yet their practice changed the wine trade in ways that challenged the brokers' role.

Changing Markets

The port records bracket a century of change; between these two dates it is much harder to know where the wine in Paris was coming from and how the city's supply crown was evolving. One piece of the evidence comes from the records of business failures of hundreds of Parisian wine merchants. The debts they owed map a partial geography of wine supplies. Wine merchants of every scale purchased some of their wine directly from brokers in the provinces, though the more modest among them bought much of their wine from Parisian wholesalers. The account books they were forced to turn over to the consular court are also sources of information about their supplies. Although these records clearly confirm the

Table 6.2
Parisian Wine Merchant Debts (in thousands of livres)

	1695–1749		1750–69		1770–89		Total	
Lower Burgundy	122.9	33%	110.8	27%	84.4	22%	313.7	28%
Upper Burgundy	48	13%	49.4	12%	97.1	25%	194.5	17%
Champagne	4.6	1%	0.2		24.3	6%	28.1	2%
Île-de-France			6.4	2%	5.7	1%	12.1	2%
Lower Loire	46	12%	56.3	14%	23.2	6%	125.5	11%
Upper Loire	104.6	28%	140.5	34%	78.6	21%	323.7	29%
South	48.6	13%	45.9	11%	68.2	18%	157.9	12%
Total (provinces)	374.7		409.5		381.5		1,163.4	
Parisian	126.7	25%	103.1	20%	416.6	52%	646.4	33%
Total	501.4		512.6		798.1		1,812.1	

geography of wine supplies revealed by the port records, they also suggest the relative lateness of the expansion of this geography.

The records from the first half of the century emphasize the importance of the traditional markets for wine, especially along the Loire. A score of Parisian wine merchants filing for business failure in this period amassed outstanding debts of a half million livres for wine purchased from wine brokers throughout the northern half of France, as well as from other wine merchants in Paris. Of the 374,700 livres owed in the provinces, 40 percent went to brokers along the Loire, mostly the upper Loire, and the brokers of lower Burgundy were owed a third of the total (see table 6.2). Upper Burgundy and the south already contributed a quarter of the wine bill, though the significantly greater expense of wine from the south had inflated its monetary importance.[62] These debts confirm the general geography of the port traffic at the beginning of the century, but the bulk of the records refer to the 1730s and 1740s, by which time Champagne was no longer contributing much, and lower Burgundy had gained a more prominent role. Similar documents from the middle of the century show relatively little change.[63]

The fact that a quarter of the wine merchants' total debts were owed to other Parisian wine merchants suggests the limits of many in the wine trade. It was easier and less speculative to buy from wholesalers in Paris, particularly for wines from a greater distance. There is some evidence that Parisians were creditors because they had bought debts owed to provincial brokers, but it is clear that many small wine merchants bought much of their wine from larger wholesale merchants in Paris.[64] The accounts of a modest wine merchant show him buying more than ten thousand livres of wine a year from the wholesale merchant Chagot.[65] These were wines from across the country, a full and varied cellar purchased solely from another Parisian. Even a large wine merchant, with debts of over 130,000 livres, relied heavily on Parisian suppliers. Dupuis owed thirty-six thousand livres to brokers in the provinces of the secondary provisioning crown, mostly to brokers in lower Burgundy, plus a little to brokers in Blois and Condrieu. Yet he acquired much of his wine through the Parisian wholesale wine merchant, Gosselin, to whom he owed his largest debt of fifty-three thousand livres.[66] The inventories of his major creditor show that Gosselin, as one of the privileged "twenty-five wine merchants of the king" with wine in his cellars worth 126,000 livres, drew on a much more extensive geography. Although three-quarters of Gosselin's wine came from Burgundy and the Loire, the rest was wine from Roussillon, Condrieu, Spain, Alicante, and lower Languedoc. These last were also very expensive wines, worth almost half the value of the inventory.[67] Evidently Dupuis relied on Gosselin to bring the more distant wines to Paris.

The leaders of the wine merchants' guild insisted on the economic importance of the large wholesale merchants, both for their commercial contacts to distant markets and for their stimulus to more local vineyards. In memoirs of 1747 defending their privilege of opening several cellars simultaneously they argued that

> one can fix the number of those who today form the guild of wine merchants at around eleven hundred; there are no more than a hundred who can maintain this commerce on a certain footing and on whom one can count for the provisioning of Paris because these hundred merchants have considerable funds with which they buy wines and pay in cash, [and] as a consequence they spread money throughout the provinces; there are even some among them whose commerce extends to four to eight thousand barrels per year. If these big merchants are reduced to the condition of the small merchants by the reduction of the number of their cellars there is reason to fear that they would be obliged to abandon this trade . . . at which point the trade would be left to the small merchants and the provisioning of Paris would risk coming up short. . . . It is only these big merchants who travel to the provinces for their purchases whereas the small merchants make use of brokers, buying as their needs arise and often on

Toward a Transparent Market

credit. It is only the big merchants who are capable of bringing wines from the provinces of Languedoc, Roussillon, and others even more distant, as they did in 1740 and 1741 when they largely remedied the dearth of wine in the center of the kingdom.[68]

The distinction offered here was based on not only the geographical reach of these big merchants but also the fact that they operated on a large enough scale to bring wines speculatively to Paris, when the rest of the wine merchants bought only as they needed wine. The claim was only partly correct, however, for the submissions to consular courts show that speculation played a role in the trade of even modest merchants.

These records, most of them the accounts of merchants in trouble, reveal how speculative the wine trade actually was and how easily money was lost on this commodity. Its transportation was expensive and uncertain. The five hundred barrels bought in Anjou and Touraine in 1754 by one merchant were left to navigate the Loire from late October to late April, using up eighty of the barrels (presumably in ouillage) and leaving the rest in terrible shape.[69] But when the wine arrived it posed further problems, particularly of storage. A small tavern keeper was caught short when the six hundred barrels of wine he had bought "in the country, in several regions" all arrived at the same time, because of the low water in the rivers. Without room to store so much, he had to put it in the Halle at considerable expense.[70] Merchants like the one who "made purchases a bit above my forces" had to scramble to store them and then to sell them. The following year, "seeing that I was burdened with merchandise and that I needed to sell it . . . [I] took a second cave in the city," for which this merchant had to pay rental.[71] These were the kinds of expenses that should have dissuaded merchants from buying speculatively, yet they continued to do so.

A more serious problem came from the fluctuations in prices that made profits terribly uncertain. In 1758 one merchant had a broker in Mâcon buy him 140 barrels, which cost him a total of 17,600 livres, at least half of which went to transportation and taxes. He was only able to sell them for 12,200 livres. In the same year, he acquired fifty-four barrels through a broker of Roanne for thirty-three hundred livres—which was again doubled by tax and transport—and brought in only four thousand. And a purchase of fifty-four barrels from a broker in Beaujeu only barely broke even. He listed purchases of nearly five hundred barrels the following year, from brokers in Châteauneuf and individuals in various places along the Loire, much of which ended up at the Halle and lost him money again.[72] There are dozens of similar examples, of merchants getting less for the wine than they had hoped, after costs had risen higher than they expected, if the wine arrived at all.

The number of wine merchants submitting their balance sheets to the juridiction consulaire provides a striking, though very rough, demonstration of the turmoil suffered by the wine trade in the last two decades of the Old Regime. Averaging only three submissions a year in the 1740s and 1750s, and seven a year in the 1760s, the failures suddenly surged to twenty a year in the 1770s, with a peak of thirty-eight in 1776. The 1780s remained nearly as troubled, with nineteen a year. Most of the later accounts give the impression of a host of small merchants sinking beneath the comparatively small waves of ten or twenty thousand livres of debt. Their plight was articulated by one small wine merchant who complained that "the vintage of 1779, where the price of wine suddenly fell and the vignerons sold their wine at retail for a low price, caused irreparable harm to a part of the merchants selling for themselves who did not have sufficient funds to withstand these losses."[73]

The records of commercial activity from debts and purchases in the last two decades of the Old Regime show pronounced growth in the wine shipments from upper Burgundy, bringing it close to the proportions depicted in the port records.[74] Upper Burgundy had more than doubled its share in the Parisian wine trade, at the expense of the Loire and lower Burgundy. Most of this wine was coming from brokers in the southern half of upper Burgundy, in Mâcon and Chalon rather than Beaune. Brokers in the south, particularly along the Rhône, had also increased their trade with Paris. The consular court confirms the evolving structure of the wine trade outlined by the port records at the end of the century, though the merchants' commercial records indicate a less dramatic transformation. The relative absence of wines from lower Burgundy in the port records, for example, is belied by the evidence for continuing trade with that region in wine merchants' debts and accounts. More generally, the merchants' records show the continued importance of traditional sources of supply and a significant rise of the southern vineyards.

Although the geography of the wine trade was changing, much of its basic organization did not. The merchants' contacts with the provinces relied heavily on a relatively small number of brokers. Of some hundred and eighty brokers identified in the Parisians' debts and accounts, forty of them accounted for over half of the entries and over half of the debt. Boyard, Monnot, and Guesnier of lower Burgundy, Cousin and Guignace of Blois, Guerin of Saint-Dyé, and Millard of Chalon were particularly prominent. The prominence of these families—for most of these names belonged to

Toward a Transparent Market

several generations of brokers—in merchants' debts demonstrate how concentrated the provincial wine trade was and remained through the century.

The business failures near the end of the Old Regime suggest, however, that the wine trade in Paris was becoming more centralized, much like the evidence from the port records. The proportion of merchants' debts to other Parisian wine merchants rose sharply in the last two decades, indicating that many small merchants were turning increasingly to the wholesalers for their supply. Of several dozen Parisian wine merchants whose business failures in the 1770s and 1780s reveal their sources of supply, the vast majority were apparently provisioning themselves from large Parisian wholesalers. The small merchants were especially dependent, like Alexis Mercier who owed half of his thirteen thousand livres in debts to Jacquier, one of the twelve privileged wine merchants of the king and one of the largest wholesale wine merchants in the capital. Even some of the largest of these merchants, like Gigard who owed over one hundred thousand livres for wine, relied heavily on Parisian wholesalers. For ten thousand livres owed to brokers in Blois, Orleans, and Auxerre, Gigard owed forty-eight thousand livres to Jacquier and to another of the biggest Parisian wholesale merchants, Lafond, plus another thirty thousand to a dozen smaller Parisian merchants.[75]

The reliance on the largest wholesalers arose in part from the demand for wines from the south, for the big merchants were most efficient at long-distance trade. In several cases, these wholesale merchants appear to have begun their careers as brokers in the south before moving to Paris. Perouze, one of the more prominent Parisian wine merchants, appeared in several balance sheets of the 1760s as a wine merchant of Condrieu, responsible for much of Paris's trade with the south in that decade. He had evidently shifted his base of operations to Paris and continued to deal in southern wine. Another broker of Condrieu, named Chanal, occasionally appeared in various debt records as a marchand forain and possibly a wine merchant of Paris. There may be a similar connection between a broker of Condrieu named Jacquier and the Jacquier who was a privileged "wine merchant of the king." At the very least, the Parisian Jacquier's accounts show him to have been in close contact with the vineyards of the south.

The accounts of the very large négociant Jacquier show nearly half of his wine coming from the vineyards of upper Burgundy and the south. He had to present his balance sheets to the consular court in 1784, with debts of over seven hundred thousand livres, although he claimed assets worth over a million.[76] The debts for wine included in his accounts give a picture of the sources of wine brought into the city that comes close to matching the port records. Indeed, he owed 143,000 livres to the receiver at the port, doubtless for entry taxes, as well as sixteen thousand to the farms operating the canals of Orléans and Briare for similar duties. An enormous amount of debt was owed to a few brokers along the Loire River: some fifty-seven thousand livres to one of Mer, as well as smaller amounts to brokers in Orléans, Rochecorbon, Chinon, and Saumur. But even more was owed in the south: twenty-three thousand livres to a broker of Mâcon and twenty-eight thousand to agents in Lyon. The debts of forty-two thousand livres owed to boatmen of Condrieu, rather than to brokers, emphasize both his connections to the town and his personal involvement in arranging the purchases of these wines.

The evidence from the port records and from major Parisian wholesalers points to a basic shift in the geography of the French wine trade. The capital's provisioning crown, which had included the principal vine regions of the north of France, expanded dramatically southward during the last half of the eighteenth century, becoming increasingly national in its scale and reach. The wine trade had evolved internally as well, in ways that subtly undermined the control enjoyed by brokers at the beginning of the century. Because of significant improvements in the country's transportation and communications, the market became increasingly transparent and allowed buyers and sellers easier contact with one another. Wine brokers continued to play an important role in the wine trade, but their virtual monopoly over the provincial markets appears to have been lost.

The organization of the wine trade changed during the eighteenth century, as a result of better transportation, strong brokerage, and wider dissemination of information. Improved communications, in particular, rendered the wine trade more transparent and more public. Changes at the Halle aux vins gradually offered opportunities for growers and provincial traders and speculators to participate in a market that had once been the effective privilege of Parisian merchants and their brokers. As the wine market became more sophisticated it encouraged the participation of a wider range of commercial agents and diminished the brokers' control of the trade. Their power had depended on concrete advantages, over access to information, to buyers, and to credit. For various reasons they began to lose these advantages. The wine trade became, gradually, a more open market, but in very new ways and without government regulations. This new open market was the result of new institutions that improved the flow of information and lowered the costs of trading. Its transparency contributed significantly toward the creation of a national market. At the same time, the increased competition in the wine trade forced provincial brokers to look for new markets and new commodities. As we shall see in the following chapters, the answer lay in developing expensive wine and securing the elite markets for this wine. Some brokers emerged at the end of the century with new power as a result of this switch in markets.

7

From Brokers to Négociants

The expansion of the Parisian catchment into upper Burgundy profoundly influenced the dynamics of the wine trade of this province. During the seventeenth and early eighteenth centuries, as the Parisian wine market became more accessible, vignerons planted vineyards through the southern end of upper Burgundy, around Mâcon, and the Beaujolais. Through the eighteenth century the region sent growing amounts of wine to Paris. The region around Beaune, in contrast, could not send wine so cheaply to Paris and so looked increasingly to international trade. Wine brokers played a vital role in both these developments, though in different ways. In southern Burgundy, as elsewhere, the brokers relieved Parisians of the need to visit the province, becoming their commission agents and handling their wines. At the same time, however, the region profited from the growing accessibility of the capital to establish rival commercial links. Provincial traders and growers increasingly bypassed brokers and speculated on shipping wine to the metropolis. Brokers around Beaune, on the other hand, developed an export trade to the rest of Europe, for which they bought expensive wines speculatively. Here, where competition was limited by distant markets, the brokers became independent négociants; in the rest of Burgundy they remained essentially dependent on the trade with Paris and subordinate to Parisian merchants.

Burgundian brokers created two distinct commercial roles for themselves in their province, one tied to markets in Paris and the other to markets abroad. Through their service as traditional commission agents, the brokers of Mâcon enabled Parisians to add their region and the Beaujolais to the capital's catchment. By offering to finance and find wines for outsiders they reduced transaction costs and made the province accessible. Yet here and in lower Burgundy, around Auxerre, brokers serving the Parisian market found limits to their commercial development. They sought to dominate access to this market, but with the growing transparency of the wine trade in the second half of the century brokers faced more competition from local growers and traders. As a consequence, Burgundian brokers remained within a largely traditional relationship to the Parisian market. The combination of increasing competition and commercial stagnation discouraged brokers from abandoning their commission trade and curbed their development toward independent commercial enterprise. The number of brokers in lower Burgundy declined, and the rapid evolution of their business methods that had so shocked contemporaries was largely arrested.

The more northern Côte de Bourgogne, between Dijon and Chalon, had less access to the Parisian market because of the greater difficulties of transportation and so turned increasingly to foreign trade. Growers developed high-quality wines for an elite market, using new techniques of vine-growing, wine production, and storage. Unlike the simple wines that had been made since the Middle Ages, vinified quickly to be drunk quickly, this region began to produce wines that lasted longer and traveled better, aimed at an international market. These new wines paid off additional production costs with increased value and wider markets. As a consequence, Burgundy, along with Champagne and Bordeaux, became the first sites of modern wine production, creating high-quality, aged wines with an increased capitalization of the winemaking process.[1] This turn to quality, in contrast to the wine sent to Paris, lent even more power to these brokers, as growers in these regions sought dispersed markets for high-quality, expensive wines. To locate an elite clientele that was, necessarily, rarer and more widely distributed, the skills of the broker became even more imperative. Markets needed to be sought aggressively, to be developed by effort and travel and imagination. Here the brokers, now liberated from their parochial commitments and horizons, transformed themselves into négociants—wholesale wine merchants with large speculative stocks of wine and far-flung markets.

Unfortunately no simple distinction between brokers and négociants allows us to chart this transformation with certainty. Theoretically the négociant worked for himself and the broker worked for others, but contemporary treatises emphasized the overlap of their functions. The négociant was not alone in trying to seek customers, as brokers drummed up trade through circulars and correspondence. The speculative character of the négociant's trade, which generally entailed the maintenance of inventories, distinguished them more surely.[2] In theory a broker had no occasion to stock wine, though the absence of stocks is not necessarily a reliable sign of brokering, since there were many reasons and opportunities for not assembling inventories. The cost of inventories, which included replacing wine lost to evaporation (ouillage) and occasional racking, led many brokers to leave wine with the grower until it should be required—a kind of dispersed inventory. The line between broker and négociant became increasingly blurred through the century, as Joly de Fleury's investigations made clear, but the brokers of the Côte de Bourgogne distinguished themselves from their counterparts in the rest of Burgundy by the energy they put into developing distant, speculative markets.

Integrating Southern Burgundy into the Parisian Market

The Paris port records and the accounts of Parisian wine merchants discussed in the previous chapter agree that southern Burgundy dramatically increased its contribution of wine to the provisioning of Paris, making the capital's catchment a progressively national market. The Parisian market had a particularly significant effect on the Beaujolais, which was practically created by the trade with Paris. These regions were integrated into the Parisian catchment by reducing the costs of two principal factors, transportation and transactions. By improving transportation, first between the Loire and Seine Rivers in the seventeenth century and then between the Saône and Loire Rivers in the eighteenth, the wines of this region became increasingly competitive in the Parisian market. The emergence of wine brokers in the late seventeenth century allowed Parisian merchants to find, identify, assemble, and finance ever greater quantities of wine. A late-eighteenth-century treatise described how they "offer their services, to take care of wine bought by Parisians . . . from which Parisian wine merchants formed business liaisons with these individuals who became always more obliging."[3] With the growth of commerce came a proliferation of wine brokers, particularly noticeable in the southern end of upper Burgundy, where only four brokers had been identified around Mâcon in 1705. By the 1780s, commercial almanacs identified seventeen brokers in Mâcon, six in Roanne, and three in Beaujeu serving the Beaujolais and Mâconnais, where wine production had risen dramatically since the seventeenth century and was aimed increasingly toward the Parisian market.[4]

The southern regions of upper Burgundy, essentially from Chalon south through the Mâconnais and, closely connected to it, the Beaujolais, had sent limited amounts of expensive wine to Paris in the mid–seventeenth century and had supplied local towns with more common wines.[5] The opening of the canal de Briare linking the upper reaches of the Loire to the Loing and then the Seine Rivers in 1642 undoubtedly encouraged such commerce. The Mâconnais enjoyed relatively easy access to the capital by its proximity to ports on the upper reaches of the Loire River at Digoin, Pouilly, or Roanne; the trip to Paris was long but cost less than half the long cart ride endured by the wines of Beaune.[6] The town of Beaujeu, through which ran several routes overland to the Loire River, could claim in 1708 that its "only commerce consists in the entrepôt of wine that are brought from everywhere to be sent to Paris."[7]

The initiative for the trade with Paris initially lay with Parisian merchants who visited the region "after the wine harvest, to make their purchases and provisions in the country of the Mâconnais, Chalonnais, Beaujolais, Roannais," according to an arrêt of 1716.[8] In 1705 the intendant in Lyon assured the controller general that "all the wine merchants of Paris and elsewhere have known the brokers [of the Roannais] for a long time."[9] Parisians found brokers in Mâcon like Claude Brosse, who may have taken his wine to Paris as a marchand forain around 1700 but was assisting Parisian merchants as a wine broker of Mâcon from 1717 to his death in 1731.[10] A curé of the Roannais regularly noted the presence of Parisians buying wine: "The Parisians have bought everything" in 1741; "they have bought a prodigious quantity in the Mâconnais" in 1742; "the Parisians have bought the greatest quantity" in 1756.[11] By the end of the Old Regime, a secretary of the estates of the Mâconnais claimed that "the wines of the Mâconnais are consumed for the largest part in Paris."[12]

South of Mâcon, the vineyards of the Beaujolais barely existed until the seventeenth century, at which point they expanded greatly, favored by untaxed access to Lyon.[13] Eighteenth-century accounts placed the region's emergence into the national market at the end of the previous century, a move helped no doubt by its incorporation into the Cinq Grosses Fermes in 1694. The northern part of the Beaujolais added some of its best wine to the stream of wine going from the Mâconnais by way of the Loire to Paris. By 1700 the region claimed to be sending some four thousand barrels to the capital, but this limited amount was little more than a supplement to the shipments arranged by brokers from nearby Mâcon. A description of the wine trade between this region and Paris in 1722 suggests that the Beaujolais was still sending only a little of its best wine to Paris and shipping the rest to Lyon.[14] Descriptions of the wine trade in the *Affiches* of Paris and the *Journal du commerce* in the 1750s make almost no mention of the region.[15] Improvements in overland and river-borne transportation through the middle of the century gradually made it possible for large amounts of the region's wines to travel to Paris. By the 1760s the region might have been sending as much as eighty thousand barrels to Paris and claimed that "the principal resource of the Beaujolais consists in the export of wine for the provision of the capital."[16]

The wine trade of Beaujolais, developing initially as an addendum to the wine trade of Mâcon, remained in the hands of brokers of Mâcon for much of the century. A barrister of the region accused them of conspiring to gain control of the wine trade: "The desire to make themselves master of the business led them to join in a partnership together . . . to form a single company that would handle all business exclusively and would make them despots in the province."[17] By the 1760s they appear to have succeeded. According to the royal prosecutor of Mâcon in 1740, "There are some brokers who buy more than ten thousand barrels of wine in recent years," much of which was coming from the Beaujolais.[18] It is not hard to see why Claude Brosse's two sons, who had followed him in the brokerage business, along with four other wine brokers paid the largest professional tax (*vingtième d'industrie*) of any group in Mâcon by 1751; their combined bill amounted to more than that paid by some fifty wine merchants.[19]

The rapid growth of the region's wine trade, along with its relative distance from and unfamiliarity to Parisians, made these brokers very important intermediaries. As in lower Burgundy they were accused of abusing their power in a variety of ways: "It often happens that a correspondent asks for wine from a particular growth and the broker sends a different wine to make a profit."[20] In 1761 one of the brokers of Mâcon, Chalandon, accused another, evidently from a junior branch of the Brosse family, of offering Beaujolais wines from the best regions for prices so low that the wines were clearly not genuine.[21] In fact, Brosse had been working for Chalandon as his secretary and had used the names and addresses of all his master's correspondents to offer them the wine bargains. By 1763 the royal advocate of Mâcon had reported to the town council that the wine trade, which was the "only income of this region," was threatened by too little regulation of its brokers. Normally, he explained,

> the wine is sold to Parisian and foreign merchants who address themselves to the merchant brokers of the province either to make the purchases or to prepare and deliver the wine. . . . This commerce has been conducted for a long time

with good faith, but for several years abuses have slipped in which will not fail to bring ruin to the region if they are not promptly remedied, for some individuals without wealth, estate, or morals, advertising themselves to the public as merchant wine brokers of the Mâconnais, have written circulars to Parisian and foreign merchants in which they offer to furnish them with wines of the first quality at a price infinitely lower than they sell for and if they succeed in acquiring some commissions they buy some third-class wine, are paid as quickly as possible, and leave the region having taken the whole harvest of poor vignerons [without paying them], which has happened very often for several years.[22]

The Beaujolais barrister Brac de la Perrière indicted the brokers of Mâcon for these and other sins. He underscored the help they offered Parisian wine merchants in finding transportation, in addition to the traditional tasks of arranging and financing wine purchases. But he claimed that the brokers had "persuaded the Parisian wine merchants that their interests required them not to come to the province because their presence, especially when they arrived without having reached an understanding with each other, made the prices rise, and besides they could easily avoid the expenses of the trip and still know the quality of the wine through samples sent by the brokers." Their success in persuading Parisians not to visit gave them a free hand to conduct the wine trade themselves, as well as the opportunity for fraudulent practices. "When the Parisian merchants stopped visiting the province some brokers were dishonest enough to send wines at prices much higher than they had bought them." Brokers also substituted cheap wines for more expensive ones. Although suspicious Parisians inquired of the wine producers about the original price, the producers were "forced by the empire that the brokers had gained in the Province . . . to make no response, for fear that, by the understanding that began to prevail among brokers, they would be left with their crops."[23] Not surprisingly, such behavior encouraged the development of alternative methods of selling wine to Paris.

The improvements in transportation connecting the province to Paris made it possible for a variety of individuals in the Beaujolais to avoid exploitation at the hands of Mâconnais brokers by trading wine on their own. The accounts of several brokers from the Beaujolais show them sending significant amounts of wine to Paris by the 1760s. The broker Teillard of Beaujeu brought over two thousand barrels to Paris after the harvest of 1764. Some of it he himself sold speculatively at the Paris ports, much as marchands forains brought wine to Paris; the rest appears to have been commissioned by Parisian buyers.[24] Other provincial traders combined speculative trading with brokering. Jean Desroches of Vauxrenard, in the Beaujolais, shipped eleven hundred barrels in 1763–64, more than half of which he had bought from just three people. From one marquis he bought 320 barrels; from another he purchased 146 barrels, "well racked and natural . . . and delivered to the port of Pouilly."[25] Desroches agreed to provide two men to do the racking in March and promised to pick up the wine sometime before September, until which time he was responsible for their condition. At least 235 barrels had been bought on commission, "in my quality as broker," but the wine of the one marquis was clearly acquired speculatively. The rest of the wine was sold in small quantities to dozens of wine merchants of Paris, though one large shipment may have gone to wine brokers in Mâcon.[26]

There was room for even smaller enterprises in this commerce: In the 1770s a partnership of two merchants in the village of "Villiers" [Villié-Morgon], in the Beaujolais, bought roughly a thousand barrels over three years. They acquired most of it in small quantities from dozens of people in the northern half of the region, though a few, like the curé of Villié, sold large quantities. In many cases, their accounts note that the wine was to be delivered to Beaujeu rather than Villié, as the staging area for most of the overland routes to the upper Loire, by which they traveled to Paris.[27] These merchants were fined along the way, however, for trying to pass some of their Beaujolais wine off as Mâconnais.[28] Growers also sent their wine speculatively, as did a local official from the Roannais, along the Loire River, who contracted in 1752 with a merchant shipper to take 140 barrels of his wine to the ports or Halle aux vins of Paris, at the shipper's expense, where it would be sold and the profits, or losses, would be split between them.[29]

A range of participants were speculating in the wine trade between Burgundy and Paris by the second half of the century, making the trade competitive enough to incur the anger of the brokers of Mâcon who had traditionally dominated it. The anonymous report of a writer who identified himself only as belonging to the "small number of négociants who conduct the wine trade in the Mâconnais" condemned the participation of the small-scale participants in this "essential commerce of the Mâconnais" for introducing too much speculation into the wine trade.[30] He and his fellow négociants, who "call themselves commissionnaires," represented "the conjunction of public confidence and the . . . collection of perfections that characterize the man of quality and the useful citizen." Who would believe, he asked, that thousands of barrels of wine are sold each year to brokers with no more than a verbal contract, a verbal promise on the price, and with no bills of exchange or promissory notes. Everything about the trade "announces the most reciprocal confidence, the most respectable accord and harmony" between the broker and the wine producers. Yet he had written to warn of "the abuses committed in this commerce," which, he claimed, were due to others who had joined the wine trade.

This broker, who spoke so proudly of the brokerage trade, condemned the growth of other, more speculative commercial links to the market. "A more harmful abuse is the dangerous practice that has arisen for some years of taking wines to be sold" in Paris, by which he meant "those who bring their wine without a destination, in the sole hope of finding a buyer." He objected, in other words, to the entrepreneurs who took the risk of bringing their wines to market without a commission. "Those who buy without orders" from Parisian correspondents "do real harm to the province," he argued. "Every owner or merchant who brings wine to Paris without a destination [a buyer who had ordered it], there finds a sort of broker [*courtier*] who profits from the seller's needs." He referred here to the Parisian port brokers, who tasted wine arriving in Paris and helped sellers find buyers.[31] The Parisian brokers worked together to offer as little as possible for the wine, "profiting from the provincial's ignorance [and] his need to sell [his wine] in order to pay the shippers and the entrance taxes." These were certainly the risks that did, indeed, assail any speculative trader and hindered growers from bringing their wines to a distant market, although it is clear from this diatribe that the numbers of those who tried were growing. But the writer was concerned less about the consequences to the trader than about what he saw as the harm done to the province as a whole.

Speculative traders desperate to sell their wine were flooding Paris with cheap wine, he argued, and so contributing to stagnant prices. "The Auxerrois gives us a striking example of this truth. Its vineyards are the most happily located, by their proximity to Paris, by the ease with which their wines can be brought at any time of the year; the Seine opens a free route to all those who hope for the best and try to succeed." The results for the Auxerrois, however, were grim: The region had "weakened its commerce and diminished its inhabitants' revenues by bringing abundance to the capital." To remedy these abuses, "it suffices only to purge the province of a multitude of traders whom I regard as so many pirates." The négociant proposed the creation of a bureau of commerce to regulate the wine trade to that end.[32]

The brokers of Mâcon might well regret the multitude of traders who competed with them, yet they were not alone in condemning the growers' speculative shipments to Paris. The barrister Brac, speaking as a winegrower and critic of brokers, was equally hostile. Although expressing sympathy for those "proprietors who, impatient with the brokers' behavior, have undertaken to bring their wines to Paris for themselves," he pointed out that they could not hope to compete with provincial wine brokers. "The wine merchants of Paris and the brokers have used all their power to thwart them and make them give up in disgust; the shippers by water and land are more expensive for them than for the brokers, they are less prompt." Brac pointed out that the unit cost of transporting two thousand barrels was bound to be less than for two hundred, which gave the advantage to brokers. In addition "there are cabals [against proprietors] to have their wine left untouched at the ports of Paris." He blamed all these "inconveniences" on the brokers' "abusive practices," but he decried the fact that "many peasants and inhabitants of the province, seeing wine at a low price, have bought some and become marchands forains, to take them to sell in Paris. . . . These alleged marchands forains hurt the proprietors by giving their wines for nothing at the ports of Paris."[33]

These two assessments, however partisan, made several important points about the Beaujolais wine trade. Both attested to the swarm of provincial traders who had joined the wine trade with Paris. Improved transportation had made Paris accessible, and the prices of Beaujolais wines allowed them to bear these costs. Large numbers of growers and small traders were clearly trying to compete with brokers in the long-distance wine trade, whether from entrepreneurial initiative or from impatience with the brokers' power. Despite both writers' insistence on the weight of structural disadvantages working against speculative traders, their concern clearly indicates that such speculation was increasing. Both asserted that brokers enjoyed significant advantages over small traders, whether because of "abusive practices" or because of their contacts with Parisian merchants. Nevertheless, these facts had not stopped participation by provincial traders. The anonymous broker, who saw this trade diminish his control over the wine trade, and Brac, who argued that it hurt the interest of growers, could agree that the practice had become widespread.

The difficulties with bringing wine speculatively to Paris became so serious that the Parisian wine merchants guild complained of it to the Parlement of Paris in 1774. In their complaint they referred to the "frequent contraventions taking place at the Halle, the Staple, and the ports against the public interest and particularly against the bourgeois of Paris, who are accustomed to furnishing themselves with wines at the Staple and the Halle, established particularly for them." The problems arose, they argued, from "so many pretended marchands forains domiciled in Paris, selling continually at the Halle, as much as from the cupidity and inexactitude of those carrying out the function of *courtiers* at the Halle and at the ports and Staple, but even more from the understandings that these *courtiers* and pretend forains have with a certain number of wine merchants connected to them."[34] Acting in collusion, the merchants and brokers at the Halle and ports preyed on the "vigneron, vineowner, or marchand forain, who brings one or several boats of wine to the port for sale." Among their favorite tactics was to direct buyers away from these provincial traders and "leave them languishing to wait for buyers." Then they would "make deals and agree on the price for the wines of the last arrivals [the provincial traders], who get tired of selling only a little and very slowly, so that they are obliged to give up their merchandise, often at a loss, to the resident forains. After having profited from these circumstance, in concert with the wine merchants with whom they have plotted, they fix whatever price they want to the wine when they have chased away those who would have sold for a better price."

In an attempt to avoid such market manipulation the Parlement prohibited wine merchants from buying the wine that vignerons and provincial traders brought to the ports and Halle aux vins. This provoked at least one, barely coherent, protest from growers of the eighty viticultural parishes around Orléans, Châteauneuf, and Beaugency. Their representatives protested that this trade had brought "abundance" to the capital and money back to the province, with which growers paid their taxes and repaid their loans. They claimed that most of the province's brokers had been bankrupted, "ruined by the Parisian wine merchants and cannot pay us." Growers had been left to take their wines to the ports and Halle of Paris on their own "in order to earn something from the fruits of their labor." If allowed to stand, this prohibition would bring "desolation and misery" to their vineyards, "more than three million barrels will remain on the hands of the poor growers," and Paris would lack wine.[35]

Winegrowers in the provinces offered different solutions to the problems of speculation. Brac called for the association and confederation of all growers in the region in a "general assembly" where they would organize a buying and selling cooperative. The cooperative would arrange for the purchase of grain for the consumption of its members and barrels for the production of their wine. The excessive cost of these items had forced some members to sell their wine too cheaply, thus hurting the interests of all. It would see to the payment of taxes for similar reasons and would pay advances for shipping. In addition the cooperative would arrange to hire a broker to work for them in Paris and in foreign markets. Brac was anxious that the province maintain control over the quality of the wine it sold, to protect its reputation and avoid the kinds of fraud that so damaged the public perception of the wine of the Beaujolais. The cooperative's broker would be under the association's control and could deal in no wines besides those of the province. The association would help its members advertise their wines in the business journals of the day, like the *Affiches* of Paris, in order to boost demand for their wine.[36]

These proposals offered a significantly different approach to the province's wine trade from the traditional desire of merely regulating brokers. They aimed to wrest power from the brokers and give control of the trade to the sellers. Brac's suggestion may seem excessively visionary, yet he had been involved in several attempts to start such an association on a small scale during the 1760s. In 1764 and again the following year, Brac and several other growers with ample means had contracted with a broker to sell their wine for them in Paris. Unfortunately these ventures barely broke even.[37] Nor did anything come of Brac's proposal, but variations of the idea continued to surface periodically among Burgundian businessmen. A broker of Chalon, Millard, suggested something similar fifteen years later in a request to the Estates of Burgundy.[38] Both in theory and in practice, growers and brokers were looking for ways to enlarge their markets.

Southern Burgundy and the Beaujolais had developed a flourishing wine trade with Paris by the second half of the eighteenth century, but speculation in wine was still a difficult and often unrewarding enterprise. Quite apart from the underhanded methods alleged against buyers in Paris, the province suffered from its own success in supplying the capital with "abundance." There was a limit to the amount of wine Parisians could consume, a limit that led other parts of the province to look elsewhere for markets.

Lower Burgundy Unreformed

The expansion of the Parisian catchment helped the economy of the Mâconnais and Beaujolais but probably hurt the regions that traditionally supplied the city with wine. The brokers of lower Burgundy, around Auxerre, now faced competition from the wines of the growing catchment, as well as from growers and traders around them who could send the wines more and more easily to the Halle and the Staple. The region turned increasingly to growing cheap wines in quantity with which it flooded the Parisian market.[39] In the face of such competition the brokers of Burgundy retained an important advantage in their relationship with

Parisian merchants. Parisian wine merchants continued to provision themselves in lower Burgundy, and, as the preceding chapter demonstrated, they continued to rely heavily on brokers for their wine. Several of the most important of the brokers did extremely well in the trade, achieving considerable social stature and using their wealth to enter the lower ranks of provincial nobility. Others did less well, and the numbers of brokers in lower Burgundy actually declined by the end of the Old Regime. The wine trade of lower Burgundy, tied as it was to provisioning Paris, does not seem to have expanded and, indeed, lost some of its relative importance in the Parisian market. The conditions of the wine trade in the second half of the century, particularly with the stagnation of the 1760s and 1780s, appear to have discouraged brokers from developing their own independent commerce and abandoning their commission relations with Parisian merchants. Instead, they remained largely tied to the Parisian market and merchants through the second half of the century.

The brokers who achieved most power and prominence in the wine trade in the second half of the century combined brokerage with some speculation, maintaining their commissions from Paris. The Boyard family offers an excellent example of this mixture, a story of social success but always within commercial limits. A brief inventory at Pierre Boyard's death in 1740 depicts a conventional broker, with several hundred barrels of wine from 1739 and 1740 in his cellars and port already "destined for different merchants." His son, Louis, who was "managing the affairs" of his father described his own purchases "for the account of different merchants" and noted that his father had just sold 149 barrels of wine from 1739, "mostly from this city" to a Parisian wine merchant, half of which had been sent but for which nothing had been paid.[40] The descriptions of the wine in the inventory suggest that this business followed the practices of a fairly orthodox commission agent—not much stock on hand, wines bought at the orders of merchants. But some of the wine—from Languedoc, Côte-Rôtie, and l'Hermitage that had been ordered through Millard and Girard, brokers at Chalon—had been shipped to Boyard "to be sent from there to Madame Boyard [his sister], wine merchant of Paris." We may wonder if the woman who would sell it eventually in Paris was independent of her father and brothers back in Auxerre, or perhaps sharing the risk with them.

Pierre's son, Louis Boyard de Forterre, continued his father's profession, and his success at brokering brought him social mobility and titles, though his rise to prominence struck many of his neighbors as too precipitous. He bought seigneuries in the 1750s as well as ennobling offices and seems to have slipped into lesser nobility even though still identifying himself as a wine broker. His ascension was reinforced by marital strate-gies, in the classic manner of seeking a noble husband for his daughter, Catherine. She had balked, unfortunately, and had eloped to the Nether-lands with one of her father's employees. Although she eventually returned and dutifully married according to her father's wishes, the family became the butt of every humorist in town. Much of the satire had a bitter edge that expressed resentment at the family's social pretensions.[41]

The most notorious of the brokers at midcentury, Edme-Pierre-Alex-andre Villetard, gave up the brokerage trade, moving his assets very visibly in the late 1740s out of the wine trade and into acquiring local lands and seigneuries. Villetard joined the landed nobility; he bought several fiefs and a château and became a conseiller secrétaire du roi by 1767.[42] At his death in 1773 he left 223,000 livres to be divided up among six children.[43] Three of his four sons went into the church, the army, and the law. But a fourth son, Edme-Germain, became a wine broker and in 1756 married Françoise Boyard, the granddaughter of Pierre and daughter of Edme, thus uniting the two principal brokering families of Auxerre.[44] For the wedding Ville-tard gave his son over twenty thousand livres in cash, plus seven arpents of expensive vines in addition to six arpents of pinot noir that "undoubt-edly produce the best and most distinguished wine of the Auxerrois wine region." These vines were clearly Villetard's prize, and handing them over as a unit posed some legal problems for having favored one child in this fashion. But, as he explained, "if the vines were divided and subdivided, as often happens with the division of family assets, each of Villetard's chil-dren would not have enough to furnish a modest cuvée, since these vines produce very little, which would force them to mix these portions of vines with others." The result, Villetard argued, would be the "loss of the repu-tation and confidence" enjoyed by this "première cuvée," and "wishing to avoid this [he] intended to perpetuate in his name its good renown, as long as it is possible for them to do so."[45]

This marriage also consolidated a business partnership. Edme-Ger-main's father-in-law, Edme Boyard, had already been an active wine broker in 1738, when he was indicted with his father, Pierre. He had gone on to acquire land and seigneuries but worked as a broker right up to his death, shortly after his daughter's wedding to Villetard. His probate inventory shows that he had joined with his son-in-law in the 1750s in frankly specu-lative ventures. With a combined sum of sixty thousand livres as their partnership's funds, they had purchased 119,545 livres in wine, which they had sold for 128,635 livres. This represents some three to four thousand barrels of wine, a measure of how large a role these two families played

From Brokers to Négociants

in the local wine trade. The profits were divided equally between the two partners, but at 7.6 percent this was little more than a simple 5 percent commission.[46] The fruits of speculative trading in wine were not enough to persuade Villetard to abandon his brokering.

Other brokers found speculation in the wine trade to be risky and unrewarding. A new broker in Auxerre, Villeneuve Delisle, formed a partnership with a Parisian in the mid-1760s to speculate on several hundred barrels of wine, for which Delisle was to receive one-fourth of the profits. But the wine sat with Delisle for two years while prices declined. As he pointed out, the bourgeois and brokers of Auxerre were selling their wines for whatever they could get. Delisle was able to sell most of the wine to other brokers in town but was reduced to selling some of it over the counter *à pot* at four sous per pinte. With great effort he was able to make some money on the wine, but the numerous costs of caring for it left very little profit. Delisle's part in the deal went beyond brokerage to being a partner in a speculative venture, for which the other partner eventually sued him.[47] Another broker, Pierre Pochet, speculated on shipments of wine to Flanders during the 1740s, as the king's armies waged war, but his business failure in 1748 suggests he was caught by the ebb and flow of military fortunes. Nearly half of the twenty thousand livres he was still owed in unpaid bills lay in Flanders, "both for wines sold by his son and for [wines] that remain there." The accounts say little about how he acquired the wine he had shipped, except for the money that he owed to brokers in Orléans and to a fellow broker, Paradis, in Auxerre.[48] Among other things, his plight shows us that a broker needed the financial resources to be able to manage more than twenty thousand livres in unpaid bills if he wished to survive the vagaries of the economy. Participation in the wine trade was an enormous financial challenge and speculative risk that could easily sink small businessmen.

Villetard engaged in some speculation but he continued to identify himself as a broker and described his actions as one to an investigation in 1767. Agents from the tax farm had asked him to verify the quantity, cost, color, and provenance of several score barrels he had sent to several Parisian wine merchants. He identified their origins with a number of growers across the region, including Irancy and Chablis, but could tell them nothing about the cost and color because he had not tasted it and, indeed, had not even bought it, for the merchants had done that themselves. Villetard referred vaguely to these merchants having been "in company with other merchants working either under the commission of Villetard or under those of his confrères." They all appear to have visited sellers together and then divided their purchases up. The agents expressed surprise that the merchants had not informed Villetard of the prices they had agreed to, since he would be obliged to pay the sellers, but he explained that "to avoid ruining the sale in the vines, the merchants buy at the agreed price of an open sale (as is the common practice)."[49] Villetard's involvement with this wine was purely that of a broker who financed the purchase for visiting merchants.

This combination of brokering and speculation caused Villetard some trouble following his ennoblement in the early 1760s.[50] The estates of Burgundy and the bailliage of Auxerre had challenged his nobility and condemned him to be reinstated in the taille rolls because of his commercial activities. An appeal to the Cour des Aides of Paris was rejected, "so long as he practices the function of commissionnaire de vins." Finally the Conseil d'état exempted him "as a noble from paying the taille, although practicing wholesale commerce in wine."[51] The language of the conseil's arrêt is confusing, since wholesale trade was formally not an impediment to ennoblement. In any case, Villetard refused to resolve the issue by the simple course of abandoning his commercial activities. He was identified as one of the chief brokers of Auxerre in several of the major almanacs of the end of the Old Regime. At the same time he became the seigneur of the villages of Vincelles, just south of Auxerre, in 1769 and there built a "very pretty château in a charming site near the Yonne." He even became embroiled in a fight with his villagers over his seigneurial winepress.[52] During the Revolution he became the mayor of Auxerre. Thus was continued commercial success joined to political and social status.

Despite their rise to social prominence, and the awkward challenges to their status leveled by various courts and their community, the Villetards and Boyards did not leave the brokering business. A new generation, now endowed with titles and seigneuries and ever greater amounts of vineyards, continued their active involvement in the wine trade.[53] With Edme Boyard's death, his wife, François Compagnot, carried on their business with their son Louis. At her death, Louis reported money still owed by wine merchants in Rouen, Blois, and Paris.[54] He married into the family of another wine broker of Auxerre with whom he formed a commercial association for the rest of their careers.[55] Compagnot had also worked with a cousin of the family, François Boyard de Saint-Martin, the son and grandson of boatmen and wine brokers. The partners were sufficiently important that they were the only brokers of Auxerre mentioned in the *Journal du commerce* in 1759.[56] Unfortunately, there were problems between the cousins; Compagnot's inventory at death spoke of wine held as a security against loans she had made to Saint-Martin, "over which there are disagreements that have not been settled." A will of Saint-Martin's, in which he disinherited his relations "both on the paternal and maternal sides," put it more bluntly: "I hold the heirs of the late Dame [Françoise] Boyard de Gastines responsible for twelve thousand livres that she stole from me . . . for which I have never received reparations."[57] Not surprisingly, his will was contested, and it took several years to straighten out his holdings after his death in 1782. He had become by then an active broker, with a large catchment area and far-flung clients.

The geography of Saint-Martin's business reached well beyond the range achieved by an earlier generation of brokers. Much of the sixty thousand livres he was still owed was for wine sent to Paris, but Rouen now also figured prominently as the target for his trade. Unfortunately for his creditors, Rouen was still suffering from war with England, and most of the nine thousand livres he was owed in Rouen was either signaled as "very difficult to recover" or already dismissed as a lost cause. He had also sent two thousand livres of wine to Moreau, the broker at the Halle aux vins, to be sold there speculatively.[58] Although Paris still dominated this broker's commercial outlets, he drew his wine from a more extensive geography than had earlier brokers. Unlike earlier brokers of Auxerre, who drew most of their wines from a few sellers in their city, Saint-Martin had suppliers throughout the countryside. He still owed twenty-four thousand livres for wines bought from seventy-two people, mostly in Coulanges and six other villages around it, but also some four thousand livres in Chablis. A little of it was even due in upper Burgundy. Unfortunately the inventory was compiled in late August, by which time he would have paid much of what he owed. Still, the number of villages and creditors and the small sums indicate that he was dealing with many small-scale sellers rather than a few notables as the brokers at the beginning of the century in Auxerre had done.[59]

The growing range of brokers' catchments in Auxerre appears to have pushed many of the brokers in the surrounding villages out of their markets; where the intendant had found fourteen brokers in six bourgs around Auxerre at the beginning of the century, the almanacs of the 1780s found only five in three bourgs.[60] Auxerre still maintained eight brokers, but Tonnerre and Chablis had far fewer brokers. Only the towns at some distance from Auxerre, like Joigny and Vermenton, had maintained or increased the number of brokers. The two lists of brokers are not really comparable, yet they suggest that Auxerre had monopolized much of the region's commerce. The brokers that survived in the bourgs, however, like Trinquet of Coulanges and Guenier of Saint-Bris, expanded the range of their markets.

Trinquet's postmortem inventory shows him dealing in large quantities, selling sixty-eight thousand livres of wine to some two dozen wine merchants in the last three months of 1752. At current prices, this amounted to more than two thousand barrels, long before the buying season was over. The recipients were principally in Paris, though a few were in Arras and Amiens. He had bought wine from scores of individuals in Coulanges and the surrounding villages, plus a little from the broker Rathier in Chablis. A quarter of the sellers, most of them identified as "Sieur," "Dame," or the "curé of Coulange," had sold more than half of the wine; the rest was in small amounts of less than twenty barrels. In several cases, Trinquet's widow mentioned that the wine already purchased "has no destination." The point is revealing, for clearly Trinquet had been buying some wine speculatively and had not yet been able to place all of his purchases.[61]

Similarly in Saint-Bris, Jules Guenier inherited a thriving brokerage business from his father, who had survived the brokerage scandal and, at his death in 1766, left over a hundred thousand livres to his heirs.[62] Jules was one of the most prominent brokers to appear in the debts and accounts of Parisian wine merchants filing for business failure, discussed in the previous chapter, but he overextended himself and had to submit his accounts to the consular court in 1787. His own account book shows that he had bought large quantities of wine in 1785, nearly four thousand barrels, for over fifty Parisian wine merchants.[63] Half of the wine went to just six individuals; others bought only a handful of barrels. Guenier's accounts remind us that Paris was still the principal market for wines from lower Burgundy, even though others in lower Burgundy were expanding the reach of their markets. A broker in Avallon, south of Auxerre, did the bulk of his business in the early 1780s with Normandy. He acquired over eleven hundred barrels of wine from around Vermenton, between Avallon and Auxerre, in 1782 and sent some 40 percent to Caen alone, with another 35 percent going to Rouen, Dieppe, and other Norman towns. Barely 20 percent was stopping in Paris, and a little went on past Rouen to northern Germany.[64]

Like Boyard de Saint-Martin, Guenier's catchment was larger than those of brokers at the beginning of the century. He drew his wine from Saint-Bris and the dozen villages around it that made up the bourg's traditional catchment area, but he also bought a quarter of it from upriver along the Yonne, particularly from Vermenton and even from Avallon.

From Brokers to Négociants

Most of his sixty suppliers sold him only two or three dozen barrels on a single occasion, no doubt the sum of their own vintage. But nearly half of the wine was sold to him by just ten people, identified as merchants, a seigneur, a lieutenant of the bailliage, and several vignerons, who were clearly petty wine dealers in their own right and had assembled one or two hundred barrels from smaller growers. In September 1787, after another full year of business, he calculated the money owed him by Parisian wine merchants at almost seventy thousand livres. He also owned enough im-movable assets—twenty arpents of vines, a huge farm of a hundred arpents in grain, plus houses, to the amount of sixty-four thousand livres—that his financial difficulties were quickly resolved.[65]

There is indirect evidence that Guenier was also taking a hand in preparing the wine. Although his accounts were careful to identify the exact provenance of most barrels—both the village and grower—a small amount, almost 9 percent, was identified generically (for example, four barrels of old wine of Coulanges). It appears that Guenier had bought these wines speculatively and was deliberately aging them to improve their value, for those that were "old" were much the most expensive—at fifty to seventy-five livres a barrel rather than the typical seventeen to twenty-five livres for the wine being sold by growers. Such speculation on old wine, if that is what he was actually doing, took Guenier a significant step toward the activities of a modern négociant-éleveur, who not only buys but also blends and ages wine, but it should not obscure the fact that the majority of what he bought was evidently still on commission.

The complaints of the tax farm in lower Burgundy at the end of the Old Regime indicate that Guenier was not alone in his activities. Because earlier laws were not enforced, the tax farmers charged,

> there are a number of brokers who abuse the privilege which is accorded to
> them of keeping wines until their departure. They buy speculatively, for a ficti-
> tious third party, and know very well how to get rid of the wine on their own.
> The presentation of the registers that they are supposed to keep, and of the
> commissions that they have received, would put a brake on a maneuver that is
> very prejudicial to the king's taxes. [But] these brokers absolutely refuse, and
> with the lapse of time and the non-compliance since [the arrêt of] 1721 leads us
> to fear that an attempt to enforce such sage ordinances, would be frowned on
> and rebuffed by the Cour des Aides. So the abuse continues.[66]

Time and official complacency had freed brokers from earlier restrictions. They now mixed functions and titles, identified in the almanacs as commissionnaire en vins but calling themselves "négociants en gros sur les vins" in a complaint addressed to the prosecutor general in the early 1780s.[67]

Despite the new titles and the purchase of land and offices, the principal wine brokers remained in the trade. And despite tentative forays into speculative buying and aging of wines, their account books demonstrate that these brokers retained much of their traditional commission relationship with Parisian merchants. Several families had transformed themselves spectacularly—from boatmen to nobility in just two generations—and most had achieved wealth, but their commercial development had reached a plateau. Once they had made the transition to buying on commission, at the turn of the century, they had been slow to become full-fledged négociants. Although they sent some wine to a rather larger geography of markets, lower Burgundy was still tied principally to the Parisian market. Brokers bought from larger, less contested catchment areas and were somewhat more independent, buying wine speculatively and even selling a little of it speculatively at the Halle. But their chief activity remained purchasing wine at the behest of wine merchants in Paris, and most of the wine appears to have been "placed" with Parisians much as before. Commercial power was still most certain in the brokering trade, so long as Paris continued to be the principal market for the province's wines, and it would be difficult to develop a fully independent provincial wine trade.

Burgundy's International Markets

In the region north of the Mâconnais, from Chalon-sur-Saône to Dijon, known as the Côte de Bourgogne, the wine trade experienced a very different evolution from the rest of the province. Here the distance from the Loire left the transportation costs to Paris excessive for all but the finest wines. Through the eighteenth century growers turned increasingly to producing fine wines for this long-distance trade. The wines of the region had been much admired in the Middle Ages, but they were simple wines. They tended to be light red in color, to have great delicacy of flavor, but not to last long. During the eighteenth century, however, growers began to vinify some of these wines differently, in order to deepen their color and their body and to extend their duration. The change was driven by markets, according to a late-eighteenth-century treatise: "Since the buyer prefers color and duration to finesse he must be contented."[68] Foreign markets were particularly important, according to another treatise from the 1760s: "We have abandoned the method of making very light wines to conform to foreign tastes. The tastes of the century guide us in our methods."[69] The

Côte de Bourgogne turned increasingly to foreign markets through the eighteenth century, led by brokers looking more and more like négociants.

Since the Middle Ages, the Côte de Bourgogne had well-established links to the distant markets of Flanders and Germany, and at the same time, small but steady amounts of their wines arrived in Paris.[70] The curé of Volnay emphasized the importance of the role played by Parisian merchants in the local wine markets, and the brokers of Auxerre routinely handled wine from upper Burgundy for Parisian clients. One enthusiastic estimate of the eighteenth century judged that as much as seven thousand muids took this route.[71] But the most important buyers had traditionally been Europeans from markets to the north and east of Burgundy, who had been coming to buy wines for centuries.[72] As the town council of Beaune boasted in 1720, the wines of Beaune, Pommard, and Volnay were the finest in the kingdom and "on their own draw the foreign, English, Flemish, and German merchants to come in a mass to this country each year," and begin their buying with the finest wines. But if these merchants "learn from the brokers they use in Beaune that the wines of the region are bad or defective they do not leave their country and buy little anywhere."[73]

This wine trade was initially in the hands of foreigners and the local intermediaries who assisted their visits to Burgundy. The costs of participating in this trade—both the costs of transportation and of the expensive wine itself—dissuaded most growers from speculation and left them passively waiting for outside demand. Thus the brokers of Beaune enjoyed a privileged position in the local wine trade, as the principal and practically unique conduit to distant markets. Like brokers elsewhere they gradually took on a more active role in buying wines speculatively, but in the face of economic difficulties they moved decisively into the wholesale wine trade during the late eighteenth century, becoming négociants who pursued markets with new initiative. They emerged at the end of the Old Regime as the most powerful figures in the province's wine trade.

The records of brokers in the region point to the importance of the export trade already in the early eighteenth century. The balance sheet of even a small broker in Beaune from 1735 claimed that most of the five thousand livres of good debts and the fifteen thousand livres of bad debt that he had declared "lost" was owed by a dozen individuals in the Netherlands.[74] Two other small balance sheets were more local, with debts owed almost entirely by individuals in France and particularly around Lille and Dijon, but one claimed three thousand livres of unsold wine in "foreign countries."[75] François Antoine, the broker of Nuits who worked frequently with the curé of Volnay, claimed before the consular court in 1725 that he was owed some thirty thousand livres for wines sent to Dresden, Hamburg, Leipzig, Cambrai, and Frankfurt. He was forced to spend three months in Stuttgart vainly soliciting payments. Some of the debts still on his books were from Paris, but far more were found in Cambrai and Strasbourg. Antoine acquired his wine right around the areas of Nuits and Beaune, although he also arranged with a merchant from Reims for champagne to be shipped to Cambrai.[76] Cambrai figured prominently in the accounts of a contemporary of Antoine, who sent more than thirty thousand livres worth of wine acquired between Beaune and Chagny to customers in northeastern France, including Saint-Quentin, Reims, and Cateau-Cambrésis.[77]

Aiming initially at markets on either side of the French border, brokers from the northern half of upper Burgundy expanded their trade increasingly into German principalities and beyond. It is instructive in this regard to see how the growers of Nuits-Saint-George involved themselves in the wine trade. With no brokers identified in the survey of 1705, the town appears to have been dependent on brokers of Beaune and Dijon to find them buyers. In 1720, however, the son of one of the town's notables, from a family making good wine, decided to seek his own buyers, taking two carts of wine to the fair at Frankfurt. Claude Marey apparently established fruitful relationships on this trip with a number of foreign merchants, who proceeded to open direct correspondence with him for the wines of Nuits. He encouraged this commerce by maintaining a large house available to visitors, combining business with hospitality. The curé of Volnay described him in 1761 as "one of the busiest and richest brokers in Burgundy."[78] To commercial success, Marey added lands and vineyards in the region, the office of mayor in the 1740s, and a charge of nobility in 1762. A son joined him in the wine trade.[79] As in Champagne, some brokers were drawn from a level of society that already enjoyed some wealth and status, significant advantages for an activity that needed to mobilize large financial resources. If the story about his trip to Frankfurt can be believed, Marey was also precocious in taking the initiative for expanding Burgundy's markets; the idea occurred to other brokers later in the century. By the 1780s the number of brokers in Beaune had increased from nine to twelve and had been joined by another seven in Nuits-Saint-George.[80]

The account books of brokers of Beaune from the middle of the century show their markets divided between France and Europe. Poulet in the 1740s was sending large shipments to Stockholm and to cities in Switzerland, Germany, and Italy. Still, the majority of roughly forty-five thousand livres of wine was shipped to cities within France: Little more than 10 percent of the total went in small amounts to Paris, as opposed to large shipments to Metz, Reims, Lisieux, and around Lille.[81] André Porte, a négociant in Beaune around the middle of the century, sold wine throughout Switzerland, Alsace, and northern France. He had particularly large debts owed him in Strasbourg, Dole, and Mande, but only trivial sums due from Paris. Yet he blamed sixty thousand livres of his losses on interest and expenses owed to Parisian bankers, and a third of his own thirty-one thousand livres of debt was owed to two bankers in Paris.[82] Beaune's major markets were to the north and east, but much of the trade was still within France.

The brokers of the Côte de Bourgogne, particularly in the northern half, sold their wines widely but acquired them from a concentrated catchment area. They specialized increasingly in the expensive wines of the Côtes de Nuits and Beaune and the elite markets that went with them. The small brokers early in the century owed money to a range of individuals for wine, among them many "bourgeois" of the local bourgs but also many vignerons.[83] The wines sold by the more serious brokers like Poulet came overwhelmingly from the Côte de Beaune; a small amount was from further south, at Chalon and l'Hermitage, that he bought through other merchants. Between 1747 and 1774 Poulet's catchment expanded minimally to include more wine from the Côte de Nuits, which was producing a stronger wine, a wine to be aged, that was increasingly popular abroad.[84] He bought in small lots, little more than a half dozen barrels at a time, and directly from the owners, who included men of law, councillors of the Parlement, merchants, and artisans, but only one styled as a vigneron. The vineyards in this part of Burgundy had been largely acquired by the notables of Dijon, who were able to produce wine of the highest quality. And with few exceptions, Poulet was acquiring very expensive wine, anywhere from one to two hundred livres per barrel, so that even small quantities could involve large sums of money.[85] Only wine of that price could bear the costs of extensive transportation across Europe.

In contrast to the brokers of Beaune, those at the southern end of the Côte de Bourgogne, in Chalon, enjoyed better transportation networks to the rest of France. As a consequence, they drew their wine from a much broader catchment and sold most of it to domestic markets. A merchant of Chalon, early in the century, was owed money in cities to his north and south, but almost entirely within France. In addition to debtors in Lille, Lyon, Paris, and Montpellier, he was owed large sums in Reims and appears to have conducted considerable trade with a brother there. His own debts suggest that he was acquiring wine from across upper Burgundy, from Nuits through the Beaujolais.[86] Another broker of Chalon reported dealing in, and losing substantial sums on, the wines of l'Hermitage, much farther to the south.[87] A partnership of several négociants in Chalon, dealing in over 180,000 livres of wine, sent almost all but a fifth of the seventeen hundred barrels they shipped in the mid-1750s to places inside France. Nearly a quarter of the total went to Paris, and a fifth remained locally in Burgundy. The rest went to several dozen towns in a broad arc east and north of the city, mostly within France, but a hundred and fifty barrels went to Amsterdam and Aachen and a little as far as Berlin. The source of these brokers' wines, in contrast, was rather more extensive than those of the brokers of Beaune. If a bit more than half of their wine came from Chalon and its environs, a further fifth came from both the region of Tain-l'Hermitage, along the Rhône River and from the area around Montpellier.[88] Connected as it was by rivers directly to the Rhône, Chalon provided a crucial contact between the vineyards of the south and the consumers of the north.

Accounts from the second half of the century map vastly expanded commercial connections, although the wine trade suffered from international disruption and the reduction of demand and prices during the 1750s and 1760s. One of the victims of the poor markets in the 1760s was the important "négociant-broker" of Beaune, Philibert Chavansot, who had expanded his trade considerably to the east. His balance sheet, left with the consular court, claimed one hundred thousand livres owed him by individuals in cities across Europe, plus another forty thousand livres that he had written off for a shipment of wines to Saint Petersburg. Only a third of this money was owed by clients in French cities, mostly to the east and north of Beaune; the rest were in cities of Germany and the Low Countries. This was a business conducted almost uniquely with other wine merchants, usually one or two in each city; there is no evidence of contacts with individual consumers. His business had also been spread remarkably widely: He had debtors in over three dozen towns and rarely more than five thousand livres concentrated in any one of them.[89] Another victim was among the largest négociants in Chalon. Antoine Verniquet's accounts deposited with the consular court identified scores of individuals in two dozen cities around Europe who owed him more than 170,000 livres. What stands out particularly about his business, besides its size, is its southward focus. A dozen Italian cities owed him fifty-one thousand livres, and individuals in Marseille owed him another thirty-two thousand and in Lyon sixteen thousand. By comparison, a few merchants in the Netherlands owed him only nine thousand livres, and Parisians owed only thirteen thousand.[90] Neither merchant's account offers explanations for his business failures, but European war clearly hurt such extended trade networks.

The 1760s were a difficult time for most viticultural communities, with the war limiting foreign markets and causing economic disruption in the country, but Burgundy was hit particularly hard. Prices and revenues for common wines in upper Burgundy rose sharply during the 1740s, only to slump in the next two decades and then gradually recover in the 1770s.[91] The trade in expensive wines probably suffered less, but provincial officials in the 1750s complained that "there have been almost no sales of wine for some years," and prices for vineyards declined.[92] A treatise on the "cultivation of vines of Beaune" in 1763 claimed that "for several years the wines of Burgundy have sold so little quantity that three-quarters of the vignerons owe considerable amounts to their employers."[93] The curé of Volnay, who had sold to Parisians in eleven of the twenty years before 1754, found only one Parisian customer in the next twenty years and had trouble selling his wines through the 1760s.[94] Finally in 1766 the provincial estates launched a general inquiry into the situation and requested reports from the principal viticultural towns.[95] As one report summarized the situation, "The commerce of wines, which is the unique resource of the region in which we live, has weakened for several years and will even disappear if the authorities do not offer the promptest remedy." It is clearly an indication of who owned the vineyards that we have the responses of not only the brokers but also of the notaries, the barristers, and the nobility of Beaune.

The responses displayed little uniformity in their diagnosis of the problem, beyond a tendency to blame it on the local brokers. Not surprisingly, the brokers dissented but had no advice for "fixing the wine trade in this town, except to continue to favor it, as has been done up to the present, by leaving it the liberty that is its soul."[96] The nobles, however, complained that "the best wine is ordinarily chosen and sent off to foreign countries each year, without establishing a price, [so that] the merchants who receive it are the masters of setting its price, which becomes the general benchmark." They wished to forbid such practices and to return to the old system whereby "the price was arranged at the Hôtel de Ville between the merchants and the notables; with honesty and rectitude conciliating all interests."[97] The town of Chalon offered a similar indictment of the harm caused by the disorganization of pricing and recommended a return to the old system whereby the price was formally set by growers and merchants meeting at the town hall of Beaune.[98] The nobles of Beaune condemned those who employed the "specious pretext that [price setting] hindered the liberty of commerce, as if all that guaranteed good faith and fidelity that are its essence were not preferable to this pretended liberty." And they blamed the fault on "these merchants who only know how to trade in contraband, against patriotism, honor, and the interests of the [public] good."[99]

If the nobles took a traditional and easily recognizable position, they did not speak for the whole community. The barristers expressed sympathy for wine merchants who were "so pressed to have wine" that they took a "certain quantity of wine" without fixing the price. "It is always good to get rid of one's merchandise," they opined, "and we cannot stop the merchants' urgency without hurting the wine trade of Beaune." They further pointed out that "in the eighty years since wines have been allowed to leave without a set price, there have only been four times when those who let them go repented of it and thirty times when the wines without set price got the best price." The barristers looked elsewhere for the most serious abuses in the wine trade.[100]

The barristers of Beaune warned that "it is of the utmost importance that brokers be men of probity, since they enjoy the confidence of the seller and buyer." They noted that "a broker of Beaune often buys and sends two hundred thousand livres of wine on his own credit"; the town had to have confidence in them. This confidence had once been well placed, apparently, even after the town had lost the right to license brokers. But more recently a "prodigious number of brokers" had set themselves up, and "the largest part of them" acted as both brokers and merchants and so tricked their customers. Their solution called for the creation of a bureau called the "Protector of the wine trade of Beaune," made up of vineowners, to license brokers once again. The notaries of Beaune agreed with the barristers that the brokers would have to be regulated again. But they also blamed wine producers for producing a "too great an abundance" of wine, at the expense of quality as well as of price. Growers who used manure and "edifices" on their vines, or who mixed mediocre with good wine, were all contributing to the problem.[101]

The account books of the curé of Volnay offered more trenchant criticism of the brokers, particularly of their speculative activities. He reported that they had stocked up heavily on wines in 1753, when "nearly all the wine of Volnay had been spoken for by the brokers long before the vintage." But they found themselves embarrassed by unsold stock the next year and so manipulated the market, according to Delachère, in order to sell it: "No one has ever seen a swindle like the brokers pulled on the wines of 1754. Although they had been denigrating the wines to all the merchants long before the harvest, the wines turned out to be good. But these people, who break the rules by being more merchants than brokers, were still holding lots of wine from 1753 that they want to sell for twice what they paid; they stopped the merchants from coming to buy," and nothing was sold till the early spring, for a very low price.[102]

Delachère complained increasingly through the 1750s and 1760s of the brokers' speculations and indicted their inventories for provoking them to manipulate the market. He blamed the trouble in 1761 on the letter one broker of Beaune wrote to "the merchants" that the wines were not good. The letter was "an enormous lie and infinitely harmful to the public and to the brokers themselves, for [much] wine remained in their cellars" unsold as late as the following harvest. In 1769, he asserted, "the brokers, all become merchants, have much old wine, which has doubled in value according to their habit." The brokers in 1771, "looking only to enrich themselves by impoverishing the bourgeois," ruined another good market. In each case the curé pointed to the stocks of wine accumulated by brokers.

In many ways, the diagnoses offered by different groups of upper Burgundy were traditional and familiar, interesting more for the limits of their reports than for the content. They were the analyses of growers, who looked to issues of production and considered issues of exchange only so far as they involved the intermediaries who lived among them. In contrast, the situation was analyzed by other Burgundians in the 1770s, who offered much different approaches to a solution, based on the search for new markets.

Among the solutions to the commercial problems of Burgundy was one offered by the négociant Perrot to the Estates of Burgundy in the mid-1770s. In his assessment, the wine trade in Burgundy was still what it had been at the beginning of the century; all commerce was in the hands of brokers, who worked for foreign merchants. The broker's activity was described as being still essentially passive, as they waited for commissions from foreign buyers. These foreigners enjoyed all the benefits from the wine trade, whereas the brokers ran all the risks. Perrot wanted to reverse the dynamics of the wine trade by taking the sale of wine to the consumer: "Why shouldn't the merchant of Burgundy have foreign brokers who would sell on commission in their countries?" He had formed the "project," he said, "of having a rich broker in several capitals who will make me known in the city, will collect all the commissions for wine from people in the capital and surrounding provinces, and I will ship the wine upon his request."[103]

In fact, the innovation in this plan was subtle, for Perrot would still act as a broker, shipping wines only when they had been requested, rather than sending them speculatively to be sold from inventory. But he had recognized the need to send representatives into the heart of distant markets in order to drum up trade. And although he was unwilling to send wines speculatively to foreign capitals, he suggested creating such a store (*magasin*) in Paris, where he would send bottles of "the most excellent wine from our Province." Sending the wine in bottles avoided the assaults committed by wagoners on the barrels they transported, all too easily tapped and the wine replaced by water. Bottles also guaranteed the unchanging quality of the wine to customers who "ignore the way to maintain a wine" in barrels. To prepare for these enterprises, Perrot had taken the step of arranging contracts (*traités*) for some of the finest wines in the province: with the count of Clermont-Montoison for his wines of Chassagne, with the chapter of Nuits for its wine of Saint-George, with a councillor of the Parlement for wines of La Tache, and with Jobert de Chambertin for his wines of Chambertin. A commercial almanac of 1775 identified him as a "correspondent" in Paris, at the Bureau d'Indications, where he offered to take "commissions for the wines of Burgundy of the first, second, and third quality at the best prices possible." [104] His request for the "protection" of the Burgundian estates was rejected, but there is ample evidence that his plans for aggressively selling French wines abroad were picked up by others.

The economic difficulties of the 1760s appear to have forced the brokers of upper Burgundy to realize that extra effort was needed to develop markets. The lack of easy access to a large market, such as Auxerre enjoyed in Paris, meant that they needed to work hard at developing outlets for their wine. Rather than waiting passively for the arrival of foreign buyers, as had been customary in upper Burgundy, or relying on correspondence with clients, as did the brokers of lower Burgundy and Champagne, brokers of Burgundy began to travel abroad in search of customers. An early and limited example of this can be found in 1734, when a merchant of Dijon set himself up in Strasbourg to broker the wines of clients in Burgundy. He spent nearly ten months in Strasbourg trying to sell wines for, among others, a noble's widow back in Chalon. He paid for all transportation, taxes, and upkeep, and had even advanced two thousand livres against the eventual sale of her wines. [105] This venture ended in a lawsuit, but négociants of Beaune began seriously in the 1770s to take the initiative for finding European markets. According to the négociants themselves, however, the trade rapidly became competitive. [106]

A remarkable expansion of the Burgundian wine trade into the rest of Europe took place at the end of the Old Regime based largely on the efforts of négociants to find business. Poulet of Beaune was using a relative to travel for him by 1776 and heard from his clients that other négociants were competing for their business.[107] The correspondence of a broker of Beaune in the 1770s shows him engaging salesmen to travel throughout Europe selling his wines. One salesman offered to go "wherever you wish, whether in Italy, in all of Germany, Poland, Russia, Sweden, Denmark, England, Spain" and undertook to "acquire good commissions, with all possible precautions to avoid bad debts, by informing myself of the resources of those with whom I will deal."[108] By the mid-1780s the practice of sending traveling salesmen east and north in search of clients was so well established that they were blanketing the continent.

Traveling in search of customers became so vital to the wine trade that all of the partners in one company of wine dealers, Bureau puiné of Dijon, spent time on the road: two of them through Germany and the north, one of them south into Provence. One of the partners, named Chardon, complained, in a series of letters back to his associates from a trip through France, Germany, and Flanders in 1783, that "the competition is incredible . . . competition has been pushed to a ridiculous point . . . there is so much competition in this unfortunate wine trade that I am not surprised that a new company is having much trouble in finding customers." He had met seven other salesmen in Frankfurt and was told that twenty of them from Chalon alone came through Montbéliard each year. Salesmen for Millard of Chalon seem to have been most pervasive and to have achieved particular success in finding business, but he spoke of competing with many others, including Bouchard of Beaune, Gilles, and Regnier of Nuits. He expressed real hostility for Perrot of Dijon (presumably the same Perrot as above), noting that "I hope to steal business at the court of Cassel from Perrot. I would be charmed to do so because I do not like this Monsieur."[109]

The worst competition came in the northeast and the Netherlands, where "they drink much common wine from Champagne, which has the advantage over us of very low transportation costs." One of his more successful competitors was a salesman from Champagne, for François, De la Motte and Company of Reims, who had been traveling for six years through Germany, Sweden, and Russia and insisted that there was much business to be found. But more regularly he reported that the salesmen he met "also sing of their misery . . . all of them grimace like me."

Such competition took on an edge of desperation in a poor economic climate. The intendant of Burgundy reported in 1785 that "wines are at a very low price and their commerce has been almost nothing for some years."[110] "In general," Chardon remarked, "France's commerce is having

a very unfavorable crisis, and the two Burgundies are not the only provinces to have the most multiplied and considerable bankruptcies." But the
real problem was simply that too many salesmen were chasing too little
consumption. "Unfortunately the richest individuals here [Cassel] drink
barely a barrel of burgundy a year," and in Frankfurt, "the richest houses
consume hardly sixty bottles of burgundy a year." The whole of Basel consumed "very little [burgundy] . . . perhaps thirty baskets of twenty-five
bottles a year." "Everywhere I look and everywhere I listen," he wrote from
Germany, "they are consuming far less of our wine than I had thought;
only the rich drink it and then only a hundred bottles a year."[111] The export figures for 1788 attest to the problem: Burgundy exported little more
than thirty thousand bottles and seven thousand barrels.[112] Still Chardon
remained confident that there were a great many Germans who might buy
their wine.

Chardon gradually discovered what other salesmen had been learning:
that they needed to sell small quantities of bottled wine to a vast number
of clients. There was a sizable market out there for small amounts of burgundy, but "we must reunite a great number of such customers to make
a passable consumption." This had forced a profound alteration in traditional commercial practices. He had come with letters of introduction
to the wine négociants of Frankfurt, but they had told him that "in the
ten years since Messieurs the Burgundians and the Champenois have been
traveling [to sell wine] in Germany and have been taking the smallest commissions from the smallest individuals, they [the négociants] have stopped
carrying the wines of Burgundy and Champagne because they could not
sell them." As a consequence it was increasingly difficult to sell whole barrels of wine to négociants; instead, salesmen were dealing directly with
individual customers. But "the richest people in Germany join together
to buy a single barrel. . . . I have commissions for several barrels that will
have to be divided up." In fact, the commissions he reported home tended
more often to be for wine in bottles. All of this was terribly inefficient:
"Judge how many clients buying sixty or a hundred bottles we will have to
pull together to compensate for the enormous expenses of finding them."

His solution in Metz, where "our wines are consumed principally by
the officers of the garrison, who are neither rich nor well enough lodged
to buy large provisions of wine," was to commission a tax official, a general receiver of gabelles, to turn his cellars into a "dépot for bottled wine"
where the wine sent by Bureau could be sold retail. The official's clerk
would advertise in the *Petites Affiches de Metz* when the wine arrived and
would sell it on commission. This amounts to much of the project that

From Brokers to Négociants

Perrot had suggested earlier, though Chardon may have intended something more speculative in the stocking of the cellar.[113]

The efforts of salesmen like Chardon transformed the northern Burgundian wine trade. Accounts from late in the Old Regime show the négociants of upper Burgundy sending wines to a huge area and to a broader range of customers than before. Poulet's market had grown by the 1770s and 1780s, aimed now mostly outside France at Flanders and Germany. Although a little was sold in Paris, far more went through Paris and Rouen to reach buyers in Poland.[114] The accounts of another merchant of Beaune from 1775 show the vast majority of his business with noblemen throughout Germany, generally selling them small quantities at a time. Some of it went to wine merchants in Berlin, or a négociant in Breslau, and Halder et Companie of Strasbourg either sold or forwarded some of his wine, but most went directly to wealthy elite customers and even the "brother of the king of Berlin."[115] The broker Verry, from Beaune, in the nine years following 1775 sold wine to 850 different clients in a hundred cities across Germany, the Low Countries, Switzerland, and Italy.[116] In the seventeen years following 1785, Paire et Maire of Beaune sent a little more than a barrel on average to each of some two thousand customers across Europe, nearly all of them in Germany, and only half that amount to French customers, principally in Normandy, from which it might have been exported.[117] By the 1770s these brokers were sending little to French markets; instead, they were working very hard to develop an entirely different kind of international market. The wines they handled were expensive and sold, necessarily, to an elite clientele. This was an increasingly dispersed market—quite the opposite of the Parisian wine trade.

The brokers of Beaune continued to draw their wine from "a very reduced viticultural region" according to one study, because theirs was overwhelmingly a trade in expensive wines produced by the best vineyards of Burgundy.[118] During the 1760s Chavansot owed large sums to a few individuals—ten thousand livres to three individuals in Gevry, seven thousand to three in Nuits, fourteen thousand to the fermier of the Cistercian vineyards in Meursault—who probably belonged to the elite producing good wine. A dozen small debts to inhabitants of Beaune show him in closer contact with the small growers of his own town, but there too he owed large sums to several merchants of Beaune. Most of the 145,000 livres that he owed was to individuals within a forty kilometer radius, though he had drawn some wines from farther away. His debts included twenty-four thousand livres for wine from Chalon, and beyond that ten thousand livres from Lyon, and sixty-one hundred livres from Languedoc and

Montpellier.[119] Two négociants in the 1770s and 1780s, buying an average of more than ninety thousand livres of wine a year, relied heavily on acquiring very local, very expensive wines, usually within ten kilometers.[120] Poulet bought from more regions, but only the best cantons in the Côte de Bourgogne.[121] Another négociant was sending the very best wine of Burgundy: from Beaune, Vosne, Chambertin, and Clos Vougeot, at 400, 600, and even 950 livres per queue [double barrel] in the 1770s. Much of this wine was described as "old," and some of it was bottled.[122]

As Delachère and Chardon and others made clear, the brokers of the Côte de Bourgogne had largely made the transition from commission brokering to wholesale commerce in the last decades of the Old Regime, though they were still identified as "négociants commissionnaires" by the almanacs of 1789.[123] As their markets diverged increasingly from those of the brokers of lower Burgundy, so did their business methods. Throughout the late Old Regime, the brokers of lower Burgundy remained dependent on the metropolitan market. Despite some speculation, and occasional shipments to more distant markets, the bulk of their business was conducted with Parisian wine merchants. In contrast, the upper Burgundian response to the commercial problems of the late Old Regime involved an aggressive search for markets, both to the east and the west. This had led many to Paris, where wines from the Mâconnais or Beaujolais found a ready outlet. The brokers of the northern part of upper Burgundy looked instead to a luxury market, spread thinly across Europe, created increasingly by their own efforts. Through the 1750s, Chavansot was selling to wine merchants across Europe but was largely dependent on them for orders. Later brokers, acting as négociants, took the initiative to find and sell directly to the customers themselves, particularly the nobility of the courts and cities. Négociants built up inventories of fine wines, aging, and sometimes bottling, them for this luxury market.

The expansion of the Burgundian wine trade into Europe, through the growth of aggressive marketing by négociants, was a response to inadequate demand and a stagnant market at home. And yet the consequences for the Burgundian wine trade were profound, for the challenges to selling wine gave négociants a distinct advantage in their commercial role. They transformed themselves and their local market, gaining greater control than they had enjoyed before. Their creation of European markets also appears to have reversed the dynamic of the early eighteenth century whereby foreign merchants visited Beaune in search of wines. One of the largest wine producers of the region, the Hospices de Beaune, recorded having sold to foreigner merchants only twice in the first half of the nineteenth century, during which time "the négociants of Beaune exercised a quasi monopoly on the purchase of the Hospices' wines."[124] By then they had transformed the wine trade, taking charge of their region's viticultural destiny and becoming salesmen to the whole of Europe.[125]

8

The Decline and Transfiguration of Champagne

In both Burgundy and Champagne, commercial difficulties pushed growers and brokers away from mass markets, which were all too stagnant from growing competition, and toward elite markets. Northern Burgundy, burdened by transportation costs that precluded any real competition in the mass market, maintained and, indeed, refined its production of superior wine. Champagne found a lively, if diminished, market in producing sparkling wine in bottles. If the outline of this process is already known, contributing as it did to the creation of two wine regions still commanding premium prices for world-famous wines, the impact of the turn to quality on the wine trade and on viticultural communities is much less clear. In Burgundy to some extent, and to an even greater degree in Champagne, the development of expensive wines enhanced the role of commercial intermediaries. The creation of new markets and new marketing techniques required brokers to turn themselves into négociants and aggressively seek clients. In Champagne, above all, commercial intermediaries also became the producers of fine wines.

Yet the producers of Champagne adopted these production techniques with reluctance and only slowly during the eighteenth century. The increased costs and risks were powerful disincentives to most producers, too poor to make the investments, and even the wealthy growers preferred not to change their traditional methods of making and selling their wines.

The changes in production came very slowly, as a consequence, spurred more by the force of commercial distress than by enterprise and requiring much of the century to transform the wine trade fully. This transformation was due largely to the wine brokers and merchants, who understood it primarily as a commercial, rather than an industrial, undertaking, aimed at solving a commercial crisis.

Brokers pursued elite clients for this new wine, taking to the highways of Europe to look for them in the last decades before the Revolution. As the brokers turned to a long-distance trade in elite wines, they began to operate increasingly as négociants, assembling stocks of wine for speculative trading. Their transition from brokerage to speculation also meant their increasing involvement in the production of luxury wine, particularly in Champagne. Their intervention into the productive sphere, well beyond the traditional role of brokering, signaled a new role for these intermediaries. Yet, however much it had angered the state and viticultural society, the brokers' shift from commission to speculation was less the result of greed than of necessity. Basic economic problems in the Champagne wine trade forced brokers to develop new systems of commerce.

The Champagne wine trade offers evidence for a rather different evolution in the viticultural economy than that expressed in the classic thesis of Labrousse. In contrast to his argument that viticulture flourished through much of the century before the crisis of the 1770s, Champagne endured economic problems early in the century that forced it to transform its wine production and trade in response. After three ebullient decades at the start of the eighteenth century, the wine trade in Champagne suffered hard times. In the face of a crisis, the winemakers turned reluctantly to a technique that ultimately made the province famous: They bottled their wine and worked to develop a luxury market. The brokers of Champagne were crucial in this transformation, providing both the financial resources to produce bottled wine and their skill at constructing new markets for a new product.

Crisis in the Champagne Wine Trade

There is much evidence to indicate the existence of a serious economic decline in the wine trade of Champagne, beginning in the second quarter of the eighteenth century. According to the intendant, by 1731, "the vine regions, once the best in Champagne, have become the most miserable."[1] The tax farm of various levies on wine, which gives a rough indication of quantities sold throughout the generality, declined by 11 percent from the late 1720s through the 1730s and early 1740s.[2] As the agent of one of the abbeys in Epernay reported at the end of the 1720s, "The wines of Champagne are so reviled that we dare not hope to make any profit from them."[3] Already in 1732, the intendant's report on the region around Epernay warned of a serious depression in the wine trade, which was the "principal occupation of its inhabitants. [But] since wine has not been selling for some time the inhabitants are not rich. . . . The disrepute of their wine has made this region one of the unhappiest in the province."[4]

In addition to much anecdotal evidence for the province's problems, the contrôle des actes testifies to the scale of the crisis. The shipments of wine from Epernay in the first three decades were the largest of the century. A sample of more than half of the years through this period yields an average of seven thousand barrels per harvest year (from October to the following September).[5] In 1729, however, there was a general and permanent decline in the number of barrels sent from Epernay: barely two thousand that year and barely three thousand the next. A sample of a dozen years between 1729 and 1750 averaged less than two thousand barrels; only 1748 reached five thousand and several years on either side of it sent less than one thousand.[6] The second half of the century was even worse; Epernay sent less than a thousand barrels in most years. A growing number of clerical errors in the contrôle des actes probably exaggerated the gravity of Epernay's commercial decline, but it is hard to imagine that the clerks missed more than a thousand barrels at most.[7] There is no question that the wine trade with Paris experienced a profound change.

Some of Epernay's decline was balanced by increasing shipments from neighboring towns, registered in different contrôles des actes. Shipments of wine in the contrôle des actes of nearby Ay actually increased through the first half of the century, from an average of eight or nine hundred barrels, in the first two decades, to two or three thousand barrels in the 1730s and 1740s.[8] The shipments of wine from Ay may explain part of Epernay's decline, but the totals of Epernay, Ay, and other villages nearby in the 1740s were still well below those of the century's first three decades.[9] The region also sent some wine east out of the country that did not appear in the contrôle, and these exports grew from roughly sixteen hundred barrels in the 1740s to twenty-five hundred in the 1770s.[10] But, for a variety of reasons, the whole region was clearly hit by a decline in its wine trade, particularly with Paris.

Bad weather caused serious disruptions in wine production through much of this period. One broker told his correspondents in 1729 that the region had produced only a third as much wine as the previous year, and the vineyards of the mountain of Reims were "completely lacking" in wine.[11] The records of a grower of Ay, Malavois de la Ganne, spoke of the "sterility" of the harvests in 1736, 1741, 1757, and 1758, the "mediocrity" of 1735, 1755, and 1756, and a drought in 1738.[12] A report in 1752 complained that "the only harvest in this election [of Epernay] since 1744 that has produced something is 1748, though it was not very considerable. The others have been a pure waste, either because there was so little or because of the bad quality."[13] Another grower spoke in 1759 of his vines having "suffered the same fate as those of everyone else, having produced nothing for four years."[14] Official estimates of the grape harvest in Epernay and Ay confirm these complaints: After averaging 5.8 barrels per arpent in the 1720s, output from 1730 to 1741 declined to 3.4 barrels and from 1745 to 1758 was only 1.2 barrels.[15]

Prices reflected declining harvests to some extent. Judging from prices paid for wines in the accounts of several brokers—not, unfortunately, a homogenous source—the price per queue of common wine in the 1720s varied roughly between forty and sixty livres in abundant years and eighty to 120 livres in the poor years. This range ignores many of the distinctions that Bertin identified in his letters to merchants. Wines from Ay tended to be a bit above the "vins de vignerons"; those from Cumières were even higher. "Bourgeois" wines could be two or three times more expensive than vigneron wines, though the "tailles" of bourgeois wines were in between. Moët also bought a range of wines, whose prices in the early 1740s tended to be similar to those in the 1720s. He paid forty-five to sixty livres per queue for vin de tailles in reasonably abundant years and roughly twice that in the poorer years at the end of the 1740s and during the 1750s. The price of Malavois's red wines between 1745 and 1754 was some 65 percent higher than in the previous fifteen years, though they lost more than half of that increase in the following decade. He reported the price of common wine (vin de vigneron) rising from forty or fifty livres per queue (double barrel) in the early 1740s to sixty to ninety livres in the 1750s.[16] Without being very precise, account books confirm the general disruption occasioned by bad weather.

Rising prices probably hurt the common wines of Champagne more than the luxury wines; they were competing with a growing supply of cheap wine produced around Paris and coming from an expanding provincial provisioning crown. The result was that merchants shied away from Champagne and often did not buy the wine that was available: Malavois complained that the wines of 1753 were "good but very little sought because the wines of the previous year had cost too much, so the merchants' cellars are still full [of unsold wine]." Abundant years like 1748 brought merchants "eagerly" looking for wine, but when the "sterility was general," as in 1758, "no merchants showed up to buy, so growers sold their wine from their houses by the pinte." Another consideration was the quality of the wine; according to Malavois, they were "excellent" in 1742 and "so sought after that we have rarely seen so many merchants," but those of 1744 were "not good quality so we have hardly seen any merchants anywhere." Through the middle of the century, the lack of demand was a frequent refrain in Malavois's accounts.

Contemporary explanations for the region's commercial stagnation tended to emphasize the declining quality of its wines. The intendant in 1732 bemoaned the fact that the wines around Epernay, once "the most esteemed in Champagne, have lost their ancient reputation for the last several unhappy years." He claimed that "most of the wine [is] of such bad quality that it cannot be shipped [to distant markets] and must be consumed in the region. . . . As for the wine from good vines, the public complains with reason that its quality is diminishing since most vignerons, looking to produce an abundance, manure their vines, which alters the quality." The wine brokers were also blamed for substituting mediocre wine for the good wine that was ordered, which "tends to drive away foreigners who are beginning to get fed up." As a result, "several reliable [vine] owners have even assured me that for seven or eight years they have barely earned enough to cover their outlays." [17]

The government blamed the loss of quality on the growing amount of inferior vines planted in the region. Indeed, one of the recurring themes found in testimony of growers and administrators alike was the contrast between the small amount of extremely expensive wine, produced in a few locations from a limited portion of their grapes, and the large and rapidly growing amount of mediocre wine produced across the region. The government had tried to resist the extension of vines throughout France on several occasions, arguing that the result was an overproduction of wine that hurt prices, along with a decline in grain production. Its campaign had culminated in an arrêt of 1731 that imposed harsh penalties on any new conversion of grain lands to vines, but growers resisted these efforts, for the simple reason that an arpent of vines was substantially more productive than an arpent of grain. [18] A family could survive—barely—on three or four arpents of vines but never on that amount of grain; so the vineyards spread.

A survey of vineyards in the parishes around Reims in 1738 confirmed the government's fears that the ban of 1731 had been ignored. [19] The principal inhabitants of sixty-five parishes admitted to a total of 257 arpents of new vines planted just in the four previous years. Although this is barely 2 percent of the vineyards estimated in these parishes later in the century, it represented a flagrant violation of the arrêt.[20] And in several cases the surveyor noted that "there have been easily sixty [more] arpents planted in the last ten to fifteen years; people are planting daily; their declaration does not seem to be sincere." The resistance to the ban was widespread; the survey named over a thousand people who had planted new vines. Most of these were local peasants who had planted a tiny new plot, but there were also outsiders from Reims, like Nicolas Ruinart who had planted some eleven arpents in several parishes.

The report of 1738 emphasized the dire consequences of spreading vines. In a few places toward the south, around Mailly and Ludes, the survey noted that "the plantations are so frequent that if there is no remedy they will have difficulty finding vignerons and manure, and in the years of dearth the inhabitants will suffer [since] many have no masters to assist them." A number of other parishes noted that the price of vine props and manure had almost doubled, and "the inhabitants of Saint-Thierry die of hunger in the years when wine is abundant." The survey expressed particular concern about a trend it noted in the southeast, around Verzenay, where "the inhabitants are planting a plant commonly called *belo* and *pandella,* which produces a very bad wine in large quantities and is ruining the region's reputation."[21] The vines continued to spread into the 1750s, when a treatise about Champagne, which asserted that "this commerce [in wine] has languished for some years," laid much of the blame on "this too great planting of vines" that had raised the price of land, manure, wood, and labor.[22]

According to a report written to Joly de Fleury, the prosecutor general in Paris in 1739, the problem lay with changing tastes:

The custom introduced into the *grand monde* for the last twenty years of not drinking champagne if it is not foamy, and which has gone to such an extent that a mediocre *mousse* is no longer enough and the cork must shoot out as soon as the strings that tie it are cut, has forced the bourgeois, in order to sell his wine, to put them in bottles, when he has not been able to sell them in barrels before March, and to seek, at considerable expense, the critical point of foaming, without which the sale of his wine is no longer possible, since still wine is presently out of style and rejected.[23]

The "grand monde" had not been the only customers for the wines of Champagne, but changing tastes had clearly contributed to the difficulties Champagne faced. The common red wines from Champagne that had supplied the mass market in Paris early in the century had to compete increasingly with a growing amount of mediocre wine produced across the north of France and increasingly with wine from upper Burgundy and the south.[24] Bourgeois growers like Malavois de la Ganne, making a more expensive white wine, had the advantage over the common grower in that the price of white wine was more buoyant. But apparently the "grande monde" was increasingly demanding that this white wine be bottled and sparkling. All of these trends contributed to a sharp diminution in the trade between Epernay and Paris, a decline that forced growers to develop new products and challenged brokers, who had dominated the trade with Paris, to find new markets.

Wine in New Bottles

Commercial difficulties led to profound structural transformations in Champagne's wine trade: A commerce based overwhelmingly on the sale of wine in barrels became predominantly a market in bottled wine. With the decline in the Parisian market for a large amount of mediocre wines, some growers turned to making better wine and selling it to elite customers. In certain cases this meant improving their red wine: A treatise on Champagne in the 1720s claimed that "some individuals have recently begun to make a wine as red as that of Burgundy. . . . These wines are good for Flanders where they are easily sold as burgundies."[25] According to a grower of Ay, "the bourgeois vignerons of Ay have learned how, in imitation of Cumières since 1743, to make first-class red wine and put it in big barrels [*grosse jauge,* after the fashion of the mountain of Reims] and so match and even surpass the quality of wines of the mountain."[26] But the more common strategy was to bottle a white wine that became foamy, or sparkling, and quite expensive. Over the course of the century, the extraregional wine trade of Champagne turned overwhelmingly to a commerce in this bottled wine.

The techniques for producing a sparkling white wine had been discovered in the seventeenth century, but they were too demanding and expensive to be widely practiced. During the seventeenth century some wine producers along the Marne River began to make a white wine with their red grapes that rapidly gained a dazzling reputation among the fashionable society of both France and England. If red grapes are pressed lightly and quickly enough, their juice is clear and results in a nearly white or "gray" wine. To make a white wine properly from red grapes, however, required substantial investment in the vines as well as access to a considerable labor force and the proper equipment. A letter to the controller general from the middle of the century complained that the only way the grower of Ay, Hautvillers, or Pierry achieved expensive, high-quality wine was by "spending lots of money to prune his vines, he cuts them extremely low, he keeps the vines from multiplying and blocking the sun by becoming too shady."[27] These low vines produced only two or three barrels per arpent, as opposed to seven or eight of normal growth. They had to be harvested early in the day, before the sun heated the grapes, which required a large labor force that could finish the job quickly. Such grapes, produced in smaller quantities and harvested with greater care, cost their grower more than did the common grapes to make common red wine.

Vinification of this first-class white wine was equally arduous. The grower raced to press the grapes, ideally at a winepress close by, to avoid heating the grapes and tinting the juice with the color of the skins. Where growers owed a tithe on their grapes, the process of collecting the tithe often delayed them from pressing and even precluded their making white wine.[28] A clear white wine depended on the precise selection of the grape juice, which in turn demanded careful use of the press. The grapes were crushed gradually, through a progressive series of pressing and easing off that produced different batches of juice of increasing body, but also increasing color. The first press produced the *vin de goute,* of great delicacy but little body. It was usually combined with the next pressing, the *vin de première taille,* to make the best white wine. The second and third tailles were pressed harder and produced more volume than did the first batches; depending on the weather and the method of harvesting, they too could result in an acceptable white wine. Alternatively the third and fourth tailles might be combined to make a rosé wine of some value. The subsequent tailles, up to a seventh pressing, produced a very red *vin de pressoir,* "a part of which is served to the infinite number of workers [the grower] is obliged to employ, and the rest being sold very cheap."[29] The cahiers of Epernay at the end of the Old Regime calculated that only a fifth of a grower's wines were first class and worth 175 livres per barrel; half of the wine was considered second class, worth sixty livres, and the rest worth only twenty-five.[30] It is not surprising to learn that, in villages like Pierry before the Revolution, "the bourgeois proprietors alone make the great white wines of Champagne [and] the small vignerons make only red and common wines," or that in Ay, "the rich bottle much of their wine, the vignerons sell it all in barrels."[31]

Preparation of this white wine also required clarifying it, both through racking and fining. Whether or not the wine was sparkling, its color was particularly important to customers like the comte d'Artagnan, who wrote to his wine broker, Adam Bertin du Rocheret, that "I do not mind [if it is bubbly] so long as its quality is not diminished . . . and it is very clear."[32] Clarifying was not merely a matter of aesthetics, however. Growers in Champagne had discovered that the process of fining, or clarifying by adding a substance to precipitate out any impurities or sediment, helped to conserve the wine. Racking, or pouring wine out of one barrel into a new one and leaving the deposits behind, appears to have been an even more recent practice, gaining general acceptance in treatises on vinification only in the 1730s.[33] Bertin still, in 1716, resisted the suggestion made by a Parisian négociant that a shipment ought to have been racked after it was fined, reminding him that "your father fined wines as he shipped them, and in his days we did not know about racking."[34] It must be remembered that all of these expensive and labor-intensive techniques were reserved for quality wine. There is little evidence of their practice before the late seventeenth century, and then only in a few regions that were beginning to produce wine for aging. Champagne was essentially the earliest to develop these techniques, to be followed shortly by areas of Bordeaux.[35]

Most of the wine produced in Champagne did not meet the standards of the best white, but those that did rapidly gained favor and important markets at home and abroad. Literary and anecdotal evidence points to the burgeoning popularity of wines of the Marne River at court during the reign of Louis XIV, and an earlier chapter noted that their prices rose rapidly.[36] They were helped, perhaps, by being served at the banquets following the consecration of the king in Reims, and he appears to have preferred these wines for much of his life. They also gained the support of nobles with a reputation for refined taste. The exile of one of these connoisseurs, Saint-Evremond, to the royal court in England extended the wine's reputation to an island of prodigious wine consumers. Saint-Evremond consciously campaigned for the wine among his new neighbors and helped to arrange their supplies.[37] The demand for this new wine grew rapidly, especially when it began to do something unusual: The wine started to become foamy.

Historians now generally agree that it was the consumers of the white Champagne wines who discovered how to turn it into a sparkling wine.[38] Some of them had bottled this wine during the spring, before it had finished fermenting, and it had become "bubbly, foamy" (*mousseux*) in the bottle. The use of bottles was not a normal part of the wine trade in the early eighteenth century, and the winemakers of Champagne rarely used bottles to store their wine. Wine was stored and shipped in barrels; it was served directly from barrels into glasses or pitchers. Consumers had discovered, however, that wine rarely survived more than two years in barrels, and the white wine of Champagne was even more vulnerable in barrels than the red.[39] Furthermore, a barrel might remain fairly airtight for a year or two, but once it was broached it quickly went bad.[40] Few wine merchants bothered themselves about conservation. Tavern keepers were usually able to finish a barrel quickly, and wholesale wine merchants hoped to sell the wine as fast as possible and start afresh with new wine in the fall. Instead, it was elite consumers, who bought wine by the barrel but drank it in small quantities, who needed to solve the problem of a barrel that might remain only partially full for long periods. The solution was to transfer the wine out of barrels and into bottles.

The fundamental process of a second fermentation, anywhere from six to twelve months after an initial fermentation, is quite natural for Champagne's white wines; they need only to be properly bottled to conserve the carbon dioxide produced by the second fermentation and make the wine "foamy." Proper bottles, with proper corks to seal them, were probably utilized first by the English in the second half of the seventeenth century.[41] There are literary references to effervescence in champagne drunk in that country from the 1660s or 1670s. The French give evidence of producing the same sparkling wine shortly thereafter, probably by the 1680s.[42] But in both cases this sparkling wine appeared first among the consumers rather than the producers because it was the by-product, initially, of conservation techniques rather than the deliberate outcome of winemaking practice. For several reasons, wine producers bottled little of their wine until the mid–eighteenth century.

The "secrets" of producing a bottle of sparkling champagne were generally known by the late seventeenth century, but they were inconvenient and expensive. Growers rarely bottled, preferring to ship their wine in barrels and leave the bottling to consumers or wine merchants in Paris and London. Despite its success in high society, sparkling wine played a very limited role in the wine trade of Champagne until well into the eighteenth century. Only gradually did the region's wine trade evolve into something fundamentally different, becoming a high-quality but low-quantity trade aimed less and less at Paris and increasingly toward export markets. It took a commercial slump in the wine trade to force growers, grudgingly, to accept the new methods of production and brokers to deal with this new commodity.

The Decision to Bottle

The transformation of the Champagne wine trade from barrels to bottles occurred gradually because the benefits it offered came only at the expense of significant investments and risks. Most producers, fearing the uncertainty and unable to bear the costs, resisted the transition, but the economic difficulties of the wine trade provided powerful incentives. Those with enough wealth to have good vines and some financial flexibility were slowly forced to adopt the new methods. Brokers were ultimately in the best position to profit from the new trade.

Wine in bottles was worth far more than wine in barrels and thus seems like an attractive business decision, but bottling required much greater production costs and sacrificed quantity of production for quality. Growers were not anxious to put their wine into bottles, for the process of making sparkling wine was a gamble. It required careful and expensive preparation of the wine: The wine had first to be racked and fined, a process that required special equipment and technique. The grower needed to wait until the right moment, during a full moon according to some authors, to bottle the wine. The bottles were expensive, as were the cost of racking and the labor for every step of the process. The intendant estimated the price of bottles at the factory as thirteen livres per hundred in the 1730s. By another estimate, the bottle cost as much as three sous, and the corks cost roughly another half sous each.[43] The delay until a spring bottling meant that a harvest brought no return for an extra half year.

One of Champagne's notables, with vines in Ay, succinctly spelled out the calculus of disincentives in a letter to the intendant in 1734:

> But given an abundant harvest, if I fail to make an elite wine, if it is tinted red, even slightly, my ruin is only accelerated by this unfortunate abundance. My expenses start up without having any income. I pay taxes on wine that I do not sell. With a successful cuvée that I cannot sell I am even more miserable: new expenses, new loans to put it in bottles. If my wine does not foam it is only worth ten sous a bottle. If it turns ropy or drops a deposit, it has to be put back into a barrel and sold in taverns. Or, if it foams, half of the bottles break, and when I sell it I have to pay brokerage fees and more taxes.[44]

Growers were reluctant, as a consequence, to bottle their wine and much preferred to sell what they could in barrels quickly at the harvest. Bottling was a second-best alternative, forced on them by the necessity of slow sales and poor conservation. A letter from Reims to the prosecutor general in the 1740s pointed out that, although "a great part of the province's red and white wines are sold quickly [*dans la primeur*], all of the white that remains unsold by the months of March and April are bottled, after which no white remains in barrels, except for mediocre wines or those of the vignerons."[45] What was not sold was bottled, for it did not last in barrels.

Even the wealthy makers of excellent wines like the abbey of Hautvillers, where Dom Pérignon had produced much-prized (though undoubtedly nonfoamy) white wine, sold little of its wine in bottles before the middle of the eighteenth century.[46] In addition to some three hundred barrels sold in the 1691 season (from October 1691 to September 1692) the abbey sold only four hundred bottles, and these went to either Châlons or Reims. This was apparently wine for local consumption; two years later, the abbey's accounts mention a thousand bottles (the equivalent of roughly five barrels) sent to Reims "to be sold over the counter [*en détail*]."[47] The abbey moved only very slowly, and well after the death of Dom Perignon, to bottling more of its wine. As late as 1713, the inventory of wines at the abbey showed nearly four hundred barrels of wine, but no bottles. An inventory of wine belonging to the abbey in 1733 listed 18 percent in bottles; the figure was 26 percent by 1743 and 1747.[48] The switch to bottling wine was a very gradual one.

The accounts of a grower in Ay, Malavois de la Ganne, clearly show the difficulties in selling wine experienced even by elite producers and how their response involved a reluctant turn to bottled wine. A previous chapter noted Malavois's insistence on the "advantage of selling early [*en primeur*]" and how much this depended upon the arrival of brokers of Epernay or Reims to take it off his hands. Alas, this occurred only three times in his first two decades; during most of those years he sold nothing until the spring and summer—late April on average—and sometimes took several years to get rid of it all.[49] In his last fifteen years, when he had firmly established his reputation with the brokers of Reims, he was favored more often and sold in an average of two months after the harvest. In the early years, however, the brokers came late or not at all, and he had to find his own markets, which took time. In years like 1731 or 1737, he only received help from local brokers for small amounts and late in the summer following the harvest, by which time the price had dropped. He was still selling the wine more than a year after the harvest.

Slow sales posed serious problems: of finances, of storage, of finding markets. Malavois tried different solutions, but slow sales usually led him to bottle his white wine. Early in his career, with wine from 1732 still on hand in the summer of 1734, he was obliged to retail it to local customers out of his own house, for six sous per quart. This was clearly a counsel of desperation and the only time he would ever do it. Although he noted in 1749 that "many were forced to sell their wine out of their houses at eight to ten sous per pinte," he refused to do likewise. That year, and in most of the others when sales were slow, he bottled his wine instead. As he explained in 1744, when the quality was poor and "we have hardly seen any merchants anywhere, . . . few people have sold their wine. I was among the great number of these unfortunates with the result that I was forced to bottle our five barrels from Cuis but did not go to this expense for those of Epernay." Otherwise, he rarely specified what provoked his decision to bottle, but the circumstances give us some clue. In the fourteen years when he bottled, his first sale took place an average of six months after the harvest; in the years when he did not bottle the first wine was sold in less than four. It was the "lack of sales," he explained about the vintage of 1759, that "forced me into the new expense of bottling, of which part [would be] foamy and part destined for not foamy."

In addition to the expense, bottling meant running very real risks. The experience of 1735 had clearly been a disaster for many in the town: "This year was very favorable for the mousse, all the wines having had this quality, but very disadvantageous in another way because of the volume of mousse, which left many with nothing but the debris of broken bottles and others with little to show for their expenses." The same thing happened in 1746: "The breakage this year has been extreme because of the great *liqueur* of the wine, and of three barrels that I bottled [worth some six hundred bottles] only 250 survived." Of the wine bottled after the harvest of 1754, more than twelve hundred bottles broke. Heavy rains in January 1741 flooded his cellar and destroyed the bottles remaining from 1739.

The losses from broken bottles had become so severe in the mid-1740s that the prosecutor general in Paris launched an inquiry into the bottle industry. He received reports from individuals in Reims claiming that the city had lost three hundred thousand livres worth of wine (probably ten to fifteen thousand bottles) from broken bottles in 1747 alone. The broker Allart de Maisoneuve, for example, had lost all but nine hundred bottles in a batch of over five thousand. The breakage was so bad that summer that his cellar "could not be entered until September without suffocating from the fumes" of the spilt wine. "Some have lost more than a quarter of their bottles," one letter reported, "others nearly a half."[50] Several reports blamed the glass manufacturers that had sprung up around Paris for selling cheaper bottles and forcing the established glass makers of the Argonne to cut costs. Since the late 1730s everyone had begun to use glass slag, with impurities in it, which weakened the bottles. "Those who have had the misfortunate not to sell their wine in barrels, or those who have bought the barrels from them run a great risk in putting their wine in bottles," according to one report, "from the great expense of bottling and from the loss occasioned by badly made bottles."[51]

Another of the risks Malavois ran in bottling his wine was the challenge of finding the necessarily selective clientele who were interested in such an expensive product. The brokers helped with some of it, particularly with finding customers to the east and south, in Arras, Strasbourg, Dijon, and Lyon. Some fifteen hundred bottles went to Hamburg through brokers in Reims in 1753, and another 250 bottles were sent to the governor general of Canada aboard a ship leaving from Rochefort in 1749. But more often he sent it to Paris, and in this market he was aided by his network of friends and relatives. When brokers failed to help him sell his wine, he turned to a brother living in Paris who brokered wine for him to a wide range of people. Another brother, a priest, helped him sell some bottles to an elaborate network of friends, many of them also priests. Although the Parisian brother normally distributed his bottled wine, one year Malavois sent six barrels of white wine to his brother in Paris that had been "racked three times and fined twice, to be put in bottles." It is not clear whether his brother sold them in barrels or did the bottling himself, but Malavois obviously preferred to avoid waiting until spring to bottle, even if he had performed many of the steps needed for bottling. The only good reason for bottling, it seems, was the extra storage time he gained, a crucial factor when some harvests took four years to sell off.

On the whole, Malavois appears to have bottled his wine with reluctance, when there was no easy sale for it. He complained of having to bottle, despite the fact that bottling his wine brought real gains, much increasing his normal gross income in his early years. His bottles of sparkling wine usually sold for thirty sous, making a barrel of white wine that sold for one hundred livres worth three hundred. But the bottles alone cost him nearly three sous apiece on average, even more in certain years, and the process added considerable inconvenience and risk. Bottling this wine was an expensive solution to a slow market, but the alternative of selling it over the counter was also inconvenient and had little appeal. Fortunately, the merchant wine brokers of Reims relieved Malavois of the necessity of bottling for much of the last fifteen years of his life. Increasingly in the 1750s and 1760s they arrived promptly in October or November to buy his best white wines at steadily mounting prices.

The brief accounts of another Champagne grower, Durand of Pierry, who operated on much the same scale as Malavois, suggest less hesitation about producing and selling bottled wine. In the late 1730s he started to sell several thousand bottles of wine to brokers in Epernay and Cumières; he provided Bertin du Rocheret with much of his wine. His accounts do not offer enough details to explain his reasons for bottling his wine, but they show him increasing his business in bottled wine. By the late 1740s, Durand's commerce had grown not only in volume but also in range. His output had reached the level of requiring the purchase of nearly nine thousand empty bottles in the spring of 1749. He was sending large shipments of three and four thousand bottles in the early 1750s to Nantes and La Rochelle, by way of an intermediary in Paris, and to Hamburg by way of a négociant in Rouen. There was no mention of local brokers involved in these large shipments, but he was selling lots of bottled wine to local brokers in smaller quantities.[52]

If Durand did well in the wine trade, his daughter who took over after his death ran into trouble with creditors by 1757. Debts of five thousand livres to merchants in Châlons led to the seizure of her furniture and wine. She also owed several thousand livres to others in surrounding villages for purchases of wines and bottles. Her creditors tried to force her to sell some ten thousand bottles of wine from 1753 and 1754 for what she considered the "vile price" of only sixteen sous per bottle, and she sent letters to various judges seeking relief until she could find a better buyer. "I was not born with a fortune," she wrote, "I was born of honest people, I have followed a profession, I have engaged in no commerce, I have retired to my house like a nun in her cloister and have occupied myself with my household and making the most of my property." Her large debts for wine purchases belie these words or, rather, show how growers of a certain size mixed production with some commerce. The market had clearly turned against her, though she blamed her problems on "this monopoly on the part of other merchants who would like to have these wines for very little." In the nick of time she was able to find a buyer. Whether it was the work of a "heaven favorable to my prayers" or, instead, of the broker Germon of Epernay "who set the price of my wine" and found her a "rich wine merchant" from Paris, she was able to get twenty-eight sous per bottle.[53] Like Malavois, she depended on merchants, and on the brokers who could contact them, for her sales.

If the ultimate product of bottling was more valuable, it was not obvious to growers that the result was worth the effort. Racking, fining, clarifying, and bottling might produce a windfall or, just as easily, an explosion. And the market was never certain. An elite clientele was willing to pay high

The Decline and Transfiguration of Champagne

prices, but this market was necessarily limited and difficult to penetrate. Brokers already enjoyed access to the elites of Paris and the rest of Europe, but growers had to scramble to sell their bottled wine. In addition to these problems, the government had also discouraged the trade in bottled wine, allowing the shipment of no more than a hundred bottles at a time.[54] As a consequence, growers like Malavois did not embrace bottling as a welcome innovation, but rather turned to it as a last resort, imposed by commercial stagnation and simple needs of conservation. It required the commercial skill and financial resources of large brokers to turn bottled champagne into a profitable business, and even they accepted the challenge reluctantly.

It is not surprising, then, to find that very little wine was shipped in bottles from Epernay at the beginning of the century, and only in small batches. Scarcely four thousand bottles sailed down the Marne in the first four years of the century, amid some twenty-five thousand barrels; half of the bottles went in one shipment, sent by an individual to Versailles "to be sold over the counter."[55] (Presumably the shipment of two thousand bottles was acceptable because the lettre de voiture specified that the wine was to be sold retail.) The number of bottles sent from Epernay increased but slowly through the first quarter of the century. The twenty thousand bottles shipped between the summers of 1713 and 1715 comprised less than 1 percent of the total volume of wine shipped. Shippers began sending larger amounts at a time, even before 1728, although the eighty-four hundred bottles sent by an individual to Le Havre, to be shipped to the "French islands of America" in 1720, were unusual.[56] Over twenty-six thousand bottles sailed in the single year following the harvest of 1724, but that was still a bit less than 1 percent of the total volume.

The government made it easier to ship large quantities of bottles in 1728, at least for shipments to and through Normandy, which facilitated the export of wine in bottles from Norman ports.[57] Yet the freer trade allowed by the revision of 1728 appears initially to have had little impact on the trade in bottled wine. The number of bottles increased slowly after 1728, though the percentage increased because the number of barrels declined. Nearly 4 percent of the wine shipped in the early 1730s was in bottles, yet this was less than twenty thousand bottles a year. By the early 1740s, the number of bottles had increased to twenty-six thousand and amounted to some 10 percent of the wine listed in the bills of lading.[58] But in a good year, like 1748 when there was more demand, the region once again sent nearly the entirety of its wine in five thousand barrels; less than 1 percent was sent as bottles. Good years like that, however, were all too rare, and such wine as was shipped went increasingly in bottles.

The modest number of bottles sent in the first half of the century—generally some ten to thirty thousand in a year and rarely more than 1 percent of the total volume—indicates their marginal role, both in wine production and the wine trade.[59] There was a gradual trend over the period of increasing numbers of bottles shipped, yet the quantities of bottles rose and fell in inverse correlation to the total volume of wine sent in a given year. Thus a very poor year like 1713 sent twice as many bottles as the following year, though it shipped only a tenth as many barrels. The number of bottles in 1724 was ten thousand less than the previous year, though the total volume of wine had more than doubled. Most of the bottles sailed in the spring, suggesting that they had just been bottled, though it is impossible to tell the age of the bottles listed in the contrôle. These rhythms describe a general pattern to the decision to bottle: When the market was good wine was sold in barrels, otherwise it was bottled.

The trade in bottled wine early in the century was originally the work of winegrowers rather than the brokers. During the first two decades, brokers rarely sent more than several hundred bottles, except in a few years when the volume of barrels declined. The vast majority of bottles were sent by the score or so of growers who occasionally showed up in the contrôle as having "charged" a small shipment of wine. Whereas these bottles made up an essentially insignificant portion of the total wine shipped from Epernay, they represented an important part—at least 10 percent—of the wine sent by non-brokers. Evidently brokers had not yet seen the point of dealing in bottled wine when their commerce in barrels was so successful.

The brokers played a more active role in shipping bottles in the 1720s, as the amount of bottles shipped gradually increased. By 1723, the number of bottles had jumped to thirty-five thousand, though this was barely 3 percent of the total wine in a good year, and the brokers shipped 40 percent of them. The rest were sent by individuals like the subdelegué (who sent twenty-eight hundred) or the receiver of the aides. Most of the bottles went to Paris, though the monks of Hautvillers sent a *panier* (a basket carrying 75 to 120 bottles) to Rome. A big jump in total wine shipments the next year led to some drop in the number of bottles, and the brokers now shipped slightly over half of them. The amounts were down to eighteen thousand in the late 1720s, of which the brokers handled only a third, but they moved to dominate the bottle trade in the following decades.

A similar shift to bottles is evident in the wine exported from the whole province. Barely 5 percent of the wine exported from Champagne in the 1720s went in some thirty-seven thousand bottles; by the late 1740s the number of bottles had more than tripled and made up 14 percent of the wine. As the town council of Reims explained to the government in 1724: "The trade in gray wine [white wine from red grapes] of Champagne has grown considerably in recent years, due to the precautions taken by growers to bottle the wine at the first moon of March in order to make it foamy, since those who drink gray wine prefer it foamy, and furthermore gray wine cannot be shipped in barrels, either in France or abroad, without totally losing its quality."[60] Detailed figures for the 1740s show that half of the 125,000 bottles were from Reims and Châlons, the rest were from "Champagne," probably referring to the Marne region. Thus the Marne was sending more bottles east toward central Europe than west toward Paris by the middle of the century. In addition, most of the fifty thousand bottles of wine identified as being "from Reims" was probably wine bought along the Marne and bottled in Reims.

By the middle of the century the largest brokers in Reims were bottling the white wine they bought from the Marne region. The "merchant-brokers" of Reims, like Tronson Sutain and De la Motte, who bought most of Malavois's white wines after 1750 were clearly bottling his wine themselves. Allart de Maisonneuve, "the most important négociant in bottles" of Reims, reportedly had thirty thousand bottles "pass through [his] hands each year" already in the 1740s. Allart bottled forty-six thousand bottles in the spring of 1747 and at least forty thousand the following year.[61] In fact, such vast stocks of bottled wine—worth seventy or eighty thousand livres—clearly distinguished Allart from most brokers, who rarely maintained inventories of that size. The essence of brokering was turnover; an orthodox broker who bought only when given a commission had no need for inventories of wine. Yet the trade in bottles was pushing brokers to make larger investments in storage and stock, to take the risks of producing and purchasing wine for speculative trade, to become, indeed, négociants. Négociants like Allart had access to the markets that bought bottled champagne, as well as the resources to bear the expense and run the risks of bottling. Malavois was happy to let them turn his wine into bottles of bubbly.

This growth in bottled champagne meant a significant improvement in the value of the province's vineyards. The transition to sending bottles was crucial to the economy because bottled champagne cost substantially more than wine in barrels. A barrel of wine, containing 196 pintes (182 liters), might be worth one hundred livres in 1748; the same amount of wine, in 196 bottles, was worth 330 livres. Thus, although only 12 percent of the eight thousand hectoliters of wine exported from Champagne in 1748 was in bottles, the bottled wine represented over one-third of the total value.[62] Such expensive wine was going to an elite clientele across Europe, a clientele that would be discovered and served by brokers looking for new markets.

The Brokers' Response

The wine brokers of the Marne enjoyed considerable commercial success in the early years of the century and saw little reason to abandon a wine trade in barrels that brought them so much business. As a consequence they had not initially embraced the new sparkling wine. Adam Bertin du Rocheret was notorious for his dislike of the foam, for his conviction early in the century that "foaming removes what is best in a good wine while giving some merit to small [poor] wines."[63] He persuaded some among his elite clients to admit that "I see how wrong I was to ask you to bottle my wine to make it foamy," and others assured him that "the less foamy the wine is . . . the more I prefer it."[64] Other clients insisted on sparkling wine, but it is clear from the contrôle des actes that neither Bertin nor the other brokers shipped much bottled wine in the early years of the century.

Adam Bertin's cellars, however, tell a somewhat different story. At the time of his wife's probate inventory in 1722, they contained over three thousand bottles from the harvest of 1720, which had been sitting there for nearly a year. The inventory valued them at only eight sous apiece, suggesting both that this wine was not foamy and how limited the advantages of bottling might really be: His wine in bottles was worth little more than the wine in barrels. Rather than seeking a profit, it is quite probable that he had bottled this wine because he could not sell it quickly, indeed, it was still on his hands a year and a half later, and only bottling could save it. The inventory also listed several thousand empty bottles, purchased "the day before" for twelve livres per hundred. This was early March, and he had over a dozen barrels of good white wine left unsold. The late purchase of the bottles suggests he had not been planning to bottle initially but had been forced, like others, to bottle what was not sold.[65]

Other brokers evinced equal reluctance to make sparkling wine or to deal in it. On several occasions the broker Guyot sent a little bottled wine, but only two or three hundred bottles a year for most of the 1720s. In most cases the accounts show that Guyot was buying the wine already bottled. But in the spring of 1729, when he sent over seventeen hundred bottles to wine merchants in Paris, he notes that he "was obliged to have [the wine] racked and fined to get it in shape to be bottled. I topped it off at my expense after the second racking and paid all the necessary costs." These costs included "advanc[ing] the bottles, bottling it, the paniers, the packaging, [and] food for the workers."[66] Guyot treated these costs in a curiously unenterprising manner: The price he charged the buyer was not for the wine in bottles, but rather for the original wine in barrels, to which he added the costs of bottling it. Evidently he was not yet thinking of bottling in speculative terms as a way to increase his profits. Yet Guyot too was won over, for by 1734 he had more than ten thousand bottles of wine in his cellars that he was waiting to sell when the price rose.[67]

The commercial disruption of the 1730s forced profound changes in the wine trade and in the role of brokers, pushing some to abandon the profession, and all to change their business practices with changing circumstances. One who had been most successful, Adam Bertin du Rocheret, remained actively involved in the brokering business until his death in 1736 but seems to have lost money at it. His son, Philippe, spoke in gloomy terms about the state of the family's finances at the time of his father's death. His father, he alleged, had lost fifty thousand livres since the death of his wife some fifteen years before. Now Philippe spoke of inheriting financial difficulties and prayed for strength to "pilot his bark to a safe shore."[68] In a declining market, all brokers needed to find new ways to carry on their commerce.

Philippe Valentin Bertin du Rocheret, who began his brokering using his father's methods, was gradually forced to pursue very different markets. In his first year of brokering (1724) he sent a thousand barrels to Paris. His business declined rather precipitously after that, amounting to less than two hundred barrels in following years and under fifty by 1730. His big shipments, in the 1720s, had been sent to wine merchants in Paris, particularly to "Regnault and associates," two of whom were privileged wine merchants. Each received several dozen barrels, three or four times during 1724 and less often in subsequent years. A letter to Regnault in October 1727, asking him if he had changed brokers, signaled the approach of hard times; he soon lost his business in Paris almost completely.

Bertin responded to the loss of his Parisian market by seeking out new markets. In the fall of 1727 he contacted a wine merchant in London, Chabannes, with a business proposition: arranging contacts in Calais and Paris for shipping and finances and the terms under which Bertin might travel to Burgundy, presumably to buy wines.[69] He soon ended the Burgundy trips; after several discouraging letters about the difficulty of finding good burgundies he finally announced that he would handle buying the wines of Champagne but that Regnault, the Parisian wine merchant, would buy from Burgundy. Bertin also wanted information about the "English tastes," which suggests that he was not simply going to take specific orders, but was left with the initiative to buy wines. In the following spring he also traveled a good deal to new markets: Brussels, Lille, and Cambrai. From 1730 on, trade to these markets and England replaced his commerce with Paris. His cultivation of this clientele pushed him into sending an increasing amount of his wine in bottles.

Bertin's correspondence made relatively little reference to bottles in his early days, during the mid-1720s, only occasionally reporting on prices for bottled wine (twenty-five sous for foamy, twenty for still), particularly after the miserable harvest of 1725. Bertin only sold his first few bottles in the summer of 1727, to Orléans, Angers, and Paris. Even the wines sent to England went in barrels, with instructions that they be bottled ("you must never keep fine wines in barrels") and when they were to be bottled: "the fifth and sixth of the moon, that is, the 13, 14, and 15 of March."[70] He sent bottles occasionally over the next several years to a distant city like Metz, Luneville, or Thionville. Yet the bottled wine was clearly marginal to his business in the early years, both in what he was sending and advertising.

Wine in bottles gradually rivaled barrels in his commerce as he focused increasingly on a small, elite clientele. His bottles of both still and sparkling wine were especially requested by notables at court, like the king's librarian, for example, who informed Bertin that the king had consumed it with pleasure.[71] Some of this was wine bought from large growers like Durand of Pierry, but some was his own wine that he bottled at the request of customers, though he told one that he was "crazy to bottle his wine here."[72] He continued to sell some of his wine in barrels and had the good fortune sometimes to sell a large quantity of it to a wine merchant early in the year. There is some suggestion that bottling was still a second choice; to one correspondent he offered three barrels at the beginning of March, and added "if not [taken] I will bottle them."[73] Bertin's business by the 1740s had become a low quantity of very high quality wine to distant markets.

However reluctantly, brokers shifted their commerce increasingly to bottled wine. Through the middle of the 1730s and early 1740s, the brokers gained considerable control of the trade in bottled wine. Over three-quarters of the bottles listed in the contrôle des actes in those years were charged by brokers. As an official in Epernay explained to Joly de Fleury in 1739:

Our brokers, who are mostly rich, are possessors of very large vineyards, so that the liberty they have of knowing the taste of the region's wines, from being given samples of all these wines, puts them in a position to accept those that they have noticed will have the most disposition to mousse, which they then take home and join to their own wine and so amass such a large quantity of bottles in their stores that it is extremely difficult for the bourgeois to promote the sale of his own, for as I have told you, merchants [from outside] no longer take the trouble to come to make their own purchases, but rely on the brokers; it is easy to believe that [the brokers] begin by sending their own wine.[74]

Although some brokers possessed large vineyards, they appear to have been buying large quantities of wine that they bottled, using their advantages from superior knowledge about the conditions of both supply and demand to profit from the market.[75]

Yet some brokers resisted the change to bottled wine and continued the trade in common wine to Paris as long as they could. Claude Moët gradually increased his control over the traditional wine trade with Paris, single-handedly sending almost two-thirds of the wine shipments in the bumper year of 1748. The following year he was given the dubious honor of paying the largest tax in a special levy of 250 livres imposed on the town's seven brokers, though he grumbled at having to pay more than La Bertinière and Chertemps père who were "more senior and have earned more than we in this business."[76] He largely aimed his shipments of wine at a few of the major wine merchants, particularly Gauthier de Rougemont, one of the twelve privileged wine merchants of the king. Moët's purchases were also limited geographically and entrepreneurially. Most of the wine he bought came from only a few individuals in Ay, Avize, and Pierry, generally from fairly large-scale sellers. For example, he bought 350 barrels and over six thousand bottles in the year following October 1743 from three dozen people, more than half of them women. But nearly half was sold by just two people, one of them the dame Geoffroy, who had extensive vines but also, as the widow of the salt tax receiver of Epernay, probably dealt in local wines. Others had assembled much of his wine for him, and others had bottled it for him.

Moët himself was responsible for bottling very little of the bottles that he shipped, thus missing the chance to add value to his product. He bottled the dozen barrels of white wine that his own vines produced in 1744 but rarely bottled the wine that he was buying from others. Instead, he bought his bottled wine from the "bourgeois" growers, including, in later years, from Malavois de la Ganne. Only ten of the barrels that he acquired in 1743 were put into (1,954) bottles before shipment, but this was done at the residence of, and presumably by, the man who had sold him the barrels of wine. Given the cost of other bottles Moët bought, these ten barrels were worth roughly four times more in bottle than in barrel, yet it is not clear who gained the profit from the operation or paid the costs. In other years he usually bought his wine already bottled.

Business for Moët, as for the whole town of Epernay, was poor through the middle of the century. He was "more and more convinced," he wrote at the end of 1750, "that our vines cost us more than they produce, as they do for many others. Nevertheless one persists from habit, and at least our commissioning trade ought to make them less expensive than for others. . . . Only the big, big bourgeois, with very choice parcels of excellent vines that they pay close attention to and who know how to acquire and maintain favorable acquaintances for the sale of their wine, can make any profit." Throughout the 1750s he rarely shipped more than three hundred barrels in any year and often less than a hundred. His total for the decade, some sixteen hundred barrels, was less than from the harvest of 1748 alone. He shipped nearly 20 percent of his wine in bottles, usually seven or eight thousand, though the volume had fallen noticeably by the end of the decade to barely two thousand. His trade in bottles was slowly sketching out a more ambitious geography than his trade in barrels—to Warsaw, Stettin, Königsburg, Danzig, as well as closer cities.

The wine trade seems to have improved generally in the 1760s, and Moët's business, now run by Claude's son, Claude-Nicolas, increased to roughly a thousand barrels a year. This constituted nearly all the barrels being registered in the contrôle des actes those years, though the ten thousand bottles Moët sent were less than a third of the registered bottles. Once again Moët profited from contacts with the major Parisian wine merchants, like Gauthier de Rougemont whom his father had cultivated, and Chagot. Over 95 percent of the barrels sent by Moët went to Paris, only three-quarters of the bottles. His was still primarily a trade in still wine with the metropolis, much as his father's had been, and his business methods continued to be essentially those of a commission broker. The account book ends in 1763, but the contrôle shows Moët dominating this Parisian market into the 1780s.

The province of Champagne moved decisively to a high-quality wine trade during the second half of the century and recuperated much of the value, if not the volume, of its previous wine trade. The amount of wine shipped from Epernay and recorded in the contrôle des actes never returned to the heady levels of the beginning of the century, but the bottles now amounted to a much larger percentage of the total than before. Less than three hundred barrels sailed in the two years following October 1752, but they were accompanied by fifty-five thousand bottles—nearly half the total volume. A better year in 1759 sent only a tenth of the wine in bottles, and the sixty-five thousand bottles sent in 1761–62 were roughly a fifth of all the wine shipped. From the late 1760s on, the wine sent in bottles rarely fell below half of the volume; over one hundred thousand bottles sent from the two years following the poor harvest of 1772 amounted to 80 percent. Roughly one hundred thousand bottles sent in 1779 and again in 1781 were some three-quarters and two-thirds of the total shipments, though the proportion of bottles fell below half in 1782.[77] At a price of roughly thirty-five sous a bottle, this bottled wine alone brought nearly as much money to the region as the average years at the beginning of the century.[78]

The brokers of the Marne River dominated this trade in bottles through the second half of the century; it was they who now shipped the largest quantities. Quatresous and Chertemps shipped almost half of the bottles in the early 1750s but played a somewhat smaller role in the 1760s. Moët alone sent a quarter of the bottles in 1752–53, and his son sent a third of the bottles in 1761–63. Moët's son, however, did not lead this movement toward bottled wine; he sent over twenty-four thousand bottles in 1772 but more often he shipped no more than several thousand. Claude-Nicolas Moët steadfastly preferred to send barrels of more common wine to merchants in Paris, much as his father had done. Instead, other brokers in the region began to appear in the 1760s, ready to meet the demand for bottled wine.

A dozen individuals, some identified as négociants of Epernay but others from surrounding villages, took up the opportunity: Germon of Epernay, for example, sent over a third of the bottles in 1762. Men like Chedel of Pierry, Doublet of Mesnil, and Marc of Epernay, or women like Germon's widow, were shipping tens of thousands of bottles by the early 1770s and continued to do so in the 1780s.[79] Arthur Young proclaimed the success of these merchants in the 1780s: "Men who not only have many arpents of their own vines, but buy the wine of all their little neighbors." He emphasized the importance of their inventories, noting that Lasnier of Ay "has from fifty to sixty thousand bottle of wine always in his cellar," and spoke glowingly about Quatresous: "Should the good genius of THE PLOUGH ever permit me to be an importer of Champagne, I would desire Monsieur Quatresoux Partelaine, merchant at Epernay, to send me some of what I drank in his fine cellars."[80]

At some point in the two decades before the Revolution, Moët embraced the more speculative production and trade in bottled wine. By the 1780s, however, the province's wine trade with Paris had reached a very low ebb, and Moët's business, as one study of the family puts it, "seems to have fallen quite low."[81] Claude-Nicolas and his son, Jean-Rémy, now identified as négociants, recognized the need to seek new markets and took to the roads of the Holy Roman Empire in the 1780s to find customers.[82] The Moëts also employed a salesman, Jeanson, to create business in England: "I have distributed samples of which I have no news," he wrote in 1790. "How the taste of this country has changed in ten years, almost everywhere they ask for dry wine."[83] With new markets came a transition to high-quality, bottled wine. The house now produced its own bottled wine from barrels bought throughout the region and bottled as much as fifty thousand bottles in 1787, although contemporaries apparently found this "prodigious and did not believe that it was possible to find markets for such a considerable quantity."[84] Moët claimed in 1790 to have stocks of one hundred thousand bottles, which he offered to sell to correspondents across France and Europe.[85] His efforts bore fruit by the end of the 1780s, with shipments of bottles rising to nine thousand on the eve of the Revolution and climbing rapidly during the Republic. By the late 1790s he was shipping seventy-four thousand bottles a year.[86]

In response to the decline in Parisian demand, the brokers of the Marne actively pursued new markets. Throughout the first half of the century, the contrôles des actes of Epernay and Ay recorded the vast majority of the wine going directly to Paris, usually to wine merchants there, who might turn around and ship the wine elsewhere. Paris was still the destination for most of the wine by the middle of the century, but a growing number of bottles shipped in the 1730s and 1740s went to places like Hamburg, Saint Petersburg, and Rotterdam. They went increasingly during the next decades to Rouen and other locations in Normandy from whence they were exported. Through the 1760s and 1770s, shipments to Rouen gradually rivaled those to Paris, although the totals exported through this port were not very great, fluctuating between three and six hundred hectoliters, much of it in bottles.[87]

By 1773 Rouen was the most frequent destination, although Paris still imported the greatest volume because of the occasional very large shipment of barrels from Moët. From Rouen the wine went to markets across Europe. Even a small enterprise like Chanlaire, selling less than seven thousand bottles in the late 1770s, was sending more than half of it to Hamburg, Frankfurt, and Ulm.[88] Through the 1780s, most shipments were not stopping at Paris. The bottled wine in particular was going beyond Paris, to Rouen, and probably to northern Europe from there. The barrels, particularly shipments of more than two or three barrels, went only to Paris, but these shipments were rare and sent almost uniquely by the largest

The Decline and Transfiguration of Champagne

remaining broker, Moët.[89] The region of Epernay had finally joined the international wine trade.

The Brokers of Reims

The international market and a growing commerce in bottled wine had already saved the wine business around Reims from much of the disruption suffered along the Marne River. Exports from the mountain of Reims increased, both in volume and value, across the century, and the number of bottles exported from Reims grew ten times. Reims continued to serve a large market north and west of the city, which remained buoyant and to which their proximity still gave them an advantage over other French wine regions. Figures for exports of wine, most of it from around Reims and mostly going to the Netherlands and Germany, remained fairly steady at some eight thousand hectoliters through the first half of the century. Exports rose rapidly afterwards, nearly doubling by the late 1770s, though they declined precipitously before the Revolution.

The majority of the exports from Champagne remained in barrels throughout the century, but the amount of bottled wine grew rapidly. Through the first half of the 1720s, some thirty-seven thousand bottles accounted for only 5 percent of the wine exported from Champagne, most of which had been sent from Reims. By the late 1740s, the number of bottles leaving the kingdom had more than tripled and comprised 15 percent of the wine sent by Champagne. The province exported an average of nearly 275,000 bottles of wine through the second half of the 1770s, making up 20 percent of total volume, and the 381,000 bottles sent in 1780 were a third of wine exports. Exports declined in the 1780s, but by 1788 nearly 290,000 bottles made up 47 percent of the province's wine exports.[90]

Most of the bottled wine exported from Champagne came from Reims and was probably sent by the city's merchant-brokers, some of whom made the transition to a commerce in bottled white wine during the middle of the century. There is scattered evidence of brokers already bottling tens of thousands of bottles in the 1740s, and the detailed records of one broker show the change quite clearly. Nicolas Ruinart had dealt almost solely in barreled wine through the 1730s, and the vast majority of this wine had been sold quite locally, mostly in Lille and to a lesser extent in Tournay and Mons. The volume of his sales had barely reached two hundred barrels a year by the end of the decade, for a total value well under twenty thousand livres. Ruinart was clearly a modest businessman at this point, operating on a smaller scale than Moët but essentially in the same manner. Three decades later his enterprise was quite transformed.

Unlike the Moëts, who remained wine brokers until the last decade of the Old Regime, Ruinart began to act very much like a négociant during the middle of the century, buying, selling, and even producing large amounts of wine. In the process, Nicolas and later his son Claude greatly increased the quality of the wine they handled and the scale of their market. Their supply zone shifted quite distinctly from the area around Reims to the most prestigious locations along the Marne River and to its south, as well as to the most expensive wines of Burgundy. By the 1760s and 1770s Ruinart was shipping some thirty thousand bottles a year to a market that spanned the continent. Bottled wine, mostly mousseux but some still, now made up over a third of the volume of wine that they sold. The rest, some two to three hundred barrels of wine, included some cheap wine sold to local tradesmen in exchange for services, and much of it was sent to local purchasers. The bottles, in contrast, went to cities and courts throughout central and Eastern Europe. These bottles, averaging a little more than two livres apiece, were the real heart of this business; the wine in bottles was worth three to five times the same amount of wine in barrels. Thus the value of Ruinart's sales had more than quadrupled through the addition of bottled wine.[91]

More significantly for understanding the success of this house, it was Ruinart who was making the investment of bottling the wines of Champagne, unlike Moët, who bottled little of the wine he sold. Although Ruinart bought several thousand bottles of wine—already bottled—each year, the vast majority of his purchases of wine was in barrels, which he then bottled himself. This meant, first of all, acquiring much of his wine from Ay, Pierry, Vertus, and other sites along the Marne River that produced white wine of considerable quality. Some of this he purchased through a broker in Ay, but the majority came directly from producers like Gosset and Pietrement who were producing enough to be making ten barrels or so of "première cuvée." Ruinart was buying this wine mainly in the late fall and then cellaring until he bottled it in the spring. His accounts include purchases of twenty to thirty thousand empty bottles a year, at a cost of nearly four sous per bottle, from a variety of suppliers. A letter from 1764 to his bottle supplier in Sedan ordered seventy to eighty thousand bottles for the following Easter and asked that he be given "preference as your first and oldest customer." The supplier's response warned him that "since many other merchants of Reims have begun to make demands on us, I ask that you request only what you will need."[92]

With the profits from bottling wine came the risks. A report from Claude Ruinart's assistant in the following decade tells us that he was dealing with very large quantities of bottled sparkling wine but suffering from its vulnerability to excessive pressure. The "fine weather" of July was wonderful for the vines but evidently contributed to massive bottle breakage throughout the city. Ruinart's cellars were full of the *vin de casse,* that is, wine from the exploded bottles. The wine ran off into pots that the assistant was busy emptying and collecting in barrels. He had already collected forty-one barrels of vin de casse, the wine from at least eight thousand broken bottles, and reported that he was having trouble finding anyone to buy it.[93] But the real challenge lay in finding customers for the bottled wine.

The Ruinarts' move into the "luxury" market meant they also dealt in modest amounts of wine from Burgundy. As their contacts with elite consumers grew they were able to serve them by acquiring other kinds of luxury wines, much as the brokers of Reims had done for centuries. They purchased this wine from the bigger brokers in Beaune and Nuits, though they also went looking for bargains from brokers in Chalon and Mâcon. Some of the wine, from a grower in Beaune with whom Nicolas exchanged testy letters, came in barrels and was "bottled shortly after its arrival" in September by Ruinart. Ruinart was clearly dealing with many customers who wished to buy their wine in bottles. Other wine he had sent by the Burgundians directly to his clients.

By 1761 Ruinart's market included more than two dozen cities in southern Germany, plus another half dozen in the Netherlands, London, and Naples. The luxury market for bottled wine in any one city was very limited, so Ruinart was obliged to sell it over a much greater geographical expanse. Very little wine went to Paris, causing his banker in Paris to write with alarm, "Has your commerce in this region died? I no longer have any bills of exchange to receive or pay; whence comes such a long and considerable interruption?"[94] Instead, Ruinart worked hard to expand his foreign markets and in a dozen years had increased them substantially, geographically if not by volume. Claude Ruinart, who joined his father in 1764 and took over on his father's death in 1769, was sending wine to four dozen towns throughout Germany and the Netherlands by the mid-1770s, as well as to a few addresses in Sweden and Denmark, Poland and Russia, Britain and Italy. There were twice as many addresses, and far more clients, in places like London and Munich, than had been found in the 1760s. The luxury market brought Claude considerable success, allowing him to acquire a seigneury and an ennobling office in the 1770s. To a large trade with clients to the east, he added the newly opened British market in

1786. By 1789 he was selling some sixty-five thousand bottles, still mostly abroad.[95]

The Ruinarts acquired their vast expanse of markets by dint of constant travel. Nicolas spent more than half of 1762 on the road, principally in central Europe and the Netherlands. He visited dozens of cities and courts and found the bulk of his customers among the German nobility and even royalty but also took orders from wine merchants in Breslau, Leipzig, and Dresden. In succeeding years he made much the same tour.[96] Claude's correspondence from the 1770s shows him equally to have been on the road for long stretches at a time. A clerk in the office at Reims kept him informed of the purchases, the commissions coming in, the receipts of money, and the state of the cellar. He received letters at least once a week as he traveled through London, Cambrai, Louvain, Brussels, and Béthune. There are few of his responses from the road, but he complains in one of the difficulty of finding any "lords" (*seigneurs*) in London in April, as they had all gone off to the countryside.[97] Ruinart found himself obliged, like the Burgundian merchants in the previous chapter, to establish his clientele directly with the upper-class customers.

Claude's son Irénée, who took over the trade in 1794, left written advice on some of these commercial matters to his own sons in 1809:

Perhaps no other commerce demands so much activity as that of Champagne's wines, these luxury wines suit the great, those who like and invest some thought to their manner of living, and so are sought by wine merchants, innkeepers, entrepreneurs of public amusements and those who procure objects of fantasy to the rich and the well-off public. . . . The first thing to do when you arrive in a commercial city is to find out who holds the finest table, sees the most people, is obliged to keep a grand house, such as ministers, civil and military high officials, and then use all your industry to discover their relations with each other, in order to make their acquaintances."

He also defined their profession for them:

The négociant is different from the merchant . . . [who] only knows how to buy a bale of merchandise and then retail it. But the perspective of the négociant extends farther. Always occupied with the different branches of his country's commerce, he occupies himself with facilitating exportation; . . . this kind of négociant should be regarded as the man who contributes most to increasing and enriching the resources of the state . . . [and] he ought always to seize every occasion that can be useful to the Nation.[98]

The Decline and Transfiguration of Champagne

The family appears to have left the opprobrium of commission brokering behind them.

Ruinart was not alone in bottling wine for a foreign luxury market, or in building European markets through aggressive marketing. An associate of Allart de Maisonneuve insisted in the late 1740s that "no one in Champagne has pushed the wine trade as far as he [Allart] has by the costly and distant voyages he has made each year, as well as his son who is now in Russia trying to extend this commerce throughout the north, where they are beginning to send considerable shipments."[99] Others in Reims were obviously bottling the premium white wine they bought from Malavois de la Ganne in the 1750s and 1760s. The export records for the 1770s indicate that the merchants of Reims had much increased their bottling of the wine they had bought from the producers along the Marne River.[100] The export figures distinguished between wines coming from "Champagne," the "mountain," "Reims," and the "river," much as the figures from the late 1740s had. The bottles identified as coming "from Reims" had increased from some forty-eight thousand in the 1740s to over two hundred thousand; those identified as "from Champagne" had diminished from sixty thousand to little over seven thousand. Since bottled wine was still overwhelmingly produced from wine grown around Epernay, it is reasonable to infer that bottles "from Reims" were principally those bottled by négociants in Reims from wine they had bought from growers like Malavois.[101] At the same time, the paucity of bottles identified as "from Champagne" suggests that the brokers of Epernay had largely abandoned their trade to the east and were sending a hundred thousand bottles west, to Paris and beyond.

Other négociants in Reims joined Ruinart in the export wine trade at the end of the Old Regime, though few exceeded his scale.[102] Philippe Clicquot, a cloth merchant, was among those who added a small business in wine to his main occupation, much as Ruinart had in the 1730s. In the 1770s Clicquot began to send wine—almost uniquely bottled wine—to clients across Europe. Although the amounts were smaller than Ruinart's —an average of only twelve thousand bottles in the late 1770s and mid-1780s—they indicate the same commercial strategy. The German courts, particularly Frankfurt and Vienna, received a large majority of the bottles in the 1770s, and the 10 percent going to Strasbourg was probably going farther east eventually. To these destinations, Clicquot added shipments to Russia, England, and America in the 1780s, though his exports had barely risen to sixteen thousand bottles by 1790; he considered the wine trade only an "accessory" to his cloth business as late as 1797. Nor did he bottle the wine he sold, as Ruinart did. Practically all the bottled wine he sold was bought from local suppliers already in bottles. Clicquot added five sous, more or less, to the price of forty sous per bottle and then resold it. The profit was good enough but did not entice the family into the wine trade seriously until the following century when his son, and then daughter-in-law, decided to devote themselves to it.[103]

Although the disruptions of the 1790s hurt Clicquot's wine trade, it grew rapidly in the first decade of the nineteenth century—to thirty-two thousand bottles in 1802 and an average of ninety-three thousand bottles in the last half of the decade. A majority of this wine was now bottled by Clicquot; the firm bought barrels of wine from large growers in Ay, Epernay, and elsewhere along the river and bottled them in Reims. The vast majority of these bottles were sold abroad. Ten and twenty thousand bottles were going yearly to Austria and Prussia, and Russia received forty and fifty thousand bottles in 1805, 1806, and 1808. Clicquot employed several traveling salesmen, who made most of these sales. Their letters home reveal, among other things, that a score of other firms, particularly Moët of Epernay and Jacob, Tronson-Jacquesson, and Ruinart of Reims, were covering eastern Europe with salesmen. There were more disruptions to the wine trade in the following decade, but the basic mechanisms of the wine trade established in the late eighteenth century would change little over the next two centuries.[104]

The Champagne wine trade was essentially a commerce in barreled wine until quite late in the eighteenth century. For a number of reasons, the growers and brokers of Champagne produced little bottled wine if they could help it; the popularity of their barreled wines at the beginning of the century gave them little incentive to change. Bottling forced growers to accept significant costs, challenges, and risks. We have seen that they bottled reluctantly, when they had trouble selling their wine in barrels. Such troubles began in the 1730s along the Marne River and gradually induced a profound transformation in the Champagne wine trade.

The wine trade observed a basic division of labor between the growers who bottled and the brokers who sold the bottles through most of the first half of the century. Growers with good wines found themselves increasingly "obliged" to bottle their white wine and to seek an elite clientele willing to pay for it. Growers along the Marne appear to have led this development for the first decades of the century. Not until the 1730s and 1740s did the brokers of the Marne begin to deal seriously in bottled wine, and the evidence suggests that they generally bought it already bottled. Moët's experience indicates that he dealt in bottles reluctantly and on a

The Decline and Transfiguration of Champagne

small scale. He bottled little of the wine he bought, preferring to sell his wine as he had bought it. Paradoxically, it was Moët's very control over the traditional market in Paris that slowed his need to seek alternatives in new markets and new techniques.

At the same time, the brokers of Reims embraced this new market earlier and more entrepreneurially, seeking the wines of the Marne and bottling what they purchased. Several dozen merchant-brokers competed in Reims for an international market; they were noticeably more specu-lative and more attuned to the tastes of an elite clientele. A few of these merchant-brokers were starting to bottle large quantities in the 1740s; they were "producing" almost as many bottles for export in Reims as were the growers along the Marne. The amount of wine bottled in Reims more than quintupled between 1748 and the 1770s, due to négociants like Rui-nart, who fundamentally redefined the role of the négociant. Ruinart and others clearly bottled a great deal of wine that they had bought in barrels and actively sought to cultivate markets in other countries.

The négociants emerging at the end of the Old Regime in Champagne looked nothing like the passive *courtiers* of the late seventeenth century, acting purely as intermediaries between visiting buyers and local pro-ducers. Like the brokers in upper Burgundy, the brokers of Reims and, more slowly, those of Epernay had also relinquished the traditional role of commission broker, assembling the existing supply for a well-established demand. They now intervened decisively in the production of wine, at its most expensive and risky stage, and went looking for customers, creating a market for their expensive product. Like merchants in other fields, they were moving from the sphere of circulation into the sphere of production and transforming it with their capital and enterprise.

Conclusion

The main outlines of the modern wine trade can already be seen in the last decades of the Old Regime. Provincial brokers had become négociants, wholesale merchants who took charge of making and marketing much of the expensive wine aimed for a foreign market. They aged it, bottled it, stocked it, and traveled the courts and cities of Europe looking for someone to buy it. Through their efforts the province of Champagne rapidly increased the bottles of wine exported, from less than four hundred thousand in 1780 to five million by the 1840s and twenty-two million by the end of the nineteenth century.[1] Many of the most prominent companies of modern Champagne owe their creation to that half century of growth spanning the Revolution. Their production of bottled wine became more sophisticated, with new techniques of *remuage* (agitation) and *dégorgement* (disgorging of the lees), and the search for foreign, elite markets became a big business. Each company vied with the others to build glamorous reputations and mount ambitious advertising campaigns. All of these improvements elaborated on functions that négociant-brokers had initiated in the Old Regime.

The pre-Revolutionary négociants of upper Burgundy were also aging their wine for an elite foreign market, though on a smaller scale than in Champagne. Only a small part of the wine produced on the Côte de Bourgogne was expensive wines, already distinguished by *climat* and *cru* in the eighteenth century. Négociants were beginning to bottle and cellar the region's best wines at the end of the Old Regime and to travel through Europe creating markets for them. The number of négociants grew rapidly in the next half century, to some thirty "important houses" and fifteen or twenty lesser ones in the 1830s, and more were created in the second half of the century.[2]

Négociants were most successful where they dealt in expensive wine aimed at a luxury market. In Champagne a relatively limited number of négociants became heads of very large businesses that dominated the province's export trade. By the 1880s the largest of these, Moët et Chandon, owned some four hundred hectares of vines, employed over a thousand people, and produced two and a half million bottles of wine.[3] The négociants of upper Burgundy were less imposing; all one hundred or so négociants in the Côte de Beaune at the middle of the twentieth century owned only eight hundred hectares of vines and employed only fourteen hundred people.[4] Where wine was cheaper and aimed at a mass market, far greater numbers of minor négociants were involved, but few were serious businesses. Growers with enough resources had already involved themselves in the domestic wine trade during the late eighteenth century. Improvements in canals and the creation of railroads by the middle of the nineteenth century reduced the cost of transportation and increased the trade in common wine. In response, many growers took out "patents" that qualified them as wholesale merchants; estimates of their numbers through the nineteenth century range from twenty to thirty thousand.[5] These were not large merchants, however; they sold their own wine and some of the wine produced by poorer vignerons around them. Over two hundred had registered by the midcentury in the Mâconnais/Chalonnais alone. By the second half of the century their numbers diminished, and those who remained became more powerful and more concentrated in the main cities. Around Sancerre, "these local négociants formed a sometimes dense network." A mass of small négociants could similarly be found in the Beaujolais by the mid–twentieth century, but only one was important enough to engage in export.[6]

Elsewhere, through much of lower Burgundy, the wine trade went into a slow decline. Increasing ease of access to the Parisian market encouraged common growers to produce cheap wine already in the eighteenth century. Through the nineteenth century the region faced growing competition from other sources of cheap wine, particularly from the south of France, as they established rail connections to the capital. Coulanges-la-vineuse had abandoned most of its vines in the first half of the nineteenth century, Auxerre by the end of the century. Only Chablis maintained its high-quality vines and only its vineyards survived to the mid–twentieth century, though with few serious négociants and its commerce in "extreme decadence."[7] The last few decades, however, have seen a resurgence of the region's wines.

During the nineteenth century brokers reappeared, called either *courtiers* or commissionnaires, and operated once again purely as finders without engaging in trade. They worked very locally, as they had in the sixteenth century, offering their expert knowledge of a limited area to négociants who wanted to buy in large quantities. They continued to be disliked by growers and accused of reducing competition, but their role has changed. Now they have no financial stake in the wine, either as lenders or as buyers; instead, they identify wine for négociants who will buy it and supervise the care of the wine until shipment.[8] Their reemergence reminds us of the technical challenges posed by the trade in a commodity with so many local variations in quality, taste, price, and availability. The broker still offered this kind of expertise, even after other commercial agents had evolved to deal with the financial aspects of the trade.

In the course of the eighteenth century the wine trade developed the basic forms of its modern organization. Viticultural communities began to produce wines that required vastly more investment in time, inventory, and capital equipment. More importantly, they began to produce the entrepreneurs who slowly took control of the wine's commercial fate. From being the largely passive suppliers to outside merchants who had dominated the trade for so long, provincials began to acquire important commercial roles and to compete in a national and international market. Brokers, in particular, initiated this process by mobilizing the financial resources of their communities and facilitating sales to long-distance markets. Gradually becoming négociants, they took responsibility for marketing and preparing wine. The emergence of such entrepreneurs brought capitalism into the midst of provincial society; they confronted viticultural communities with fundamental economic changes. Thus the evolution of their role and of the wine trade in the eighteenth century reveals much about the early modern economy.

Wine was not a simple commodity. Its pervasive role in people's diet and sociability gave it unusual prominence in early modern culture. In sacraments, ceremonies, contracts, and reconciliations, wine stood for unity and trust. In pictures, poetry, drinking songs, and police ordinances, wine was glorified or vilified and given iconic status. But the significance of wine consumption, its cultural complexity, and even its romance should not be allowed to obscure the fact that wine was also an important commodity, and, as such, it played a crucial role in the early modern economy. The wine trade stimulated the evolution of a market economy, commercializing those regions of the country in which wine was produced or through which it was transported. By the seventeenth century the wine trade connected viticultural regions with markets across France and throughout Europe. Through the eighteenth century the wine trade gained sophistication, developing new wines, new markets, and new methods of organizing the market.

The wine trade alone cannot answer the questions raised at the beginning of this study, questions dealing with the pace and impact of commercialization in the early modern French economy. The wine trade was already more commercial than most of French society and thus hardly representative of the country's economy, but it can suggest some of the forces and limits that operated in this economy, limits only partially overcome even in the wine trade. Vinegrowers faced very real limits on the scale of their markets and the degree to which the market organized their economic activity. Most wine was exchanged locally, sold in neighboring taverns or bartered in payment for debts. Much wine was sold through informal channels of friends and relatives, even over long distances. The market's ability to set prices was unsophisticated, based as it was theoretically on formal negotiations between buyer and seller but often distorted by ignorance and fraud. Prices were usually set long after the wine exchanged hands. Accounting and credit were still informal and personal, legacies of the small-scale local wine trade but inappropriate to the growing long-distance commerce. Thus, even viticultural communities, which were more commercial than most of rural society, reveal the primitive nature of much economic exchange.

Local markets offered little reward to the wine producer, who sought better prices instead through long-distance trade. The southwest of France was fortunate in having access to international maritime trade, but most of the country could look only to nearby cities, at best to Paris, for a large market. Interregional trade became the goal of all wine producers, but one available only to an elite favored by having excellent wines, good contacts, enough wealth to offer credit, or the resources to speculate on finding buyers. Taxes and the cost of transportation made wine too expensive for most growers to send to distant markets without the certainty of a sale. The wine trade clearly shows both the disproportionate value of long-distance trade to the early modern economy and the impediments to its realization.

The wine trade was unusually dependent on the development of transportation and communication networks, more so than most commodities. The creation of canals between the Loire and Seine Rivers through the seventeenth century had greatly facilitated the spread of the Parisian catchment, and improvements in road networks in Burgundy helped the growth of the Beaujolais wine trade. Yet the growth of interregional trade depended on improvements in communications as well. Ignorance of local conditions, of the state of harvests and prices, of dealers, buyers, and sellers, and the risks of commercial exchanges between people who did not know each other, all raised the costs of doing business over long distances. It was precisely this need that brokers addressed by sending news to the metropolis throughout the century, to be joined belatedly by a fledgling commercial press. The gradual growth of information, about prices, agents, quality, and local conditions, made distant markets more accessible.

The existence of wine brokers since the Middle Ages underscores the weight of transaction costs, especially when local communities dealt with distant markets and unfamiliar merchants. The uncertainties about local measures, standards, and customs and the distrust of outsiders all raised the cost of doing business with the outside world, and all demonstrate the need for intermediaries to reduce these costs. As public officials, brokers provided the legal guarantees that alleviated much of the risk arising from exchanges between strangers. Their emergence as independent agents also emphasizes the universal demand for credit, particularly at the local level, where cash was always scarce and bills of exchange were distrusted and avoided. Brokers financed a growing segment of the wine trade on their own and provided the bookkeeping and authority to further mobilize the financial resources of local communities. Trust was crucial to overcoming the scarcities and costs of the early modern economy, trust in people's credit and in their word, and brokers initially enjoyed that trust.

The provincial wine trade in the eighteenth century was delicately balanced between power and transparency. The medieval marketplace had institutionalized commercial transparency through elaborate regulations that articulated a classic vision of open competition and just price. It aimed also at balancing the power of outside purchasers, whose commercial initiative clearly controlled the wine trade, with the needs of the viticultural community. Official brokers were a major part of the community's defense of its transparency, designed to mediate its contact with outsiders and organize the market. Yet the dynamics of the wine trade changed in the eighteenth century as provincial brokers took increasing initiative and control of their own markets.

The wine brokers gained considerable power in their communities through their superior access to large markets. In many cases they became the chief agents for distant merchants and reduced the market to a handful of buyers. So long as commercial contacts between the local economy and its remote market ran through relatively few hands, those hands had power. They began to use their power to profit from the wine trade, manipulating prices and exploiting producers. They may have enhanced this power by operating in collusion, but in reality their power was structural and needed little help from conspiracies. It was based in part on advantages of asymmetrical information, the exclusive possession of "the secrets of the market." Their control over information gave them power over prices and clients, which in turn gave them unprecedented control over the market. But that very power obscured the transparency of the market and added a very real cost to transactions by taking profits from other people's ignorance and commercial weakness. Their use of power diminished their trustworthiness, and they violated the widely shared conception of how markets should operate. Critics complained that the broker's word was no longer good, that self-interest had diverted him from serving the public good and made him a predator on the viticultural community.

Power in the wine trade exhibited the classic forms of commercial capitalism, based on the control not of production but of the market. Brokers intervened in the production process in only limited ways, most frequently as barrel merchants and brokers. Their loans to small growers enhanced their local power, but more indirectly. Raw materials were less crucial to the broker's power than they were to merchants in the rural industries; barrels and vine props were essentially subsidiary to land as instruments of winemaking, and small vineyards were not hard to acquire. Rather, access to markets gave brokers their primary leverage. Indeed, growers often bought materials from them simply in order to gain their help in marketing. Unlike the rural textile trade, where some studies have argued that intermediaries enjoyed little advantage in access to markets, the wine trade operated through a hierarchy of markets, and few besides brokers had access to the most important markets. As a consequence, growers willingly gave brokers the job of marketing their wine and granted them a 5 percent commission as fair recompense. Yet growers began to object when a broker's commercial power was used against them, when a broker forced them to charge lower prices for their wine or pay more for barrels, or when he paid them less than he charged his client. They were objecting, in part, to the perception that brokers increasingly controled all access to the market as they replaced visiting merchants. Growers resented a situation they identified as a monopoly.

Through the late eighteenth century, however, the market was changing in ways that restored some of its transparency. Improvements in communications, transportation, and financing made distant markets more accessible to more participants. The growth of commercial journalism initiated a public forum for advertising; it fostered greater understanding of the intricacies of the wine trade and more sympathy for commercial enterprise. The increasing financial strength and sophistication of agents at the Halle aux vins in Paris facilitated speculative trade with the capital and opened new lines of communication to the provinces. The Halle offered credit to those who brought their wine to Paris looking for buyers, credit to help pay for the outlay that preceded any income. Provincials could consign their wines to brokers at the Halle who provided credit, information, and a proxy for their interests. Distant speculation became cheaper, but it did not solve the problem of demand; provincial brokers who worked for Parisian wine merchants still enjoyed privileged access to secure sources of demand. Brokers never lost their advantages in the market, yet viticultural communities slowly found alternatives to the brokers' services and diminished, somewhat, their power.

The wine trade reminds us that a premodern market was more vulnerable to manipulation than a more modern one, that unsophisticated communications created asymmetries of information and thus of power. The transition from public to private marketing was awkward because, for a time, the old forms of publicly imposed transparency were abandoned and new forms of commercial integration were only beginning to function. If authorities feared manipulation of markets it was not without reason. The polemics over government regulation revolved around the grain trade, where so much was at stake, but officials could draw conclusions from the wine trade as well.

The wine trade also lends weight to the classic dichotomy between the core of France and its peripheries. The differences highlighted by the controversies over the broker tax at the beginning of the eighteenth century, between the roles played by brokers along the Atlantic coast and in the interior, were essentially repeated at the end of the century in the diverging development of brokers addressing themselves to domestic and international markets. The brokers in the domestic market gained their power from superior access to the Parisian market, but they remained dependent on this commerce. As their advantages of information and access waned, so did their power in the market. There is little evidence for entrepreneurial growth beyond this market in the eighteenth century, except where brokers lost, or never had, access to the Parisian market. Brokers in upper Burgundy and Champagne turned increasingly in the eighteenth century to markets outside of France rather than to Paris. Both regions responded to stagnant markets by developing expensive wines for elite markets. In both cases brokers moved beyond selling wines made by others to intervening decisively in the production of expensive wine. Whether aging the wine or bottling it, both regions invested in more expensive production techniques, requiring new wines, new materials, and new inventories. Brokers in both regions played a key role not only in finding markets for these wines but also in producing the wine.

The provinces' experience of the wine trade spanned the range of the early modern economy—from barter to bills of exchange, from local trade in marketplaces to long-distance trade with international entrepôts, from communal control to private enterprise—and testifies therefore to the evolution of cultural assumptions about exchange. As the capitalist sophistication of international trade, with its complex credit, speculation, and proxy, met a more bounded world of local trade based on face-to-face exchange, the brokers at the intersection of these worlds bore the brunt of this confrontation. The history of the eighteenth-century wine trade suggests that these worlds did not accommodate each other easily.

Viticultural communities embraced the market with profound ambivalence. The market was essential for all wine producers, but many at the bottom of this society limited their involvement. Sharecroppers appear often to have left their landlords in charge of marketing the wine they produced, preferring to borrow regularly against the eventual sale. Wine producers with the reserves to wait until the harvest, to wait for the right offer, perhaps even as long as a year before finding a buyer, were more completely involved in the market and played a more effective commercial role. Selling their wine for a good price brought them honor in the community, a public confirmation of the quality of their wine and the astuteness of their business dealings. But they resented the rapid evolution of commercial exchanges and referred at times to a past when issues of price were settled more amicably between buyer and seller. In contrast to the divisiveness of commercial competition they invoked the interests of the community and of the province. At the same time, commercial changes brought opportunities. The Halle aux vins encouraged speculation by a growing number of provincial growers and traders who eagerly gambled on weather and rising prices. Viticultural communities engaged themselves in the market but were slow to give up old attitudes about how the market should function.

Wine brokers focused much of the viticultural community's ambivalence about exchange. They facilitated and financed sales to distant buyers and made it possible for more growers to participate in long-distance commerce. Wine producers avidly sought larger markets through interregional trade, but even well-off growers found that their relative economic power dwindled upon a larger stage. They discovered their own impotence in their lack of control over the value of their wine, the terms of its payment, the speed of its sale, and, above all, their relationship to the broker. Brokers came to represent the incursions of commercial capitalism, of unequal economic power, which distorted an idealized market where goods were exchanged equitably and without advantage. Brokers reminded their society that economic exchange was a contest of power as much as a satisfaction of needs.

Notes

Introduction

1. R. H. Britnell, *The Commercialisation of English Society 1000–1500* (Cambridge, 1993); S. R. Epstein, "Regional Fairs, Institutional Innovation, and Economic Growth in Late Medieval Europe," *Economic History Review* 47 (1994): 459–82, offers evidence for the proliferation of markets even during a period of demographic decline and argues for concomitant growth in domestic trade; Jean-Marc Moriceau, *Les fermiers de l'Île-de-France, XVe–XVIIIe siècle* (Paris, 1994), pp. 61–72, shows the commercial involvement of large farms around Paris in the late Middle Ages, as does Guy Bois, *The Crisis of Feudalism, Economy and Society in Eastern Normandy c. 1300–1550* (Cambridge, 1984), pp. 244–55. But see Jean-Christophe Agnew, *Worlds Apart: The Market and the Theater in Anglo-American Thought, 1550–1750* (Cambridge, 1986), pp. 1–56, for the limits on local markets.

2. Georges Lefebvre, "La Révolution française et les paysans," in G. Lefebvre, *Etudes sur la Révolution française* (Paris, 1954); Albert Soboul, "The French Rural Community in the Eighteenth and Nineteenth Centuries," *Past and Present* 10 (1956): 78–95; Barrington Moore, *Social Origins of Dictatorship and Democracy* (Boston, 1966), pp. 40–110.

3. *Afterthoughts on Material Civilization and Capitalism,* trans. Patricia Ranum (Baltimore, 1977), p. 17. According to François Crouzet, "England and France in the Eighteenth Century," in François Crouzet, *Britain Ascendant* (Cambridge, [1966] 1990), p. 26, "In France the quasi-autarchic subsistence sector was still important and prevailed in extensive areas, acting as a brake on the growth of the economy as a whole."

4. *The Ancien Régime: French Society, 1600–1750,* trans. Steve Cox (New York, 1973), p. 69; Abel Poitrineau, *La vie rurale en Basse-Auvergne au XVIIIe siècle* (Paris, 1966), pp. 426–27, also asserts that the "general rule is attenuated autarky."

5. Jean Meuvret, *Le problème des subsistances à l'époque Louis XIV,* 3 vols. (Paris, 1977–88), 3:97–143, presents the grain trade in the seventeenth century as a barely

organized mass of small-scale traders. Paul Butel, *L'économie française au XVIIIe siècle* (Paris, 1993), pp. 184–86, sees little overall growth in the grain trade, but improved efficiency. Steven L. Kaplan, *Provisioning Paris: Merchants and Millers in the Grain and Flour Trade during the Eighteenth Century* (Ithaca, 1984), p. 598, concludes that the "striking fact about the Paris supply system was its fragmentation." But Moriceau, *Les fermiers de l'Île-de-France,* pp. 638–62, shows the large producers around Paris increasingly integrated into regional and long-distance commerce in the late seventeenth century.

6. Eugen Weber, *Peasants into Frenchmen: The Modernization of Rural France, 1870–1914* (Stanford, 1976), p. 117.

7. *La banque protestante en France de la révocation de l'édit de Nantes à la Révolution,* 2 vols. (Paris, 1961), 2:24–25.

8. Edward W. Fox, *History in a Geographical Perspective* (New York, 1971), p. 174; J. Tarrade *Le commerce colonial de la France à la fin de l'ancien régime* (Paris, 1972), cited by L. M. Cullen, "History, Economic Crises, and Revolution: Understanding Eighteenth-Century France," *Economic History Review* 46 (1993): 651, who contests this position.

9. Fernand Braudel, *The Perspective of the World,* trans. Siân Reynolds (New York, 1984), pp. 339–51.

10. Cullen, "History, Economic Crises," pp. 635–39, criticizes Labrousse and his legacy; Robert Brenner, "Agrarian Class Structure and Economic Development in Pre-Industrial Europe," in T. H. Aston and C. H. E. Philpin, eds., *The Brenner Debate* (Cambridge, 1985), similarly criticizes the work of Le Roy Ladurie. A parallel charge has been made against historians of British industrialization and of European proto-industrialization, in Maxine Berg, ed., *Markets and Manufacture in Early Industrial Europe* (London, 1991), pp. 3–6.

11. Bois, *The Crisis of Feudalism,* pp. 365–67; Alan McFarlane, *The Origins of English Individualism: The Family, Property, and Social Transition* (London, 1978).

12. Maurice Aymard, "Autoconsommation et marchés: Chayanov, Labrousse ou Le Roy Ladurie?" *Annales ESC* 38 (1983): 1392–1410; but Meuvret, *Le problème des subsistances,* 3:13–46, emphasizes the minimal commercialization of most grain in the seventeenth century and notes that "the primitive constitution of the principal stocks of grain can seem not to have obeyed commercial motives but to have been the consequence of a social system to which commerce had to adapt itself."

13. Jonathan Dewald, *Pont-St-Pierre, 1398–1789: Lordship, Community, and Capitalism in Early Modern France* (Berkeley, 1987), pp. 5, 51; Philip T. Hoffman, *Growth in a Traditional Society: The French Countryside, 1450–1815* (Princeton, 1996), pp. 35–80; Liana Vardi, *The Land and the Loom: Peasants and Profit in Northern France 1680–1800* (Durham, 1993), pp. 1–14; Colin Jones, "Bourgeois Revolution Revivified: 1789 and Social Change," in Colin Lucas, *Rewriting the French Revolution* (Oxford, 1991), pp. 78–88.

14. Pierre Léon and Charles Carrière, "L'appel des marchés," in Fernand Braudel and Ernest Labrousse, eds., *Histoire économique et sociale de la France,* vol. 2, *Des derniers temps de l'âge seigneurial aux préludes de l'âge industriel (1660–1789)* (Paris, 1970), p. 162, add that "it is not at all a question of two juxtaposed domains, even less of individual specializations which . . . exist practically not at all, but with a permanent interpenetration at every level."

15. Pierre Léon, ed., *Aires et structures du commerce français au XVIIIe siècle* (Paris, 1975), iii; Anne-Marie Cocula, "Pour une définition de l'espace aquitain au XVIIIe siècle," in idem; Butel, *L'économie française,* pp. 193–99; Jean-Pierre Poussou, *Bordeaux et le Sud-Ouest au XVIIIe siècle* (Paris, 1983), pp. 261–73.

16. David Weir, "Les crises économiques et les origines de la révolution française" *Annales ESC* 46 (1991): 917–23; Hoffman, *Growth in a Traditional Society,* pp. 170–84; William Parker, *Europe, America and the Wider World: Essays on the Economic History of Western Capitalism* (Cambridge, 1984). See also Charles Tilly, "The Geography of European Statemaking and Capitalism since 1500," in Eugene D. Genovese and Leonard Hochberg, eds., *Geographic Perspectives in History* (Oxford, 1989), pp. 159–62.

17. The pessimistic assessment of grain production by Michel Morineau, "Y a-t-il eu une révolution agricole en France au XVIIIe siècle?" *Revue historique* 239 (1968): 299–326, and idem, *Les faux-semblants d'un démarrage économique: agriculture et démographie en France au XVIIIe siècle* (Paris, 1971), is still persuasive. Hoffman, *Growth in a Traditional Society,* pp. 81–142, finds only a few regions that contradict Morineau. But see Jean-Marc Moriceau, "Au rendez-vous de la 'révolution agricole' dans la France du XVIIIe siècle: à propos des régions de grande culture," *Annales ESC* 49 (1994): 27–63; Butel, *L'économie française,* pp. 184–99, for more optimistic evaluations of capital investments, new techniques, and market integration.

18. Emmanuel Le Roy Ladurie, "De la crise ultime à la vraie croissance, 1690–1789," in Georges Duby and Armand Wallon, eds., *Histoire de la France rurale, de 1340 à 1789,* 4 vols. (Paris, 1975), 2:392.

19. Poussou, *Bordeaux et le Sud-Ouest,* p. 266, is quoting Henri Enjalbert, *Histoire de la vigne et du vin, l'avènement de la qualité* (Paris, 1975), p. 60.

20. Meuvret, *Le problème des subsistances,* 3:91–92.

21. Marcel Lachiver, *Vins, vignes et vignerons: histoire du vignoble français* (Paris, 1988), pp. 604–5, and Ernest Labrousse, *La crise de l'économie français à la fin de l'ancien régime* (Paris, 1944), have offered rough estimates of total wine production at the end of the Old Regime between 27 and 30 million hectoliters, at a price of roughly 10 livres per hectoliters, making the value of wine probably equal to one-third of the value of cereal production in 1791, as cited in Emmanuel Le Roy Ladurie, *The French Peasantry 1450–1660,* trans. Alan Sheridan (Berkeley, 1987), p. 325. But since some 15 percent of cereal is saved for seed, and as much as half is consumed by the producer, little was left to be sold—less than 30 percent according to Ernest Labrousse, "Les ruptures périodiques de la prosperité," in Braudel and Labrousse, eds., *Histoire économique et sociale de la France,* 2:534. Thus the value of wine on the market was nearly as great as the value of cereal.

22. See E. A. J. Johnson, *The Organization of Space in Developing Countries* (Cambridge, Mass., 1970), pp. 85–91, for a discussion of dendritic markets.

23. Alan Everitt, "The Marketing of Agricultural Produce," in Joan Thirsk, ed., *The Agrarian History of England and Wales 1500–1640* (Cambridge, 1967), p. 588. See also Fernand Braudel, *The Wheels of Commerce,* trans. Siân Reynolds (New York, 1982), pp. 403–20. François Olivier-Martin, *La police économique de l'ancien régime* (Paris, 1945), pp. 198–221, provides the analogous French regulations for what he calls the "public market."

24. Roy Dilley, "A General Introduction to Market Ideology, Imagery and Discourse," in Roy Dilley, ed., *Contesting Markets: Analyses of Ideology, Discourse and Practice* (Edinburgh, 1992), p. 15.

25. For example, Douglass North, *Structure and Change in Economic History* (New York, 1981), pp. 143–57; Vardi, *The Land and the Loom*, pp. 8–13, 117–21; Hilton L. Root, *Peasants and King in Burgundy: Agrarian Foundations of French Absolutism* (Berkeley, 1987), p. 17; idem, "Politiques frumentaires et violence collective en Europe au XVIIIe siècle," *Annales ESC* 45 (1990): 167–89; idem, "The Case against George Lefebvre's Peasant Revolution," *History Workshop Journal* (1989): 88–102, but see Peter Jones, "Response," in ibid., pp. 103–6.

26. Jürgen Schlumbohm, "Relations of Production—Productive Forces—Crises in Proto-industrialization," in Peter Kriedte, Hans Medick, and Jürgen Schlumbohm, *Industrialization before Industrialization,* trans. Beate Schempp (Cambridge, 1981), pp. 98–107. Tessie P. Liu, *The Weaver's Knot: the Contradictions of Class Struggle and Family Solidarity in Western France, 1750-1914* (Ithaca, 1994), emphasizes the relative ease of access in the eighteenth century, but increasingly difficult access in the nineteenth. E. P. Thompson, "The Moral Economy of the English Crowd in the Eighteenth Century," *Past and Present* 50 (1971): 76–136; Charles Tilly, *The Vendée* (Cambridge, Mass., 1964); Louise Tilly, "The Food Riot as a Form of Political Conflict in France," *Journal of Interdisciplinary History* 2 (1971): 23–57; Olwen Hufton, "Social Conflict and Grain Supply in Eighteenth-Century France," *Journal of Interdisciplinary History* 14 (1983): 303–31. Elizabeth Fox-Genovese, "The Many Faces of Moral Economy: A Contribution to a Debate," *Past and Present* 58 (1973): 161–68, and J. Stevenson, "The 'Moral Economy' of the English Crowd: Myth and Reality," in A. Fletcher and J. Stevenson, eds., *Order and Disorder in Early Modern England* (Cambridge, 1985), survey some of the criticism of Thompson; Cynthia A. Bouton, *The Flour War: Gender, Class, and Community in Late Ancien Régime French Society* (University Park, Pa., 1993), pp. 1–36, offers a useful discussion of the debates about the "moral economy."

27. See the interesting discussion of historical models of the market in Thomas L. Haskell and Richard F. Teichgraeber, eds., *The Culture of the Market* (Cambridge, 1993), pp. 1–17.

28. Karl Polanyi, *The Great Transformation* (Boston, [1944] 1957), pp. 56–67. Walter C. Neale, "The Market in Theory and History," in Karl Polanyi, Conrad Arensberg, and Harry Pearson, eds., *Trade and Market in the Early Empires: Economies in History and Theory* (New York, 1957).

29. Everitt, "The Marketing of Agricultural Produce"; Agnew, *Worlds Apart.*

30. Though Dominique Margairaz, *Foires et marchés dans la France préindustrielle* (Paris, 1988), shows us the survival of numerous marketplaces up to and through the Revolution.

31. William M. Reddy, *The Rise of Market Culture: The Textile Trade and French Society, 1750-1900* (Cambridge, 1984), pp. 1–18.

32. Braudel, *Afterthoughts,* p. 50, uses the term "transparent" exchanges for those "which involve no surprises, in which each party knows in advance the rules and the outcome, and for which the always moderate profits can be roughly calculated beforehand." He is using the word very differently from P. W. Klein, *De trippen in de 17e eeuw* (Assen, 1965), summarized in Kristof Glamann, "The Changing

Patterns of Trade," in E. E. Rich and C. H. Wilson, eds., *The Economic Organization of Early Modern Europe* (Cambridge, 1977), pp. 277–78, as the "monopolistic practices [that] diminished the risks and thus also the costs of transactions." Braudel, *The Wheels of Commerce,* pp. 422–23, criticizes Klein and carefully distinguished transparent exchange from "capitalism: the latter being an accumulation of power (one that bases exchange on the balance of strength as much or more than on the reciprocity of needs)."

33. As R. H. Coase, *The Firm, the Market, and the Law* (Chicago, 1988), p. 9, argues for modern markets, "for anything approaching perfect competition to exist, an intricate system of rules and regulations would normally be needed. . . . They exist in order to reduce transaction costs and therefore to increase the volume of trade." Paul Alexander, "What's in a Price?" in Dilley, ed., *Contesting Markets,* p. 82, points out that an earlier tradition of identifying peasant markets with the "idealised" market has been replaced by an emphasis on the imperfections caused by structural uncertainties in premodern markets. At the same time, a recent school of transaction cost analysis posits "the impossibility of perfect competition" in all markets; Malcolm Sawyer, "The Nature and Role of the Market," in Christos Pitelis, ed., *Transaction Costs, Markets and Hierarchies* (Oxford, 1993), p. 30.

34. Raymond de Roover, "Concept of the Just Price: Theory and Economic Policy," *Journal of Economic History* 18 (1958): 421–29. According to de Roover, "Monopoly Theory Prior to Adam Smith: A Revision," *Quarterly Journal of Economics* 65 (1951): 511, " 'freedom of trade' was the antithesis of 'restraint of trade' and of monopoly," and he points out that the medieval ideal of just price was still current in scholastic thought in the seventeenth century.

35. Everitt, "The Marketing of Agricultural Produce," p. 563.

36. Braudel, *Afterthoughts,* pp. 50–53; Braudel, *The Wheels of Commerce,* p. 22.

37. Westerfield, "Middlemen in English Business: Partly between 1660–1760," in *Transactions of the Connecticut Academy of Arts and Sciences* 19 (1915; repr. Newton Abbot, 1968); John Chartres, "The Marketing of Agricultural Produce, 1640–1750," in John Chartres, ed., *Agricultural Markets and Trade, 1500–1750* (Cambridge, 1990).

38. John Baldwin, *Medieval Theories of the Just Price* (Philadelphia, 1959), p. 67.

39. Georges Weulersse, *Le mouvement physiocratique en France (de 1756 à 1770)* (Paris, 1910), 1:309. Max Beer, *An Inquiry into Physiocracy* (London, 1939), passim, makes a similar case, though he is criticized by some authors for emphasizing the scholastic elements of physiocracy too exclusively.

40. Mirabeau, *L'ami des hommes,* translated and discussed by Elizabeth Fox-Genovese, *The Origins of Physiocracy* (Ithaca, 1976), pp. 162–65.

41. See J.-P. Hirsch, "Les milieux du commerce, l'esprit de système et le pouvoir, à la veille de la Révolution," *Annales ESC* 30 (1975): 1345; Simone Meyssonnier, *La balance et l'horloge: la genèse de la pensée libérale en France au XVIIIe siècle* (Paris, 1989), pp. 224–25.

42. Quesnay, *L'analyse,* ed. and trans. Ronald Meek, *The Economics of Physiocracy* (Cambridge, Mass., 1963), pp. 164–65. See Lüthy, *La banque protestante,* 2:22, for similar quotes from Quesnay.

43. See Albert O. Hirschman, *The Passions and the Interests: Political Arguments for Capitalism before Its Triumph* (Princeton, 1977); Daniel Gordon, *Citizens with-*

out *Sovereignty: Equality and Sociability in French Thought, 1670–1789* (Princeton, 1994), pp. 129–37, for the idea of "commerce" in political thought.

44. Steven L. Kaplan, *Bread, Politics and Political Economy in the Reign of Louis XV* (The Hague, 1976).

45. Tilly, *The Vendée*, p. 32.

46. See, for example, Christian Huetz de Lemps, *Géographie de commerce de Bordeaux à la fin du règne de Louis XIV* (Paris, 1975); A. D. Francis, *The Wine Trade* (Edinburgh, 1972); Paul Butel, *Les négociants bordelais, l'Europe et les iles au XVIIIe siècle* (Paris, 1974); Tim Unwin, *Wine and the Vine: An Historical Geography of Viticulture and the Wine Trade* (London, 1991).

47. The obvious exceptions to this statement is the classic work by Roger Dion, *Histoire de la vigne et du vin en France des origines au XIXe siècle* (Paris, 1959).

48. Thus Leo Loubère, *The Red and the White: The History of Wine in France and Italy in the Nineteenth Century* (Albany, N.Y., 1978), devotes a single chapter to the "Human Element." Or see Pierre Goujon, *Le vignoble de Saône-et-Loire au XIXe siècle (1815–1870)* (Lyon, 1973); René Pijassou, *Un grand vignoble de qualité, le Médoc*, 2 vols. (Paris, 1980); Rolande Gadille, *Le vignoble de la côte bourguignonne* (Paris, 1967).

49. Lachiver, *Vins, vignes*, p. 13.

50. Marcel Lachiver, *Vin, vigne et vignerons en région parisienne du XVIIe au XIXe siècles* (Pontoise, 1982), has all the demographic strengths and commercial weaknesses of this genre; Georges Durand, *Vin, vigne et vignerons en Lyonnais et Beaujolais (XVIe–XVIIIe siècle)* (Paris, 1979), and Jacques Beauroy, *Vin et société à Bergerac du moyen âge aux temps modernes* (Saratoga, Calif., 1976), are more balanced.

51. Labrousse, *Crise*, pp. 594–97.

52. Lachiver, *Vins, vignes*, p. 245, puts self-sufficiency at 1.5 to 2 hectares, or roughly 3 to 4 arpents.

53. Moriceau, *Les fermiers de l'Île-de-France*.

54. Meuvret, *Le problème des subsistances*, 3:92, argues that the grain trade in the seventeenth century "played only a limited role" in the circulation of goods within and from France.

55. Agnew, *Worlds Apart*, pp. 23–46. Hoffman, *Growth in a Traditional Society*, pp. 198–205, refers to the "moral hazards" inherent in economic transactions, which were much diminished by the communal pressures of a local market yet "worsened when trade stretched over longer distances."

Chapter 1 *Wine into Wealth*

1. Labrousse, *Crise*, p. 596.

2. Thomas Brennan, "Towards the Cultural History of Alcohol in France," *Journal of Social History* 23 (1989): 71–92, reviews some of the evidence for this statement.

3. Dion, *Histoire de la vigne*, pp. 117–66; Lachiver, *Vins, vignes*, pp. 19–55; Unwin, *Wine and the Vine*, pp. 113–19. These three authors offer excellent summaries of the literature on wine in the classical and medieval periods.

4. For a more detailed discussion of these developments, see Dion, *Histoire de la vigne,* pp. 171–94.

5. Le Roy Ladurie, *The French Peasantry 1450-1660,* p. 319; Guy Fourquin, *Les campagnes de la région parisienne à la fin du moyen âge,* p. 113, cited in Pierre Thibault, "Les parisiens et le vin à la fin du XVe siècle," in *Mémoires de la société de l'histoire de Paris et de l'Île-de-France* 35 (1984): 245.

6. Dion, *Histoire de la vigne,* pp. 245–46, quoting the monk Salimbene.

7. Jean Tanguy, *Le commerce du port de Nantes* (Paris, 1956), pp. 49–57; Hugues Neveux, "Déclin et reprise: la fluctuation biséculaire (1340–1560)," in Duby and Wallon, *Histoire de la France rurale,* 2:100–101.

8. Jean Eon [Mathias de Saint-Jean], *Le commerce honorable ou considerations politiques* (Nantes, 1646), pp. 87–88.

9. Beauroy, *Vin et société à Bergerac,* pp. 240–43.

10. Dion, *Histoire de la vigne,* pp. 425–60; Eon, *Le commerce honorable,* p. 90.

11. Tainturier, "Remarques sur la culture des vignes de Beaune et des circonvoisins," BM Dijon, Fonds Baudot, ms. 455 (1763). He identifies the change "since about eighty years."

12. Nicolas Delamare, *Traité de la police,* 4 vols. (Paris, 1705–38), 3:681, 688, arrêt of 14 August 1577. See Dion, *Histoire de la vigne,* pp. 540 ff. for a discussion of the impact of this arrêt.

13. Paul Jeulin, *L'évolution du port de Nantes, organisation et trafic depuis les origines* (Paris, 1929), pp. 237–38.

14. Mémoire of Tours, quoted in Monique Merlet, "Le péage de la cloison d'Angers: Histoire d'un impôt municipal, apercu du trafic de la Loire au XVIIIe siècle" (thèse de l'Ecole des Chartes, 1967), p. 132. See also James B. Collins, *Classes, Estates, and Order in Early Modern Brittany* (Cambridge, 1994), pp. 50–60, for the Breton wine trade in the seventeenth century.

15. Report of the échevins of Blois, 28 December 1667, in H. Trouessart, *Le commerce de Blois de 1517 à la fin du XVIIIe siècle d'après les registres municipaux,* 2 vols. (Blois, 1898), 2:380.

16. Auguste Chauvigne, *Monographie de la commune de Vouvray et de son vignoble* (Tours, 1909), p. 65; the lettres patentes of 10 May 1723 forbade the wines of the Touraine from being shipped to the colonies.

17. Françoise de Persan, "Les voituriers par eau et le commerce sur la Loire à Blois au XVIIe siècle," thèse de 3e cycle (Tours, 1984), pp. 216–20, finds that sixty-eight of a sample of seventy-three lettres de voiture, mostly in the 1660s and 1670s, were aimed at Paris rather than the Atlantic.

18. Marcel Lachiver, "Les aires d'approvisionment de Paris en vin au début du XVIIIe siècle," *Bulletin de la société de l'histoire de Paris et de l'Île-de-France* 35 (1984): 277–87.

19. AD Indre-et-Loire, C 91, reports to the intendant, 1756.

20. According to Norbert Wach, *Histoire des habitants de l'Orléanais* (Paris, 1982), p. 149, "The last exports to England [from the region around Orléans] occurred in 1607. Henceforth the land owners specialized in low-quality wine . . . becom[ing] entirely dependent on Parisian demand."

21. See Dion, *Histoire de la vigne,* pp. 468–70; Georges Lefebvre, *Etudes orléanaises,* 2 vols. (Paris, 1962), 1:49–50.

22. BN, Coll. Joly, ms. 1392, fol. 306, mémoire of Duchesne of Blois to Joly de Fleury, 26 January 1782. Henri Roland, *L'organisation corporative à la veille de la révolution française: essai sur l'organisation corporative et vie économique à Blois au XVIIIe siècle* (Paris, 1938), p. 203, cites the presidial of Blois in 1782 that "vines gave a value of 500 to 1,000 livres to sterile land that was otherwise worthless."

23. Geneviève Gavignaud, *Propriétaires-viticulteurs en Roussillon, XVIIIe au XXe siècle* (Paris, 1983), pp. 136–50.

24. Robert Vivier, "Un problème d'histoire économique: les essais de limitation de la culture de la vigne en Touraine au XVIIIe siècle," *Revue d'histoire économique et sociale* 24 (1938): 26–38.

25. These figures come from AN, F[20] 560, tableau par départements de l'étendue et de la culture de la vigne et de la quantité de ses produits en 1788 et 1829; see Lachiver, *Vins, vignes*, pp. 594–605, for these figures.

26. The figures for vine growing from the same survey are subtly different from those of wine production: the geography of production does not coincide exactly with the geography of vines. The disparity is most striking in the northeast, where vines appear to produce twice the national average, and the interior of the southwest, where yields appear to be little more than half the national average. But since production was measured from various sales taxes, the apparent disparity in yield is more a measure of greater commercialization in the north than in the south. For this reason, the production figures are more useful to a study of the wine trade than the vineyard figures.

27. Figures for vineyards in 1789, in Lachiver, *Vins, vignes*, pp. 594–96, are over 1.5 million hectares. Antoine Lavoisier, *Résultats extraits d'un ouvrage intitulé: de la richesse territoriale du royaume de France* (Paris, 1791), p. 26, estimates two and a half million vignerons and those who worked for them.

28. Although Root, "The Case against George Lefebvre's Peasant Revolution," p. 94, claims the existence of a more general struggle between lords and peasants over "equal access to the kingdom's growing market economy," Jones, in his "Response to Hilton Root," p. 105, argues instead that "the majority of peasants practised a semi-subsistence way of life which sought to limit contact with the market place."

29. Labrousse, *Crise*, pp. 556–57, arrives at this figure by adding the fallow land and pasture land needed to produce grain; Lachiver, *Vin, vigne*, p. 331, is more modest: "two to three arpents of vines would assure the revenue that ten arpents of grain and fallow would barely furnish."

30. Lachiver, *Vin, vigne*, pp. 439–41; Arthur Young, *Travels during the Years 1787, 1788, 1789*, 2 vols. (Dublin, 1793), 2:209, commented that "very few possess more than 20 to 30 arpents of vines," but in my experience ten arpents seems to be only very rarely exceeded.

31. Durand, *Vin, vigne*, pp. 414–48, calls vines a "capital factor in the reduction of inequalities," and the "providence of the little people." See also Lachiver, *Vin, vigne*, pp. 460–66, 488; Poussou, *Bordeaux et le sud-ouest*, pp. 222–23.

32. See Moriceau, *Les fermiers de l'Île-de-France*, for the definitive study of this group. For a recent summary of some of the huge bibliography on this question, see Bouton, *The Flour War*, pp. 42–61.

33. Durand, *Vin, vigne*, p. 414.

34. Ibid. and Lachiver, *Vin, vigne,* have studied landholding in considerable detail, as has Marc Venard, *Bourgeois et paysans au XVIIe siècle* (Paris, 1957), pp. 26–29, based on an enquête of 1717. Edouard Gruter, *La naissance d'un grand vignoble: les seigneuries du Pizay et Tanay en Beaujolais au XVIe et au XVIIe siècles* (Lyon, 1977), pp. 90–121, finds examples of peasant-owned vines in the Beaujolais, but also places where peasants had lost most of their vines to outsiders.

35. Gavignaud, *Propriétaires-viticulteurs en Roussillon,* pp. 81–84.

36. Lachiver, *Vin, vigne,* pp. 363–79; Durand, *Vin, vigne,* pp. 406–48. Jacquart's study of the Île-de-France in the seventeenth century, as cited in Le Roy Ladurie, *French Peasantry,* pp. 165, 196, argues for 69 percent of vines in the hands of village peasants, but an average holding of less than one hectare in vines.

37. Lachiver, *Vins, vignes,* p. 246. Much the same argument is made by Labrousse, *Crise,* pp. 210–12, and by Robert Dauvergne, "La vigne dans les environs de Paris au temps de Louis XIV," *Bulletin de la société de l'histoire de Paris et de l'Île-de-France* 91 (1964): 64. Tilly, *Vendée,* p. 116, points out that winegrowing regions in the nineteenth century were the part of rural France that "most consistently voted for traditional republicanism."

38. Lachiver, *Vin, vigne,* pp. 272–76. The taxes on wine defy any easy summary, but the principal taxes owed in the central part of France by the eighteenth century included a *droit de gros* that amounted to 5 percent of the wine's estimated value, plus an *augmentation,* owed shortly after harvesting. Wine sent to Paris, however, owed the gros upon entering the city, along with a long list of other entrance taxes. Wine sold wholesale also owed a flat *droit de courtage* at each sale and *droit de jaugeur* at the first sale, plus separate *droits de courtiers jaugeurs.* There were several taxes on wine sold retail, and tolls along roads and rivers added to transportation costs. For details see Lefebvre de la Bellande, *Traité général des droits d'aydes* (Paris, 1770).

39. Gaston Roupnel, *La ville et la campagne au XVIIe siècle: étude sur les populations du pays dijonnais* (Paris, 1955), pp. 268–70; Gadille, *Le vignoble de la côte bourguignonne,* pp. 354–58.

40. Robert Laurent, *Les vignerons de la "Côte d'Or" au XIXe siècle,* 2 vols. (Dijon, 1958), 2:47–61, provides a very detailed analysis of the land distribution at Nuits-Saint-George and Savigny in the 1780s. The average vigneron in Savigny possessed almost one hectare of vines; the average at Nuits was half of that.

41. Paul Butel, "Les grands propriétaires et production des vins de Médoc au XVIIIe siècle," *Revue historique de Bordeaux et du département de la Gironde* (1963): 129–41; Butel, *Les négociants bordelais,* pp. 350–62; J.-P. Poussou, "Les structures foncières et sociales des vignobles de Caudéran et du Bouscat en 1771," in *Vignobles et vins d'Aquitaine, histoire, économie, arts* (Bordeaux, 1970), pp. 155–73; Robert Forster, "The Noble Wine Producers of the Bordelais in the Eighteenth Century," *Economic History Review* 14 (1961): 18–33.

42. Pijassou, *Un grand vignoble de qualité,* 1:344–64.

43. Lefebvre, *Etudes orléanaises,* 1:51, quoting a report of 1648 about the village of Saint-Jean de la Ruelle.

44. AD Marne, C 429, statistique de la fin du XVIIe siècle (1691); AN, G^2 26 in the 1780s; M. Pélicier, "Cahiers de doléances des communes du bailliage d'Epernay en 1789," *Mémoire de la société d'agriculture du département de la Marne* (1898–99): 375.

45. AD Marne, C 818, assiette de taille for Ay, 1789.

46. Jean Nollevalle, *Ay en Champagne* (Ay, 1984), pp. 156–59. His figures for property sizes appear to be based on a survey in 1790.

47. AD Marne, C 429, statistique de la fin du XVIIe siècle (1691) and, for Avenay, Pélicier, "Cahiers de doléances," p. 354.

48. The vines were "situated in the most part in Sillery and Verzenay"; Gustave Laurent, *Reims et la région rémoise à la veille de la Révolution* (Reims, 1930), ccv.

49. René Gandilhon, *Naissance du champagne: dom Pierre Pérignon* (Paris, 1968), p. 100; Laurent, *Reims et la région rémoise*, ccxlvii, 639, cahiers of Hautvillers.

50. A. Nicaise, *Journal des états tenus à Vitry le François en 1744, rédigé par Bertin du Rocheret* (Paris, 1864), pp. 241–42. The opinions are those of Bertin du Rocheret.

51. Pélicier, "Cahiers de doléances," p. 361.

52. Paul Richard, "Le vignoble auxerrois en 1787," *Bulletin de la société des sciences historiques et naturelles de l'Yonne* 98 (1959–60): 33–40; Jean-Paul Rocher, ed., *Histoire d'Auxerre des origines à nos jours* (Roanne, 1984), pp. 228–29.

53. According to an early-nineteenth-century cadastre, "the greatest number" of the villages vines belonged to the forains; Centre auxerrois de l'université pour tous de Bourgogne, *Vaux, village viticole 1850–1914* (Dijon, 1990), pp. 106–7, 158.

54. AD Yonne, 3E 11-31, 9 March 1759, 3E 11-10, 11 March 1759.

55. The investigation of 1666, quoted in Max Quantin, "Recherches sur l'état sociale des habitants du comté d'Auxerre, 1666," *Annuaire de l'Yonne* 52 (1888): 38. But we must be careful in interpreting these categories; in a study on property ownership in villages elsewhere in Burgundy, J. Loutchitsky, "De la petite propriété en France avant la Révolution et de la vente des biens nationaux," *Revue historique* 59 (1895): 88–91, discovered that the tax rolls identified only a small minority as "property-owners," even when most inhabitants owned some property, especially vines.

56. AN, G², 31, report of the régie from the 1780s.

57. AN, F²⁰ 273, Statistique de l'Yonne, an IX, quoted in J.-P. Moreau, *La vie rurale dans le sud-est du bassin parisien* (Dijon, 1958), p. 82. Moreau, p. 87, notes that 62 percent of the citizens in the region of Chablis and 70 percent in the region of Auxerre qualified as property owners in 1790.

58. AD Yonne, 38B 118, 128, 130; 3E 24-2, 6, 7, 8; 3E 11-129, 167; 3E 14-796, 801, 804; 3E 6-385; 3E 7-281.

59. Lachiver, *Vin, vigne,* pp. 435–38; Lachiver, *Vins, vignes,* p. 245.

60. Lachiver, *Vin, vigne,* pp. 435–39.

61. For examples of such contracts in the Burgundian archives, see Henri Forestier and Claude Hohl, *Extraits analytiques des minutes déposées aux Archives de l'Yonne* (Auxerre, 1977), passim.

62. See Gandilhon, *Naissance,* pp. 95–120 for a vivid description of the work required in the vineyards.

63. Arnoux, *Dissertation sur la situation de Bourgogne et sur la manière de cultiver les vignes . . . vins qu'elle produit . . . deux moyens pour les faire venir à Londres* (London, 1728), p. 26.

64. Ibid., p. 22.

65. Mack Holt, "Wine, Community and Reformation in Sixteenth-Century Burgundy," *Past and Present* 138 (1993): 58–93.

66. Nollevalle, *Ay en Champagne*, p. 149.

67. Arnoux, *Dissertation sur la situation de Bourgogne*, pp. 22–23.

68. AD Yonne, 9B 798, 18 September 1722, 12 September 1723. The assembly of inhabitants asked to gather on the 13th, and the general harvest would begin on 23 September.

69. Delamare, *Traité de la police*, 3:533.

70. Arnoux, *Dissertation sur la situation de Bourgogne*, p. 20.

71. See Gandilhon, *Naissance*, pp. 109–21, and Pierre de Saint-Jacob, *Les paysans de la Bourgogne du Nord au dernier siècle de l'ancien régime* (Paris, 1960), pp. 260–91, for details about viniculture. Young, *Travels*, 2:208–9, notes the "promiscuous" planting of vines in parts of Burgundy too.

72. Labrousse, *Crise*, p. 210.

73. Delamare, *Traité de la police*, 3:526, ordonnance of 30 January 1350.

74. Edict of 1393, in Maugis, "La journée de huit heures et les vignerons de Sens et d'Auxerre devant le Parlement," *Revue historique* 145 (1924): 203–18. This is part of a general attempt to limit the increasing wages enjoyed by many different workers at this time. See also Marcel Delafosse, "Les vignerons d'Auxerrois (XIVe–XVIe siècle)," *Annales de Bourgogne* 20 (1948): 22–25.

75. Dion, *Histoire de la vigne*, pp. 461–71; Delafosse, "Vignerons," pp. 22–34.

76. AD Marne, B 9109, 30 March 1738.

77. Laurent, *Reims et la région rémoise*, ciii, ccv, testimony of the procureur du roi, 12 May 1789.

78. Archives Privées, account book of Malavois de la Ganne, 1755. I wish again to thank Jean Nollevalle and François Bonal for making these accounts available to me.

79. Laurent, *Vignerons de la "Côte d'Or,"* pp. 59–60, finds only sharecropping in Savigny and suggests that vignerons distinguished themselves from day laborers by not working for daily wages. Labrousse, *Crise*, pp. 536–37, categorizes money rental (*fermage*) as "exceptional" in viticulture; in his more detailed study of the Lyonnais, Durand, *Vin, vigne*, pp. 480–83, finds the vast majority of contracts for vineyards to be sharecropping rather than renting. See Hoffman, *Growth in a Traditional Society*, pp. 62–69, and Philip Hoffman, "The Economic Theory of Sharecropping in Early Modern France," *Journal of Economic History* 44 (1984): 309–19, for an analysis of risks and advantages of sharecropping.

80. Marc Bloch, *French Rural History: An Essay on Its Basic Characteristics*, trans. Janet Sondheimer (Berkeley, 1966), pp. 147–48.

81. AD Côte d'Or, G 4167, accounts from 1726–81.

82. Maurice Fondet, *Le domaine et les vins de l'Hôpital de Beaune* (Dijon, 1910), pp. 31–49.

83. In contrast, he rarely sold the sharecropper's half of wine in his vineyards at Mavilly, probably because the vines were at some distance from Volnay and the wine was not very good. Saint-Jacob, *Les paysans de la Bourgogne*, pp. 252, 291, notes that "the proprietor often bought their [sharecroppers'] wines," and that the monks of Saint-Denis de Nuits bought their sharecroppers' wines at a discount.

84. Accounts of Nicolas Grozelier, prêtre de l'oratoire, with Claude Mussy, vigneron of Beaune, 1750–51, in Louis Fournier, *Vignes et vins de Beaune: documents*

pour servir de la contribution à leur histoire (Beaune, 1907), pp. 30–33. Here too the priest deducted expenses like the brokerage fee from the vigneron's profits.

85. BM Epernay, Fonds Chandon, ms. 150, livre de Sebastien Boulley, vigneron à Volnay, 1682–1719. The sale of 1698 was the last one entered. See Bavard, *Histoire de Volnay* (Beaune, 1870), pp. 285 ff., for wine prices.

86. AD Yonne, 38B 128, assembly of inhabitants, 19 November 1724.

87. Godinot, *Manière de cultiver la vigne et de faire le vin en Champagne* (Reims, 1722), pp. 9–14.

88. AN, G² 26, in a discussion of Ay, no date.

89. Young, *Travels*, 2:209.

90. Lachiver, *Vin, vigne,* pp. 405–10; Young, *Travels,* 2:214–15.

91. AN, G² 26, régie of the tax farm, generality of Châlons, direction Epernay, from the 1770s.

92. Laurent, *Reims et la région rémoise,* cci.

93. AP, Malavois de la Ganne.

94. Lavalle, *Histoire de la vigne,* pp. 56–61.

95. AN, G² 26, report of the régie of the tax farm, 1771.

96. AP, Malavois de la Ganne. To complicate matters, he was not always able to sell, or even to make, his white wine each year, and occasionally he sold it in bottles rather than barrels. He also noted that the wine was often sold more than a year after the harvest. Thus the price might reflect both the quality of one year with the market conditions of the following.

97. The price of his white wine rose from 120 livres per queue (a double barrel of four hectoliters that was the standard measure of account) in the 1730s to 380 livres in the 1760s. The best reds sold for 95 livres per queue in the 1730s; they averaged 157 livres between 1745 and 1754 and 125 livres in 1755–65. The second range of reds rose from 73 livres in the 1730s to 96 livres in the 1760s.

98. Lavalle, *Histoire de la vigne,* pp. 56–61; the common wines from the "low lands" (*pays bas*) were worth only 20 percent more in 1720–39 (33.5 livres per queue) than they had been in 1680–99 (27.8 livres per queue) and were worth 78 percent more by 1760–79 (49.4 livres per queue); the best wines, from around Nuits, had increased 135 percent by 1720–39 (159.7 livres per queue from 68 livres per queue) and 261 percent by 1760–79 (245 livres per queue).

99. Lachiver, *Vin, vigne,* pp. 324–25; Mantellier, "Les marchands fréquentant la Loire," *Mémoires de la société archéologique de l'Orléanais* 5 (1862): 272–79; Henri Hauser, *Recherches et documents sur l'histoire des prix en France de 1500 à 1800* (Paris, 1936), pp. 281–83.

100. According to Durand, *Vin, vigne,* pp. 150–51, prices in Béziers changed little between the 1690s and 1750s, whereas in Draguignan they remained steady until the 1740s and then rose sharply; see also René Baehrel, *Une croissance: la basse Provence rurale de la fin du XVIe siècle à 1789* (Paris, 1961), pp. 561–63, for prices in Draguignan, and in Marseille where they remained fairly steady until 1770. Prices in Grenoble, according to Hauser, *Recherches et documents,* pp. 400–406, were essentially stagnant from 1700 to 1770.

101. Lachiver, *Vin, vigne,* pp. 303, 325. The wine harvests from 1766–77 were the latest of the century, according to M. Baulant and E. Le Roy Ladurie, "Une synthèse provisoire: les vendanges du XVe au XIXe siècles," *Annales ESC* 33 (1978):

763; Rosemary George, *The Wines of Chablis and the Yonne* (London, 1985), p. 199, indicating unusually cold weather.

102. Labrousse, *Crise*, pp. 428–54, does calculate, however, that revenues during the 1770s were substantially higher than in the 1780s.

103. BN, FF 21664, objections to an arrêt de conseil of 26 October 1715 by the wine merchants of Orléans, cited in an arrêt de conseil of 15 December 1716.

104. AN, G² 26, referring to Damery, no date but among reports from the 1770s and 1780s.

105. AN, G⁷ 1511, no date, written in response to efforts by the intendant of Lyon to exempt collectors in his generality from the tax of 1710.

106. Ibid.

107. Ibid.

108. AN, G⁷ 1512, letter of 23 June 1712.

109. Nollevalle, *Ay en Champagne*, p. 159; this refers, however, to their possessions in Ay alone.

110. AP, accounts of Malavois de la Ganne.

111. Young, *Travels*, 2:205–9, estimates the cost of vine tending, harvesting, casks, and taxes in Epernay at 259 livres, though he also adds 150 livres for the interest on the purchase of the land, which would put the cost at two-thirds the 600 livres of income. Labrousse, *Crise*, pp. 493–97, puts the ratio of cost to income at something closer to two-fifths.

112. Nollevalle, *Ay en Champagne*, p. 152, quotes a letter from Bertin du Rocheret to the intendant with that figure and finds it echoed in other documents.

113. Delamare, *Traité de la police*, 3:546.

114. AD Côte d'Or, G 4167, accounts from 1726–81.

115. Labrousse, *Crise*, pp. 428–87, 554–64, placed considerable emphasis on the advantages enjoyed by the vine producer who could wait to sell his wine.

116. Butel, *Les négociants bordelais*, pp. 138–39, makes the same point.

117. The report of the régie, AN, G² 26, at the end of the century indicates the existence of five distillers in the villages around Reims and a "small number" along the Marne but suggests that the region produced little eau-de-vie (brandy). Most of the brandy produced in France came from the west: around Nantes and up the Loire as far as Anjou, around Bordeaux, in Armagnac and Cognac, and some in bas Languedoc; little was made in Burgundy or Champagne. See Lachiver, *Vins, vignes*, pp. 261–71.

118. AD Côte d'Or, G 4167, accounts from 1726–81. Delachère owned 1.5 hectares, of which half produced "good wine" and the rest a common red. To this he added the "vin de passion"—wine he received as a tithe—which usually equaled roughly the amount of good wine he produced on his own. In 1748 he bought a further two hectares of vines in Mavilly, some eight kilometers northwest of Volnay.

119. Lachiver, *Vin, vigne*, pp. 441–50. He also invokes Pierre Goubert for this equation.

120. Bavard, *Histoire de Volnay*, p. 249.

121. "The villages of Volnay, Pommard, Savigny and the town of Beaune are estimated to have produced a thousand barrels of fine wine at the most, and nothing between Beaune and Dijon." AD Côte d'Or, G 4167. This is at a time when

Arnoux, *Dissertation sur la Bourgogne,* pp. 26–27, could assert that the normal harvest of the slopes from Chambertin to Chagny "amounts to more than 20,000 queues of wine."

122. AD Côte d'Or, BII Suppl. 255, 4 June 1725, business failure of François Antoine of Nuits.

123. Tainturier, "Remarques sur la culture des vignes de Beaune," p. 186.

124. AD Côte d'Or, G 4167, 29 December 1758.

125. See the discussion in William M. Reddy, *Money and Liberty in Modern Europe* (Cambridge, 1987), ch. 3.

126. AD Côte d'Or, G 4167, receuil des jours de la vendange de Vollenay avec un mémoire de la production des vignes de la cuve dudit Vollenay et des frais de vendange, 1748, 1749.

127. Ibid., 1727. 128. Ibid., 1735.

129. Ibid., 1751. 130. Ibid., 1743.

131. Ibid., 1762, 1749.

Chapter 2 *The Provincial Wine Trade*

1. Since the pessimistic conclusions of Morineau, *Les faux-semblants d'un démarrage économique,* about the lack of an agricultural revolution, historians have rallied to a modest optimism about growth in certain sectors of agriculture and gradual structural change in the rural economy; see, for example, James L. Goldsmith, "The Agrarian History of Preindustrial France: Where Do We Go from Here?" *Journal of European Economic History* 13 (1984): 175–99; Moriceau, "Au rendez-vous de la 'révolution agricole,'" pp. 27–63. For the importance of the market, see also Weir, "Les crises économiques," pp. 917–23; Butel, *L'économie française au XVIIIe siècle,* pp. 193–99; George Grantham, "Agricultural Supply during the Industrial Revolution: French Evidence and European Implications," *Journal of Economic History* 49 (1989): 43–72.

2. See, for example, François Crouzet, *De la supériorité de l'Angleterre sur la France* (Paris, 1985). As Goldsmith, "The Agrarian History of Preindustrial France," p. 185, notes, the lack of figures and studies on the internal market makes "coming to grips with the domestic market . . . the more difficult task."

3. Poitrineau, *La vie rurale en basse-Auvergne,* p. 435; see the discussion and critique of this and other authors in Poussou, *Bordeaux et le sud-ouest,* pp. 262–68.

4. Léon and Carrière, "L'appel des marchés," p. 167.

5. Baehrel, *La basse-Provence rurale,* p. 77.

6. The term "vent for surplus" is applied to protoindustrialization by Kriedte, Medick, and Schlumbohm, *Industrialization before Industrialization,* pp. 22, 47, drawing on earlier work by Hla Myint, "The 'Classical Theory' of International Trade and the Underdeveloped Countries," in H. Myint, ed., *Economic Theory and the Underdeveloped Countries* (New York, 1971).

7. Poussou, *Bordeaux et le sud-ouest,* pp. 258–73.

8. Georges Frêche, "Etudes statistiques sur le commerce céréalier de la France méridionale au XVIIIe siècle," *Revue d'histoire économique et sociale* 49 (1971): 10–25.

9. Cocula, "Pour une définition de l'espace aquitain," p. 304.

10. Quoted by Georges Frêche, *Toulouse et la région Midi-Pyrénées au siècle des lumières, vers 1670–1789* (Paris, 1974), p. 786.

11. Frêche, "Etudes statistiques," p. 191.

12. Frêche, *Toulouse et la région Midi-Pyrénées,* pp. 794–95.

13. Frêche, "Etudes statistiques," p. 191.

14. Meuvret, *Le problème des subsistances,* 3:141, 126.

15. Moriceau, *Les fermiers de l'Île-de-France,* pp. 645–62.

16. Kaplan, *Provisioning Paris,* pp. 82, 123, and much else of this remarkable book.

17. Léon and Carrière, "L'appel des marchés," pp. 198–200, provides a similar overview.

18. Meuvret, *Le problème des subsistances,* 3:92–94, notes that "wine dominated" the commerce along the upper Loire at Cosne, the French maritime trade with Amsterdam, the trade of Nantes, and the plans to improve various French waterways.

19. Poussou, *Bordeaux et le sud-ouest,* p. 235.

20. Gaston Rambert, "Toulon et l'exportation des vins provençaux par Marseille au XVIIIe siècle," *Provence historique* (1962): 18–30; P. Boissonnade, "La production et le commerce des céréales, des vins et des eaux-de-vie en Languedoc, dans la seconde moitié du XVIIe siècle," *Annales du Midi* 17 (1905): 344–60.

21. See, for example, Huetz de Lemps, *Géographie du commerce de Bordeaux;* Beauroy, *Vin et société à Bergerac;* Guillaume Géraud-Parracha, *Le commerce des vins et des eaux-de-vie en Languedoc sous l'ancien régime* (Mende, 1958).

22. Butel, *Les négociants bordelais,* pp. 152–62; Pijassou, *Un grand vignoble de qualité, le Médoc,* pp. 502–12.

23. See Jacques Savary, *Le parfait négociant,* 2 vols. (Paris, 1645), 2:143–47, for a description of commissionnaires.

24. Huetz de Lemps, *Géographie du commerce de Bordeaux,* pp. 101, 183; Butel, *Les négociants bordelais,* pp. 132–40; Cocula, "Pour une définition de l'espace aquitain," p. 301.

25. Dion, *Histoire de la vigne,* pp. 241–43.

26. Renée Doehaerd, "Un paradoxe géographique: Laon, capitale du vin au XIIe siècle," *Annales d'histoire économique et sociale* 5 (1950): 145–65.

27. Gérard Sivery, *Les comtes de Hainaut et le commerce de vin au XIVe siècle et au début du XVe siècle* (Lille, 1969); Jan Craeybeckx, *Un grand commerce d'importation; les vins de France aux anciens Pays-Bas, XIIIe–XVIe siècle* (Paris, 1958), p. 36; Jean-Pierre Devroey, *L'éclair d'un bonheur: une histoire de la vigne en Champagne* (Paris, 1989), pp. 157–58.

28. Dion, *Histoire de la vigne,* pp. 619–21, argues for the importation of pinot noir in the fourteenth century, though Gandilhon, *Naissance,* pp. 109–11, insists on a later date.

29. Godinot, *Manière de cultiver la vigne,* pp. 19, 34. In the early seventeenth century, according to François Bonal, *Le livre d'or du champagne* (Lausanne, 1984), p. 29, the wines of the mountain normally sold for half the cost of wines of the river; but the wines exported from the mountain in 1747, AD Marne, C 481, were worth roughly as much.

30. Nearly two-thirds of the wine exported in 1747–48 came from the mountain and Reims (AD Marne, C 481), as did the exports of the late 1770s; AN, F^{12} 242, 1775–80. Reims probably handled much of the wine sent from the rest of the region as well.

31. Pierre Desportes, *Reims et les Rémois au XIIIe et XIVe siècles* (Paris, 1979), pp. 662–63.

32. Ibid., p. 663; Devroey, *L'éclair d'un bonheur,* pp. 141–45. The barrel [*poinçon*] used along the Marne river normally held 1.82 hectoliters, whereas the barrel of Reims and the mountain was 2.05 hectoliters.

33. Lettres patentes of 1412; Pierre Varin, *Archives législatives de la ville de Reims,* 6 vols. (Paris, 1840–53), 1:432; Devroey, *L'éclair d'un bonheur,* p. 156.

34. AD Marne, C 481, for figures on exports in 1748, and C 669 for Etat des vins vendus en gros, 1746–48. The figures for exports in 1748 refer only to those registered at the Bureaus of Châlons and Charleville; they miss champagne exported through Normandy, but Rouen exported only forty-one barrels in 1728 and half that in 1730, according to Pierre Dardel, *Navires et marchandises dans les ports de Rouen et du Havre au XVIIIe siècle* (Paris, 1963), p. 167.

35. The report of the intendant of Champagne, 1697.

36. Desportes, *Reims,* p. 664, is speaking here of the early fifteenth century.

37. The city had bought the privilege in 1692, according to a memorandum for the mayor and échevins of Reims, 1706, AN, G^7 1508.

38. Devroey, *L'éclair d'un bonheur,* p. 177.

39. AD Reims, 17B 1579, fraudulent bankruptcy of François de la Vieville, in the act of succession of Drouin Regnault, 3 October 1693. Another of Regnault's heirs is Adam Regnault, conseiller du roi, assesseur de l'hôtel commun de Reims, and a very important broker in 1705. The balance sheet is also from October 1693.

40. AD Reims, 18B 629, inventory of Jean Clicquot, 1718. Thus he pays Millon, marchand commissionnaire à Beaune, 2,762 livres and notes shipments of Burgundy received from Parisot and Etienne of Beaune, Brosse of Mâcon, and Massonnet of Chalons, who is probably Masson of Chalon. This wine was costing him twenty-three and twenty-seven livres per barrel just for shipment to Reims.

41. AD Reims, 18B 60*, register of the communauté des tonneliers, 1658–1716.

42. BM Epernay, Fonds Chandon, ms. 329, fol. 20, letter of Simon Bertin de la Bertinière, 13 October 1691.

43. AN, G^7 1512, letters from the "merchants and wine brokers of Reims" to Desmaretz and the traitants, September 1712.

44. He describes the purchase being from Pietremont "vigneron of Cumières" but it was probably the Pietremont who was taxed in 1705 as a broker, given the size of the purchase.

45. AD Reims, 17B 1608, fraudulent bankruptcy of Jean Mallo, maitre tonnelier commissionnaire en vins, 1731. He was in prison because he had sold some of the wines surreptitiously to pay various expenses.

46. Archives privées, Ruinart Père et Fils, Livre de 1729. Again I would like to thank Ruinart for their assistance and welcome.

47. See AD Marne, C 669, for production figures in 1746–48, and Laurent, *Reims et la région remoise,* ccix–ccx, for prices in 1749.

48. It is safe to assume that the inhabitants of Reims, estimated between 25,000

(Lynn Hunt, *Revolution and Urban Politics in Provincial France: Troyes and Reims, 1786-90* [Stanford, Calif., 1978], pp. 9–11) and 35,000 (AD Marne, C 669) people, consumed roughly a barrel per head.

49. AD Marne, C 669, mémoire pour la ville de Reims, no date, but referring to a controversy taking place in 1752.

50. Lachiver, "Les aires d'approvisionnement de Paris," pp. 284–85.

51. AD Marne, C 430, fols. 84–87; these are figures for 1773 that include terre laborable, pré, and bois, as well as vignes, in each parish.

52. AD Marne, C 429.

53. Cited in Devroey, *L'éclair d'un bonheur*, p. 177.

54. Edme Baugier, *Mémoires historiques de la province de Champagne* (Châlons, 1721), p. 305.

55. AD Marne, C 4371. Legally, the contrôle des actes entered every lettre de voiture from a given area, but in most cases the citation was too cryptic to be of any use. This is a very unusual contrôle des actes, in that it gives the amounts sent in each shipment, as well as whom it was "charged by." Unfortunately 1702 is the earliest register to survive from Epernay.

56. Quoted in Pierre de Saint-Jacob, "Une source de l'histoire du commerce des vins: les lettres de voiture," *Annales de Bourgogne* 28 (1956): 124–26.

57. Delamare, *Traité de la police*, 3:681, explains the system of lettres de voiture and declarations as they apply to the wine trade.

58. Saint-Jacob, "Les lettres de voiture," p. 125, points out, "One would find mention of [lettres de voiture] in the contrôle des actes, but without details and so without value to the historian." Nor, with rare exceptions, do the contrôles in the archives of the Yonne, Reims, Loir-et-Cher, Indre-et-Loire, or Maine-et-Loire offer any useful details.

59. AN, Z^{1h} 337, fol. 11.

60. Lachiver, "Les aires d'approvisionement de Paris," pp. 280–82, is based on records for only 6 percent of the city's imports between 1702 and 1705, but is the only source offering monthly figures for Paris.

61. AD Cher, 43H 178, péage de Cosne, July 1733 through June 1734.

62. Jean Nollevalle, *Le vin d'Ay à l'origine du champagne* (Reims, 1988), p. 42, quotes Saint Evremond: "Champagne gives us the wine of Ay, Avenay, [and] Hautvillers until the spring; [the mountain of Reims] for the rest of the year."

63. AD Marne, C 4372–C 4377, contrôle des actes, 1702–31.

64. AN G^7 1179, report on the produit net des marchands de vin de Paris, 1712, identifies a yearly average of 600,000 hectoliters of wine brought into Paris by wine merchants between 1702 and 1708. Similar figures for 1720–25 in G^7 1182 averaged 760,000 hectoliters Parisians also consumed a considerable amount of local wine in the guinguettes around the outskirts of the city.

65. Lachiver, "Les aires d'approvisionnement de Paris," pp. 277–87.

66. Although the wine merchants identified their membership at some 1,950 in 1701 and 1702, after having fallen as low as 1,400 in the late 1690s, the tax farm insisted that there were over 2,500 of them; AN G^7 1179, memoirs for and against the wine merchants in 1704.

67. Thomas Brennan, *Public Drinking and Popular Culture in Eighteenth-Century Paris* (Princeton, 1988).

68. Delamare, *Traité de la police*, 3:680–82.

69. One of the brokers of Epernay, Bertin, identifies a Mopinot in the wine trade as a cousin—possibly the same one; letter of 13 October 1691, cited in R. Chandon de Briailles, "Recherches sur les origines des vignobles et du vin mousseux de Champagne," *Bulletin du laboratoire expérimental Moët et Chandon* 2 (1908): 306.

70. See Abraham du Pradel, *Le livre commode des adresses de Paris pour 1692*, ed. E. Fournier, 2 vols. (Paris, 1878), 1:310–12, for a list of the privileged merchants.

71. AD Marne, C 4371, 16 November 1702, 21 October 1703.

72. These are figures offered in 1773 for normal years, in AD Marne, C 430. The arpent in this document is 0.51 hectares. Godinet, *Manière de cultiver la vigne*, p. 6, estimates the average yield of vines along the river, where vines tended to be pruned low, at "two barrels per arpent, sometimes less, rarely three, and much more rarely four."

73. AD Marne, C 669, letter to Machault d'Arnouville, 1752.

74. AD Marne, C 4470, contrôle des actes, Hautvillers, 1708–30.

75. The accounts of the abbey of Hautvillers, AD Marne, H 1070, vins vendus, September 1691–September 1692, show some six hundred hectoliters of very expensive wine being sent to the north and east.

76. AD Marne, C 4320, contrôle of Damery; la Vieville was one of the two from Reims, though he only shipped twenty-seven barrels. Geoffroy of Cumières purchased over one hundred barrels, and he figures prominently in earlier years as well.

77. AD Marne, C 4140, for the years 1706–8.

78. AD Marne, BR 1393, inventaire après décès of Marie Lallement, wife of Adam Bertin, 2 March 1722.

79. Nicolas Bertin and another courtier were called in as expert witnesses to judge wine in Vertus in 1680, cited in Gandilhon, *Naissance*, p. 170.

80. Chandon de Briailles, "Recherches sur les origines," pp. 301–2, notes the presence of courtiers in less than a third of the wine sales made by the abbey of Epernay, in 1561.

81. According to C. Moreau-Berillon, *Au pays du Champagne* (Reims, 1925), pp. 214–15, "The commerce of wine in Epernay was little developed until the edict of 1691. . . . The wine that proprietors did not sell to friends or family was sent to merchants of Reims." See also R. Chandon de Briailles and H. Bertal, *Sources de l'histoire d'Epernay*, 2 vols. (Paris, 1906), 1:xi; Emile Roche, *Le commerce des vins de Champagne sous l'ancien régime* (Châlons-s-Marne, 1908), pp. 79–81; Chandon de Briailles, "Recherches sur les origines," pp. 301–5. Devroey, *L'éclair d'un bonheur*, pp. 133–35, argues instead for lively competition among different towns in the Middle Ages, though he says little about the early modern period.

82. AD Marne, 4E 16052/53, marché between Antoine Salmon and Charles Triboulet, 13 October 1685.

83. BN. Coll. Joly, ms. 1336, fol. 270, letter to Joly de Fleury, 4 March 1739.

84. Letter of Simon Bertin de la Bertinière, in Paris, to his brother, Adam Bertin du Rocheret, 29 July 1690, in BM Epernay, Fonds Chandon, ms. 329, fol. 20.

85. Philippe Bertin sent a circular advertising wines to 115 négociants in 1724; BM Epernay, ms. 209, fol. 1.

86. See, for example, AD Marne, 4E 16052/53, marché of 5 December 1685 be-

tween Chertemps, "commissionnaire," and Jean Thibaut, merchant of Saint-Martin d'Ablois, to deliver six thousand barres à barrer from a local forest. An identical marché for two thousand grandes barres can be found in 4E 16051, 23 December 1684, cited in Gandilhon, *Naissance*, p. 273. As Durand, *Vin, vigne*, p. 107, explains, a barrel would have a barre put on its top and bottom to reinforce it before shipment. There is a contract with a boatman to ship two hundred barrels to Paris in 4E 16055, 23 November 1686. See AD Marne, B 9075, inventory of Chertemps's widow, 24 January 1721, for reference to a sack containing his "provisions d'assesseur et de courtier," but there is no date for when he had the office.

87. See the reference to an état de compte fait entre Chertemps and Quatresous du 11 July 1707 touchant leur société, and a register—au premier page la vente de vin que j'ay fait à mon neveu 24 October 1711–28 January 171—in the inventory of 24 January 1721 in AD Marne, B 9075.

88. He had two presses, one *à tesson* [*taisson*], and a smaller one *etiqueté*. The *pressoir à taissons* is described by Lachiver, *Vin, vigne*, p. 112, as very large and expensive—nearly one thousand livres in eighteenth-century inventories around Paris— but the two belonging to Chertemps were either smaller or in poor shape since they are worth only two hundred livres together; inventory of 24 January 1721 in AD Marne, B 9075.

89. BM Châlons, ms. 125, pp. 372–73.

90. AD Marne, B 9076, inventaire après décès of Antoine Quatresous, 30 December 1732.

91. Kaplan, *Provisioning Paris*, pp. 136–38, 332–35, 390–91, 518–23.

92. Chandon de Briailles, "Recherches sur les origines," pp. 302–3; Chandon de Briailles and Bertal, *Sources de l'histoire d'Epernay*, 1:xlv; the grandfather was supposedly "one of the first to practice soutirage of the wine before its sale."

93. The inventory and the total of the movables are identified in the contrôle des actes for 1 February 1706, AD Marne, C 4372. Most inventories did not record the "immovable" assets (chiefly property), which required a separate assessment and valuation.

94. By comparison, the average for officials and professional men in Paris at the beginning of the century was twenty-seven thousand livres and for nobles was sixty-two thousand; Daniel Roche, *La culture des apparances; une histoire du vêtement (XVIIe–XVIIIe siècle)* (Paris, 1989), p. 95. Robert was closer to the average of fory-one hundred livres found among artisans and shopkeepers.

95. AD Marne, C 4374, 26 February 1720, marriage to Elizabeth de Villers.

96. This was more than five-sixths of the "merchants" of Bordeaux, and one-third of the "négociants," according to Poussou, *Bordeaux et le sud-ouest*, p. 315. For vinedressers and provincial nobles, see Durand, *Vin, vigne*, p. 450; for Paris, see Adeline Daumard and François Furet, *Structures et relations sociales à Paris au milieu du XVIIIe siècle* (Paris, 1961).

97. AD Marne, BR 1393, 2 March 1722, inventory of Marie Lallement. The total assets amounted to eighty-nine thousand livres and debts to fifty-five thousand livres. The average for movable wealth of fermiers between 1671–1743 was thirty-nine thousand livres, if debts and "avances de succession" are subtracted; Moriceau, *Les fermiers de l'Île-de-France*, p. 746. The average movables for rural merchants in one Norman bourg was forty-five hundred livres; Dewald, *Pont-St-Pierre*, p. 20.

98. Chandon de Briailles and Bertal, *Sources de l'histoire d'Epernay,* 1:xlviii, identifies the membership in Epernay as "les familles récemment enrichies ou nouvelles venues."

99. This is according to the registers of the town council of 31 July and 7 September 1712, in Auguste Nicaise, *Epernay et l'abbaye Saint-Martin* (Châlons, 1869), pp. 210–12.

100. See chapter 7 for a discussion of the arquebusiers in Auxerre.

101. See the copies of the various procès verbaux, from 11 June 1727 on, in BM Epernay, ms. 114, fols. 440 ff.

102. BN, Coll. Joly, ms. 1336, fol. 197, mémoire of Villetard of Auxerre, no date, but roughly 1740.

103. The two Merlins of Ay ran inns, according to AP Malavois de la Ganne, and Nicolas Chanlaire was tavern keeper in Epernay as of 8 October 1724 in AD Marne, 4E 15889.

104. Gandilhon, *Naissance,* p. 234, cites Arthur Michel de Boislisle, *Correspondance des contrôleurs généraux des finances avec les intendants des provinces,* 3 vols. (Paris, 1874–97), 2:279, for Desmaretz; the shipment is in AD Marne, C 4372, 7 January 1706.

105. BM Epernay, Fonds Chandon, ms. 329, fol. 34.

106. A comparison of every lettre de voiture in Bertin's *agenda,* BM Epernay, ms. 209, with the contemporary contrôles des actes reveals that his shipments were always attributed in the contrôle to a Nicolas Richard, who was described in the contrôle as a "broker of Epernay." Yet Bertin dealt with the shippers, received the payments from the wine merchants, and paid the growers: the details in his correspondence leave no doubt that he was actually the broker. Indeed Bertin describes Richard as "my domestic" in the agenda and sent him off to ride after shipments with messages and on other errands. We can only speculate that Bertin used Richard's name because he wished to distance himself from the business, perhaps because of his judicial offices.

107. BM Epernay, ms. 209, 27 November 1725.

108. AD Reims, 25B 61. See Jacqueline-Lucienne Lafon, *Les députés du commerce et l'ordonnance de Mars 1673, les juridictions consulaires: principe et compétence* (Paris, 1979), for these courts and pp. 113–34 especially for business failures. As Kaplan, *Provisioning Paris,* p. 154, points out, "Filing for failure was very similar to what we call filing for bankruptcy today, but in the old-regime French context bankruptcy necessarily implied fraud and was harshly punished and thus was carefully distinguished from *faillite,* or failure."

109. AD Côte d'Or, BII Suppl. 261, 12, 24, 29 December 1756.

110. Serge Chassagne, "Faillis en Anjou au XVIIIe siècle: contribution à l'histoire économique d'une province," *Annales ESC* 25 (1970): 477–97.

111. In addition there are small purchases by the Marquise du Chartres, a garde du Trésor royal "pour conduir à son château," a garde and lieutenant du roi, and a sergent au château de Vincennes.

112. AD Marne, F 148, mémoire sur l'état actuel de la généralité de Champagne, 1732, by the intendant Lepeletier de Beaupré, p. 166.

113. Moët is described as "living in Paris, at present in his maison de vendange

à Epernay" in 20 December 1718 and 16 October 1719, but as a bourgeois or commissionnaire of Epernay at many dates around these two; AD Marne, C 4374.

114. AP, Moët et Chandon, journal of 1743. I would like to thank the people of Moët et Chandon again for their remarkable kindness.

115. Ibid., 19 October 1748.

116. Ibid., 11 March 1749; 5 and 13 December 1748.

117. Ibid., 31 January 1749. See chapter 1, note 38, for these taxes.

118. Ibid., 16 January 1749.

119. AD Seine, D5B⁶ 143, letter of Chavansot of Beaune to Collas of Paris, 15 March 1743.

120. AP, Moët et Chandon, journal of 1743, 19 July 1744.

121. Ibid., 30 August 1755: "It is the excessive delay of my eldest son's voyage from Paris that causes this dearth, and those who have borrowed money from me have waited too long to repay."

122. Ibid., 11 September 1751.

123. Ibid., 22 December 1748.

Chapter 3 *From Public Office to Private Entrepreneur*

1. Jean-Louis Mestre, *Introduction historique au droit administratif français* (Paris, 1985), pp. 33–37, 71–73; François Olivier-Martin, *Histoire du droit français des origines à la Révolution* (Paris, 1948), pp. 144–46, 170–71; Thomas Brennan, "Public, Private, and la Police," in *Proceedings of the Western Society for French Historical Studies* 18 (1991): 582–91.

2. Charles Loyseau, *Traité des seigneuries,* 4th ed. (Paris, 1614), p. 90.

3. Cardin Le Bret, *De la souveraineté du roy* (Paris, 1632), p. 683.

4. See Gordon, *Citizens without Sovereignty,* pp. 11–23, for interesting reflections on later conceptions of *police.*

5. Agnew, *Worlds Apart,* pp. 19–27.

6. There is a large literature on transaction costs, much of it looking back to Ronald Coase, "The Nature of the Firm," *Economica* 4 (1937): 386–405, and O. E. Williamson, *Markets and Hierarchies* (New York, 1975). Useful discussions of this subject can be found in Pitelis, *Transaction Costs;* North, *Structure and Change in Economic History;* Douglass North, *Institutions, Institutional Change and Economic Performance* (Cambridge, 1990).

7. "Transaction Costs, Institutions, and Economic Performance," *Occasional Papers of the International Center for Economic Growth* 30 (1992), p. 14.

8. Michel Mollat, "Les hôtes et les courtiers dans les ports normands à la fin du moyen âge," *Revue historique* 24 (1944–45): 49–64, describes the profession as a "public function." Roger Price, *An Economic History of Modern France, 1730-1914* (New York, 1981), p. 29, notes about the late eighteenth century that "intermediaries with a certain commercial expertise had an increasingly important part to play, and began to replace the face to face character of many transactions between farmer and merchant. The mass of small vine cultivators or workmen in rural industry, with limited knowledge of market conditions themselves, were especially dependent upon intermediaries."

9. J.-A. Van Houtte, "Les courtiers au moyen âge: origine et caractéristiques d'une institution commerciale en Europe occidentale," *Revue historique de droit français et étranger* 15 (1936): 118–29, argues that courtiers in all medieval trades throughout Europe shared this double function, though very few of his examples are French. He concludes that "courtage in the Middle Ages thus appears to have been a system of surveillance rather than of mediation." See also Mollat, "Les hôtes et les courtiers dans les ports normands," pp. 49–64.

10. Delamare, *Traité de la police,* 3:629. The *Coutumes de la cité et ville de Rheims . . . avec commentaires par J. B. Buridan* (Paris, 1665), p. 833, noted that this unusual situation contradicted Roman law and was uniquely "a privilege or private law that the custom or ancient usage has introduced for wine merchants."

11. Arnoux, *Dissertation sur la situation de Bourgogne,* pp. 32–33.

12. A. Mollin, "Statuts et règlements des métiers de Beaune," *Mémoires de la société d'histoire de Beaune* 23 (1898–99): 151–59.

13. The denunciation is that of Cleirac, *Les us et coutumes de la mer,* quoted in Francisque-Xavier Michel, *Histoire du commerce et de la navigation à Bordeaux,* 2 vols. (1867), 2:391.

14. Paul Butel, "Bordeaux et la Hollande au XVIIIe siècle: l'exemple du négociant Pellet," *Revue d'histoire économique et sociale* 1 (1967): 72.

15. Delamare, *Traité de la police,* 3:629–30.

16. For Beaune, see the statuts des courtiers of 31 August 1607, reprinted, along with other documents from the registres de délibérations de la Chambre de la Ville de Beaune, in J. Délissey and L. Perriaux, "Les courtiers gourmets de la ville de Beaune: contribution à l'histoire du commerce du 'vin de Beaune' du XVIe au XVIIIe siècle," *Annales de Bourgogne* 34 (1962): 46–57. See also P. Destray, "Le commerce des vins en Bourgogne au XVIIIe siècle," in J. Hayem, *Mémoires et documents pour servir à l'histoire du commerce et de l'industrie en France,* 2d series (Paris, 1912), pp. 51–53. For Reims, see ordonnances of 3 June and 4 September 1654, in Roche, *Le commerce des vins de Champagne,* p. 62. See also Devroey, *L'éclair d'un bonheur,* pp. 138–40. Gérard Sautel, *Histoire du contrat de commission jusqu'au Code de Commerce* (Paris, 1949), p. 38, points out that the Code Michau of 1629 actually prohibited courtiers in all trades from taking commissions. It should be noted that in most cases I use the term broker interchangeably for courtier and commissionnaire.

17. Claude Tournier, "Le vin à Dijon de 1430 à 1560: ravitaillement et commerce," *Annales de Bourgogne* 22 (1950): 170.

18. Marcel Delafosse, "Le commerce du vin d'Auxerre (XIVe–XVIe siècle)," *Annales de Bourgogne* 13 (1941): 205–27; Jean Richard, "Production et commerce du vin en Bourgogne aux XVIIIe et XIXe siècles," *Annales cisalpines d'histoire sociale* 3 (1972): 29; Gadille, *Le vignoble de la côte bourguignonne,* pp. 375–76.

19. Michel, *Histoire du commerce et de la navigation à Bordeaux,* 2:382–97.

20. Savary, *Le parfait négociant,* 2:145.

21. [C. Brac], *Le commerce des vins, réformé, rectifié et épuré, ou nouvelle méthode pour tirer un parti sûr, prompt et avantageux des récoltes en vins* (Amsterdam and Lyon, 1769), pp. 12–15.

22. AN, G^7 1508, arrêt du conseil d'état, 30 June 1692; ordonnances of 3 June

and 4 September 1654, in Roche, *Le commerce des vins de Champagne,* p. 62. See also Bidet, *Mémoire pour servir à l'histoire de Reims,* 4 vols. (1749), 4:68–69.

23. Deliberations of the town council, 28 December 1632, quoted in Persan, "Les voituriers par eau," pp. 225–26.

24. Deliberations of the town council, 8 October 1674 and 24 November 1684, cited in Délissey and Perriaux, "Courtiers gourmets de Beaune," pp. 56–57.

25. AM Beaune, carton 4, no. 5, extraits des registres des délibérations de la chambre du conseil de l'hôtel de ville de Beaune, 14 October 1682. Documents relating to the case can also be found in AM Beaune, carton 4, no. 1 and 3; AD Côte d'Or, C 874.

26. See de Roover, "The Concept of the Just Price," pp. 418–34. See also chapter 5 for more discussion of this issue.

27. AM Beaune, carton 4, no. 5, extraits des registres des délibérations de la chambre du conseil de l'hôtel de ville de Beaune, 14 October 1682.

28. J. Accarias de Serionne, *Les intérêts des nations d'Europe developpés relativement au commerce,* 2 vols. (Leipsich, 1766), 2:252.

29. Butel, *Les négociants bordelais,* p. 134, notes for example, that "in the area of finances the role of the bordelais commissionnaire was very important, for he made advances to the merchants of the Haut Pays who only disposed of limited means."

30. Edict of November 1691, in Delamare, *Traité de la police,* 3:632.

31. Edict of 27 March 1627, in ibid., 3:630.

32. BN, Coll. Joly, ms. 1336, fol. 16.

33. Edict of 27 March 1627, Delamare, *Traité de la police,* 3:630.

34. Ibid., 2:630–31, edict of 27 March 1627, edict of June 1691 (which also refers to the edict of July 1656).

35. Edict of June 1691, in ibid., 3:631–33.

36. See the arrêt du conseil d'état of 6 May 1692 in BM Epernay, Fonds Chandon, ms. 149, fol. 99.

37. See letters from 2 July, 16 August, 13 October, 22 October 1691, and 1 July, 8 November 1692, in BM Epernay, Fonds Chandon, ms. 329 fols. 20 ff., ms. 155, fols. 125 ff.

38. Quoted in Trouessart, *Le commerce de Blois,* 2:351.

39. The town had to borrow the money and, when the king later suppressed the office, the *Coutume du comté et baillage d'Auxerre avec notes et actes de notoriété . . . par Edme Billon* (Paris, 1693), pp. 294–95, 301, asserted that "this caused the beginning of the town's misfortunes and its debts."

40. AN, G⁷ 1508, arrêt du conseil d'état, 30 June 1692. See also Roche, *Le commerce des vins de Champagne,* pp. 56–78, for an extensive discussion of the courtiers of Reims and part of the text of this arrêt.

41. AN G7 1507, memoir of Nantes, no date; memoir of Bordeaux, no date. Gail Bossenga, *The Politics of Privilege: Old Regime and Revolution in Lille* (Cambridge, 1991), pp. 121–28, discusses the impact of royal "fiscalism" as it applied to a range of offices in the city of Lille.

42. Edict of November 1704, in AN G⁷ 1508.

43. AN, G⁷ 1507, extrait de la lettre du Sr Stalpaert à M Chamillart, 21 April 1705, with the traitant's response appended. Like a tax farmer, the traitant ad-

vanced money to the government for the right to sell the offices; see J. F. Bosher, *French Finances, 1770–1795, from Business to Bureaucracy* (Cambridge, 1970), p. 9, for the role of traitants.

44. AN, G⁷ 1507, extrait des registres du conseil d'état, 22 April 1692; letter from the élus généraux des états de Bourgogne, 7 March 1705; extrait des registres du conseil d'état, 18 August 1705.

45. Ibid., placet of Sr Tassier, fermier des aides de Champagne, no date. See similar warnings from the intendant at Lyon about brokers in Roanne, in AN, G⁷ 360, letter of 25 November 1705.

46. Letter of 18 September 1691, and summaries of letters from the intendant to the controller general, 23 February and 10 March 1705, in Boislisle, *Correspondence des contrôleurs généraux*, 1:259; 2:234–35. See Butel, *Les négociants bordelais*, pp. 180–87, for confirmation of this advice.

47. AN, G⁷ 1508, état du traité des courtiers de vin ainsy qu'il avoit été arreté par Mgr Desmarets, 21 May 1706, gives a list of sums to be paid by each generality to buy out the new offices. Most owed less than thirty thousand livres, except for Bordeaux, Châlons, and Orléans.

48. Ibid., mémoire sur l'affaire des courtiers de vin de Bretagne [Nantes 1705], unsigned. The memoir is not sympathetic to the brokers' complaints, so its author probably worked for the traitant.

49. AN, G⁷ 1507, placet de Sr Tassier, fermier des aides de Champagne, no date. In response the traitant accused him of "acting more in favor of and in concert with the courtiers commissionnaires than in the interests of his [tax] farm." Communication between the traitant and the marquise de Louvois, as holding the comté de Tonnerre, no date. G⁷ 1508, memoir of the maire et échevins de Reims, no date, with traitant's response.

50. AN, G⁷ 1507, mémoire des négociants de Nantes au Roi et nosseigneurs de son conseil, no date.

51. Ibid. In a survey of legal and commercial treatises on the subject, Sautel, *Histoire du contrat de commission,* p. 38, asserts that "this distinction between commissionnaire and courtier has always been made with remarkable precision." For example, Guyot, *Répertoire universel et raisonné de jurisprudence* (Paris, 1784), 4:160, "Commissionnaires must not be confused with courtiers. The latter are public men who cannot, at the same time, conduct commerce in their name . . . whereas commissionnaires are only the proxies [*mandatoires*] of merchants."

52. AN, G⁷ 1507, mémoire sur l'affaire des courtiers de vin de Bretagne [Nantes 1705], unsigned; letter to controller general, dated 12 May 1705, signed by J. Descasaux, juge consul, and others.

53. Letter of 18 September 1691, in Boislisle, *Correspondence des contrôleurs généraux,* 1:259. AN, G⁷ 1508, letter of négociants de Bordeaux, no date.

54. AN, G⁷ 1507, undated letter from Jacques Stalpaert, Jean VanBerchem, et al., followed by the traitant's response. See also a letter to Chamillart by Stalpaert on 21 April 1705, and an unsigned letter to Darmenonville of 30 April 1705.

55. Ibid., letter from DeMontmiy to Chamillart, dated 18 January 1705 at Marseille.

56. Ibid., traitant's response to letter by Stalpaert et al.; G⁷ 1508, response of the fermiers généraux de droits des courtiers-commissionnaires de la province de

Bretagne aux mémoires données par le procureur général syndic des Etats de Bretagne, no date, but à propos their legal pursuit of the case into 1709.

57. Savary, *Le parfait négociant*, 2:145, 191.

58. Ibid., 2:143–45. The edition of Savary published a hundred years later (1777) gave essentially the same definitions of commissionnaire. The treatise written by his son, Jacques Savary des Bruslons, *Dictionnaire universel de commerce* (Paris, 1760), 2:126, was also very similar.

59. Etienne Bonnot de Condillac, *Le commerce et le gouvernement considéré relativement l'un à l'autre*, 2 vols. in one (Paris, 1776), 1:34–38.

60. Lachiver, *Vin, vigne*, pp. 244–57, offers a quick survey of these taxes. For more detail see Lefebvre de la Bellande, *Traité général des droits d'aides*, pp. 4–14, 328–33.

61. Lefebvre de Bellande, *Traité général des droits d'aides*, pp. 332–33.

62. Almost sixty years earlier, Eon, *Le commerce honorable*, pp. 87–90, had described the domination achieved by Dutch merchants over the wine trade of the western Loire region. For Dutch business sophistication, see Jonathan I. Israel, *Dutch Primacy in World Trade, 1585-1740* (Oxford, 1989), though there is little about contacts with Nantes. For Dutch involvement in the wine trade of the lower Loire, see also Dion, *Histoire de la vigne*, pp. 423–29, 449–60.

63. One of them, named Stalpaert, complained, "I am always included with the foreign merchants even though I have been naturalized for thirty-six years and established here since 1660"; AN, G^7 1507, extrait de la lettre du Sr Stalpaert de Nantes à M Chamillart 12 April 1705. In response, the intendant of Brittany wrote shortly after to the controller general: "Jan Stalpaert, originally of Bruges, has been established at Nantes for thirty years and there has a large commerce in wines and brandy to foreign countries, with reputation"; 30 April 1705, Boislisle, *Correspondence des contrôleurs généraux*, 3:245.

64. AN, G^7 1508, roll of courtiers de vin, 31 January 1707.

65. There are six rolls of fines, with 1,074 names, drawn up between February and April 1705, in AN, G^7, 1507, 1508, 1509.

66. Braudel, *Perspective of the World*, pp. 339–51.

67. The brokers in Epernay and some of the surrounding villages can be identified quite exactly with the records of the contrôle des actes; AD Marne, C 4140, 4371. Those in lower Burgundy can be identified through taille and notarial records; see chapter 4.

68. AN, G^7 1509, undated letter of Jean Prevost.

69. AN, G^7 1507, Placet of Sr Tassier, tax farmer in Champagne, no date.

70. Ibid.

71. Brokers taxed only 500 livres averaged 3,700 livres of wealth. Those fined 1,000 livres averaged 9,000 livres, and those taxed 2,000 livres averaged 21,000 livres. Those in the highest bracket, of 3,000 livres averaged 42,000 livres.

72. Letter from intendant at Limoges, 10 January 1705, in Boislisle, *Correspondence des contrôleurs généraux*, 2:234. He also pointed out that the wine produced closer to La Rochelle, in the Angoumois, was purchased without the aid of brokers.

73. AN, G^7 1507, mémoire concernant l'état du traité des offices de courtiers-commissionnaires, 27 March 1705.

74. Gadille, *Le vignoble de la côte bourguignonne*, pp. 370–72; Brac, *Le commerce des vins*, pp. 9–10; Enjalbert, *Histoire de la vigne*, pp. 110–11.

75. Braudel, *Perspective of the World*, pp. 339–51; Fox, *History in a Geographical Perspective*, p. 174.

76. Of course some of the wine that reached Paris was also destined for the international export market, and according to an Etat des vins de la sénéchaussée de Bordeaux qui se chargent dans le port, année commune, AN, F^{12} 1500, over one-quarter of the wine exported from Bordeaux in the middle of the eighteenth century returned to Brittany or northern France.

77. The intendant offered no more information about brokering in Provence than a detailed list of the wine produced and sold in each locale, in an Etat des lieux de vignobles, AN G^7 1507, along with an "estimation" that the province could support 226 brokers, of which only six were assigned to Marseille. Charles Carrière, *Négociants marseillais au XVIIIe siècle* (Marseille, 1973), p. 357, identifies an average of forty thousand hectoliters of wine exported from Marseille between 1725 and 1727, which is only one-quarter the exports from Nantes and one-twentieth of that from Bordeaux. Géraud-Parracha, *Le commerce des vins*, pp. 121–22, 170–79, identifies Montpellier, Sète, and Béziers as the principal ports for wine exports from Languedoc, but Sète only exported thirty-five thousand hectoliters and Boissonnade, "La production et le commerce des céréales, des vins et des eaux-de-vie," p. 355, says that the majority of wine exported from Languedoc left by way of Bordeaux.

78. This is the suggestion made by Braudel, *The Wheels of Commerce*, pp. 184–85.

79. According to Delamare, *Traité de la police*, 3:630, "courtiers shall be distributed among and bounded by their parishes."

80. Deliberations of the chambre de ville, 16 September 1683, cited in Délissey and Perriaux, "Courtiers gourmets de Beaune," p. 57.

81. Henri Enjalbert, "Comment naissent les grands crus: bordeaux, porto, cognac," *Annales ESC* 8 (1953): 318–21.

82. Huetz de Lemps, *Géographie du commerce de Bordeaux*, p. 137.

83. Beauroy, *Vin et société à Bergerac*, pp. 243–48. Butel, *Les négociants bordelais*, pp. 134–37, also identifies the "relative independence" of upstream producers from a map of courtiers created in a dozen upstream villages in 1761, but without knowing the size of their operations, they may have been no more impressive than the marginal upstream brokers identified in 1705.

84. Huetz de Lemp, *Géographie du commerce de Bordeaux*, pp. 181–83.

85. However, a revised list from 1706, in AN, G^7 1508, which had reduced the total fines to only seventy-two thousand livres shifted the burden between Bordeaux and its hinterland, by raising the percentage of the total paid by the surrounding towns from 10 to 25.

86. Dion, *Histoire de la vigne*, pp. 448–53, is quoting the intendant at Blois in 1707.

87. Gandilhon, *Naissance*, pp. 160–61; Dion, *Histoire de la vigne*, pp. 618–19.

88. The top quartile in Nantes owed 58 percent, in Laon owed 52 percent, and in Bordeaux owed 43 percent. Of fifty-five brokers in Orléans, over half owed less than a thousand livres, and only six were fined more than two thousand livres; the top quartile owed 44 percent. Orléans's situation was unusual. It did not appear

on the original rolls because of delays by the local intendant, and the sums were low by the standards of the Loire, as if the traitants had already agreed to a diminution by the time this roll appeared.

89. AN G⁷ 1507, the first roll was dated 10 February 1705; the second was dated 17 March. Brokers in the top quartile in Bordeaux were fined four thousand livres each and owed nearly half the city's total fines.

90. See the map of wine production in this area in Lachiver, *Vin, vigne,* p. 189. For Soissons, see Doehaerd, "Laon, capitale du vin au XIIe siècle," pp. 145–65; Dion, *Histoire de la vigne,* pp. 234, 544–45.

91. This does not include the election of Tonnerre, which was nominally in the generality of Paris but geographically part of lower Burgundy, or the election of Château-Thierry, along the Marne.

92. See the discussion of guinguettes in Brennan, *Public Drinking,* pp. 176–86; and the description of this market in Lachiver, *Vin, vigne,* pp. 272–82.

93. This average does not include the fines for Orléans, since the surviving roll is evidently not the original but the subsequent list of diminished fines.

94. Auxerre also exhibited a clear hierarchy among its brokers, with the five paying five or six thousand livres, accounting for nearly three-quarters of the town's tax. Another five paid between one thousand and twenty-five hundred livres, and two paid five and six hundred livres.

95. Delafosse, "Le commerce du vin d'Auxerre," p. 204, based on the farm for aides. See Thomas Brennan, "The Anatomy of Inter-Regional Markets in the Early Modern French Wine Trade," *Journal of European Economic History* 22 (1994): 581–617, for a fuller discussion.

96. AD Seine, D5B⁶ 695, journal of Paul Herbelin, marchand de vin en gros, 1713–14. Herbelin paid the broker in Auxerre, Robinet, for the "expenses" of wine shipped from Chalon and Beaune through Auxerre. Two Robinets, listed in the tax rolls for five and six thousand livres, were among the five biggest brokers in Auxerre.

97. Johnson, *The Organization of Space in Developing Countries,* pp. 85–91. Carol A. Smith, "Regional Economic Systems: Linking Geographical Models and Socio-economic Problems," 1:34–39, and Klara Bonsack Kelley, "Dendritic Central-Place Systems," 1:221–34, both in C. A. Smith, *Regional Analysis,* 2 vols. (London, 1976), treat the dendritic system as a tool for analyzing wholesale trade, whereas traditional central place theory has theoretical application only to retail networks. For a study considering the trade networks of a single commodity that uses the dendritic model, see Gordon Appleby, "Export Monoculture and Regional Social Structure in Puno, Peru," in Smith, *Regional Analysis,* 1:291 ff.

98. Carol A. Smith, "Economics of Marketing Systems: Models from Economic Geography," *Annual Review of Anthropology* 3 (1974): 177–78.

99. AN, G⁷ 1507, mémoire of 27 March 1705.

100. AN, G⁷ 1508, letter from Charles Huet et Edme Mathieu, no date.

101. AN, G⁷ 1507, request presented to the king in his council, no date. The brokers' complaints were incorporated into an arrêt de conseil of 28 July 1705 that forbade anyone without the office to involve themselves in the brokerage.

102. AN, G⁷ 1508, mémoire of Merite, dated 4 June 1706. See also G⁷ 1507, for the contract by which Pierre Charles Dubois, bourgeois de Paris agreed to pay

15,500 livres, plus a 10 percent surcharge, to the traitant for these six offices. Merite says he acquired them "under the name of Dubois."

103. One of the brokers, Edme Beau was actually the son of a "merchant of Coulanges," but Edme had married the daughter of a merchant of Tonnerre (29 July 1681) and identified himself as a commissionnaire of Tonnerre in 1688; AD Yonne, 3E 11-102; 3E 11-104, 23 June.

104. AD Yonne, 2CC 2 [Archives communales de Tonnere], acte d'assemblée des habitants de . . . Tonnerre, 3 March 1715; memoir to the bailly of Tonnerre, 13 January 1713; memoir of countess of Tonnerre, 23 October 1713.

105. BN, Coll. Joly, ms. 1336, fols. 12–15; the memoir is unsigned and undated but was clearly provoked by an incident in 1739 and may well have been written by Joly de Fleury; see chapter 5.

106. Lefebvre de la Bellande, *Traité général des droits d'aide,* p. 418. The taxes associated with the office, such as the droits de courtier-jaugeur and droit de courtage, were still owed by the seller, however.

Chapter 4   *The Brokers of Burgundy*

1. Schlumbohm, "Relations of Production," p. 99.

2. Reddy, *The Rise of Market Culture,* p. 26. Liu, *The Weaver's Knot,* p. 58, says, "With open access to buying and marketing, those who did not engage in production, especially petty traders, were vulnerable."

3. Vardi, *The Land and the Loom,* p. 191; Schlumbohm, "Relations of Production," p. 104.

4. A study of scattered lettres de voiture in the Burgundian notarial archives by Saint-Jacob, "Les lettres de voiture," pp. 124–26, offers a purely impressionistic report: that the senders were almost always merchants and brokers rather than the growers, much like the evidence from bills of lading in Champagne.

5. See the reservations against the use of these documents expressed by J.-P. Poisson, "De quelques nouvelles utilisations des sources notariales en histoire économique, XVIIe–XXe siècles," *Revue historique* 249 (1973): 5–22, especially as to the systematic underreporting of assets.

6. Dion, *Histoire de la vigne,* pp. 245–46.

7. Roger Dion, "Le commerce des vins de Beaune au moyen âge," *Revue historique* 214 (1955): 209–10.

8. Ordonnance of 22 August 1578, in Delamare, *Traité de la police,* 3:689.

9. Charles Estienne, 1637, and Le Paulmier, 1588, cited in Nollevalle, *Vin d'Ay,* pp. 7–9.

10. "Mémento d'un propriétaire auxerrois," *Almanach de l'Yonne* (1855): 38–41, (1865): 57–59; Rocher, *Histoire d'Auxerre,* pp. 229–30.

11. BN, FF 22214, Déscription du Duché de Bourgogne par Ferrand, intendant, 1698, p. 405.

12. AN, G^2 31, régie of 1787.

13. AD Yonne, 3E 7-178, the farm of a tax at Auxerre, 2 October 1654, in Henri Forestier, *Extraits analytiques des minutes déposées aux archives de l'Yonne par Me André Guimard, notaire à Auxerre* (Auxerre, 1954), p. 189; Max Quantin, "His-

toire de la rivière d'Yonne," *Bulletin de la société des sciences historiques et naturelles de l'Yonne* (1885): 450.

14. Richard, "Production et commerce du vin en Bourgogne," pp. 23–24, statistics from 1812 and 1833.

15. Challe, "Documents statistiques sur des villes, bourgs et autres communautés d'habitants du comté d'Auxerre," *Annuaire de l'Yonne* (1853): 301–59.

16. AN, G² 31, régie of 1787.

17. AD Yonne, 3E 11-6, remonstrance by half a dozen tonneliers, 14 February 1691, cited in Forestier, *Extraits analytiques,* pp. 21–22. According to the registers of the conseil d'état, 30 June 1681, cited in 3E 11-102, 17 September 1681, a fire in 1676 had reduced the bourg to an "extreme misery" and had done 250,000 livres in damage.

18. From the registers of the Bureau de la Ville, February 1555, cited in Marie-Edmée Michel, "Recherches sur la 'Compagnie française' au XVIe siècle d'après le commerce vinicole parisien," *Mémoires publiées par la fédération des sociétés historique et archéologique de Paris et Île-de-France* 15 (1965): 64. See also Thibault, "Les Parisiens et le vin," pp. 231–49.

19. Delafosse, "Commerce du vin," pp. 214–29, gives a very thorough explanation of this thesis for the fifteenth and sixteenth centuries.

20. Delamare, *Traité de la police,* 3:548. The term "marchand forain" denotes itinerancy, "qui, sans résidence fixe, s'installe sur les marchés et les foires de n'importe quelle localité"; *Petit Robert* (Paris, 1972), s.v. forain.

21. Quoted in Dion, *Histoire de la vigne,* p. 548

22. Arrêt of August 1662, in Delamare, *Traité de la police,* 3:551–52. It is interesting that the petitions of 1648, 1656, and 1661 came from traders of lower Burgundy alone and included none from Champagne or the Loire.

23. "Favorable opinion" by eighteen marchands bourgeois of Auxerre in support of the entrepreneurs, AD Yonne, 3E 7-185, 10 April 1661. There are similar opinions from marchands bourgeois of Vaux, Champs, Cravant, and Vermenton, in 3E 7-185, 11 and 12 April.

24. Ibid.

25. Extrait des registres de Parlement, 13 May 1675, in BN, FF 21665, fol. 42, about a request sent by them in 15 December 1670.

26. The average for the Halle is based on figures for the years 1702–8, taken from an affidavit by the commis aux aides at the Halle, dated 8 May 1712; AN, G⁷ 1511. The average for the wine brought in by Parisian wine merchants comes from a report on the produit net des marchands de vin de Paris, in AN, G⁷ 1179, no date but internal evidence indicates the summer of 1712.

27. AN, G⁷ 1511, two different memoirs concerning the edict of January 1710 taxing wine merchants.

28. AN, G⁷ 1180, proposal of the tax farm to let Parisian wine merchants provision within the twenty league limit, 29 October 1711; AN, G⁷ 1511, report of a tax farmer, Noble, 14 July 1712.

29. Lefebvre de la Bellande, *Traité général des droits d'aides,* p. 28.

30. AD Yonne, 3E 11-145, 9 November 1670, cited in Forestier and Hohl, *Extraits analytiques.*

31. AD Yonne, 3E 11-150, 22 February 1725.

32. AD Yonne, 8B 4, 19 September, 10 October 1725, 8B 5, 27 May 1729; 8B 6, 17 November 1729, 27 February, 12 June, 27 December 1730, 5 March 1731. In the few cases where the wine had been commissioned by a Parisian, the boatmen sued the Parisian and his broker; see, for example, 8B 6, 19 August 1729.

33. AD Yonne, 8B 6, 13 May 1732; 8B 7, 26 February 1734, 12 May and 27 November 1738, referring to contracts in 1730 and 1732. These suits essentially disappear after the 1730s.

34. See, for example, AD Yonne, 3E 7-251a, 10 December 1740, inventory of Charles Marion, worth 11,923 livres. For boatmen elsewhere, see Anne-Marie Cocula-Vaillieres, *Un fleuve et des hommes, les gens de la Dordogne au XVIIIe siècle* (Paris, 1981), pp. 220–24; Denis Luya, "Port, quartiers et gens de rivière à Roanne (fin du XVIIe siècle à 1858)," *Cahiers d'histoire* 29 (1984): 24–29. According to Meuvret, *Le problème des subsistances,* 3:81, boatmen in the seventeenth century "were most often only small entrepreneurs with restricted capital and short commercial horizons. They were mostly helped by the members of their family."

35. Le Roy Ladurie, "De la crise ultime à la vrai croissance," pp. 448–50; Dion, *Histoire de la vigne,* p. 552. The story is originally told in Nicolas Rétif de la Bretonne, *La vie de mon père.*

36. According to the report of the régie in 1787, AN, G^2 31, Sacy produced 350 muids a year, making it only marginal to the region's wine trade.

37. BN, Coll. Joly, ms. 1335, fols. 42–46, correspondence in October 1739 with the controller general about extending this caisse to wine brought to Paris by cart. An edict of September 1719 originally created the caisse to loan traders the price of their wine at a rate of six deniers per livre [2½ percent].

38. BN, FF 21664, fols. 92–93, arrêt du conseil d'état of 19 March 1724.

39. BN, Coll. Joly, ms. 1335, fols. 42–46, correspondence in October 1739.

40. In 1770, Lefebvre de la Bellande, *Traité général des droits d'aydes,* p. 28, noted that "few merchants made use of this ability to borrow against the price of their wines; it cost a great deal to operate this caisse, which did not respond to the utility that had been proposed; so that, by the arrêt and letters patent of 16 September 1727, the loan was reduced to [cover] the entry tax as it is still today."

41. BN, Coll. Joly, ms. 1336, fol. 204, printed factum of Soufflot, no date, but appealing a judicial sentence of March 1739. See chapter 5 for the case.

42. Ibid. He set the number of Parisian wine merchants at twelve hundred or more.

43. BN, Coll. Joly, ms. 1336, fols. 195–200, factum of Villetard, no date, but appealing a judicial sentence of 1739.

44. Challe, *Histoire de l'Auxerrois* (Paris, 1878), p. 555.

45. Delafosse, "Le commerce du vin d'Auxerre," p. 206. Dion, *Histoire de la vigne,* p. 250, notes that in 1387, the jaugeurs of Auxerre were "performing their functions at Chablis" of buying wine for outsiders.

46. Etienne Fernier, one of the maire's courtiers and seventy-five years old in 1623, had earlier formed an association with his son for seven years to share "half the profits and losses of brokering and reliages of the wines they will buy" in and around Auxerre. At that point both identify themselves as "merchants of Auxerre"; 3 April 1605, AD Yonne 3E 7-375. Etienne Fernier, l'ainé and Edme Deserin gave

expert testimony, in their capacity as courtiers, on the condition of some disputed wine, in AD Yonne, 3E 7-387, 30 June 1618; both documents in Forestier, *Extraits analytiques.*

47. Jean-Paul Desaive, "D'Auxerre à Paris et retour: un témoignage inédit de 1644," *Bulletin de la société des sciences historiques et naturelles de l'Yonne* (1991): 22. Jehan, or Jean, would identify himself as a "marchand courtier" in 1632.

48. Drinot, twenty-nine years old, and yet already in office for twelve years, mentions that he had received the office from his father-in-law, Jehan Henot, who is identified as a voiturier par eau in 27 May 1588; AD Yonne, 3E 7-94. Navarre, aged sixty-two, and having held office for some twenty-five years, seems also to have belonged to such a dynasty; a Guillaume Navarre was courtier de vins at Chablis up to 1687 (AD Yonne, B 5e suppl., 199, extrait of his inventaire après décès, 29 October 1687) and an Etienne Navarre of Auxerre owed the large sum of 6,000 livres in 1705. At the same time, Jean Drinot and a "nommé Drinot fils" were fined 6,000 and 2,500 livres, AN, G[7] 1509. Pierre and Jean Robinet were fined 5,000 and 6,000 livres, and a "nommé Ragot" was fined 6,500 livres at Chablis.

49. Charles Demay, "La juridiction consulaire d'Auxerre," *Bulletin de la société des sciences historiques et naturelles de l'Yonne* (1894): 182–89.

50. AD Yonne, 3E 7-214, 10 March 1691, cited in Forestier, *Extraits analytiques.*

51. AD Yonne, 3E 7-156, inventaire après décès, François Potin, 23 October 1702. The *nommé* Potin who owed the fine was probably his son.

52. AD Seine, D5B[6] 695, journal of Herbelin, 1713–14.

53. AD Yonne, 3E 7-161, 11 September 1719. Navarre's nephew purchased some five hundred barrels in 1718 and was paid a commission of ten sous by his uncle for each double barrel (muid). In addition to his nephew Navarre, another nephew, François Ragot, and a son-in-law, François Boyard, were also wine brokers; in 9 December 1719, AD Yonne, 3E 7-161.

54. AD Yonne, 3E 7-160, inventaire après décès of Marie Legate, wife of Etienne Navarre, 19 March 1717; 3E 7-161, inventaire après décès of Etienne Navarre, 11 September 1719. Among the heirs were several brokers, including François Boyard, as the husband of Marguerite Navarre, the widow of a voiturier par eau.

55. AD Yonne, 3E 3-20, 9 September 1718, contrat d'atermoiement entre Jean-Achille Sallé, marchand commissionnaire de vins, et ses créanciers. Sallé is not on the list of brokers in 1705 but is probably related to two master boatmen with the same last name listed among the nineteen in Auxerre in 1702.

56. AD Seine, D5B[6] 695, journal of Herbelin, 1713–14.

57. AD Yonne, 3E 3-19, 14 and 17 May 1714. Sallé was protesting the condition of the wine on its arrival and turned to several local brokers to give testimony as to its condition.

58. AN, G[2] 31; the production in Coulanges and five villages around it at the end of the Old Regime was over seventeen thousand hectoliters. Courtepée, *Description générale et particulière du duché de Bourgogne,* 4 vols. (Dijon, 1847–48), 4:359, calls it a small town in the middle of the century, but the residents insisted it was "not a town but only a mean little bourg" at the end of the seventeenth century.

59. AD Yonne, 3E 11-104, marriage of Millon, 24 April 1688. Guy Pilleron was both lieutenant au bailliage and a "commissionnaire" working for the Parisian wine merchant, Triboullot, 3E 11-3, 10 September 1676, 8 April 1679, cited in For-

estier and Hohl, *Extraits analytiques*. His father had been lieutenant au bailliage and "courtier" before him; AD Yonne, BB 65, 27 November 1620, 26 January 1621.

60. AD Yonne, 3E 11-6, is receveur of Gy l'eveque, 24 June 1692; 3E 11-23, 22 June 1705; 3E 11-26, 31 January 1705; 3E 11-7, 1 April 1699; cited in Forestier, *Extraits analytiques*. See Moriceau, *Les fermiers de l'Île-de-France,* passim, for the economic behavior, and power, of these positions.

61. AD Yonne, 3E 6-21, inventaire après décès of Claude Millon, 1 October 1718. His heirs include his widow, Catherine Devilliers, and daughter, Catherine, married to Germain Soufflot, the lieutenant au bailliage of Irancy and son of the deceased Jacques, lieutenant au bailliage and its sole broker in 1705. Another heir was Madeline Soufflot, the widow of Jean Millon, who was identified as a [living] marchand commissionnaire of Coulanges-la-Vineuse in 3E 7-160, 21 May 1718. Claude Millon is identified in 1704 as fermier of the land and seigneurie of Coulanges belonging to Mgr Daguesseau, procureur général du roi au Parlement; AD Yonne, 9B 273.

62. There is little evidence for prices, except occasional references in the account book of his sales to Parisians, where the prices range from 44 to 63 livres per muid (two barrels) and a few barrels of "old wine" worth 105 livres per muid. These prices probably included significant transportation costs and taxes.

63. BN, Coll. Joly, ms. 1336, fol. 202, factum for Soufflot, broker of Irancy and Coulanges, no date, but it appeals the sentence against him of 17 March 1739.

64. It is possible to identify many of the names using the extracts of the local notarial archives in Forestier and Hohl, *Extraits analytiques.*

65. AD Yonne, 3E 11-5, 14 February 1692. See 3E 11-5, 10 July 1688 for such contracts.

66. AD Yonne, 3E 11-3, 7 January 1676; 3E 11-4, 5 October 1681; 3E 11-5, 10 December 1685, cited in Forestier and Hohl, *Extraits analytiques.*

67. AD Yonne, 8B 10, Benoit Liger, commissionnaire de Coulanges-la-vineuse vs. Jacques Gousjoin, cordonnier de Coulanges-la-vineuse, 19 July 1766.

68. AD Yonne, 3E 6-210, appeal against Boyard Forterre, 10 October 1754.

69. The inventory only quoted accounts that were not closed, in this case Parisians who still owed the estate. Most of the extracts come from AD Yonne, 3E 6-21, inventaire après décès of Claude Millon, 1 October 1718, fol. 50 and beyond, relating to 1716 and 1717.

70. AD Yonne, C 3458–3461, contrôle des actes de Saint-Bris, 1697–1700.

71. AD Yonne, 3E 11-6, 20 January 1691.

72. Several Soufflots appear in numerous documents edited and abridged in Forestier and Hohl, *Extraits analytiques;* AD Yonne, E 458, has the marriage between Jean Soufflot, avocat and son of Jean the lieutenant of the bailliage of Irancy, with Barbe Rigollet, daughter of Jean, élu du roi in the élection of Vézelay.

73. He is one of the brokers visited by Herbelin in 1714; AD Seine, D5B⁶ 695.

74. AD Yonne, 3E 14-801, inventaire après décès of Jacques Sourdeau, wine merchant of Paris, 29 December 1735, lists some two thousand livres of movables in his house, and the wine in that year's vintage was worth 1,260 livres.

75. Jean Felix Regnauldin, a wholesale wine merchant in Paris, also had a house and fifteen arpents of vines in Saint-Bris; AD Yonne, 3E 14-801, 26 October 1735. The grandson, Guillaume, would be described as a broker in 1766 and son-in-law

of another broker; AD Yonne, 3E 3-66, 17 February 1766. See Etienne Meunier, "La famille Regnauldin, marchands de vin à Saint-Bris-le-vieux," *Cahiers de généalogie* 2 (1984): 45–48, for more about the family.

76. See sales on 23 July, 4 and 9 August, 6 September, and 12 October 1709 in AD Yonne, 3E 14-797 and C 2270. But Boyard's brother-in-law, Nicolas Guyon, does not appear in the 1705 list of brokers.

77. Dion, *Histoire de la vigne*, p. 553.

78. AN, G^7 1507, letter to Desmaretz, May 1705. Forty years earlier, a widow Girault, presumably the mother-in-law of Alexandre's wife, had been actively continuing the business of her husband, a "merchant commissionnaire" of Chablis, in association with a merchant of Auxerre.

79. AD Yonne, 3E 24-2, 9 February 1718. He was fined sixty-five hundred livres.

80. AD Yonne, 3E 66-29, inventaire après décès of Jean Soufflot, 25 May 1689.

81. The vines included ten arpents of vines in and around Chablis and another three at Irancy [where the vines were worth 25 percent less than in Chablis—369 livres vs. 497 livres per arpent]; AD Yonne, 3E 66-49, partage of communauté de biens between Jeanne Henry and Edme Petit, 13 May 1705.

82. AD Yonne, 3E 24-2, inventaire après décès of Edme Petit, 26 November 1717; partage of Petit, 1 February 1718. Moriceau, *Les fermiers de l'Île-de-France*, p. 747.

83. AD Yonne, 3E 24-1, inventaire après décès of Rathier, 9 March 1716; partage, 12 March 1716. His meubles, assessed at 3,000 livres, plus 150 livres of wine and 60 livres of wood for barrels (described as the "things necessary for the use of the wine broker"), describe a very modest household, though he also owned 13 arpents of vines, worth about 5,000 livres, which made him a large proprietor.

84. AD Yonne, 3E 24-2, inventaire après décès of Elizabeth Froment, veuve Rathier, 1 June 1719.

85. AD Yonne, 3E 24-2, 4 November 1719. By June she had only paid 40 percent of what she owed these people, repaying the big and little debts to about the same extent. A later inventory said that her estate still owed thirty-four thousand livres to one hundred people who had sold her wine.

86. Lambert's postmortem inventory, AD Yonne, 3E 66-65, 5 May 1741, suggests that he was a small-scale broker, with Parisian wine merchants owing him little more than three thousand livres at his death.

87. AD Yonne, 38B 128, inventaire après décès of Marie Le Prince, 1724, refers to a donation by the widow Navarre to Ragot and Le Prince, his wife, in 11 August 1708.

88. The inventory does not give the value of this land, but in 1705 Ragot, identified as a merchant, bought three and a half arpents of grand cru, at Grenouille, for 750 livres per arpent; AD Yonne, 3E 66-50, 1 December 1705.

89. According to figures for the end of the century, AN, G^2 31, the parishes of Chablis, Poinchy, and Chichée were producing an average of 3,140 muids. Milly was probably included in the parishes of Poinchy and Chablis and is today technically part of the town of Chablis. Fleys was not included in the survey.

90. One of these four was a Villetard; see the following chapter for more on him.

91. The prices of wines shipped from Chablis to Paris appear to be little differ-

ent from those for wine shipped from Coulanges; this suggests that Chablis could not yet lay claim to higher quality wine.

92. The date of the harvest in Coulanges, which could not have been much different from that of Chablis, was 2 October in 1724, according to George, *The Wines of Chablis and the Yonne,* p. 199.

93. Delamare, *Traité de la police,* 3:681; see chapter 5.

94. BN, FF 22214, Description du duché de Bourgogne, pp. 382–83.

95. AD Yonne, 38B 128, inventaire après décès of Jacques Rigolley, 28 November 1724; 3E 24-3, inventaire après décès of Claude Guine, 15 January 1722; 38B 128, inventaire après décès of Pierre Vinot, 6 May 1724; inventaire après décès of the wife of Edme Goulley, 17 March 1724; 38B 130, inventaire après décès of Anne Feuillebois, wife of Edme Vinot, 11 May 1726.

96. For more evidence of their importance to Parisian merchants, see the analysis of faillite records in chapter 6.

Chapter 5   *Power in the Vines*

1. Kaplan, *Bread, Politics and Political Economy,* offers the best overview of this crisis. See the various contributions in Dilley, *Contesting Markets,* for a recent theoretical approach to models and discourses of markets.

2. Thus the many works on food riots; but see Lionel Rothkrug, *Opposition to Louis XIV: the Political and Social Origins of the French Enlightenment* (Princeton, 1965); Meysonnier, *La balance et l'horloge.*

3. See Bouton, *Flour War,* pp. 1–36, for a recent summary of the literature on moral economy. For sans-culotte as consumer, see Albert Soboul, *The Sans-Culottes: The Popular Movement and Revolutionary Government, 1793–94,* trans. Rémy Inglis Hall (Princeton, 1972), pp. 42–44.

4. Even some of the best work on guilds, like James Farr, *Hands of Honor: Artisans and Their World in Dijon, 1550–1650* (Ithaca, 1988), and Ménétra, *Journal de ma vie: Jacques-Louis Ménétra, compagnon vitrier,* ed. Daniel Roche (Paris, 1982), have little to say about attitudes toward the market economy, but Liu, *The Weaver's Knot,* is especially good.

5. An obvious and honorable exception is Jean-Pierre Hirsch, *Les deux rêves du commerce, entreprise et institution dans la région lilloise* (Paris, 1991).

6. Robert B. Ekelund Jr. and Robert D. Tollison, *Mercantilism as a Rent-Seeking Society: Economic Regulation in Historical Perspective* (College Station, Tex., 1981) are particularly extreme. Kaplan, *Bread, Politics and Political Economy,* is still the best analysis of the government's position.

7. Eli Heckscher, *Mercantilism,* trans. Mendel Shapiro, 2 vols. (London, 1935), pp. 129–30, identifies the "general social ethic of the middle ages, formed . . . on an Aristotelian foundation." Max Beer, *An Inquiry into Physiocracy* (London, 1939), pp. 56–67, discusses the Thomistic condemnation of "trafficking" (*negotiatio*). Raymond de Roover, "Scholastic Economics: Survival and Lasting Influence from the Sixteenth Century to Adam Smith," *Quarterly Journal of Economics* 69 (1955): 166–80, contrasts scholastic economics, which "considered equity in distribution and exchange as the central problem," and mercantilist policies, which "all too often . . . serve as a screen for private interests."

8. See Kaplan, *Bread, Politics and Political Economy,* pp. 3–8, for a formulation of the "policy of provisioning as a means of social control."

9. Thompson, "The Moral Economy of the English Crowd," pp. 83–97.

10. Tilly, "The Food Riot," p. 26. Dewald, *Pont-Saint-Pierre,* pp. 238–50, shows how "the seigneurial officials' anxieties about public order" led them to regulate both the grain trade and the cotton business.

11. Dilley, ed., *Contesting Markets,* p. 4.

12. See the discussions by de Roover, in "The Concept of the Just Price," pp. 418–34, and "Scholastic Economics."

13. According to de Roover, "Scholastic Economics," p. 179, "Scholastic writers regarded trade as an occupation which, although not evil in itself, endangered the salvation of the soul, as the merchants almost unavoidably succumbed to the temptations of usury, cheating, and unlawful gain." Baldwin, *Medieval Theories of the Just Price,* pp. 62–67, agrees that the "profession of trade remained characteristically a sordid business." Kaplan, *Bread, Politics and Political Economy,* pp. 52–56, discusses the persistence of this hostility in the old regime.

14. Everitt, "The Marketing of Agricultural Produce," p. 466, identifies the "more or less rigorous regulation and vigilant, ordered system summed up in the contemporary phrase 'the open market.'" See his discussion of this concept, pp. 563–88, especially p. 570, where he notes the belief that "every agricultural transaction both could and should be 'equitable.'"

15. Gérard Sautel, *Le bureau de police d'Aix-en-Provence* (Paris, 1946), pp. 84–98, discusses the range of market restrictions. See Delamare, *Traité de la police,* 2:621–22, for regulation of the grain trade and 3:680–90 for regulation of the wine trade.

16. Kaplan, *Provisioning Paris,* pp. 27–32. Everitt, "The Marketing of Agricultural Produce," pp. 568–88, is a classic treatment of the issue of the regulated, or "open," market, which is useful for the Continent as well. See also Westerfield, *Middlemen in English Business.*

17. According to Kaplan, *Bread, Politics and Political Economy,* p. 58, "The merchant was not condemned for his trading practices per se. . . . What made them illicit and dangerous was the effect they had on the price structure." According to Fox-Genovese, *The Origins of Physiocracy,* p. 25, "The authorities and the people concurred in damning free market capitalism in matters of grain supply." Tilly, "The Food Riot," pp. 27–35, also emphasizes "protecting the consumer" through price fixing. See also Olivier-Martin, *La police économique,* for a classic overview of commercial regulation that emphasizes the grain trade. I will use the terms "monopoly" and "monopolistic" to refer to behavior that is technically oligopolistic and oligopsonistic, for the simple reason that contemporary texts did.

18. Kaplan, *Provisioning Paris,* p. 27. "Consumers were the chief beneficiaries of the regulatory structure [because] . . . the regulations were social contrivances aimed at redressing a social imbalance [between supplier and consumer] which menaced the peace and well-being of the community"; Kaplan, *Bread, Politics, and Political Economy,* p. 66.

19. Charles Tilly, "Food Supply and Public Order in Modern Europe," in Tilly, ed., *The Formation of National States in Western Europe* (Princeton, 1975).

20. Rothkrug, *Opposition to Louis XIV,* p. 416, and passim.

21. Meyssonnier, *La balance et l'horloge,* pp. 149–51. Thomas J. Schaeper, *The*

French Council of Commerce, 1700–1715 (Columbus, Ohio, 1983), pp. 55–66, makes similar points for the beginning of the century as does Hirsch, "Les milieux du commerce," pp. 1337–70, for the end of the Old Regime.

22. Boisguilbert admonished merchants to seek a "just division of profits" in order to "share the utility" of market exchanges; Meysonnier, *La balance et l'horloge,* pp. 40, 224–25.

23. Montesquieu, *The Spirit of the Laws,* trans. Thomas Nugent (New York, 1949), p. 322.

24. Quesnay, "Dialogue on the Work of Artisans," in Meek, *Economics of Physiocracy,* p. 214, and discussion, p. 378, where Meek defends this unregulated "free competition" as a "description of an 'ideal' economy."

25. Letter to *Journal économique,* May 1754, quoted in Kaplan, *Bread, Politics and Political Economy,* p. 61, and attributed by him to the marquis d'Argenson. "Monopoly is exclusive selling or buying supported by the authorities"; Mirabeau, *La philosophie rurale,* quoted in Weulersse, *Le mouvement physiocratique,* 2:504.

26. Root, "Politiques frumentaires," p. 169. See also Stevenson, "The 'Moral Economy' of the English Crowd: Myth and Reality," for criticisms of the concept among English historians.

27. See Reddy, *The Rise of Market Culture,* pp. 31–40; Liu, *The Weaver's Knot,* pp. 60–74.

28. AD Yonne, 4B 160, monitoire, 18 October 1737, and a later version, dated 10 February 1738. A very brief introduction to this case has already appeared in Horace Marcoux, "Commissionnaires auxerrois en vins poursuivis en justice (1737)," *Bulletin de la société des sciences historiques et naturelles de l'Yonne* 104 (1971–72): 125–31. Marcoux appears unaware that the case went to Paris and eventually took on national proportions.

29. Billon, *Coutume du comté et bailliage d'Auxerre* (Auxerre, 1743), pp. 301–2. It is perhaps no coincidence that this coutume was republished in Auxerre shortly after this scandal.

30. In a factum published in his defense, BN, Coll. Joly, ms. 1336, fols. 193–94, Villetard criticized the monitoire for not having kept its accusations anonymous.

31. Villetard, Pierre Boyard (thrice), Pochet (twice), and Monnot; ibid., fol. 151, Noms des juges et consuls et agens (no date, but probably 1738). It should be noted that three of the six seats held by these men were as *agent* of the court, and therefore they do not appear in the list provided by Demay, "La juridiction consulaire d'Auxerre," pp. 180–89. Demay does show that Pierre Boyard had been either juge or consul three times between 1723 and 1728.

32. BN, Coll. Joly, ms. 1336, fol. 81, motifs de la déclaration proposée concernant les commissionnaires de vin, no date.

33. AD Yonne, C 1221, contrôle des actes of Chablis, 1706; 3E 24-1, 9 March 1716, inventory of Rathier; C 85, rolles des tailles, 1725–27. Edme is identified in notarial records around the time of the trial as an assessor of the town hall of Auxerre; AD Yonne, 3E 6-171, 23 January 1735.

34. AD Yonne, 3E 6-138, marriage of Germain Soufflot and Catherine Millon, 3 June 1713. Soufflot's only real claim to fame is probably as father of the architect of the église Sainte-Geneviève, now the Panthéon, in Paris. Another broker accused rather tangentially of fraud, Jean-Louis Trinquet, was still a broker in Coulanges.

35. The rumor is reported by the intendant of Burgundy, BN, Coll. Joly, ms. 1336, fol. 39. Boyard's son was also in the brokerage trade and under indictment. Another broker caught in the scandal, Jean Guenier, was still a broker in Saint-Bris. He had married Marie Guyon and so was quite possibly an in-law of Boyard.

36. AD Yonne, 3E 7-237, list of all the boatmen of Auxerre, assembled to divide up a tax among them, 16 March 1702. Monnot is identified as a nephew in 16 February 1737, BB 34.

37. AN, G⁷ 1509, Bordereau du rolle, premier rolle. It is reasonable, but not certain, that Roch Liger, le jeune was identified in the roll of fines as le nommé Liger fils, paying two thousand livres and was the nephew of Edme Liger, paying five thousand. Only three other families had paid the very big fines: two Robinets, who were still occasionally active as brokers, Etienne Navarre, whose son was still a prominent broker, and two Drinots, who had left the business. Some on the roll had obviously died before 1737, but none of the culprits even shared the last name with those on the list.

38. AD Yonne, 4B 157, depositions taken for Villetard, 16 December 1737.

39. BN, Coll. Joly, ms. 1336, fol. 193, printed memoir for Villetard, no date.

40. Most of the witnesses in AD Yonne, 4B 160 can also be found in BN, Coll. Joly, ms. 1336, fols. 83–121.

41. BN, Coll. Joly, ms. 1336, fol. 40, summary of remarks.

42. Billon, *Coutume du comté et bailliage d'Auxerre*, p. 302.

43. See Craig Muldrew, "Interpreting the Market: The Ethics of Credit and Community Relations in Early Modern England," *Social History* 18 (1993): 163–83, on the role of trust in the early modern market.

44. Testimony of Marguerite du Toureau, widow of Pierre Thienot, bourgeois of Auxerre; Marie Merat, widow of Jean Dujon laboureur of Jussy; Etienne Naudier, laboureur of Jussy; AD Yonne, 4B 160.

45. BN, Coll. Joly, ms. 1336, fol. 109; see fols. 110–11 for other witnesses from Vaux with the same information. Eon, *Le commerce honorable*, p. 89, complained, in the 1640s, that the Dutch had introduced the system of buying wine from the grower without agreeing to any price other than "the common price." As a consequence, "Our good people [the French] . . . do not perceive that this is to sell at the price that pleases the foreigners, who are thus masters and absolute arbiters of the value of their wines."

46. BN, Coll. Joly, ms. 1336, fol. 113.

47. Brac, *Le commerce des vins*, p. 32.

48. BN, Coll. Joly, ms. 1336, fols. 114–15. This curé did not receive a dîme in wine, according to Courtépée, *Description générale et particulière du duché de Bourgogne*, 4:382, and was sufficiently involved in local winemaking that he kept a record in the parish register of the weather and its effects on the vines. Almost exactly three months after he gave his testimony, for example, he noted that "the vines froze on 2 May [1738] so that in the surrounding countryside one makes so little wine as to be none at all"; Pierre Bourgoin, *Un village de vignerons auxerrois: Augy au moyen âge et sous l'ancien régime* (Clamecy, 1982), p. 110.

49. AD Yonne, 8B 7, 15 January 1740, complaint of Toussaint Robinet de Pontagny.

50. Bourgoin, *Un village de vignerons auxerrois*, p. 110, quotes the parish regis-

ters to the effect that frosts caused widespread damage both on 2 May 1738 and 7 October 1740.

51. *Coutume du comté et bailliage d'Auxerre*, p. 291, Article 141, said that the seller could be expected to hold the wine no more than twenty days after the sale. See Pijassou, *Un grand vignoble de qualité*, 1:344–60, for a discussion of what maintaining wine entailed.

52. AD Yonne, 4B 160, letter from procureur du roi to the Prévôt d'Auxerre, 2 December 1737.

53. BN, Coll. Joly, ms. 1336, fols. 149–51; the district attorney even appended a list of the men sitting on the merchants' court to show that, indeed, seven of the previous ten years had seen at least one broker among the four judges, though not all from this group of accused.

54. AD Yonne, 4B 160, testimony of Millot, docteur en médecine d'Auxerre, 12 December 1737.

55. BN, Coll. Joly, ms. 1336, fol. 208, letter of Regnauldin to Joly de Fleury, 11 July 1739.

56. Ibid., fol. 118; 101–2.

57. *Encyclopédie méthodique: jurisprudence*, 10 vols. (Paris, 1782–91), 3:397, s.v. courtier.

58. Royal ordinance, 30 January 1350, in Delamare, *Traité de la police*, 2:595–96; arrêt de conseil d'état, 10 October 1721, in BN, Coll. Joly, ms. 1336, fols. 162–68. According to Lefebvre de la Bellande, *Traité général des droits d'aides*, p. 332, "These dispositions are meant to identify and follow the purchases made by brokers, and to restrain the different kinds of fraud they can practice on the wine that they buy for their account."

59. For something of the role and audience of factums, see Sara Maza, *Private Lives and Public Affairs: The Causes Célèbres of Prerevolutionary France* (Berkeley, 1993), pp. 2–37.

60. AD Yonne, 8B 6, 12 January 1730, Boyard vs. Germain Navarre.

61. Technically, Villetard's defense is in AD Yonne, 4B 160, 20 February 1739, but his description of the evolution of the wine trade, and quotes from it in the following paragraph, come from a (printed) Mémoire pour Villetard, BN, Coll. Joly, ms. 1336, fol. 193–200.

62. The records of Parisian merchants' business failures give ample testimony to the truth of this statement. See any of scores of dossiers in the AD Paris-Seine, D4B6 series, but especially D4B6 2-117, 15-715, 22-1087, and 22-1096 for a total of more than twenty-four thousand livres owed to Boyard alone.

63. BN, Coll. Joly, ms. 1336, fols. 195, 205, factums of Villetard and Soufflot.

64. Ibid., fol. 189, letter to "nos seigneurs de Parlement en la chambre de la Tournelle criminelle" from Paradis, Monnot, and Pierre Boyard.

65. Ibid., fol. 203, (printed) factum pour Germain Soufflot (no date, but it appeals the sentence against him of 17 March 1739).

66. Savary, *Le parfait négociant*, 2:151.

67. According to Léon and Carrière, "L'appel des marchés," p. 214, "The two ways of treating merchandise were inextricably mixed."

68. See Westerfield, *Middleman*, pp. 354–62, for an excellent explanation of the typical commercial categories.

69. According to the survey of contemporary jurisprudence in Sautel, *Histoire du contrat de commission,* pp. 31–41, the merchant was solely responsible when the broker acted "in the name of" the merchant, although if the broker acted "in his own name" authors were divided about who should be held responsible. Sautel, p. 34, cites an arrêt de Parlement of 21 July 1742, between some Parisian wine merchants, a broker, and a wine seller from Mâcon, which held the broker alone responsible for the purchase (Jean-Baptiste Denisart, *Collection de décisions nouvelles et de notions relatives à la jurisprudence actuelle,* 4 vols. 7th ed. [Paris, 1771], 1:553) to argue that brokers in general were normally held responsible, but fails to recognize that the legal responsibilities of wine brokers were not typical of brokerage in general.

70. BN, Coll. Joly, ms. 1336, fol. 138, letter from the lieutenant criminel of Auxerre to Joly de Fleury, 1 March 1738.

71. For the "projet de déclaration," see ibid., fols. 52–55. Correspondence between Joly de Fleury and Orry indicates that the projected declaration was drawn up in March 1738.

72. Of course, Orry is famous for ordering national investigations into a variety of administrative, commercial, and industrial matters. Unlike Joly de Fleury's investigation, however, Orry's *enquêtes* were handled by intendants and subintendants. See Michel Antoine, *Louis XV* (Paris, 1989), pp. 319–24.

73. Steven L. Kaplan, *The Famine Plot Persuasion in Eighteenth-Century France* (Philadelphia, 1982), pp. 27–46.

74. AM Beaune, carton 94, no. 53, mémoire pour les habitans de Beaune au sujet des commissionnaires de vin, 1735.

75. AM Beaune, carton 4, no. 5, factum of the mayor, échevins, and inhabitants of Beaune against Philibert Bouzereau, notary, procureur, and merchant commissionnaire, 22 April 1732. Arnoux, *Dissertation sur la situation de Bourgogne,* pp. 32–33, had only recently assured English consumers that "if [the brokers of Beaune] charged more for the wine from the person to whom they are sending it than they had to pay for it in the cellars, they risk being hung, without remission, by order of the Parlement of Bourgogne, which made a law to ensure the fidelity of the wine trade." Arnoux exaggerated but was clearly addressing an important concern among consumers.

76. AM Beaune, carton 94, no. 52, mémoire des maires et échevins de Beaune, 10 November 1732, "What happened to the Carthusian monks of this town at the last harvest is proof of the mistrust we ought to have for the brokers' maneuvers; three of the brokers bought wine from five or six bourgeois at the [benchmark] price that the reverend fathers of the monastery would sell theirs, but the three brokers agreed among themselves at the same time not to buy the wine of the monks although they were accustomed to taking it formerly, and the monks were obliged to abandon the best part of their wines at ten pistoles per queue less than the price that these same brokers got for the wines they produce."

77. Ibid.

78. AM Beaune, carton 94, no. 53, mémoire pour les habitans de Beaune au sujet des commissionnaires de vin, 1735.

79. Regrettably, the polling did not include cities outside of the jurisdiction of the Parlement of Paris, and even then managed inexplicably to miss Reims.

80. BN, Coll. Joly, ms. 1336, fols. 65–70.

81. The correspondent in Anger explained that he had given copies of the indictment to "the largest guilds" and to the merchants' judge, ibid., fol. 63. Roche, *Le commerce des vins de Champagne*, pp. 109–13, found a copy of the memoir in the papers of Bertin de Rocheret, a président de l'élection and former wine broker of Epernay, and attributes it mistakenly to Bertin.

82. BN, Coll. Joly, ms. 1336, fols. 33–39.

83. Ibid., fol. 239, Beaugency; fols. 76–80, Anger; fols. 291–92, Saumur; fol. 277, Mâcon.

84. Ibid., fols. 251–52, memoir of Blois.

85. Ibid., fol. 255, Chartres; fol. 232, Baugé; fol. 280, Mantes.

86. The report from Château-Thierry, ibid., fol. 263, adds, "All these brokers are usually no better off than the bourgeois and vigneron who are very unhappy in this region; the broker only earns three or four hundred livres a year from his commissions." Such brokers were essentially still courtiers.

87. AM Blois, BB 28, fols. 1–2, 31 August and 1 December 1733.

88. AN, F^{12} 80, pp. 811–14, 15 October 1733.

89. The memoir from Blois, BN, Coll. Joly, ms. 1336, fol. 253, commented that the brokers' opposition was "founded on the liberty that each should have to deliver and dispose of his merchandise as he wishes, nevertheless . . . public interest would seem to prevail over this liberty." As late as 1777, according to a commentary by Fourré in the *Coutumes générales du pays et comté de Blois* (Blois, 1777), p. 673, "An ordinance of the [presidial] court declared all sales of wine without prices to be null; but, on the appeal that the brokers made to the council, the execution [of the ordinance] has been provisionally blocked, and the appeal remains undecided."

90. AD Côte d'Or, G 4167. See also Pierre de Saint-Jacob, "La vente du bon vin de Volnay au XVIIIe siècle," *Annales de Bourgogne* 19 (1947): 44–51.

91. BN, Coll. Joly, ms. 1336, fols. 241–43, two letters to Joly de Fleury signed by a dozen master coopers of Baugency (sic), 4 November and 17 December 1739. The procureur of Beaugency condemned brokers for much the same reasons; fols. 239–40.

92. AN, F^{12} 662-70, 1 February 1723, cited in Braudel, *The Wheels of Commerce*, p. 414.

93. BN, Coll. Joly, ms. 1336, fol. 78, mémoire of Angers.

94. AD Loir-et-Cher, E 749, mémoire pour la communauté des maîtres tonneliers de Blois, no date.

95. The brokers appear in the rolls of those to be fined for their unofficial brokering, most of them paying three thousand livres; AN G^7 1507, Bordereau du rolle, 2e rolle, 10 February 1705.

96. BN, Coll. Joly, ms. 1336, fols. 315–16, memoir from Vendôme (annotations on the memoir sent by Joly de Fleury); fols. 277–78, memoir from Mâcon. The response from Angers, fols. 76–78, denied that brokers had to make the "kinds of advances that they would have us believe" but argued that a broker of Angers, who had to buy "150 bariques of anjou wine with the most *liqueur* and sweetness" for a Dutch merchant, was performing a harder job, and deserved a larger reward, than the broker of Orléans who simply assembled a thousand barrels of local wine.

97. Ibid., fol. 271, memoir from Epernay; fol. 251, memoir from Blois; fol. 290, memoir from Orléans.

98. Ibid., fols. 289–92, memoir from Orléans.

99. Ibid., fols. 318–20, memoir from Villefranche.

100. Ibid., fols. 63–64, letter to Joly de Fleury from Angers; fols. 76–77, memoir from Anger; fol. 270, memoir of Epernay.

101. Ibid., fols. 63–64, letter to Joly de Fleury from Angers; fol. 270, memoir of Epernay; fol. 299, memoir from Tours.

102. Géraud-Parracha, *Le commerce des vins,* pp. 170–73.

103. Lefebvre de la Bellande, *Traité général des droits d'aides,* 1:332, arrêt de la Cour des Aides de Paris, 8 May 1739; Denisart, *Collection de décisions nouvelles,* 1:553, arrêt rendu 4 September 1747 sur les conclusions de M. le procureur général.

104. Lefebvre de la Bellande, *Traité général des droits d'aides,* 1:332, arrêts of 22 August 1742, 17 July, and 19 September 1744, 30 August 1746, 14 March 1749.

105. Emile Magnien, *Histoire de Mâcon et du Mâconnais* (Mâcon, 1971), p. 177.

106. AD Loir-et-Cher, E 749, [printed] mémoire pour la communauté des maîtres tonneliers de Blois, 1752; extrait du livre des résultats et délibérations de l'hôtel de ville de Blois, 3 September 1753.

107. Ibid.

108. Ibid.

109. Ibid., p. 11.

110. AD Loir-et-Cher, F 3, 1749. The partnership came to a premature end in 1749 when the son and his wife, Anne Guerin (daughter of another négociant broker), both died. Both families were well represented among the brokers of Blois at the beginning of the century. Coullange's grandfather, also a broker, left an inheritance of seventy-eight thousand livres, according to Persan, "Les voituriers par eau," p. 295. The widow was fined three thousand livres in 1705, as were three of the Guerin family.

111. Ibid. A stray accounting from 1724, in with the rest of the papers from 1747 and 1749, relates the purchase of 295 barrels of wine for Violet, a Parisian wine merchant, based on "commissions that he has made to us." He shipped a small quantity of this wine to Frankfurt on Violet's orders. The partnership's assets also included a shop and twelve thousand livres, which the father had given the son as his wedding portion. Guerin had given the couple vineyards and three thousand livres.

112. Ibid.

113. AN, G² 28, report of the régie on Blois, October 1777.

114. AD Loir-et-Cher, E 749, suits of 18 January 1782, 12 April 1783.

115. AP, Malavois de la Ganne, 1754. AD Côte d'Or, G 4167, recueil des jours de la vendange de Vollenay avec un mémoire de la production des vignes de la cuve dudit Vollenay et des frais de vendange, 1754.

116. Brac, *Le commerce des vins,* pp. 19, 27, 29, 133.

117. Ibid., p. 31

118. Ibid., p. 19.

119. AD Côte d'Or, G 4167, recueil, 1772.

120. AD Côte d'Or, G 4167.

121. Durand, *Vin, vigne,* pp. 93–101.

122. Cited in Roche, *Le commerce des vins de Champagne,* pp. 74–78.

123. See Kaplan, *Famine Plot Persuasion,* pp. 1–4, 62–72, for the complex interplay of perception and reality underlying the fear of famine plots.

Chapter 6 *Toward a Transparent Market*

1. Figures for Parisian wine consumption are difficult to find; an estimate in 1637 put it at 240,000 muids. The tax farm recorded an average 218,000 muids of wine paying entrance taxes between 1700 and 1708 (AN, G⁷ 1179) and an average 285,000 muids between 1720 and 1725 (AN, G⁷ 1182). To this should be added a further 5 percent that was tax free. These figures do not tell us about the growing amount of wine that was consumed outside the tax barriers in the guinguettes. Similar tax figures for 1744–57, in Lachiver, *Vin, vigne,* pp. 275–76, recorded 228,000 muids, of which 174,000 muids was wine brought to Paris by wine merchants, but in the late 1750s the wine merchants insisted that they delivered an annual 250,000 muids; AD Seine, D3 AZ 90, mémoire pour le corp et communauté des marchands de vin de la ville et faubourgs de Paris contre les administrateurs de l'hôpital général de Paris, p. 3; there is no date for this memoir, but it refers to an arrêt of 1756 as a recent event.

2. AD Seine, D3 AZ 90, mémoire pour le corp et communauté des marchands de vin, p. 3.

3. See Delamare, *Traité de la police,* 3:682–91, for these regulations.

4. BN, FF 21664, fol. 225, sentence of 26 January 1722.

5. AD Seine, D3 AZ 90, mémoire pour le corp et communauté des marchands de vin, pp. 6–7.

6. Ibid., pp. 6–11.

7. Ibid., p. 7.

8. The Halle received about 7 percent of the city's wine; see chapter 4.

9. BN, Coll. Joly, ms. 1335, letter to the controller general, no date but roughly October 1739.

10. His earliest letters, in AN, Y 15529, go back to 1773, but his accounts, especially AD Seine, D5B⁶ 1038, are from the 1780s. His office appears to be distinct from the official courtiers of Paris, who were responsible for assisting the sale of wine sold at the ports, according to Delamare, *Traité de la police,* 3:594–629, but I have no evidence for the origins of his office.

11. See B. C. Gournay, *Almanach général du commerce, des marchands négociants, armateurs de la France, de l'Europe et des autres parties du monde* (Paris, 1789–90), p. 532, for Ladureau Chevesier, Damoneville, Boulard, and Rathouis.

12. See, for example, AD Seine, D5B⁶ 4800, p. 3; D5B⁶ 4980, fol. 16.

13. AN, Y 15527, letter from Girault, 14 October 1780.

14. AN, Y 15529, 30 November 1773, 18 April, 20 June 1774, 18 January 1775.

15. AN, Y 15527, 1 and 12 September 1780.

16. AD Seine, D5B⁶ 6214, letter of 7 May 1782 to François Grammont, the ancien directeur de la megisserie royalle de la ville d'Orléans.

17. The best source for his accounts is AD Seine, D5B⁶ 1038.

18. AD Seine, D5B⁶ 6214, 8 and 23 August, 6 October, 26 September 1782.

19. Ibid., 12 and 8 August 1782. AN, Y 15529, 4 January 1781.

20. AD Seine, D5B⁶ 6214, 28 September 1780. This is a very large register, with copies of all the letters he sent from 1780–83.

21. AN, Y 15527, letter of Girault, 14 October 1780.

22. Ibid., letter from Bizoteau, 2 October 1780.

23. See, for example, ibid., lettres de voiture from December 1780 and the following January from Saint-Dyé.

24. AD Seine, D5B⁶ 6214, letter of 15 August 1782.

25. Ibid., letter of 8 August 1782.

26. Ibid., 12 and 16 May 1782, 26 July 1780, 23 and 28 August 1780.

27. Ibid., letter of 8 October 1780.

28. AN, Y 15529, letter from Rathouis fils of Orléans, 15 April 1778.

29. AD Seine, D5B⁶ 6214, 1 September 1780, 8 August 1782, 7 and 8 October 1782.

30. Ibid., letters of 6 October 1780, 2 October 1782, 2 May 1782, 2 August 1782.

31. Delamare, *Traité de la police*, 3:681.

32. AD Seine, D5B⁶ 6214, letter of 17 May 1782.

33. Ibid., letter of 5 May 1782.

34. This is the *Annonces, affiches et avis divers* published for the provinces, usually known as the *Affiches de province*. See Eugene Hatin, *Histoire politique et littéraire de la presse française,* 8 vols. (Paris, 1859–61), 2:58–60; Colin Jones, "The Great Chain of Buying: Medical Advertisement, the Bourgeois Public Sphere, and the Origins of the French Revolution," *American Historical Review* 101 (1996): 13–40, for discussions of the *Affiches*.

35. Although Habermas, *The Structural Transformation of the Public Sphere: An Inquiry into a Category of Bourgeois Society,* trans. Thomas Burger (Cambridge, Mass., 1989), pp. 23–24, makes the point that as the "private sphere of civil society" becomes "the subject of public interest" it becomes a public sphere in opposition to the public sphere of the state.

36. *Annonces, affiches, et avis divers,* 24 May 1752, 27 September 1752.

37. Ibid., 16 October 1752.

38. Ibid., 8 November 1752.

39. Gadille, *Le vignoble de la côte bourguignonne,* p. 377. See Gilles Feyel, "Négoce et presse provinciale en France au 18e siècle: méthodes et perspectives de recherches," in Franco Angiolini and Daniel Roche, eds., *Cultures et formations négociantes dans l'Europe moderne* (Paris, 1995); Hugh Gough, *The Newspaper Press in the French Revolution* (Chicago, 1988), pp. 5–11, for the pre-revolutionary provincial journals.

40. Feyel, "Négoce et presse provinciale," pp. 492–93, based on the issues from 1778.

41. *Journal du commerce et de l'agriculture* (August 1759): 146, 148.

42. Ibid., (August 1759): 146–48, 162–63; (December 1759): 168–69, 178–79.

43. *Almanach général des marchands, négociants, armateurs et fabricans de la France et de l'Europe* (Paris, 1778): s.v. Beaujeu, Beaune, Epernay, Reims.

44. Gournay, *Almanach général du commerce* (1789–90): s.v. Bourgogne, Champagne.

45. Ibid., 1788 and 1789–90. See René Durand, "Le commerce en Bourgogne à la veille de la Révolution française," *Annales de Bourgogne* 2 (1930): 221–34, 326–36, for a summary of this information.

46. Gournay, *Almanach général du commerce* (1789–90); for Vertus, *Almanach* (1779). The later edition skipped some of the smaller towns mentioned in the 1788 edition, according to Durand, "Le commerce en Bourgogne," p. 222, though few without brokers in Burgundy. Most of the small towns in Champagne are not listed, but Ay and Mareuil-sur-Ay have an entry and no mention of brokers.

47. Gournay, *Almanach général du commerce* (1789–90): s.v. Nuits[-Saint-Georges].

48. AN, Z[1h] 337; see Lachiver, "Les aires d'approvisionnement de Paris," pp. 277–87, for a discussion of this document; AD Seine, DC[2] 5–13.

49. Lachiver, "Les aires d'approvisionnement," pp. 280–87.

50. AD Seine, DC[2] 5–13. The port of Saint-Paul in 1702 received 39 percent of the wine listed in the register in AN Z[1h] 337. The origins of the wine at the port of Saint-Paul were closely similar to the rest of the wines in this document.

51. Labrousse, *Crise*, pp. 363–70.

52. Vivier, "Un problème d'histoire économique," pp. 23, 51–52 is quoting reports on the generality of Tours written in 1698 and in 1762, plus a report on Chinon written in 1756.

53. Léon Blin, "La route beaujolaise de Saône à Loire au XVIIIe siècle, ses affinités mâconnaises," *Mémoires de la société pour l'histoire du droit et des institutions des anciens pays bourguignons* 8 (1942): 84–126.

54. The principal boatmen from Cosne, Legrand and the associates Quillier and Frossard, are identified by Durand, *Vin, vigne*, p. 113, as "entrepreneurs" shipping the wines of Beaujolais to Paris.

55. AD Cher, 43H 178, records for July 1733 through June 1734.

56. Léon and Carrière, "L'appel des marchés," p. 183.

57. Brac, *Le commerce des vins*, p. 5, speaks of eighty thousand barrels as an upper limit.

58. Labrousse, *Crise*, p. 242, is quoting the opinions of the local intendants.

59. The Canal d'Orléans, opened only a decade before the first port survey of 1702, undoubtedly encouraged boatmen from the western end of the river to participate in the provisioning of Paris, just as the Canal du Loing, opened in 1723, encouraged producers from both ends of the river to send their wines.

60. Blin, "La route beaujolaise de Saône à Loire," pp. 88–90; Brac, *Le commerce des vins*, pp. 9–10.

61. See the *Tablettes royales de renomée ou de correspondance et d'indication générales des principales fabriques, manufactures, maisons de commerce* (Paris, n.d.), for a list of some of the magasins en gros de vins in Paris.

62. AD Seine D4B[6] 1-29, 12 September 1695; 1-35, 8 October 1695; 1-67, 29 April 1737; 1-82, 25 March 1739; 2-98, 12 March 1740; 2-101, 17 March 1740; 2-107, 28 April 1740; 2-117, 13 September 1740; 3-144, 8 July 1741; 3-147, 17 July 1741; 3-173, 18 January 1742; 5-222, 6 February 1743; 7-330, 30 August 1747; 7-354, 27 April 1748; 7-359, 18 May 1748; 8-389, 12 April 1749; 8-396, 4 June 1749; 8-399, 17 June 1749; D5B[6] 143 (1741–44); 695 (1713–14); 3680 (1716); 3804 (1744–45). The D4B[6] series consists of dossiers listing debts and assets; the D5B[6] series contains various kinds of account books.

63. AD Seine, D4B[6] 10-460, 29 April 1751; 10-488, 23 February 1752; 14-642, 13 September 1754; 14-662, 6 February 1755; 14-695, 24 July 1755; 15-715, 31 Decem-

ber 1755; 21-1020, 29 November 1759; 22-1087, 20 August 1760; 22-1092, 8 October 1760; 22-1096, 23 October 1760; 22-1102, November 1760; 22-1139, 26 April 1761; 23-1198, 18 May 1762; 24-1216, 7 August 1762; 24-1233, 11 October 1762; 24-1254, January 1763; 24-1257, February 1763; 26-1343, 12 March 1764; 26-1372, 26 May 1764; 26-1380, 3 July 1764; 26-1382, 7 July 1764; 26-1389, 8 August 1764; 26-1391, 17 August 1764; 29-1535, 17 May 1766; 29-1547, 2 July 1766; 29-1561, 21 August 1766; 29-1563, 26 August 1766; 29-1567, 10 September 1766; 29-1571, 23 September 1766; D5B⁶ 4828 (1753–60).

64. See, for example, AD Seine, D4B⁶ 26-1380, 3 July 1764, for the sale of debts.

65. AD Seine, D5B⁶ 2415 (1760–73).

66. AD Seine, D4B⁶, 8-396, 4 June 1749.

67. AD Seine, D4B⁶ 8-389, 12 April 1749.

68. Arrêt of 12 April 1747, *Ordonnances, statuts, et règlements des marchands de vin* (Paris, 1732), p. 173. The publication date of this collection appears to be inaccurate.

69. AD Seine, D4B⁶ 24-1254, January 1763.

70. AD Seine, D4B⁶ 14-695, 24 July 1755.

71. AD Seine, D4B⁶ 23-1169, 9 January 1762.

72. AD Seine, D4B⁶ 24-1254, January 1763.

73. AD Seine, D4B⁶ 94-6504, August 1785.

74. AD Seine, D4B⁶ 39-2116, 31 August 1770; 39-2137, 30 September 1770; 39-2144, 10 October 1770; 39-2148, 12 October 1770; 39-2149, 12 October 1770; 39-2160, 31 October 1770; 43-2417, 30 December 1771; 43-2429, 15 January 1772; 43-2448, 4 February 1772; 47-2769, 11 February 1773; 47-2786, 27 February 1773; 47-2787, 2 March 1773; 47-2828, 6 May 1773; 47-2839, 21 May 1773; 52-3198, 1 July 1774; 52-3227, July 1774; 52-3234, 16 August 1774; 53-3278, 14 October 1774; 53-3298, 7 November 1774; 53-3314, 6 December 1774; 53-3320, 14 December 1774; 53-3323, 23 December 1774; 63-4066, 11 June 1777; 75-4935, November 1779; 75-4953, December 1779; 75-4976, January 1780; 75-4978, January 1780; 75-4987, January 1780; 76-5035, February 1780; 76-5039, February 1780; 76-5082, March 1780; 88-5998, September 1783; 88-6003, 7 October 1783; 88-6015, October 1783; 88-6029, November 1783; 89-6092, January 1784; 93-6420, 18 March 1785; 94-6504, August 1785; 94-6519, 9 September 1785; 99-6915, April 1787; 99-6961, 23 August 1787; 104-7345, December 1788; D5B⁶ 1762 (1773–75); D5B⁶ 3232 (1780–88); D5B⁶ 2479.

75. AD Seine, D4B⁶ 88-6029, November 1783; 89-6092, January 1784.

76. AD Seine, D4B⁶ 89-6105, 10 February 1784. The debts included 112,000 livres for wine from the upper and lower Loire; 119,000 livres from upper Burgundy and the south; and 20,000 livres for wine from lower Burgundy, Sancerre, and Bordeaux. He gave the value of his office of privileged wine merchant as 33,000 livres. Because of its size, this balance sheet was not included in table 6.2. His fortunes revived, and in 1788 he was listed in the port entries of Saint-Paul, AD Seine, DC², as having received several thousand barrels of wine, mostly from the south through Roanne and Cosne, but he does not show up as having a magasin en gros de vins in the *Tablettes royales de renommée* of that year.

Chapter 7 *From Brokers to Négociants*

1. Lachiver, *Vins, vignes,* pp. 254–305; Enjalbert, "Comment naissent les grands crus," pp. 457–65. Unwin, *Wine and the Vine,* p. 255, and more generally pp. 233–69, associates this new production with the growth of "an acquisitive capitalist awareness."

2. Richard, "Production et commerce du vin en Bourgogne," p. 33, particularly emphasizes the distinction of inventories.

3. Brac, *Le commerce des vins,* p. 11.

4. *Almanach général du commerce* (1788, 1789–91). See also Durand, "Le commerce en Bourgogne," pp. 221–34, 326–36. The *Almanach général des marchands, négociants, armateurs et fabricans* (Paris, 1774), identified ten wine négociants in Chalon, but the almanacs at the end of the 1780s listed only one.

5. Blin, "La route beaujolaise de Saône à Loire," pp. 88–90; Brac, *Le commerce des vins,* pp. 9–10. Nevertheless, a late-seventeenth-century description of the region, discussed in L. Champier, "La situation des vignobles mâconnais et chalonnais à la fin du XVIIe siècle," *Société des amis des arts et des sciences de Tournus* 51 (1951): 3–6, portrayed the Mâconnais as much less dominated by vineyards than the Chalonnais to its north.

6. In the 1760s, overland carting from Beaujeu to the port of Pouilly cost 4 livres per barrel, plus another 9.5 livres for the boat trip to Paris; Durand, *Vin, vigne,* p. 111. According to Abel Poitrineau, "L'économie du transport fluvial: une esquisse," *Revue historique* 285 (1991): 113, the cost of the boat trip had been roughly 6.3 livres in 1664 and 9.2 livres in 1737. The cost of carting a barrel from Beaune to Paris was 25 to 30 livres, roughly half what it had been at the end of the seventeenth century; Saint-Jacob, *Les paysans de la Bourgogne,* p. 304. The trip from the Beaujolais also added 57 livres in a variety of taxes, detailed in Léon Lex, "La culture de la vigne et le commerce des vins à Mâcon à la fin du XVIII siècle," *Annales de l'académie de Mâcon* (1903): 228–29, many of which would be inflicted on wine from Beaune. See also Laurence Evans, "Gulliver Bound: Civil Logistics and the Destiny of France," *Historical Reflections/ Réflexions historiques* 10 (1983): 19–44.

7. Blin, "La route beaujolaise de Saône à Loire," p. 89.

8. Quoted in Dion, *Histoire de la vigne,* p. 586.

9. AN, G^7 360, letter of 25 November 1705.

10. Maurice Charnay, *Claude Brosse et le commerce du vin mâconnais* (Clamacy, 1984), pp. 7–19.

11. Robert Bouiller, *La vigne et les hommes en côte Roannaise* (n.p., 1984), p. 117, is quoting from the parish registers of the curé of Renaison.

12. Lex, "La culture de la vigne," p. 226; Blin, "La route beaujolaise de Saône à Loire," p. 110, quotes a mémoire by the same official stating that "two thousand barrels of mâconnais wine are embarked at the port of Digoin . . . more than four thousand barrels at the port of Pouilly, without including those at the ports of Igrande and de la Roche." The *Journal du commerce et de l'agriculture* (December 1759): 163–64, declared that "the wines of Châlons [sic] and the Mâconnais are much inferior to the other wines of upper Burgundy. They send little wine abroad." The journal did not even mention the wines of the Beaujolais.

13. Durand, *Vin, vigne,* pp. 211–24; Dion, *Histoire de la vigne,* pp. 578–80. See

Gruter, *La naissance d'un grand vignoble,* pp. 66–72, for examples of this spread of vines.

14. Dion, *Histoire de la vigne,* pp. 585–86.

15. *Annonces, affiches, et avis divers* (16 October, 8 November 1752); *Journal du commerce et de l'agriculture* (August, December 1759).

16. Brac, *Le commerce des vins,* p. 5; Blin, "La route beaujolaise de Saône à Loire," pp. 99–100, quotes a mémoire au conseil of 1763; Guy Arbellot, "La grande mutation des routes de France au milieu du XVIIIe siècle," *Annales ESC* 28 (1973): 767–91.

17. Brac, *Le commerce des vins,* pp. 20–21.

18. BN, Coll. Joly, ms. 1336, fol. 282, report of the district attorney of Mâcon, 7 March 1740.

19. AD Saône-et-Loire, CC 33, roll of 1751. The six brokers, assessed a total of 840 livres, paid over a fifth of the town's vingtième d'industrie.

20. BN, Coll. Joly, ms. 1336, fol. 278, report of the procureur du roi, 7 March 1740.

21. This is reported by Charnay, *Brosse,* pp. 152–53, without identifying its source.

22. AD Saône-et-Loire, C 490, fol. 100, 27 January 1763.

23. Brac, *Le commerce des vins,* p. 20.

24. Durand, *Vin, vigne,* pp. 93–101; the *Tablettes royales de renommée* (1788), s.v. Beaujeu, identified Teillard as one of three négociants-commissionnaires in the town.

25. Brac, *Le commerce des vins,* p. 17, notes that brokers often made sellers pay the shipment of their wine to the "first depot," thus diminishing the real return on the wine.

26. AD Seine, D5B⁶, 2956, 5675; in one he describes himself as marchand forain of "Vaurenard" en Beaujolais, but in the other he gives a residence in Paris.

27. AD Seine, D5B⁶, 4923, achapts des vins par Pierre Sallé and Benoit Terrel, 1770–73. Prices had risen substantially since Desroches's purchases in the 1760s, from 20–25 livres a barrel to between 60 and 70 livres.

28. AD Saône-et-Loire, C 764, Sallé fined 120 livres for declaring nineteen barrels of beaujolais en route to Paris as mâconnais, 1773.

29. Bouiller, *La vigne,* pp. 116–17.

30. AD Saône et Loire, C 536, no. 39, projet . . . d'un citoyen négociant sur different objets concernant le commerce essentiel du Mâconnais. The pamphlet bears no name and no date but refers to Mirabeau's *L'ami des hommes* (1756) and appears to be from near the end of the Old Regime.

31. The Parisian *courtiers* were licensed officials working at the ports of the city to aid Parisian buyers to find sellers, much as the provincial brokers did; Delamare, *Traité de la police,* 3:594–629. Unlike provincial brokers, however, Parisian *courtiers* remained subordinate to Parisian wine merchants.

32. AD Saône et Loire, C 536, no. 39, projet . . . d'un citoyen négociant.

33. Brac, *Le commerce des vins,* pp. 36–38.

34. Arrêt de la cour du Parlement, 1 August 1774, in BN, Recueil Z le senne 207 (5). It includes extracts from a general assembly of the wine merchants' guild of 30 April 1774.

35. AN, Y 15530, unsigned, undated letter, found in a collection of Moreau's papers dating from the 1770s.

36. Brac, *Le commerce des vins,* pp. 44–85. The *Journal économique* (October 1769): 443–50, ran a very favorable and very detailed review of Brac's book, commenting that the book "is only a project, but it would be good to put it into effect in all the cantons of the kingdom that grow wine."

37. Jean Fayard, "Les vins du Beaujolais au XVIIIe siècle," *Revue d'histoire de Lyon* 1 (1902): 281–89.

38. The request is printed in Jean Richard, "L'académie de Dijon et le commerce du vin au XVIIIe siècle: à propos d'un mémoire présenté aux Etats de Bourgogne," pp. 227–31.

39. Dion, *Histoire de la vigne,* pp. 548–54.

40. There was no formal inventory for Pierre, but the procès verbal, AD Yonne, 4B 90, 15 November 1740, gives a quick indication of the state of his business. There is some confusion about Louis Boyard's name: It is found equally in notarial records as Pierre-Louis and Louis-Pierre. Etienne Meunier, "La famille Boyard, voituriers par eau à Auxerre," *Cahiers généalogique de l'Yonne* 2 (1984): 2–7, confuses the issue enormously by identifying him as two different people. For convenience I shall refer to him as Louis.

41. AD Yonne, G 1629, monitoire of 4 April 1769; Barrey, "La poésies humoristique de Basse Bourgogne," *Bulletin de la société des sciences historiques et naturelles de l'Yonne* 92 (1938): 214–26.

42. AD Yonne, 3E 7-225, purchase of several fiefs for the sum of 16,600 livres, 20 March 1746; in 1750 (3E 7-259) he is paying someone three hundred livres to dig a canal to bring water to his chateau; cited in Forestier, *Extraits analytiques.* See Roland Mousnier, *The Institutions of France under the Absolute Monarchy 1598–1789,* trans. Brian Pearce (Chicago, 1979), pp. 437–39, for a discussion of this office. Unlike the Deponts, studied by Robert Forster, *Merchants, Landlords, Magistrates* (Baltimore, 1980), pp. 14–24, Villetard seems to have moved quite consciously away from commerce toward nobility.

43. AD Yonne, 3E 7-282, division of inheritance, 8 October 1773.

44. They became a canon of the cathedral of Auxerre, a captain in the regiment of Guyenne, and a conseiller honoraire au bailliage et présidial sur les fait des Aides.

45. AD Yonne, 3E 7-265, 26 May 1756. A marriage portion of over thirty thousand livres for the groom alone puts this dowry three and four times above those of the fermiers studied by Moriceau in *Les fermiers de l'Île-de-France,* pp. 614–22, and in the range of Parisian nobility studied by Daumard and Furet, *Structures et relations sociales.*

46. AD Yonne, 3E 7-266, inventaire après décès of Edme Boyard, sieur de Gastines, 11 November 1757.

47. AD Yonne, 8B 9, 20 July 1767. Villeneuve Delisle identified himself in the suit as a sergeant and guard of the eaux et fôret of Auxerre and commissionnaire de vin.

48. AD Seine, D4B⁶ 7-354, Pierre Pochet aisné, 27 April 1748.

49. AD Yonne, 3B 17, 23 March 1767.

50. Except for several years in the 1720s, the elder Villetard appeared in the taille records as an assesseur and he always identified himself in notarial archives as

seigneur rather than broker; AD Yonne, C85, taille rolls of 1725, 1726, 1727, 1730, 1732–36.

51. BM Auxerre, Coll. E. Lorin, v. 12, fols. 77–80, extrait du conseil d'état, refers to a sentence du bailliage d'Auxerre, 24 April 1765, a certificate of the secrétaire des états de Bourgogne, of 7 March 1765, and an arrêt du cour des aides de Paris of 3 September 1766.

52. Courtepée, *Déscription générale et particulière du duché de Bourgogne,* 4:409. G. Finatier, "Comment en 1774 Pelerin Truchon vigneron à Vincelles osa lever l'etendard de la révolte," *Echo d'Auxerre* 45 (1963): 37–39. Villetard had inherited the fight with Truchon from the previous seigneur, but he was still fighting with local vignerons over the banalités in 3 November 1787; AD Yonne, 3E 11-47.

53. The Boyards were the largest owners of the vines of Auxerre, sharing 31 arpents (15.5 hectares) among them; the Villetards, with 25 arpents, were close behind; Richard, "Le vignoble Auxerrois en 1787," p. 38.

54. AD Yonne, 3E 7-271, inventaire après décès of Françoise Campagnot, 15 January 1762.

55. Anne Perrette Moreau was the daughter of Etienne, identified as a broker in the 1750s (AD Yonne, C 86, rolle de tailles) and the sister of Louis Etienne, who with Louis Boyard, as "merchant wine brokers associated," would be owed over eleven thousand livres for wines delivered to a Parisian wine merchant in AD Seine, D4B⁶ 29-1547, 2 July 1766. Their partnership is simply identified as Boyard Moreau in commercial almanacs at the end of the Old Regime; *Tablette royale de renommée,* s.v. Auxerre.

56. *Journal du commerce et de l'agriculture* (August 1759): 163; (December 1759): 178.

57. AD Yonne, 3E 7-271, inventaire après décès of Françoise Compagnot, 15 January 1762; 3E 3-82, inventaire après décès of Boyard Saint-Martin, 23 August 1782. The will was dated 12 July 1771.

58. AD Yonne, 3E 3-88, sequestre de bien de Boyard, 3 June 1788, which includes the depouillement of the inventaire après décès of Boyard de Saint-Martin of 23 August 1782. He appears to have been the grandson of Pierre Boyard's cousin, François Boyard, who began his career as a marchand voiturier par eau and ended it as a broker, after marrying into the brokering family of the Navarres. See chapter 6 for a discussion of Moreau.

59. Ibid., and inventaire après décès of Boyard de Saint-Martin of 23 August 1782; see chapter 4.

60. *Almanach général du commerce* (1788, 1789–91).

61. AD Yonne, 3E 11-129, inventaire après décès of Jean Louis Trinquet, 9 January 1753. His assets included 15 arpents of vines and 2 arpents of terre, worth 10,000 livres plus a house in Coulanges worth 7,000 livres plus 120 barrels of wine in his cellars.

62. AD Yonne, 3E 3-66, inventory after death of Jean-Baptiste Guenier, 10 March 1766. The two brokers are his son and his son-in-law, Guillaume Regnauldin, grandson of the procureur fiscal of Saint-Bris.

63. AD Seine, D5B⁶ 1198, account book of Jules Guenier, starting September 1785.

64. AD Seine, D5B⁶ 2024, Ruffier négociant of Avallon, 1782.

65. AD Seine, D4B⁶ 99-6975, 25 September 1787. He is still listed as one of the three brokers of Saint-Bris in the 1789 issue of the *Almanach général du commerce*.

66. AN, G2 31, report of the régie, 1787.

67. *Almanach général du commerce* (1789–90). It is curious that Guenier and the rest in Saint-Bris are identified as négociants commissionnaires, whereas those in Auxerre are just commissionnaires; BN, Coll. Joly, ms. 1391, fols. 357–58. Although this letter to Joly de Fleury is undated, it is in a collection of materials relating to a debate about barrels in the early 1780s.

68. Pezerolle de Monjeu, *Conseils que donne un vieux vigneron aux habitants de Pommard et de Volnay,* cited in Gadille, *Le vignoble de la côte bourguignonne,* p. 187.

69. Tainturier, *Remarques sur la culture des vignes de Beaune,* p. 218.

70. A. Dubois, *Les foires de Chalon et le commerce dans la vallée de la Saône à la fin du moyen âge* (Paris, 1976), pp. 441–50.

71. Cited in J. Fromageot, "Le commerce des vins de Haute et Basse Bourgogne vers la région parisienne avant 1850," *Bulletin annuel de la société d'archéologie et d'histoire du Tonnerrois* 12 (1959): 31, but this is part of a report justifying the opening of the Armançon River and should be taken with a grain of salt.

72. Gadille, *Le vignoble de la côte bourguignonne,* pp. 369–70, notes the preponderance of the trade toward the northeast and quotes a report from 1666, that only "sometimes they [growers of the Côte de Nuits] sell wine to Parisians."

73. AN, G⁷ 169, Mémoire of the maire, échevins, syndics et habitants de Beaune, 1 May 1720.

74. AD Saône-et-Loire, 11B 228, balance sheet of Bernard Joly, 1735.

75. AD Saône-et-Loire, 11B 227, balance sheet of Desbordes and Lebeault, 1738, whose loss of five horses in Flanders and Lorraine suggests where this wine might have been; 11B 228, Nostre, 1717.

76. AD Côte-d'Or, BII Suppl. 255, bilan of François Antoine, marchand à Nuits, 4 June 1725. He identified over ten thousand livres of assets, of which nearly half was wine, plus thirteen thousand livres of active debts. He continued to buy from Delachère until the late 1740s.

77. AD Seine, D5B⁶ 15, anonymous account book of 1723–24.

78. AD Côte-d'Or, G 4167, Receuil des jours de la vendange de Vollenay avec un mémorial de la production des vignes, 1761.

79. Emmanuelle de Blic, *La famille Marey-Monge* (Dijon, 1951), pp. 7–10. The son, Marey "the elder," is listed in the *Almanach général du commerce,* p. 525, as one of the négociants commissionnaires en vins of Nuits in 1789, as well as being a large proprietor of vineyards.

80. *Almanach général du commerce* (1788, 1789–91).

81. Archives privées Chauvinet, Grand livre of Poulet, for 1747 and 1748.

82. AD Côte-d'Or, BII Suppl. 261, bilan of André Porte, négociant à Beaune, 26 May 1756. Porte claimed over 68,000 livres in assets, including some 19,000 livres of wine, in addition to 29,443 livres of active debts.

83. AD Saône-et-Loire, 11B 228 Nostre, 1717; Joly, 1735.

84. See Gadille, *Le vignoble de la côte bourguignonne,* pp. 186–90, for a comparison of the vinification of the côtes de Beaune and Nuits.

85. AP Chauvinet, Grand livre of Poulet, for 1747 and 1748.

86. AD Saône-et-Loire, 11B 244, bilan of Rigobert Rozé, merchant of Chalon,

in 1716. The claim by Arnoux, *Dissertation sur la situation de bourgogne,* p. 14, that "the wines of Dijon and Chalon do not leave the regions where they are produced to be transported to Great Britain, the Empire, or the Low Countries, as are those grown between" Chambertin and Chagny, was only partly correct.

87. The fragmentary records of Jean Millard, wine broker of Chalon in 1746, AD Saône-et-Loire, 11B 242, suggest he was sending, and losing money on, wine to Paris, Strasbourg, and Liège, without giving the relative importance of the losses.

88. AD Saône-et-Loire, 11B 206, report of experts at the dissolution of a partnership between Poucet Voyer, Nicolas Flochon, and J. B. Guillemardot, négociants at Chalon, 18 April 1759.

89. AD Saône-et-Loire, 11B 227, Philibert Chavansot, 1762.

90. AD Saône-et-Loire, 11B 246, 1768.

91. Prices for common wines of upper Burgundy, identified as those of pays bas, are in Lavalle, *Histoire et statistique,* pp. 58–61. Revenues, based on these prices times the yields for Volnay, in Bavard, *Histoire de Volnay,* pp. 285–90, averaged 163 livres per arpent in the 1740s, 111 in the 1750s, 108 in the 1760s, 143 in the 1770s, and 170 in the 1780s. Prices for fine wines rebounded much higher in the 1770s than did prices for common wines. Prices in the Beaujolais are less available, but those recorded for Lyon by Durand, *Vin, vigne,* especially in the graph of the "courbe des minima," hors texte, look much like the prices in Lavalle.

92. Saint-Jacob, *Les paysans de la Bourgogne,* pp. 317–18, 394; he is quoting the subdelegate of Nuits in 1756.

93. Tainturier, *Remarques sur la culture des vignes de Beaune,* p. 131.

94. AD Côte-d'Or, G 4167; Saint-Jacob, "La vente du bon vin," p. 50, misses several of the Parisian buyers in the first half of the accounts. Having sold his first wine in October or November in almost every year from 1727 to 1753, he could not sell before January or February for nine of the next sixteen years.

95. See Saint-Jacob, *Les paysans de la bourgogne du nord,* pp. 318–64.

96. AM Beaune, carton 94, no. 53, 11 December 1766, signed by Germain, Paul Blandin, Berbizotte et Bollinot, Tainturier, Bouchard, Bourgeois, Regnier fils, David frères, Gastinel.

97. Ibid., letter of 10 December 1766. It can also be found as a printed "Avis de MM de la noblesse de Beaune" in AD Côte d'Or, C 874. Interestingly, one of the nobles who signed this letter, Parigot de Santenay, was also identified by Delachère as having "made the price" of Volnay wines in 1762 with the wine merchant Geoffroi, AD Côte-d'Or, G 4167.

98. In a "Mémoire sur le commerce des vins de Bourgogne et les causes de sa décadence" of 1766, discussed in Destray, "Le commerce des vins en Bourgogne," p. 67.

99. AM Beaune, carton 94, no. 53, letter of 10 December 1766.

100. Ibid., no date.

101. Ibid., 5 December 1766.

102. AD Côte-d'Or, G 4167, recueil des jours de la vendange de Vollenay avec un mémoire de la production des vignes de la cuve dudit Vollenay et des frais de vendange, 1754. The brokers did much the same the next year, leaving most of the wine until spring. They allowed prices to rise only a little, and "used the same stratagems to drop [the price of] the wines of Pommard and Beaune."

103. Destray, "Le commerce des vins en Bourgogne," pp. 77–80, reprints Perrot's request to the estates of Burgundy, rejected in the session of 30 January 1777. The request refers to an earlier proposal on the same subject.

104. *Premier trimestre des tablettes royales de renommée pour servir de supplément* (1775), s.v. vin, which identifies some twenty Parisian wine merchants and the correspondents Perrot, le jeune, and Vincent.

105. AD Côte-d'Or, BII Suppl. 257, 24 March 1736, Dame Huguette Desir versus her "commissionnaire" Renée Dechaux.

106. Morelot, *Statistique de la vigne dans le département de la Côte d'Or* (Dijon, 1831), p. 222.

107. L. Perriaux, *Grand livre cotté A: bicentenaire de la maison de vins Poulet* (Beaune, 1952), p. 22.

108. François Glantenay, "Les débuts du négoce beaunnois au XVIIIe siècle," *Cahiers de la Bourgogne moderne* 2 (1973–74): 19, letter to Amyot père, 22 July 1778.

109. Solange de Montenay, "Les tribulations d'un voyageur de commerce à la fin de l'ancien régime," *Annales de Bourgogne* 39 (1967): 197–235, has published extracts from dozens of Chardon's letters back to his associates dating from a trip that he took through eastern France, Germany, and Flanders between July 1783 and February 1784. Chardon had a quarter interest in Bureau puiné.

110. Saint-Jacob, *Les paysans de la Bourgogne,* pp. 480–509; Labrousse, *Crise,* pp. 329–31. In fact prices for elite wines in the 1780s, from Lavalle, *Histoire et statistique,* pp. 58–61, were no lower than the average prices of the 1750s and 1760s, and common wines were only 12 percent lower, but contemporary evidence suggests real distress in the viticultural economy.

111. Montenay, "Les tribulations d'un voyageur de commerce," pp. 197–235.

112. Jean-Antoine-Claude Chaptal, *Traité théorique et pratique sur la culture de la vigne,* 2 vols. (Paris, 1801), 1:137. The total was essentially unchanged since the 1720s, but there had been no bottles at the earlier date.

113. Montenay, "Les tribulations d'un voyageur de commerce," pp. 197–235.

114. Perriaux, *Grand livre cotté A,* pp. 16–27, discusses the figures for 1774 and 1789.

115. AN, 63 AQ 5, Livre d'expedition, beginning 5 September 1775, anonymous but identified in guide as a marchand de vin of Beaune.

116. Glantenay, "Les débuts du négoce beaunnois," pp. 1–22.

117. Sandrine Touratier, "Le commerce des vins de Bourgogne à la fin du XVIIIe et au début du XIXe siècles," mémoire de maitrise, Dijon, 1991.

118. Glantenay, "Les débuts du négoce beaunnois," p. 8.

119. AD Saône-et-Loire, 11B 227, Philibert Chavansot; he also listed 170,000 livres of property.

120. Glantenay, "Les débuts du négoce beaunnois," pp. 7–8, based on the account books of Verry, 1775–83, and of Amyot, 1785–98.

121. Perriaux, *Grand livre cotté A,* pp. 16–23.

122. AN, 63 AQ 5, Livre d'expedition.

123. *Almanach général du commerce* (1788, 1789–91), s.v. Beaune, Nuits.

124. Laurent, *Les vignerons de la Côte d'Or,* p. 232.

125. See Françoise Grivot, *Le commerce des vins de Bourgogne* (Paris, 1964), for their later development.

Chapter 8 *The Decline and Transfiguration of Champagne*

1. Laurent, *Reims et la région rémoise,* liv.

2. This is based on what the tax farm paid to collect the tax in 1726, and every six years until 1744, given in ibid., liv–lv.

3. Rapport annuel du procureur de l'abbaye de Saint-Martin d'Epernay pour 1729–30, AD Marne C 487; cited in Chandon de Briailles, "Recherches sur les origines," p. 349.

4. AD Marne, F 148, mémoire sur l'état actuel de la généralité de Champagne by Lepeletier de Beaupré, 1732, pp. 165–66.

5. AD Marne, C 4371–C 4376, contrôle des actes of Epernay, 1702–29.

6. AD Marne, C 4377–C 4381, contrôle des actes of Epernay, 1730–52.

7. Where the entries can be checked against another source, such as the accounts of Moët or Guyot, they reveal occasional errors: The clerk dropped a zero from 50, for example, a one from 147. At least one broker contributed to the inaccuracies of the contrôle by regularly underreporting the number of bottles he shipped, "to avoid having the merchant pay the entrance [tax into Paris] on bottles that will break before they arrive"; AP Moët et Chandon, Journal de 1743, 7 April 1745. But Moët rarely slipped more than 5 percent of his bottles past the authorities and could not try that with barrels. More seriously, a few years are full of vague allusions to "many barrels;" records for the vintage of 1731 are virtually useless for their lack of precision, and several other years in the 1730s and 1740s are nearly as bad.

8. AD Marne, C 4140–C 4143, contrôle des actes of Ay, 1705–55. Unfortunately the records in the 1750s become far too vague to be useful.

9. The contrôle des actes of Damery, AD Marne, C 4320–C 4323, are not consistently informative but suggest little more than a thousand barrels sent throughout this period, with little change.

10. It appears that wines sent east were leaving from a different port, for they did not appear in the contrôle des actes. Thus Bertin lists shipments with carters from Reims in his agenda, BM Epernay, ms. 209, that often do not show up in the contrôle. Rather, exports for 1747–48 are listed in AD Marne, C 481; exports for 1775–80 are in AN, F 12 242. Both records distinguish wines "from Reims," "from the mountain," and "from Champagne," which refer to the barrel sizes, or *jauges* used around Reims and along the Marne.

11. BM Epernay, ms. 209, 21 October, 7 November 1729. The harvest was again "half of the previous year" in 8 October 1731.

12. AP Malavois de la Ganne, account book.

13. AD Marne, C 669, mémoire to Machault, no date, but a cover letter is dated 1752.

14. AD Marne, C 303, petition of Billecart for relief of his debts, 20 July 1759. Most of his twelve arpents of vines were in Avenay.

15. BM Epernay, Fonds Chandon, ms. 325, fols. 125–26. The harvests in 1742–44 averaged nine barrels; output returned to an average of 4.2 between 1759 and 1789.

16. Accounts of Bertin du Rocheret, BM Epernay, ms. 209; of Guyot, AD Reims, 25B 61; of Moët, AP Moët et Chandon; of Malavois, AP Malavois de la Ganne.

17. AD Marne, F 148, mémoire by Lepeletier de Beaupré, pp. 165–66, 189.

18. See Vivier, "Un problème d'histoire économique," pp. 15–56, for a general discussion of this effort.

19. AM Reims, FA 690, Etat des vignes qui ont été planté sur les terroirs des paroisses de l'élection de Reims sans permission pendant 1734–37, no date but conducted in response to the intendant's ordinance of December 1737.

20. Official estimate in AD Marne, C 430, reproduced in Laurent, *Reims et la région rémoise,* ccix–ccx.

21. AM Reims, FA 690, Etat des vignes.

22. Bidet, *Mémoires pour servir à l'histoire de Reims,* 4 vols. (1749), 4:69.

23. BN, Coll. Joly, ms. 1336, fol. 270, letter from Collet, 4 March 1739.

24. Dion, *Histoire de la vigne,* pp. 593–607; see chapter 6.

25. Godinot, *Manière de cultiver la vigne,* pp. 18–19. Laurent, *Reims et la région rémoise,* ccxvii, observes that after the 1720s "during the course of which there was excess production [of white wine], a reaction set in; a crisis of declining sales forced vignerons to return to [making] red wine."

26. AP Malavois de la Ganne, 1747.

27. AD Marne, C 669, memoir to Machault, no date, but from internal evidence it appears to be from 1752. According to Godinot, *Manière de cultiver la vigne,* pp. 6–11, the vines needed to be pruned to a height of three feet, instead of four or five.

28. Laurent, *Reims et la région rémoise,* lxix, ccxliii–lvi, points out that this caused real bitterness against the tithe collectors.

29. AD Marne, C 669, memoir to Machault, 1752.

30. Gandilhon, *Naissance,* pp. 126–27, 136–39. Laurent, *Reims et la région rémoise,* lxii–lxiii, procès-verbal de l'assemblée d'élection d'Epernay, October 1788.

31. Bonal, *Livre d'or du champagne,* p. 55, quoting a report from 1780; AN G² 26, report of the régie from the 1780s.

32. Letter of d'Artagnan to Bertin de Rocheret, 27 December 1712, BM Epernay, Fonds Chandon, ms. 329, p. 39.

33. See the judgments of the Grand Conseil and the Grand Prévôt against wine merchants using fish gelatin, and discussion in Gandilhon, *Naissance,* pp. 149–151. Godinot's treatise of 1718 still recommended keeping wine on the lees. Not until Pluche's treatise in the 1730s did the lees, and air, become the "two plagues of wine."

34. Letter from Adam Bertin to D'Arboulin, one of the twelve privileged wine merchants, 21 February 1716, BM Epernay, Fonds Chandon, ms. 329, p. 58, which adds, "although our grandfathers practiced it (so I believe) for my grandfather Bertin, famous commissionnaire of Reims, owned a bellows and pipe for racking."

35. According to Pijassou, *Un grand vignoble de qualité: le Médoc,* 1:345–62, the new techniques were introduced in Bordeaux in the 1680s and 1690s. See also Lachiver, *Vins, vignes,* pp. 224–26.

36. See chapter 2 and Bonal, *Livre d'or du champagne,* p. 30, for much of this evidence.

37. Dion, *Histoire de la vigne,* pp. 634–36.

38. Historians have found no contemporary evidence to support the legend that Dom Pérignon "invented" the champagne method and some to refute it, leaving him nonetheless the prestige of producing very fine wines with considerable skill

and a certain amount of innovation. See Bonal, *Livre d'or du champagne,* pp. 26–36, for discussion of the debate.

39. Godinot, *Manière de cultiver la vigne,* p. 28.

40. One seller reported that it took a week to sell a barrel by the quart, but the wine was worthless before the barrel was half empty; AD Yonne, 3E 3-88, succession sous sequestre of Boyard Saint-Martin, 3 June 1788.

41. Gandilhon, *Naissance,* p. 184.

42. See Bonal, *Livre d'or du champagne,* pp. 35–36, for the literary evidence for much of this.

43. AD Marne, F 148, mémoire sur l'état actuel de la généralité de Champagne, 1732, p. 84. The bottle remained at or a little below this through much of the century, and corks varied between three and six sous for ten; Gandilhon, *Naissance,* pp. 184, 187, n. 160.

44. Quoted in Nollevalle, *Vin d'Ay,* pp. 72–73.

45. BN, Coll. Joly, ms. 264, fol. 142, Reims, 24 August 1747.

46. The governor of Epernay, writing to Bertin for barrels of wine from the region, specified that "I think it will be better to have some [wine] from Hautvillers than from any other spot. . . . Please ask it for me from Father Prior and Dom Pérignon"; BM Epernay, ms. 155, Puyseulx, 28 September 1690.

47. AD Marne, H 1070, Extrait des vins vendus en broc, October 1691 to September 1692; état des vins que Ms les religieux d'Hautvillers ont fait conduire à Reims pour vendre en détail, October 1693 to March 1694.

48. AD Marne, H 1071, inventaire des vins, 24 November 1712; AD Marne, H 1070, déclaration des vins des religieux de l'abbeye d'Hautvillers, 14 October 1733; inventaire des vins 1743, mémoire des vins 1747. In addition to 622 barrels of new wine and 105 of old that was still in barrels, the inventory of 1743 listed forty thousand bottles (equal to roughly two hundred barrels) from 1742 and nine thousand from 1741. But these inventories were made for tax purposes shortly after the vintage and so occurred before the new wine was bottled and after some of the old bottled wine had been sold. The number of bottles from 1742 still in the cellar suggests that the abbey would have bottled more than a third of its wine.

49. AP, Malavois de la Ganne, account book, 1747, at which point he noted that the only other time that he had only sold early once before.

50. BN, Coll. Joly, ms. 264, fols. 133, 142, letters from le Gras to Joly de Fleury, 24 August 1747, 18 April 1748.

51. Ibid, fols. 145–49, mémoires of Mouton and le Gras to Joly de Fleury, no date.

52. AD Marne, B 9151, succession of Durand, no date but latest documents are from 1757. Unfortunately the records offer little evidence about his business from the mid-1730s to the late 1740s.

53. AD Marne, C 303, letters and reports concerning Benoist Durand, fille majeure of Pierry. Her identification of the rich wine merchant and of Germon is in AD Marne, B 9151. A wine merchant of Reims spoke up for her character but admitted that he had been unable to get good prices for her wine.

54. Tax courts presumed that wine sent in bottles was aimed at the retail trade, which bore a higher tax than wine sold wholesale. See the discussion in Gandilhon, *Naissance,* pp. 190–91.

55. AD Marne, C 4371, the two thousand bottles were sent 23 October 1702 by Parchappe, a conseiller au prévôté.

56. AD Marne, C 4374, 6 May 1720.

57. Gandilhon, *Naissance*, p. 191, emphasizes the importance of the new law in 1728 because he presents it as the end of the restriction covering all of France, whereas Bonal, *Livre d'or du champagne*, p. 58, and Chandon de Briailles, "Recherches sur les origines," p. 378, make it clear that the restriction was lifted only in Normandy.

58. AD Marne, C 4380, lists 52,000 bottles between October 1743 and September 1745 and only 2,319 barrels. Similarly Ay was sending five and six thousand bottles in the 1730s, but this was only 1 or 2 percent of the total; C 4141, 4142, 1727–45.

59. AD Marne, C 4371–C 4380, 1702–49. Again, these are harvest years, beginning in October and running through September of the following year.

60. This is a petition to reverse the impediments to shipping wine in bottles, in Varin, *Archives législatives*, 4:222.

61. BN, Coll. Joly, ms. 264, fol. 133, 142, letters of le Gras to Joly de Fleury, 24 August 1747, 18 April 1748.

62. The figures for the early 1720s are in Chaptal, *Traité sur la culture*, p. 136. The figures for 1747 and 1748, in AD Marne, C 481, refer only to wines sent east through the bureaux of Charleville and Châlons.

63. BM Epernay, ms. 155, fol. 349, letter to le maréchal de Montesquiou, 20 December 1713.

64. Quoted in Bonal, *Livre d'or du champagne*, p. 42.

65. AD Marne, BR 1393, 2 March 1722, inventory of Marie Lallement.

66. AD Reims, 25B 61.

67. Chandon de Briailles, "Recherches sur les origines," p. 377.

68. BM Châlons, ms. 125, letter of Philippe Valentin Bertin du Rocheret to abbé Bignon following the death of Adam Bertin du Rocheret in 1736.

69. Ibid., 18 November 1727.

70. Ibid., letters to Chabanne, 26 January 1728, 8 October 1731.

71. René Gandilhon, "Un amateur de vin de Champagne: l'abbé Bignon, bibliothécaire du roi," *Bibliothèque de l'Ecole des Chartes* 141 (1983): 122–26.

72. BM Epernay, ms. 209, 27 January 1751, 13 February 1751, 1 January 1753. He identifies Durand as being from Ay, but the account book of Durand of Pierry, AD Marne, B 9151, records some of the commerce with Bertin.

73. Ibid., 15 November 1752; 1 March 1749.

74. BN, Coll. Joly, ms. 1336, fol. 270, letter from Collet, 4 March 1739.

75. Nicolas Chertemps had twenty arpents of vignes in 1720, AD Marne, B 9075 12 December 1720; Adam Bertin had only four arpents, BR 1393, 27 February 1722.

76. AP Moët et Chandon, account of 1743, May 1749.

77. AD Marne, C 4381–C 4386, particularly the years 1750–54, 1760–63, 1769–71, 1779–83.

78. The price of a bottle of sparkling wine covered a range from thirty to forty sous, according to the records of Moët and Malavois in the 1750s and 1760s and the records of Ruinart and Clicquot in the 1760s and 1770s. The price of a barrel

of red wine in the 1720s, according to the records of Guyot, and in the 1740s according to Moët, was roughly twenty-five livres.

79. AD Marne, C 4386, contrôle des actes, 1773–74. According to the *Almanach général du commerce, des marchands négociants, armateurs de la France* (1779), p. 488, "Gilles Doublet is the only one at Vertus who is engaged in the wine trade, not only in this bourg, but also at Mesnil, where he has a beautiful vintage house [vendangeoir];" it identifies Marc and Germon, with Moët, Partelaine, and five others as négociants in Epernay (p. 200).

80. Young, *Travels*, 2:210.

81. Gilbert Nolleau, "La maison Moët-Chandon, un siècle d'existence (1743–1843)," mémoire de maitrise (Reims, 1972), p. 64.

82. Since 1778, the *Almanach général des marchands* had identified Moët the elder among the "principal négociants" of Epernay, and by 1788 it was Moët père et fils.

83. Quoted in Henry Vizetelly, *A History of Champagne* (London, 1882), p. 207.

84. The remark is first made by Max Sutaine, "Essai sur l'histoire des vins de Champagne," *Séances et travaux de l'académie de Reims* 3 (1845–46): 207, and repeated in M. Salle, "Rapport sur un mémoire de M. Louis Perrier sur l'histoire des vins de Champagne," *Mémoires de la société d'agriculture, commerce, science et arts du département de la Marne* (1858): 126. Both refer to "one of the first houses" of Epernay, which most historians have taken to mean Moët.

85. AD Reims, 18J 1, accounts of barrels of wine carted to Epernay in 1789; 18J 500, register of correspondence of 1790, especially letter of 10 August 1790.

86. Nolleau, "La maison Moët-Chandon," p. 66.

87. Dardel, *Navires et marchandises dans les ports de Rouen*, pp. 167–68, distinguishes the wine shipped in barrels and bottles only in 1766, when the thirty-nine thousand bottles were three-quarters of the champagne wine exported from Rouen.

88. BM Epernay, Fonds Chandon, ms. 329, accounts of Chanlaire, 1776–77.

89. Calculations made by Nolleau, "La maison Moët-Chandon," pp. 40, 60, show that the proportion of wine sent by the house to addresses in Paris rarely fell below 90 percent before 1762 and remained above 70 percent in the late 1780s.

90. Figures for 1720–25 and 1788 in Chaptal, *Traité sur la culture*, pp. 133–36; AD Marne, C 481, figures for 1747–48; AN, F ^{12} 242–248, for exports from 1775–80.

91. Archives privées, Ruinart Père et Fils still has account books for part of the 1760s and 1770s, to which they very kindly gave me access. I am extremely grateful for their assistance.

92. AP Ruinart, letter of 19 November 1764.

93. Ibid., letter from Wetz to Ruinart, 22 July 1775

94. Ibid., letter from Guyet of Paris, 11 November 1764.

95. Patrick de Gmeline, *Ruinart, la plus ancienne maison de Champagne* (Paris, 1994), pp. 38–41.

96. Gmeline, *Ruinart*, pp. 28–31.

97. AP Ruinart, letter of 18 April 1775.

98. Ibid., ms. "Instructions et renseignements donnés par Mr. Ruinart de Brimont à ses fils Thierry et Edmond pour le commerce des vins de Champagne," 1809, quoted in Gmeline, *Ruinart*, pp. 142–43.

99. BN, Coll. Joly, ms. 264, fol. 143, letter of le Gras to Joly de Fleury, 24 August 1747.

100. AN, F^{12} 242–248, 1775–1780.

101. Even at this late date the mountain was producing very little white wine, though its best red wines were bottled and enjoyed a reputation as good as those of Burgundy; *Almanach générale des marchands* (Paris, 1779), p. 404.

102. Although several of today's champagne wine companies can trace their origins back to the late eighteenth century, few retain records from that period. Henri Abelé, Lanson Père et Fils, and Piper-Heidsieck could offer nothing and Taittinger apparently lost all the records of the earlier Fourneaux family in a fire. The faillite records of the less successful firms remain in the archives, but they are smaller enterprises. For example, the business failures of Jean-Joseph Lefebvre and Nicolas Grosselin, AD Reims, 18B 2006, 5 January 1787 and 24 March 1787, show them selling modest amounts of wine in barrels to French cities north and east of Reims. One of Etienne Dona's account books records some nine thousand livres owed by individuals in eastern France and the Netherlands, 18B 2004, 9 December 1779. Only the tangled accounts of Loubeau Saint-Frajou, AD Reims, 18B 2002, 19 April 1768, indicate a merchant on the scale of Ruinart, buying large amounts of wine in both barrels and bottles.

103. Archives privées, Veuve Clicquot, brouillard of 1775–80; brouillard of 1784–89. I wish to thank the people of Veuve Clicquot again for their kindness and help in using their archives.

104. This paragraph is based on the extremely informative study of the firm in the first decade of the nineteenth century by Michel Etienne, *Veuve Clicquot Ponsardin, aux origines d'un grand vin de Champagne* (Paris, 1994).

Conclusion

1. Leo A. Loubère, *The Red and the White: the History of Wine in France and Italy in the Nineteenth Century* (Albany, 1978), p. 281.

2. Richard, "Production et commerce du vin en Bourgogne," p. 45, quoting the préfet in 1835.

3. Patrick Forbes, *Champagne: the Wine, the Land and the People* (London, 1967), p. 422.

4. Grivot, *Le commerce des vins de Bourgogne,* pp. 119–20.

5. Loubère, *The Red and the White,* p. 244.

6. Pierre Goujon, *La cave et le grenier: vignobles du chalonnais et du mâconnais au XIXe siècle* (Lyon, 1989), pp. 216–21; Gérald-Jack Gilbank, *Les vignobles de qualités du sud-est du bassin parisien, évolution économique et sociale* (Paris, 1981), pp. 339–40; Grivot, *Le commerce des vins de Bourgogne,* pp. 164–65.

7. Grivot, *Le commerce des vins de Bourgogne,* p. 170.

8. Ibid., pp. 94–96; Loubère, *The Red and the White,* pp. 242–43; Goujon, *La cave et le grenier,* p. 222.

Select Bibliography

Manuscript primary sources came from the Archives Nationales, Archives Départementales of the Cher, Côte d'Or, Indre-et-Loire, Loir-et-Cher, Maine-et-Loire,
Marne, Saône-et-Loire, and Yonne, Annex of the AD Marne in Reims, Archives
du Département de la Seine et de la Ville de Paris, Archives Municipales of Angers,
Beaune, Blois, and Reims, Bibliothèque Nationale, and Bibliothèques Municipales
of Auxerre, Châlons, Dijon, Epernay, and Reims.

Printed Primary Sources

Arnoux. *Dissertation sur la situation de Bourgogne et sur la manière de cultiver les vignes
. . . vins qu'elle produit . . . deux moyens pour les faire venir à Londres.* London, 1728.
[Brac]. *Le commerce des vins, réformé, rectifié et épuré, ou nouvelle méthode pour tirer
un parti sûr, prompt et avantageux des récoltes en vins.* Amsterdam and Lyon, 1769.
Delamare, Nicolas. *Traité de la police.* 4 vols. Paris, 1705–38.
Eon, Jean [Mathias de Saint-Jean]. *Le commerce honorable ou considerations politiques.*
Nantes, 1646.
Godinot, *Manière de cultiver la vigne et de faire le vin en Champagne.* Reims, 1722.
Gournay, B. C. *Almanach général du commerce, marchands, négociants.* Paris, 1788.
Lefebvre de la Bellande. *Traité général des droits d'aydes.* 2d ed. Paris, 1770.
Savary, Jacques. *Le parfait négociant.* 2 vols. Paris, 1675.
Young, Arthur. *Travels During the Years 1787, 1788, and 1789.* 2 vols. Dublin, 1793.

Secondary Sources

Agnew, Jean-Christophe. *Worlds Apart: The Market and the Theater in Anglo-
American Thought, 1550–1750.* Cambridge, 1986.
Baehrel, René. *Une croissance: la basse-Provence rurale de la fin du XVIe siècle à 1789.*
Paris, 1961.
Baldwin, John. *Medieval Theories of the Just Price.* Philadelphia, 1959.

Beauroy, Jacques. *Vin et société à Bergerac du moyen âge aux temps modernes.* Saratoga, Calif., 1976.

Blin, Léon. "La route beaujolaise de Saône à Loire au XVIIIe siècle, ses affinités mâconnaises." *Memoires de la Société pour l'histoire du droit et des institutions des anciens pays bourguignons* 8 (1942): 84–126.

Boislisle, Arthur Michel de. *Correspondance des contrôleurs généraux des finances avec les intendants des provinces.* 3 vols. Paris, 1874–97.

Boissonnade, P. "La production et le commerce des céréales, des vins et des eaux-de-vie en Languedoc dans la seconde moitié du XVIIe siècle." *Annales du Midi* 17 (1905): 344–60.

Bonal, François. *Livre d'or du champagne.* Lausanne, 1984.

Bouton, Cynthia A. *The Flour War: Gender, Class, and Community in Late Ancien Régime French Society.* University Park, Pa., 1993.

Braudel, Fernand. *The Perspective of the World.* Translated by Siân Reynolds. New York, 1984.

———. *The Wheels of Commerce.* Translated by Siân Reynolds. New York, 1982.

Brennan, Thomas. *Public Drinking and Popular Culture in Eighteenth-Century Paris.* Princeton, 1988.

Butel, Paul. *Les négociants bordelais, l'Europe et les iles au XVIIIe siècle.* Paris, 1974.

———. *L'économie française au XVIIIe siècle.* Paris, 1993.

Chandon de Briailles, Raoul. "Recherches sur les origines des vignobles et du vin mousseux de Champagne." *Bulletin du laboratoire expérimental Moët et Chandon* 2 (1908): 301–10, 347–50, 368–78.

Cocula, Anne-Marie. "Pour une définition de l'espace aquitain au XVIIIe siècle." In Pierre Léon, ed., *Aires et structures du commerce français au XVIIIe siècle.* Paris, 1975.

Courtépée, C. *Description générale et particulière du duché de Bourgogne.* 4 vols. Dijon, 1847–48.

Dardel, Pierre. *Navires et marchandises dans les ports de Rouen et du Havre au XVIIIe siècle.* Paris, 1963.

Daumard, Adeline, and François Furet. *Structures et relations sociales à Paris au milieu du XVIIIe siècle.* Paris, 1961.

Delafosse, Marcel. "Le commerce du vin d'Auxerre (XIV–XVIe siècle)." *Annales de Bourgogne* 13 (1941): 203–30.

Demay, Charles. "La juridiction consulaire d'Auxerre." *Bulletin de la société des sciences historiques et naturelles de l'Yonne* (1894): 156–89.

Destray, P. "Le commerce des vins en Bourgogne au XVIIIe siècle." In J. Hayem, *Mémoires et documents pour servir à l'histoire du commerce et de l'industrie en France.* 2d series. Paris, 1912.

Devroey, Jean-Pierre. *L'éclair d'un bonheur: une histoire de la vigne en Champagne.* Paris, 1989.

Dewald, Jonathan. *Pont-St-Pierre, 1398–1789: Lordship, Community, and Capitalism in Early Modern France.* Berkeley, 1987.

Dilley, Roy, ed. *Contesting Markets: Analyses of Ideology, Discourse and Practice.* Edinburgh, 1992.

Dion, Roger. *Histoire de la vigne et du vin en France des origines au XIXe siècle.* Paris, 1959.

Doehaerd, Renée. "Un paradoxe géographique: Laon, capitale du vin au XIIe siècle." *Annales d'histoire économique et sociale* 5 (1950): 145–65.

Durand, Georges. *Vin, vigne et vignerons en Lyonnais et Beaujolais (XVIe–XVIIIe siècle).* Paris, 1979.

Durand, René. "Le commerce en Bourgogne à la veille de la Révolution française." *Annales de Bourgogne* 2 (1930): 221–34, 326–36.

Enjalbert, Henri. "Comment naissent les grands crus: bordeaux, porto, cognac." *Annales ESC* 8 (1953): 315–28, 457–74.

———. *Histoire de la vigne et du vin: l'avènement de la qualité.* Paris, 1975.

Everitt, Alan. "The Marketing of Agricultural Produce." In Joan Thirsk, ed. *The Agrarian History of England and Wales 1500–1640.* Cambridge, 1967.

Forestier, Henri. *Extraits analytiques des minutes déposées aux archives de l'Yonne par Me André Guimard, notaire à Auxerre.* Auxerre, 1954.

Forestier, Henri, and Claude Hohl. *Extraits analytiques des minutes déposées aux Archives de l'Yonne.* Auxerre, 1977.

Fox, Edward W. *History in a Geographical Perspective.* New York, 1971.

Fox-Genovese, Elizabeth. *The Origins of Physiocracy.* Ithaca, 1976.

Gadille, Rolande. *Le vignoble de la côte bourguignonne.* Paris, 1967.

Gandilhon, René. *Naissance du champagne. Dom Pérignon.* Paris, 1968.

George, Rosemary. *The Wines of Chablis and the Yonne.* London, 1985.

Géraud-Parracha, Guillaume. *Le commerce des vins et des eaux-de-vie en Languedoc sous l'ancien régime.* Mende, 1958.

Gordon, Daniel. *Citizens without Sovereignty: Equality and Sociability in French Thought, 1670–1789.* Princeton, 1994.

Gruter, Edouard. *La naissance d'un grand vignoble: les seigneuries du Pizay et Tanay en Beaujolais au XVIe et au XVIIe siècles.* Lyon, 1977.

Hirsch, Jean-Pierre. "Les milieux du commerce, l'esprit de système et le pouvoir, à la veille de la Révolution." *Annales ESC* 30 (1975): 1337–70.

Hoffman, Philip. *Growth in a Traditional Society: The French Countryside, 1450–1815.* Princeton, 1996.

Huetz de Lemps, Christian. *Géographie de commerce de Bordeaux à la fin de la regne de Louis XIV.* Paris, 1975.

Johnson, E. A. J. *The Organization of Space in Developing Countries.* Cambridge, Mass., 1970.

Kaplan, Steven L. *Bread, Politics and Political Economy in the Reign of Louis XV.* The Hague, 1976.

———. *Provisioning Paris: Merchants and Millers in the Grain and Flour Trade during the Eighteenth Century.* Ithaca, 1984.

Labrousse, Ernest. *La crise de l'économie française à la fin de l'ancien régime et au début de la Révolution.* Paris, 1944.

Lachiver, Marcel. "Les aires d'approvisionement de Paris en vin au début du XVIIIe siècle." *Bulletin de la société de l'histoire de Paris et de l'Île-de-France* 35 (1984): 277–87.

———. *Vin, vigne et vignerons en région parisienne du XVIIe au XIXe siècles.* Pontoise, 1982.

———. *Vins, vignes et vignerons: histoire du vignoble français.* Paris, 1988.

Laurent, Gustave. *Reims et la région rémoise à la veille de la Révolution.* Reims, 1930.

Laurent, Robert. *Les vignerons de la "Côte d'Or" au XIXe siècle*. 2 vols. Dijon, 1958.

Lavalle, J. *Histoire et statistique de la vigne et des grands vins de la Côte-d'Or*. Paris, 1855.

Léon, Pierre, and Charles Carrière. "L'appel des marchés." In Fernand Braudel and Ernest Labrousse, eds., *Histoire économique et sociale de la France*. Vol. 2. *Des derniers temps de l'âge seigneurial aux préludes de l'âge industriel (1660–1789)*. Paris, 1970.

Le Roy Ladurie, Emmanuel. "De la crise ultime à la vraie croissance, 1690–1789." In Georges Duby and Armand Wallon, eds. *Histoire de la France rurale, de 1340 à 1789*. 4 vols. Paris, 1975.

———. *The French Peasantry 1450–1660*. Translated by Alan Sheridan. Berkeley, 1987.

Liu, Tessie P. *The Weaver's Knot: The Contradictions of Class Struggle and Family Solidarity in Western France, 1750–1914*. Ithaca, 1994.

Meuvret, Jean. *Le problème des subsistances à l'époque Louis XIV*. 3 vols. Paris, 1977–88.

Meyssonnier, Simone. *La balance et l'horloge: la genèse de la pensée libérale en France au XVIIIe siècle*. Paris, 1989.

Moriceau, Jean-Marc. "Au rendez-vous de la 'révolution agricole' dans la France du XVIIIe siècle: à propos des régions de grande culture." *Annales ESC* 49 (1994): 27–63.

———. *Les fermiers de l'Île-de-France, XVe–XVIIIe siècle*. Paris, 1994.

Morineau, Michel. *Les faux-semblants d'un démarrage économique: agriculture et démographie en France au XVIIIe siècle*. Paris, 1971.

Nollevalle, Jean. *Le vin d'Ay à l'origine du champagne*. Reims, 1988.

North, Douglass. *Structure and Change in Economic History*. New York, 1981.

Olivier-Martin, François. *La police économique de l'ancien régime*. Paris, 1945.

Pélicier, M. "Cahiers de doléances des communes du bailliage d'Epernay en 1789." *Mémoire de la société d'agriculture du département de la Marne* (1898–99): 337–511.

Persan, Françoise de. "Les voituriers par eau et le commerce sur la Loire à Blois au XVIIe siècle." Thèse de 3e cycle. Tours, 1984.

Pijassou, René. *Un grand vignoble de qualité: le Médoc*. 2 vols. Paris, 1970.

Pitelis, Christos, ed. *Transaction Costs, Markets and Hierarchies*. Oxford, 1993.

Poitrineau, Abel. *La vie rurale en basse-Auvergne au XVIIIe siècle*. Paris, 1965.

Poussou, Jean-Pierre. *Bordeaux et le Sud-Ouest au XVIIIe siècle*. Paris, 1983.

Reddy, William M. *The Rise of Market Culture: The Textile Trade and French Society, 1750–1900*. Cambridge, 1984.

Richard, Jean. "Production et commerce du vin en Bourgogne aux XVIIIe et XIXe siècles." *Annales cisalpines d'histoire sociale* 3 (1972): 9–47.

Richard, Paul. "Le vignoble Auxerrois en 1787." *Bulletin de la société des sciences historiques et naturelles de l'Yonne* 98 (1959–60): 33–40.

Roche, Emile. *Le commerce des vins de Champagne sous l'ancien régime*. Châlons-sur-Marne, 1908.

Root, Hilton. "The Case against George Lefebvre's Peasant Revolution." *History Workshop Journal* (1989): 88–102.

———. "Politiques frumentaires et violence collective en Europe au XVIIIe siècle." *Annales ESC* 45 (1990): 167–89.

Roover, Raymond de. "Concept of the Just Price: Theory and Economic Policy." *Journal of Economic History* 18 (1958): 418–34.

Saint-Jacob, Pierre de. "Une source de l'histoire du commerce des vins: lettres de voiture." *Annales de Bourgogne* 28 (1956): 124–26.

———. *Les paysans de la Bourgogne du Nord au dernier siècle de l'ancien régime.* Paris, 1960.

———. "La vente du bon vin de Volnay au XVIIIe siècle." *Annales de Bourgogne* 19 (1947): 44–51.

Sautel, Gérard. *Histoire du contrat de commission jusqu'au Code de Commerce.* Paris, 1949.

Schlumbohm, Jürgen. "Relations of Production—Productive Forces—Crisis in Proto-Industrialization." In Peter Kriedte, Hans Medick, and Jürgen Schlumbohm, eds., *Industrialization before Industrialization.* Translated by Beate Schempp. Cambridge, 1981.

Stevenson, J. "The 'Moral Economy' of the English Crowd: Myth and Reality." In A. Fletcher and J. Stevenson, eds. *Order and Disorder in Early Modern England.* Cambridge, 1985.

Thibault, Pierre. "Les parisiens et le vin à la fin du XVe siècle." *Bulletin de la société de l'histoire de Paris et de l'Île-de-France* 35 (1984): 231–49.

Thompson, E. P. "The Moral Economy of the English Crowd in the Eighteenth Century." *Past and Present* 52 (1971): 56–97.

Tilly, Louise. "The Food Riot as a Form of Political Conflict in France." *Journal of Interdisciplinary History* 2 (1971): 23–57.

Trouessart, H. *Le commerce de Blois de 1517 à la fin du XVIIIe siècle d'après les registres municipaux.* 2 vols. Blois, 1898.

Unwin, Tim. *Wine and the Vine: An Historical Geography of Viticulture and the Wine Trade.* London, 1991.

Vardi, Liana. *The Land and the Loom: Peasants and Profit in Northern France 1680–1800.* Durham, 1993.

Varin, Pierre. *Archives législative de la ville de Reims.* 6 vols. Paris, 1840–53.

Vivier, Robert. "Un problème d'histoire économique: les essais de limitation de la culture de la vigne en Touraine au XVIIIe siècle." *Revue d'histoire économique et sociale* 24 (1938): 15–56.

Weir, David R. "Les crises économiques et les origines de la Révolution française." *Annales ESC* 46 (1991): 917–47.

Westerfield, "Middlemen in English Business: Partly between 1660-1760." *Transactions of the Connecticut Academy of Arts & Sciences* 19 (1915; repr. Newton Abbot, 1968).

Weulersse, Georges. *Le mouvement physiocratique en France (de 1756 à 1770).* 2 vols. Paris, 1910.

Index

for workers, 19; ideal of, 143, 150, 169;
with traders, 214–18
consular court (*juridiction consulaire*), 67,
91, 123, 148, 153, 200–205, 224, 227, 230
contrôle des actes: of Champagne, 52–60,
62, 106–7, 242, 255–56, 258, 262–64,
297nn. 55, 58, 333nn. 7, 9, 10; of lower
Burgundy, 113–14, 131
controller general, 59, 88, 91–92, 97, 108,
121, 160
coopers, 27, 48–49, 70–71, 85, 129–30, 165,
167, 170–71, 181
correspondence, commercial, 62, 66, 70, 86,
180–87, 234–37, 260
Cosne, 54, 199
Coulanges-la-vineuse, 14, 98, 105, 115–16,
124–32, 154, 223–24, 273, 311n. 58
Coullange, Joseph, 171–72, 321n. 110
credit, 106, 232, 275–78; access to, 112–13,
150, 206; arranging, 79, 113; availability
of, 42; at the Halle aux vins, 180, 278,
310nn. 37, 40; manipulation of, 163;
offered by boatmen, 120–21; offered by
brokers, 73, 84, 135–39, 153–57, 165–67,
178; offered by winegrowers, 24, 34–35,
71–72, 81, 275; selling on, 89, 109, 183,
203. *See also* debts; financing
Cumières, 13, 18, 28, 60, 98, 243, 246, 254

Damery, 52, 59–60, 69, 98
debts, 151, 161, 224, 235; networks of, 35,
113, 130; owed by brokers, 124–26, 137,
229, 237, 254; owed by vinedressers, 19–
21, 32, 48, 129–30, 135–39, 165; owed by
wine merchants, 34, 47, 63, 125, 134–
39, 201–6, 224, 227–29. *See also* credit;
financing
Delachère, abbé, 19–20, 31–38, 165, 174,
227–28, 231–32
De la Motte, 191, 235, 257
Dijon, 11, 34, 80, 98, 229, 234–36
Dion, Roger, 133, 286n. 47
Durand, 253–54, 260

economic growth, 39–40, 44
economic power, xvii, xx, 8, 24, 59, 95, 212,
226, 276–80; of brokers, xx, 60, 64, 81,
94, 106–7, 112–14, 122, 139, 141, 145–
46, 150, 153–55, 159–76, 178, 206, 209;
through debts, 48, 128–30; inequalities

of, xii, xiv, xviii, 143–46; in rural industries, 111–12. *See also* debts; marketing;
markets, access to
Epernay, 26, 103, 166, 246–47, 260–65;
bourgeois of, 12; wine trade of, 52–73,
168–69, 242, 255–56
exchange, ix–x, xii, xiii–xv, 19, 77, 93, 143,
145, 275–76, 279–80

factums, 155
fermiers (large-scale farmers), xvii, 1, 10, 63,
128, 135
financing, 59, 66, 177, 181–83, 187, 210, 251,
255; of wine purchases, 69–73, 78, 112–
14, 121, 126, 137–39, 213. *See also* credit;
debts
Frankfurt, 228, 235–36, 264, 269
Froment, Elizabeth, 136

Garonne River, 43, 102
Germon, 254, 263
Gosset, 57, 266
grapes, 6–7, 23, 32, 36, 183; harvest, 16–17,
27, 33, 54, 147–49, 152, 243, 292n. 101;
ownership of, 9
Guenier, Jules, 224–25
Guignace, 165, 204
guinguettes, 10, 54, 56, 104
Guyot, Bernard, 67–69, 258–59

Halle aux vins, 57, 68, 118–21, 131, 178–87,
198, 203, 214, 216–18, 223, 226, 278–79
Hautvillers, 52, 247; abbey of, 13, 18, 251,
256, 335n. 48

intendants, 7, 52, 68, 87, 89, 91–92, 163–64,
241–42, 244, 250; fining brokers, 94–97,
100, 107–8
intermediaries, commercial, xiv–xv, 24, 39,
41, 57–58, 69, 74, 79, 145, 155
inventories of wine, 63, 171, 210, 233–34,
237
Irancy, 98, 105, 108, 115–16, 120, 127, 130–
32, 134–36, 148, 157, 194, 221

Jacquier, 200, 205–6
Joly de Fleury, Guillaume-François, 159–70,
210, 245, 250, 260
Journal du commerce, 190–91, 212, 222
journalism. *See* press

Index   347

Kaplan, Steven, 42

Labrousse, Ernest, xvii, 1, 28
land: ownership, xvii, 1, 9–15, 290n. 55;
    value, 7, 12–13
La Rochelle, 3–4, 95
Loire River, 3–6, 8, 12, 54, 81, 97, 102,
    192, 210; lower, 8, 97–100, 103, 106, 198;
    upper, 6, 11, 97–100, 105, 187, 196–201
Lot River, 43
Lyon, 30, 97, 211–12

Mâcon, 33, 81, 98, 163, 166, 212
Malavois de la Ganne, Jean-Claude, 19, 22–
    23, 25–33, 37–38, 51, 172–73, 243–44, 246,
    251–55, 257, 261, 269
Mallo, Jean, 48–49, 103
Marey, Claude, 228
marketing, xviii, 9, 112, 240, 277–79; by
    brokers, 153, 209, 233–38, 267–72, 274;
    by winegrowers, 7, 10–11, 19–20, 25–27,
    29–32, 251–55
marketplaces, xiii, 76, 143–46, 150, 276, 279,
    284n. 30
markets, xiii, 1, 76–78, 141–46, 150; den-
    dritic, xii, 106, 283n. 22, 307n. 97; domes-
    tic, 5–6, 39, 94, 100–101, 278; export, xi,
    2–5, 39, 74, 226–30, 235–38, 249, 253–
    55, 259–60, 262–65, 267–71; geography
    of, 30, 114, 226; information about, xviii,
    xx, 9, 35, 66–67, 77–79, 150, 163, 178,
    180, 183–87, 277; international, 2, 30, 100,
    103–4, 265, 271, 274, 278; interregional,
    2, 5, 11, 23, 33, 37, 40, 94, 103–4; national,
    33, 178, 191, 195, 206, 210–11; open, xii,
    143–46, 149, 178–79, 206, 278, 283n. 23,
    315nn. 14, 16; private, xii–xvi, 107–10,
    159, 278; regional, x, xviii, 2, 30, 33, 167;
    regulation of, xiii–xvi, 76–78, 142–46,
    150, 160, 176, 179, 206, 278; systems, 41,
    78, 94, 97–105, 134, 178
markets, access to, 8, 11, 24, 41, 45, 104,
    187, 209, 234, 284n. 26; through brokers,
    153–55, 182–83, 257; inequalities of, 15,
    21, 111–14, 117, 150, 276–77. See also eco-
    nomic power; marketing; transparency;
    transportation
markets, local, 3, 66, 81, 84, 86, 112, 168,
    238, 281n. 1, 286n. 55; competition in, 2,
    9–11; for grain, 42; for wine, 23, 33
Marne River, 45–46, 48–57, 101–2, 246,
    248, 266, 269

Marseille, 43, 92, 100, 230; merchants of, 41
merchants, 144, 158; grain, 25, 41–42, 58,
    63, 143–44
Meuvret, Jean, xi, 42
Millard, Jean, 126, 204, 218–19, 235, 331n. 87
Milliard. See Millard
Millon, Claude, 127–31, 135, 136, 148, 157,
    312n. 61
Moët, Claude, 18, 69–72, 243, 261–63, 266
Moët, Claude-Nicolas, 262–65
Moët, Jean-Remy, 263–65
Moët et Chandon, 273
Monnot, Germain, 148, 204
moral economy, xiii, 141–46, 284n. 26
Moreau, 180–87, 198, 223

Nantes, 4, 6, 87, 90–92, 98–101, 103, 106
Navarre, Etienne, 123–25, 311n. 53, 317n. 37
Navarre, Guillaume, 123
Navarre, Jean, 136
négociants, xiv, 41–43, 81, 91, 254, 272–74;
    brokers as, 93–94, 167, 178, 190–94, 214–
    15, 229–30, 233–41, 257, 269, 271; brokers
    becoming, 75, 174, 208–10, 226–27, 272.
    See also brokers
notaries, 52–53, 69, 181
Nuits[-Saint-George], 22, 32–34, 37, 194

Orléans, 6, 7, 12, 23, 98–99, 105, 107, 166–
    69, 171, 181, 217, 260

Parlement: of Dijon, 83; of Paris, 5, 26, 159,
    165, 216–17
Paris, 30, 72–73, 152, 177–87, 192–93, 234,
    243, 252–53; police, 5; port registers, 53,
    196–200; ports, 178, 182, 196–200, 216–
    17, 324n. 50; prévôt des marchands of,
    156, 178; staple, 178–80, 216; wine trade
    of, 55, 100, 104, 115–22, 125–27, 132–34,
    137–40, 177–87, 192–93, 196–211, 213–
    19, 224–31, 259–61. See also catchment:
    Parisian; wine merchants, Parisian
Pérignon, Dom Pierre, 13, 58, 65, 251,
    334n. 38
Perrot, 233–35
physiocrats, xv, 144–45, 285n. 39
Pierry, 13, 52, 59–60, 247–48, 253, 261
police, 76–79, 85, 88, 142–45, 173, 176, 187
postmortem inventories (inventaires après
    décès), 15, 62–63, 113–14, 124, 128, 134–38,
    219–20, 223, 258
Poulet, 228–29, 234–35, 237–38

Library of Congress Cataloging-in-Publication Data

Brennan, Thomas Edward.
Burgundy to Champagne : the wine trade in early modern France / Thomas Brennan.
      p.   cm. — (The Johns Hopkins University studies in historical and political science ;
   115th ser., 1)
   Includes bibliographical references and index.
   ISBN 0-8018-5567-5 (alk. paper)
   1. Wine industry—France—History.   I. Title.   II. Series.
HD9382.5.B74   1997
338.4'76632'00944—dc21   97-2188
                                                                           CIP